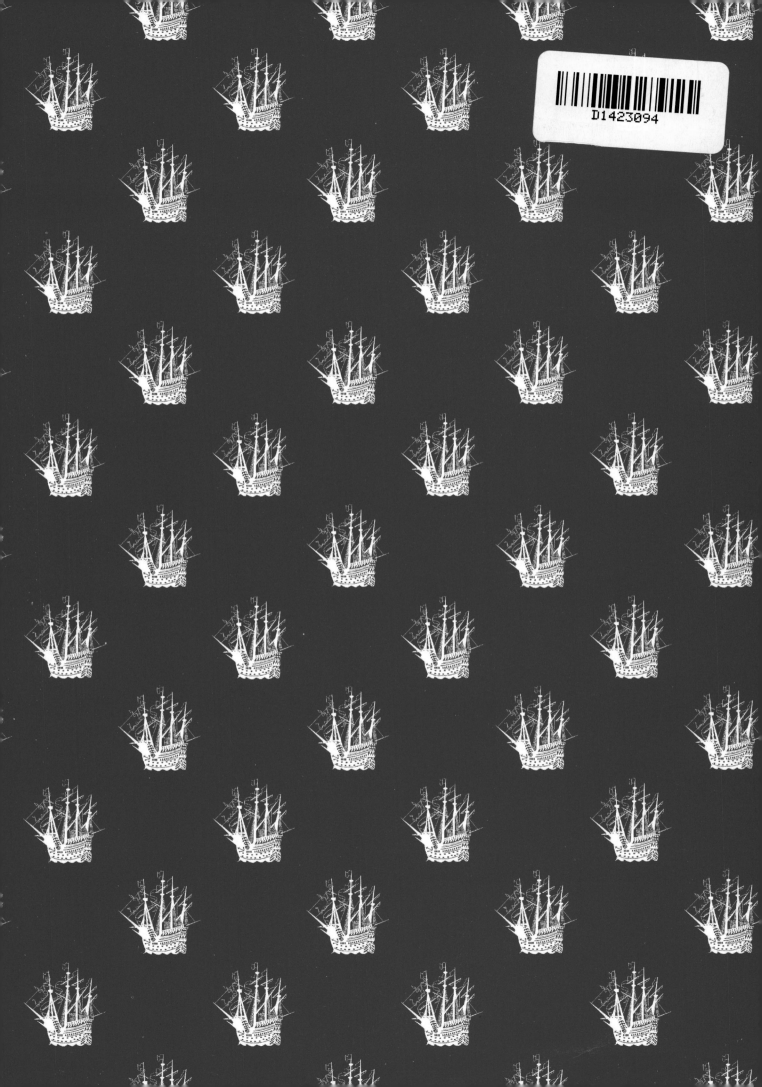

SEALED BY TIME

The Loss and Recovery of the *Mary Rose*

Peter Marsden

The Mary Rose Trust has always relied on the support of many volunteers who have given freely of their time, energy and experience. *The Archaeology of the Mary Rose* is dedicated to them all, and in particular to the many volunteer divers who worked in the most atrocious underwater conditions, under the direction of professional archaeologists, to complete the difficult task of excavating the hull. And to one of their number, Louise Mulford, who tragically died on 2 July 1980 while making her fourth dive onto the wreck

SEALED BY TIME

The Loss and Recovery of the *Mary Rose*

Peter Marsden

with contributions from

K. Collins, Richard Harrison,
J. Mallinson and Wendell Lewis

The Archaeology of the *Mary Rose*
Volume 1

2003

Published 2003 by The Mary Rose Trust Ltd
College Road, HM Naval Base, Portsmouth, England PO1 3LX

British Library Cataloguing in Publication Data
A catalogue record for this book is available from the British Library

ISBN 0–9544029–0–1

Series Editor: Julie Gardiner
Series Editor (graphics): Peter Crossman

Designed by Julie Gardiner and Peter Crossman
Produced by Wessex Archaeology

Printed by Cromwell Press, Trowbridge, England

The publishers acknowledge with gratitude grants from Hampshire County Council and the Heritage Lottery Fund towards the cost of publishing this volume

Cover illustration: Artist's impression of the *Mary Rose* under excavation (watercolour by Jon Adams)

Contents

I can remember vividly the excitement of the recovery of the Tudor warship, The Mary Rose, in 1982. For me, and countless others, it was a memorable day, lashed with driving rain, fraught with difficulties and with the successful outcome far from certain. That was over 20 years ago and, since then, an incredible amount has been achieved to recover and conserve both the ship and her artefacts. While the hull itself is impressive, it is the breathtaking collection of items found in and around the wreck, from the guns to the tiny personal possessions, that captivate so many.

As the excavation on the sea-bed progressed, I became engrossed in the project and was thrilled to have had a number of opportunities to dive on the wreck. Thereafter, as the proud President of The Mary Rose Trust, I have watched the conservation process of the 19,000 artefacts recovered, aware of the painstaking work involved in the cataloguing of the finds.

To understand and interpret the vast archive of research material from such an important excavation has been the task of archaeologists and historians, many of whom are distinguished specialists in their particular field. Their work has been drawn together to form a publication of five volumes, of which this book is the first. I know that this has been eagerly awaited by the academic world, but it will also, I am sure, appeal to the wider public who remain fascinated by the story of the Mary Rose.

The Mary Rose provides us with a unique and fascinating insight into Tudor life and this publication will enhance our understanding still further. Volume one is a fine record of an extraordinary excavation carried out in the difficult, indeed treacherous, waters of the Solent. I believe it recounts one of the Twentieth Century's greatest achievements in archaeology.

List of Illustrations and Colour Plates

Acknowledgements

This volume is the first of five in the series *The Archaeology of the Mary Rose*, and is the first account to be published by the Mary Rose Trust since the ship was discovered. It does not intend to be regarded as definitive, but should be seen as the most authoritative statement possible at the present time.

It describes the work of discovery by hundreds of people over a period of more than 160 years. Some people are referred to in the text, and many more would have been mentioned had there been space. It is important to recognise that it is not only those who were involved in the archaeological work that are important, but also those who raised funds, provided accommodation and materials, administered the project and helped in many more ways. As someone who originally viewed from the sidelines with incredulous admiration the success of the project, and then was asked to write this volume for the Mary Rose Trust, I can only say that I am all too aware of how essential was everybody's contribution to the ultimate success. The dedication of this book by the Mary Rose Trust to everyone who took part is heartfelt.

The true archaeological work on the *Mary Rose* began almost 40 years ago when, in 1965, Alexander McKee began the search, and once the ship was found it was investigated in great detail under the leadership of Margaret Rule. The resulting huge paper archive, and the mass of objects and samples recovered from the seabed, including the ship itself, is testament to the dedication of everyone involved.

Special thanks are due to Hampshire County Council and to the Heritage Lottery Fund for their generous funding of this volume, and to the leadership by successive Chief Executives of the Mary Rose Trust, Martyn Heighton and Charles Payton. The Editorial Board, under the Chairmanship of David Price, and its members Professors Barry Cunliffe and Seán McGrail, have guided the publication programme and have smoothed the way. Gill Andrews has been a valuable and constructive link between the Heritage Lottery Fund and the Mary Rose Trust providing help and guidance with this volume.

The debt due to Dr Julie Gardiner of Wessex Archaeology, both as the Series Editor and for arranging the laser survey of the ship itself, cannot be underestimated. Her enthusiasm and skills have ensured that the volume reached publication in reasonable time. The financial management by Richard Langrishe of the Mary Rose Trust and Charlotte Matthews of Wessex Archaeology has been an essential element, as has been the quiet support from Sally Tyrrell at the Trust.

Special thanks are, of course, due to the contributors of chapters: Richard Harrison, Wendell Lewes, Ken Collins and Jenny Mallinson. It was important that as much as possible of this volume should be written by those who undertook the work and therefore have a first hand knowledge.

Christopher Dobbs at the Mary Rose Trust not only provided a huge amount of information about the ship, and guided me through the Trust's archives, but also applied his great skills in text editing, and helping to root out many of my mistakes. Andrew Elkerton, the Trust's Collections Manager, has been enormously supportive by providing essential data from his comprehensive computer database. The transfer instantly of information electronically between the Trust's office in Portsmouth, my office in Hastings, the offices of Wessex Archaeology in Salisbury, and the homes of contributors has been a feature of this publication, and has saved much time and cost. Finally, thanks are due to Peter Crossman, the Trust's Archaeological Illustrator, who compiled some of the drawn illustrations in this volume, to Dr Douglas McElvogue, who prepared the plan of the Hold, and to Dr Mark Jones, Head of Collections, who facilitated my entry into the ship itself.

Many others have kindly provided essential information and checked draft text, though this does not necessarily mean that they agree with everything that is published here. Responsibility for errors is mine. My thanks is particularly due to the family of Alexander McKee, and to Jonathan Adams, Adrian Barack, John Bevan, Richard Endsor, Andrew Fielding, Alexzandra Hildred, Prof. David Loades, John Rhodes, Margaret Richards, Dr Margaret Rule and Rosemary Weinstein.

I am grateful to HRH The Prince of Wales, President of the Mary Rose Trust, for responding to my questions on his part in the project, and for supplying a message to accompany this volume.

The publication programme has clarified a sense of direction for the Mary Rose Trust regarding future research and publication needs. It is hoped that this volume will encourage scholars to tackle outstanding work, particularly on the Trust's archives. These include plotting out the finds and studying the record of archaeological deposits in the ship sector by sector and interpreting their significance; transcribing fully the contemporary documentary records and assessing them in the light of the records of other Tudor warships, such as the *Sovereign* whose remains were found at Woolwich in 1912; recording and interpreting the ship when all the dismantled structure has been reassembled; and, finally, excavating and recovering the remaining collapsed parts of the ship still in the seabed. Only then will it be possible to undertake a more definitive study of the *Mary Rose*.

Peter Marsden
5 High Street, Hastings

Preface to the Series

No one who, on Monday 11 October 1982, witnessed the *Mary Rose* emerge from the waters of the Solent will forget the sight. Here, for the first time since that catastrophic Sunday in July 1545, Henry VIII's greatship was exposed again to public gaze. Perhaps a few hundred at most had seen her heel over and sink. Millions saw the *Mary Rose* break surface, one of the most memorable events of live television, an outstanding achievement for British archaeology and a dazzling demonstration of the power of maritime history not only to command public attention but to offer one of the most vivid and eloquent of insights into mid-sixteenth century life.

The importance of the *Mary Rose* lies in the wealth, the diversity and the immediacy of the meanings encapsulated in the remains of the hull and its related artefacts. For, in the main, our view of the past is almost invariably abbreviated by uncer-tainties. These stem from unanswered and usually unanswerable questions, of date or provenance, or information lost through decay or incompleteness. The tragedy of the *Mary Rose* was instantaneous, such that of nearly 500 men aboard all but a couple of dozen perished. In the few minutes that it took for the ship to go down they lost their lives but by fateful fortune left us with a portrayal of how they had lived without precedent in its detail and vividness, preserved in the mud and sand of the bed of the Solent. Today, archaeologists, historians, scientists, and – importantly – the general public, can come closer than anywhere to the reality of the past. That shock of the real is all the more palpable because it pierces the anonymity of those sailors, soldiers and gunners, and lays wide open the everyday life of a nation.

The *Mary Rose* was one of the earliest great English warships, novel in concept as one of the first to be able to mount a large complement of guns arranged behind gun ports on several decks. Her rediscovery in the 1970s, after abortive salvage attempts in the sixteenth and nineteenth centuries, to the successful recovery of the hull and its contents a few years later itself represented an astonishing achievement. But this was really a beginning; the start of a forensic process of immense complexity, of recovery, identification, conservation and presentation that has made the *Mary Rose* uniquely famous throughout the world.

Excavation of the ship and the wreck site produced nearly 26,000 artefacts and pieces of timber, most in an extraordinarily good state of preservation. These provide for the first time a detailed view of the armoury and operation of a sixteenth century warship and the conduct of Tudor warfare. Chests of longbows and arrows; bills, pikes and halberds – the staff weapons needed to repel boarders – and swords and daggers for hand-to-hand fighting, together with ordnance and all the associated paraphernalia of shot made of iron, lead and stone, represent the largest and most comprehensive range of sixteenth century weapons to have seen service and survived. These lay amongst the personal possessions of the crew; hooks and fishing lines, musical instruments, leather jerkins, shoes, hats and buttons, buckles and laces; the medical kit of the Barber-surgeon, the tools of the ship's carpenters, and the food and utensils of the galley.

Although in generally good condition, hardly any of these items did not need some kind of scientific treatment. The conservation programme for the *Mary Rose* and her contents proved to be one of the largest and most complex ever to have been undertaken on archaeological finds. But the results, now on museum display, are not the end of the story either. The initial work of remedial conservation demanded immense and painstaking care in order to achieve a stabilised state in which long-term protection could be contemplated with some confidence. Today, the emphasis is on preventative care, carefully controlling the environment in terms of temperature and relative humidity, light levels and atmospheric pollution. That work will continue for as long as we need to look after the *Mary Rose* and her precious contents.

The other crucial requirement was that there should be a permanent record of all that has been done. Without it much of the immensity of the endeavour, the application of skill and scholarship, of science and history, would have evaporated. For excavation is essentially a destructive process. The site cannot be interrogated in the same way again. And, despite the powerful voices of the objects themselves, their meaning is ultimately diminished without a lasting affirmation of the knowledge that attaches to them. Publication therefore represents the ultimate obligation, to the ship and her crew, to history and learning. Paradoxically, it is the completeness of the material evidence, intact after more than 450 years, that makes that obligation all the more potent.

The publication of these five Mary Rose volumes also forms a significant milestone in maritime archaeology in the United Kingdom. It is the first major publication of a shipwreck investigation and I am particularly pleased that the Heritage Lottery Fund, with its first award of this kind, has made this outstandingly important publication project possible. With these volumes maritime archaeology might be said to have come of age after an over-long childhood and adolescence. The Mary Rose Project provided avaluable and symbolic opportunity, at a formative stage in the developmentof the discipline, for professional archaeologists and volunteer divers to gain experience – and some understanding of each others' points of view – in the challenging waters of the Solent.

With the passing of the *National Heritage Act* 2002, English Heritage now joins the equivalent agencies in Scotland, Wales and Northern Ireland in taking responsibility for the underwater historic environment. By developing a formal policy on maritime archaeology and advocating a seamless approach to the study and care of the archaeological resource, irrespective of the environment in which it lies, we may at last be starting to fulfil our wider responsibilities as a nation to one of the most important and largely overlooked bodies of information and knowledge about ourselves as a people and a nation.

This report on the *Mary Rose* and all that she represents is the culmination ofover 40 years of

dedication and commitment. It will not be the last word, nor is it the end of the story. We can be reasonably confident that advances in forensic investigation, in science and archaeology, and wider historical understanding, will continue to reveal new evidence from what we now hold. But what this report does provide is a rounding off of the massive project of recovery that had its most vivid expression in the minds of most people as the ship and the cradle that held her rose above the water's surface in 1982.

Sir Neil Cossons
Chairman, English Heritage

The Archaeology of the Mary Rose

This volume is the first in a series of five entitled *The Archaeology of the Mary Rose*. As the title indicates, the series is concerned with the presentation and interpretation of the vast assemblage of timbers and objects recovered by archaeological excavation from the wreck site of the Tudor warship – of the vessel itself, the artefacts, bones and other materials that survived more than 450 years buried in the silts of the Solent. It also covers the massive programme of conservation that has been necessary to preserve this unique collection for the benefit and enjoyment of future generations.

In 1545 the *Mary Rose* was a fully-fitted, heavily armed warship carrying over 400 sailors, soldiers and gunners. When she was sunk, on 19 July of that year during an engagement with the French Fleet, she took all her contents – and nearly all those men – with her. During the centuries that followed, as she lay at the bottom of the Solent, more than half the ship was destroyed or simply decayed but, astonishingly, the part – most of the starboard side – that became buried by the shifting muds and silts was preserved in remarkable condition, the soft sediments concealing a precious time capsule of Tudor life on board ship.

The recovery of the *Mary Rose* reclaimed that time capsule but, because of the nature of archaeological excavation, recovery was only achieved piece by piece. Most memorable was the raising of the greater part of the surviving hull in 1982 – watched by millions on television – the culmination of years of painstaking work already undertaken under water in very difficult conditions. The excavation itself marked a milestone in the development of maritime archaeology. The re-

assembling of all those pieces, the remaking of a 3-dimensional jigsaw, is ever the goal of archaeological research. Unlike most sites, however, where the nature and context of the material being excavated is only known in general terms beforehand, the truly thrilling reality of the *Mary Rose* was that the archaeologists knew all along what it was they were excavating, roughly what she should have looked like when re-assembled, more-or-less how the wreck got to be where it was, and exactly at what date the 'site' came into being. Such fore-knowledge is a rare luxury indeed.

Remaking the jigsaw has been no easy matter. Great difficulties are faced, for instance, in attempting to interpret the effects of a violent sinking and subsequent decay and collapse of the ship's hull and decks upon the nature and original distribution of contents that were once confined within a structured interior. More significantly, however, the vast majority of the nearly 26,000 objects and timbers, and the hull itself, have required careful and often long-term conservation treatment to stabilise and preserve them for study and display. And conservation could not wait; objects removed from the specific anaerobic conditions of the seabed began to decay immediately on removal from them. The programme has not finished yet, nor shall it do so for years to come. The hull itself will not be fully conserved before about 2015 – more than 30 years after its recovery. The result of this has been that detailed analysis of many of the component parts of the overall asemblage has simply had to wait until it has been physically possible to handle and examine enough objects to be able to achieve a reasonable under-standing and interpretation of them. In the case of some classes of object – for instance, the archery equipment, some of the hand weapons, items of clothing and personal objects belonging to the crew – it has been particularly important to study and discuss as many related objects together as possible as these classes have only rarely, if ever, been recovered before, and certainly not in the condition that they have been found in here. The Mary Rose Trust has chosen, quite deliberately and in spite of pressures from an eagerly awaiting public, not to publish its findings piecemeal but to wait until such time that the authors and editors of the series could be confident in presenting at least an outline story of the ship as a whole – as the 'living' and working entity that she was in 1545. Inevitably, therefore, there has been a considerable delay between the completion of the excavation and the first presentation of that story.

The Archaeology of the Mary Rose is the first comprehensive publication about the ship and her contents but it will certainly not be the last. These five volumes present the results of work to date and the sum of our knowledge about the structure, contents and working of the vessel at a moment in time. Some of the opinions and conclusions to be found within its pages will not stand the test of time but such is the nature of research. There is a great deal of work to do, many avenues to explore, and it will be decades, if ever, before the *Mary Rose* truly gives up all her secrets.

It is important for the reader to note that the series is not a museum catalogue. The presentation of an item by item listing of all material recovered from the wreck is a matter for future publication, at a time when it has been possible to examine and verify the identification of everything. Meanwhile, all the details so far recorded are stored in the archive, on paper and database, along with the artefacts (either in wet or dry storage depending on their place in the conservation programme) at the premises of the Mary Rose Trust in Portsmouth, where they may be examined. These volumes aim to tell the story of the *Mary Rose* and the men who were aboard her when she sank through the description and discussion of the structure of the ship itself and of related groups of objects as we currently understand them. The presentation throughout is thematic and the level of detailed description varies according to the rarity and significance of the material recovered. The authors and editors are well aware of the gaps in information, that ambiguities and contradictions exist, and that some seemingly simple questions that we might ask about various aspects of the structure, appearance, operation, contents, and, indeed, the circumstances of the sinking, of the ship, still cannot be definitively answered. These are questions for future analysis to address.

Nevertheless, the publication of this series is of great importance, both for the Mary Rose Trust specifically and all those who have worked to achieve its publication, and to maritime archaeology in general. This is the first 'full' publication of an historic ship wreck and the Trust is proud to set the precedence. *The Archaeology of the Mary Rose* is not the end of the Project it represents, but a stepping stone on a long road of discovery and the task of travelling that road will continue. Therefore, while not definitive, we present the most authoritative work yet written on this fascinating subject.

The Archaeology of the Mary Rose

Throughout the five volume the series is cross-referenced simply as *AMR*, vol. 1–5 as appropriate.

Volume 1. *Sealed by Time: the loss and recovery of the* Mary Rose, by Peter Marsden (2003)

Volume 2. *Your Noblest Shippe: anatomy of a Tudor warship*, edited by Peter Marsden (publication due 2006)

Volume 3. *Weapons of Warre: the armaments of the* Mary Rose, edited by Alexzandra Hildred (publication due 2004)

Volume 4. *Before the Mast: life and death aboard the* Mary Rose, edited by Julie Gardiner (publication due 2004)

Volume 5. *For Future Generations: conservation of a Tudor Maritime Collection*, edited by Mark Jones (publication due 2003)

John Lippiett
Chief Executive, The Mary Rose Trust
May 2003

Summary

This is the introductory volume in the series of five on the *Archaeology of the Mary Rose*. It traces the history of the ship from construction and completion in 1512, through three wars with France, to her sinking in 1545 with the loss of nearly 400 men. She was one of the first English warships built to accommodate guns on several decks.

The discovery and partial salvage of the wreck in 1836 and 1840 resulted in John Deane making the first record of objects from the wreck, and this drew the attention of historians to the story of the ship for the first time.

The nineteenth century records provided vital clues to where the wreck lay, and were used by Alexander McKee in his search for the site. The wreck was rediscovered in 1971, and a survey and trial excavation showed that a substantial part of the hull and its contents remained. The wreck site was soon protected by law, and once the Mary Rose Trust was created the Ministry of Defence, owner of the *Mary Rose*, transferred its rights to the Trust.

The excavation of the ship continued until 1982 under the direction of Margaret Rule, and the procedures are described in some detail. Raising the ship in 1982 required untried techniques, but were successfully completed, and the ship was brought ashore into Portsmouth Dockyard where it was made ready for exhibition next to HMS *Victory*. The opening of the Mary Rose Tudor Ship Museum in 1984 ensured that the public could see the ship and many objects, and since then it has been one of the top most-visited museums in Britain.

Much archaeology still remains in the seabed, and this is annually monitored by the Trust. A study of the seabed environment shows that the hull had sunk deeply into an ancient submerged silt-filled river valley, and that this resulted in much of the ship having survived. Had it sunk only a few hundred metres to the north the *Mary Rose* would have settled on hard gravel and would have eroded away.

The stratigraphy, the silt layers filling the ship, show how the wreck broke up and became buried. These layers preserve crucial objects which provide conclusive circumstantial evidence for the identity of the wreck as the *Mary Rose*.

A summary description of the ship introduces the reader to the remains, and shows that about one-third of the vessel has survived, mostly on the starboard side.

This is because the ship had sunk into the seabed at an inclined angle, ensuring the preservation of parts of the Orlop, Main, Upper and Castle decks. The bow is lost or collapsed, together with much of the port side.

The contents of the ship, its furnishing and the possessions of the crew are described in a summary form, and conclusions are drawn about the use of parts of the vessel.

The human remains represent a minimum of 179 individuals, with 92 fairly complete skeletons. They represent men and boys, with an age range of *c*. 12 to 40+. Their locations in the wreck show that at the time of sinking they were working at all levels in the vessel, particularly in the Hold, on the Orlop deck, and on the Upper deck under the Sterncastle.

The guns and their locations are summarised, and an overview of the size and types of shot show that the ship was mainly fitted out for her narrower gauge guns.

The cause of the loss of the ship, by heeling over with open gunports, is discussed. The sixteenth century belief, that the ship had fired her guns on one side and was turning to fire guns on the other, is doubted because most of the discovered guns from both sides were found loaded. That only 30-40 men survived from about 400 is explained by the fact that anti-boarding netting had covered the vessel and stopped men reaching safety.

The place of the *Mary Rose* in the development of warship design and methods of fighting is described, from the thirteenth century vessels with temporary castles, to ships with permanent fighting castles by the fifteenth century. Guns were introduced on the upper deck of ships during the fifteenth century, and several masts and sails replaced the earlier single mast and sail. But it was the establishment of new building techniques around 1500 that enabled ships like the *Mary Rose* to have gunports cut in the hull so that guns could be placed on several decks.

The discovery and recovery of the *Mary Rose* has contributed much to the discipline of nautical archaeology by ensuring that techniques of investigation and publication are developed, together with a system of handling the huge archive of records and objects. The Mary Rose Trust has tried to show that just because a ship lies in the seabed there is no reason why it cannot be investigated to standards similar to those used on land.

1. History of the *Mary Rose*

Many sixteenth century documents exist from which it is possible to reconstruct the story of the *Mary Rose*, and to show how she was used and behaved in various weather conditions and at peace and war. A knowledge of these is essential for an understanding of the archaeological evidence for they and the personal artefacts tell a strong story about people, sadly unnamed, with their personalities transcending the centuries.

There are important limits, however, for in spite of the clarity of the contemporary records there is, unfortunately, little information about the form and construction of the ship itself. Nowhere is there a written reference to the ship being a carrack, for example, and this is only established by the picture in the *Anthony Roll* of 1546 [143]. Consequently, her method of construction can only be understood by studying the remains of the ship, and the daily life on board is mostly understood from the archaeological evidence. By combining the richly documented story of the ship, and the detailed technical and personal information available from its remains, we can gain a much clearer picture than either the historical or archaeological sources alone can give.

Some caution is needed in interpreting the archaeology for it reflects the moment in 1545 when the ship capsized and sank, whereas the documentary sources show that the crew and soldiers, the victuals and even the armament were frequently changing over the decades before the sinking. Moreover, the evidence, both documentary and archaeological, is partial and depends upon what survived.

Throughout this volume reference is made to the contemporary documents given in the Appendix (eg. [143]), though many of the documents have only been published in a summary form, mostly in the *Calendar of State Papers of Henry VIII*. Some have recently been fully published in *Letters from the Mary Rose* (Knighton and Loades 2002).

Assembling and transcribing the historical documents has been a difficult task, and neither the list given in the Appendix nor the references given in this chapter should be considered exhaustive. Other records undoubtedly exist, and they will augment the story reconstructed here.

Political background to the *Mary Rose*

The construction and fitting out of the *Mary Rose* in 1510–1512 has to be set against the expansion of the navy of Henry VIII, and against the political background of that time, to understand the justification for the huge expenditure of money, materials and labour. During the reigns of Henry VII (1485–1509) and Henry VIII (1509–1547) there were political struggles between the great power blocks of Europe, particularly between France, the Holy Roman Empire, and Spain. Others were also involved, such as the Papacy and the republic of Venice. The result was that the control of parts of Europe was frequently changing. Although England was a small nation on the periphery of Europe and had limited resources, the ambitions of the king of France were viewed with particular concern. Six weeks after Henry VIII's reign started in 1509 he, aged 18, married Princess Catherine of Aragon. This created an alliance between England and Spain, and King Henry quickly adopted ambitions in Europe. In 1511 he placed England on a war footing, and joined the Holy League, a combination of King Ferdinand of Spain, Pope Julius II and the republic of Venice, to act in concert against France. Henry planned to reconquer Bordeaux, while King Ferdinand, the Pope and the republic of Venice intended to attack other French possessions. Henry led an army into France in 1513 and captured Tournai, though the Scots, an ally of France, invaded northern England.

Under Henry VII there had been the nucleus of an English navy, including the two large carracks *Regent* and *Sovereign*. But this was insufficient for future needs, especially in dealing with threats from France and Scotland.

Who ordered the construction of the *Mary Rose*?

On his accession to the throne in 1509 Henry VIII (Fig. 1.1) immediately embarked upon a major expansion of his navy, by building the *Mary Rose* and the *Peter Pomegranate* [130]. That, at least, is the most likely explanation. But, on further analysis of the date when both ships were launched, it is clear that the construction commenced very soon after the death of Henry VII, thereby raising the question as to who actually ordered their construction, Henry VII or Henry VIII? The answer is not necessarily a foregone conclusion, particularly as both had cause to enlarge the navy.

Central to the answer are the facts that Henry VII died on 21 April 1509, and that, within 27 months, the *Mary Rose* and her sister ship *Peter Pomegranate* had

Figure 1.1 King Henry VIII (by courtesy of the National Portrait Gallery, London)

been built, launched and had been sailed to London for fitting out, all before 29 July 1511.

As early as 30 December 1509, just eight months after the death of Henry VII, a private Venetian letter from England [1] stated that Henry VIII was already building four ships at Southampton. Although apparently garbled hearsay, this may have contained a basis of truth by referring to the two ships being built at Portsmouth.

More certain, however, is a warrant for building two new ships, dated 29 January 1510 and initialled by Henry VIII [2]. The ships are not named, and neither is their place of construction given, but they are almost certainly the *Mary Rose* and *Peter Pomegranate* for no other major warships were built about then. The only point of doubt is the fact that the ships were to be of 400 and 300 tons, whereas the *Mary Rose* and *Peter Pomegranate* were eventually of about 500 and 450 tons. But, as tonnage figures given for any king's ship in the early sixteenth century usually varied considerably in contemporary documents, this disparity is probably not significant. What they do show, however, is that the two new ships were of a similar size, one being only a little larger than the other, as indeed became the case with the *Mary Rose* and *Peter Pomegranate*.

As the royal accounts of 1511 were compiled on a monthly basis, it is probable that the voyage of the *Mary Rose* and *Peter Pomegranate* from Portsmouth to London (Fig. 1.2) occurred in June or July 1511 [4]. Consequently, if the warrant of 29 January 1510 refers to these two ships, then both vessels must have been built, launched and sailed to London for fitting out in just 18 months.

Confirmation of whether or not the construction of the ships was possible in so short a time is difficult to find, for ideally it is necessary to find records of how long it took to build other warships of similar size. Nevertheless, records concerning the construction of the much larger *Henry Grace à Dieu* (1000 tons) show that building commenced on 4 December 1512, and that she was 'hallowed' (ie. dedicated) at Erith on 13 June 1514, a construction period of 19 months (Oppenheim 1896, 49). This shows that it would have been possible to build the much smaller *Mary Rose* in under 18 months, and strengthens the view that the warrant [2] does indeed refer to the construction of the *Mary Rose* and *Peter Pomegranate*.

The fact that only eight months after the death of Henry VII a letter was written to Venice referring to the construction of new ships, and that a warrant to build the two ships was signed by Henry VIII only nine months after the death of his father, all suggest that Henry VIII might have been confirming a decision to build the ships made by his father. A possible reason might be that Henry VII had cause to fear the French towards the end of his reign. The marriage of Anne of Brittany to Charles VIII in December 1491 had given France valuable arsenals and ports on its north-west coast opposite England, particularly the heavily defended port of Brest. Moreover, when Charles VIII died in 1498 and was succeeded by Louis XII, the English king probably expected a change in French territorial ambitions. It is significant that Henry VII tried to delay the union of Brittany and France and that, as early as 1512, Henry VIII saw the northern French ports of Brest and Morlaix, in Brittany, as a threat, and that the primary use of the *Mary Rose* throughout her service was to attack those ports (Oppenheim 1896, 45–6).

Although Henry VII's policy was to keep England apart from continental intrigue and ambitions and to maintain peace with Scotland, France and Spain, he could have planned to build the *Mary Rose* and *Peter Pomegranate* as a defensive measure. Whatever the case, it took his son, Henry VIII, to confirm the order for the ships, and when they were ready, to turn the defensive plan into an offensive one with attacks on ports in Brittany.

Construction of the *Mary Rose*, before July 1511

The State Papers of Henry VIII show that the construction of the hull of the *Mary Rose* must have occurred during 1510 for, by July 1511, the ship had been launched. However, she was then far from ready for active service and was fitted out during the next eight months. The earliest reference to the ship by name occurs in a document of 9 June 1511, in which she is called the *Marye Rose* [3]. Her construction was part of a shipbuilding programme as is shown by the list of

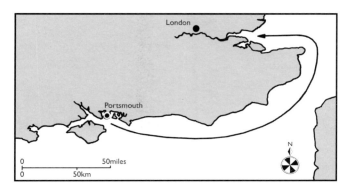

Figure 1.2 The voyage from Portsmouth to London for fitting out in 1511

ships of more than 40 tons, together with their ages, that was compiled in October 1525 [130], though its accuracy on all dates is not wholly certain.

Ships completed in:

1510	*Gabryell Royall*, 700 tons	
	Mary James, 260 tons	
1511	*Mary George*, 240 tons	
1512	*Marye Rosse*, 600 tons	
	Petur Pomgarnet, 340 tons	
	Barke of Bullen, 80 tons	
	The Gryffyn, 80 tons	
1513	*John Baptiste*, 400 tons	
	Great Henry Grace Dieu, 1500 tons	
1514	*The Grette Bark*, 200 tons	
	The Lesse Barke, 160 tons	
	John of Grenewyche, 50 tons	
1515	none	
1516	none	
1517	none	
1518	none	

There is no reference to the launching ceremony for the *Mary Rose*, though it presumably resembled the ceremony for the *Henry Grace à Dieu* described in the King's *Book of Payments* under the date 13 June 1514, which records a payment of 6s. 8d. 'at the hallowing of the King's great ship' the *Henry Grace à Dieu* at Erith (CSP II–II, pp. 1464–5). The *Oxford English Dictionary* describes 'hallowing' as consecration, dedication or sanctification.

It is probable that the *Mary Rose* was built at Portsmouth for, on 29 July 1511, following her construction, payment was made for the conveyance of the *Mary Rose* from Portsmouth to the Thames for fitting out [4], and for the wages of the master, mariners and soldiers, and their victuals [8, 9].

How the *Mary Rose* was built is not recorded, and even her tonnage is not clear. The considerable variation in the tonnage assessment of the *Mary Rose* indicates that there was no fixed formula, and the increasing tonnage as time progressed may well be due to changing methods of calculation by different people,

rather than to there being an increase in overall weight which would have increased her draught:

500 tons (April 1512) [24]
500 tons (April 1512) [27]
600 portage (1513) [45]
600 portage (Mar. 1513) [50]
600 tons (July–Aug. 1513) [87]
600 tons (?1522) [123]
600 tons (Oct. 1525) [130]
700 tons (1545) [143]
800 tons (1545, ?June) [145]
700 tons (1546) [143]

Fitting out the *Mary Rose*, July 1511–April 1512

The master for the first voyage of the *Mary Rose*, from Portsmouth to the Thames at London, was John Clerke, and payment was made in September 1511 for coats of white and green, each costing 6s. 10d., for the master, the quartermasters, the boatswain, and 24 soldiers [8]. A further payment was made for coats of white and green, each costing 6s. 8d., for the master and 34 of his company, both mariners and soldiers [9]. As some costs are spread between the *Mary Rose* and the *Peter Pomegranate* it is uncertain how many men served in each ship. These coats were presumably a type of uniform. Soon after, in November 1511, John Lawden appears to have taken up the duty as purser in the *Mary Rose* [13].

The destination for this first voyage was probably a mooring close to the Tower of London from which the guns could be installed in the ship. It appears that both the *Mary Rose* and the *Peter Pomegranate* were towed to London for it was there that they were rigged and decking was constructed [11, 12].

From September 1511 to April 1512 fitting out payments were made for decking, rigging, making streamers to fly from the masts, and stocking the ship with guns. Thomas Sperte was then the master and David Boner was the purser [11].

Cornelius Johnson, gun maker, was responsible for new stocking and repairing the guns [10, 18], and the need to carry out repairs shows that some had been used elsewhere. The payments to carpenters and sawyers [18] for stocking the ship with guns presumably reflects the construction of timber gun carriages and other supports. The fitting out ended in April 1512 with a payment of £77 0s. 3d. to Cornelius Johnson for making guns, gunstocks, bands, chambers, etc., for the ships [23]. Moreover, he was also paid £38 6s. 2d. for delivering gun-chambers, that is powder chambers, to the ships (*CSP* I–II, 3608, p. 1501).

William Botrye, a London mercer (a dealer in textile fabrics), supplied the material from which the banners and streamers were made [20]. The actual decoration

Figure 1.3 The Mary Rose
as she is depicted in the
Anthony Roll (top), with
an explanation of the masts
(bottom) (Anthony Roll
reproduced by courtesy of
Magdalene College,
Cambridge)

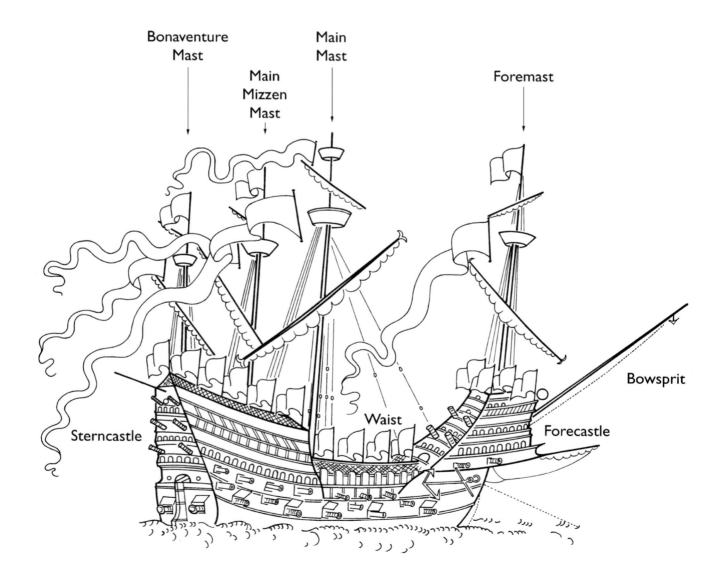

Bonaventure
Mast

Main
Mizzen
Mast

Main
Mast

Foremast

Bowsprit

Sterncastle

Waist

Forecastle

was undertaken by John Browne, a painter of London [20]. Their decoration and size are suggested by the banners for some unnamed warships, referred to on 8 April 1513, also decorated by John Brown, who is described as the King's painter. Seven banners of linen cloth and buckram (a coarse cloth stiffened with gum or paste) were painted with divers arms; and he also completed a streamer 51 yards (46.63 m) long with a 'Cadow fringe', and other streamers, banners and flags, for the ships *Henry Grace à Dieu* (about 1000 tons) and *Gabriel Royal* (about 700 tons) (*CSP* I–II, 2799, pp. 1221–2). One of the last payments to be made in respect of the *Mary Rose*, in April 1512, was to John Browne of London, painter, for 'stuff delivered', presumably the streamers, flags and banners, and for painting the ships [23]. An inventory of the *Mary Rose* taken in 1514 shows that there were 3 streamers for the tops, 18 gilded flags, 28 small flags, and 15 standard staffs for flags [106].

The completed *Mary Rose*

The only contemporary illustration of the *Mary Rose* is on the *Anthony Roll*, dated to 1546 (Fig. 1.3), but as the ship sank in 1545 it must have been drawn at least a year earlier. To what extent this shows what the ship looked like when first built is not clear from the historical sources. However, the archaeological remains show that there had been considerable repairs to the ship and so, in 1545, she might have been somewhat different from when first built.

The hull

The *Anthony Roll* illustration shows that, in 1545, the ship was a carrack, with a 'waist' separating a huge Sterncastle from a large overhanging Forecastle (Fig. 1.3). The stern is squared-off with a transom of diagonal planks. In the main lower body of the ship up to the Upper deck, there are three rows of gunports as if to reflect three decks, but the excavated ship shows that there were only two gun decks. The Sterncastle has guns protruding from three rows of gunports, as if reflecting three decks there too. And in the forecastle there are also three rows of guns, again suggesting three decks. It is not clear if the gunports were an original feature of the ship, but the illustration suggests that the larger guns were lower and the lighter were higher in the ship. It is also worth noting that in a picture depicting the major warships of Henry VIII's navy assembled at Dover in 1520 all have gunports. This picture, however, was painted about 20 years later and may not be a completely accurate representation of the ships in 1520. The *Mary Rose* inventory of 1514 [106] which lists many guns is the main clue, and these may suggest that gunports were an original feature of the ship.

The rig

On the *Anthony Roll* [143] the *Mary Rose* is shown as having four masts (Fig. 1.3): a bowsprit, a foremast, a main mast, a main mizzen mast, and a bonaventure mizzen mast. The illustration also shows the ship at anchor, with all the sails furled. When linked to the 1514 inventory of the ship [106] it is possible to reconstruct the rig (Fig. 1.4).

Bowsprit
A spritsail is shown on a yard below the bowsprit, and is furled in its position when not in use. The 1514 inventory shows that its yard carried a spritsail, with a bonnet or extra piece of canvas to make the sail larger, so as to give extra speed.

Foremast
The foremast carried two sails, the fore sail with two bonnets and two bowlines, and the fore topsail, with two bowlines, carried on a yard hanging from the foretopmast. 'Chains of iron with bolts' fastened the shrouds to the hull.

Main mast
The main mast carried three square sails hanging from yards, the main course or main sail, the main topsail and the main topgallant. The inventory of 1514 also describes the mast as having three sections: the main, top and topgallant masts. It had a main yard and sail, with two bonnets, and there were two bowlines, one no doubt on each side of the sail to catch a side wind. The topsail, hung from a top yard, also had two bowlines; and the topgallant sail hung from a yard, also with two bowlines. The mast and sails were all supported with lifts, braces, stays and shrouds, and iron chains fastened the shrouds to the sides of the ship.

Main mizzen mast
The main mizzen mast carried a lateen mizzen sail, with a small square sail on a yard above. The 1514 inventory says that it had one yard and sail, and a main mizzen top and yard, but there is no mention of a sail. 'Iron chains with bolts' fastened the stays to the hull.

Bonaventure mast
The bonaventure mast carried a lateen mizzen sail: the 1514 inventory shows that this was a single mast, with one yard but *two* sails, one perhaps being a spare. Although shrouds supporting the mast are mentioned, there is no reference to any chains attaching them to the sides of the ship. The *Anthony Roll* shows that this mast had an upper yard and topsail.

A useful clue exists in the Calendar of State Papers of Henry VIII regarding the height of a mast of the *Mary Rose*, for on 21 March 1538, G. Lovedaye wrote to Wriothesley: 'There is making for the Admiral a ship of the same fashion as the *Peterpomegarnet*, but greater.

Figure 1.4 An explanation of the sails and mast construction

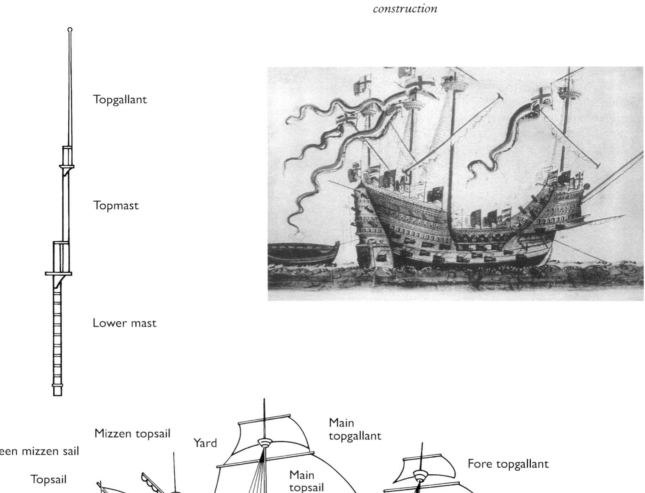

Topgallant

Topmast

Lower mast

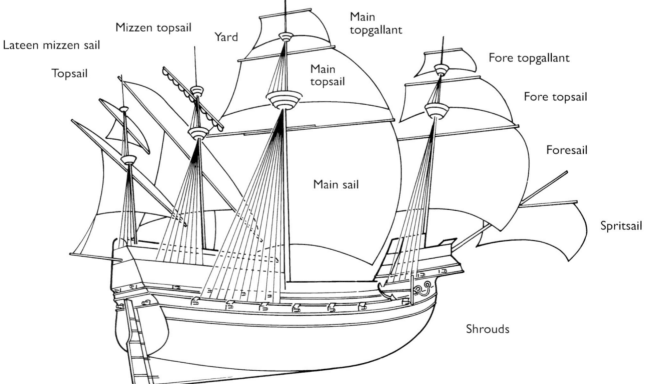

Lateen mizzen sail

Mizzen topsail

Yard

Main topgallant

Topsail

Main topsail

Main sail

Fore topgallant

Fore topsail

Foresail

Spritsail

Shrouds

Her mast is 150 feet long' (*CSP* XIII–I, 1538). As the size of a ship's mast is in proportion to the hull size, and the *Peter Pomegranate* was roughly two-thirds of the size of the *Mary Rose*, then it is likely that this was the approximate height of a mast of the latter. What is unclear is which mast this refers to, though it seems probable that it was the main mast.

The masts also supported 'fighting tops', and the *Anthony Roll* of 1546 shows that there was one on the foremast, two on the main mast, one on the main mizzen mast, and one on the bonaventure mizzen mast. Small guns appear to have been located on some fighting tops, for three 'top guns', with 75 chambers, are listed in the 1514 inventory, and two top guns with 20 stone shot are listed in the 1546 inventory.

Sailing the Mary Rose

There are some valuable indications of how well the *Mary Rose* sailed, for in March 1513 the Admiral, Sir Edward Howard, brought the fleet, including his flagship the *Mary Rose*, along the north-east coast of Kent, where he ordered a race to test their abilities [55] (Fig. 1.5). When they had reached Girdler Head the wind veered from WNW to ENE forcing them to anchor until the wind came to WSW: 'which was very good for us'. They did not start in a line, but instead some were as much as 4 miles (about 6.5km) ahead of the *Mary Rose*. Nevertheless, the order of arrival revealed which were the fastest ships: *Mary Rose, Sovereign, Nicholas, Leonard of Dartmouth, Mary George, Henry of Southampton, Anne, Nicholas Montrygo, Katherine* and *Mary James*. Howard stressed 'to bear record that the *Mary Rose* did fetch her at the talyl on her best way'.

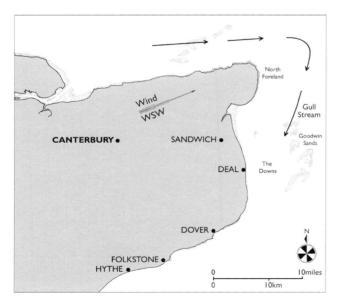

Figure 1.5 Map of the North Foreland and the race of 1513

A sailing technique used on the *Mary Rose* is mentioned by Howard in a letter to Henry VIII [55]:

'*Sir, within a mile sailing left her an fly ... at the sterne; and she al the other, saving a v. or syx smal shipps which cut o[ver the] Foreland the next wey. And, Sir, then our curs chanced [ie. course changed], and went hard uppon a bowlin ... the Forland, wher the* Mary Rose, *your noble shyp, fet the* Mary George, *the* Katerryn Prove, *a bark ... Lord Ferys hyryd, the* Leonard *off Deartmowth; and som of them weer iiij. long myle afore m[e] or ever I cam to the Foreland. The next shipp that was to me, but the* Sovereyn, *was iiij. myl behynd ... but the* Sovereyn *past not half a myle behynd me. Sir, sche is the noblest shipp of sayle [of any] gret ship, at this howr, that I trow be in Christendom'.*

He concluded that 'we went both slacking and by a bowline, and a cool ... [?] a course and a bonnet, in such wise that few ships lacked no water in over the lee wales'.

This is difficult to read, but it is possible to reconstruct the race which started with the ships sailing eastwards along the north coast of Kent, with the wind from WSW, that is from astern. Howard could let the *Mary Rose* 'fly' with this following wind, and it is here that he probably added 'bonnets' to the lower sails to give extra canvas and so increase her speed. In time the ships had to round the North Foreland at the north-east corner of Kent, whilst keeping to the deeper water. They turned south-east with some of the larger ships as much as 4 miles (about 6.5km) ahead of the *Mary Rose*, but the nearest ship following was 3 miles (about 5km) behind. On this more southerly heading the *Mary Rose* now found the wind coming from the starboard side, so the bonnets may have had to be removed. The crew pulled on the bowlines, the ropes that pulled the sails as far around as possible to catch the side wind, with the result that the *Mary Rose* heeled to port to such an extent that water probably came up to the gunwale. She responded excellently to this expert handling, and her speed enabled her to pull ahead of the other ships and so end the trial half a mile ahead of the *Sovereign*, the next ship. Howard concluded that the *Mary Rose* 'is the noblest ship of sail of any great ship, at this hour, that I know in Christendom'.

Howard's letter is a very personal statement: 'When I came to an anchor, I called for pen and ink to mark what ships came to me, for they all came by me to an anchor ... one after another'. With the wind rising they left the North Foreland and tried to reach the Downs, the safe deep water between the east coast of Kent and the Goodwin Sands, by way of the Gull Stream, a deep channel on the west side of the Sands. But when the fleet was between Brake Sand and the Goodwin Sands the wind veered and put them in danger, probably of running aground, and some of the vessels were obliged [fain] to tack [put about].

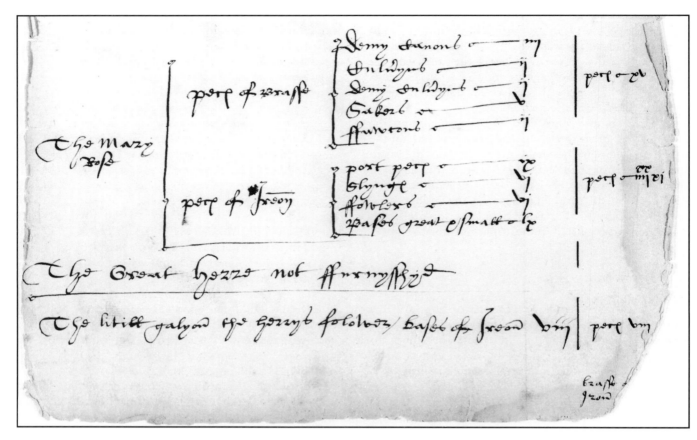

Figure 1.6 Document listing the guns of the Mary Rose *(Public Record Office: PRO E101/60/3)*

There are specific references to features of the rig of the *Mary Rose* that have not been found in the excavation and are not shown in the *Anthony Roll* picture of the ship. Mention of the 'bowline' is important, for this was the rope attached with a bowline knot to the leech or side of a square sail. Its purpose, when hauled hard in, was to keep the weather edge of the sail taut and allow the ship to sail as close to the wind as possible. The 'bonnet' was an additional strip of canvas laced to a sail to enlarge it, so as to give extra speed. The 'course' refers to the lower sails to which bonnets were attached (Kemp 1979).

There are clues to the average speed of the *Mary Rose* on some of her longer voyages, such as in a warrant of 1513 [53]. Although tidal currents and weather conditions are unknown, some documents give the number of days that it took the ship to sail from one port to another, and by dividing the distance in nautical miles by the number of hours, it is possible to arrive at an average speed. Of course, the precise times of departure and arrival are unknown, as are the exact distances and whether or not there were any intermediate stops. Also, the daily tidal movements carried the ship in various directions, so that at no time could she sail in a straight line. Nevertheless, some calculations are possible. For example, it took the *Mary Rose* 47 days to sail westwards along the English

Channel from Sandwich to Dartmouth, a distance of about 217 nautical miles [53] (a nautical mile measures approximately 2025 yards or 1.85km). This gave an average speed of 0.2 knots. Sailing eastwards, with the prevailing wind, gave slightly faster times, and it took her 12 days to sail from Dartmouth to Southampton, a distance of about 97 nautical miles, at an average speed of 0.3 knots. The voyage from Portsmouth to Sandwich, a distance of 135 nautical miles, took 14 days, and was accomplished at an average of 0.4 knots.

A faster speed is indicated by a letter [105] written off Portland on 14 June 1514. This refers to landing soldiers on the previous day near Cherbourg, a distance of about 60 nautical miles. If 24 hours is allowed for the *Mary Rose* to cover that distance, this would give a speed of 2.5 knots; and if 36 hours is allowed, which is probably too much bearing in mind the amount of devastation that the army wrought on the French countryside, then the speed would be about 1.6 knots. A maximum cruising speed of about 2 knots would seem to be about average for this voyage.

A method of moving the ship in light or contrary winds was to use the tidal drift to carry her forward from anchorage to anchorage. This is shown on 23 June 1522, when she was under sail westwards off St Helens, at the east end of the Isle of Wight, under a light north wind [117, 118]. They were bound for Dartmouth, but

	27 July 1514	1541	1545/6
Brass guns			
Great Curtows and chambers	5	–	–
Murderers and chambers	4	–	–
Falcons	2	2	1
Falconets	3	–	–
Little brass gun without chamber	1	–	–
Cannons	–	–	2
Demi cannons	–	4	2
Culverins	–	2	2
Demi culverins	–	2	6
Sakers	–	5	2
Iron guns			
Great murderers and chamber	1	–	–
Murderers and chambers	2	–	–
Cast pieces and chambers	2	–	–
Murderer and chamber	1	–	–
Demi slings and chambers	2	–	3
Stone guns	26	–	–
Top guns and chambers	3	–	–
Serpentines and chambers	28	–	–
Port pieces	–	9	12
Slings	–	6	2
Quarter slings	–	6	1
Fowlers	–	–	6
Bases (great and small)	–	60	30
Top pieces	–	–	2
Hail shot pieces	–	–	20
Total	78	96	91

by 27 June the fleet had only reached Portland due to a contrary wind 'and with force of the ebbs stopping the floods'. On that day the Admiral, Surrey, wrote to the King from the *Mary Rose* that he had little victual on board, and that he had 'plied the tides' that they might make some progress [119].

Armament

The mounted gun armament of the *Mary Rose* is listed several times and shows changes in her weaponry between 1514 and 1545 (Fig. 1.6):

Officers

The 'officers' of the *Mary Rose* are listed in various documents, the ranks referred to being: Admiral, Captain, Master, Purser, Surgeon, Gunner and Ship Keeper.

Sept 1511	Master: John Clerke
Oct–Nov 1511	Master: Thomas Sperte; Purser: David Boner.
Nov 1511–Jan 1512	Master: Thomas Sperte; Purser: John Lawden.
Feb. 1512	Purser: John Lawden (in Feb. 1513 JL is described as 'late purser').
April–July 1512	Chief Captain and Admiral of the Fleet: Sir Edward Howard.
Oct 1512	Admiral: Sir Edward Howard; ? status: Sir John Wyndeham.
1512, ?Oct	Master: Thomas Spert.
1513	Captain: Sir Edward Howard (killed by 25 April 1513); Master: Thomas Sperte.
May–August 1513	Admiral: Lord Thomas Howard; Captain: Edward Braye.
1513, July	Surgeon: Rob. Symson;
1513	Purser: John Brerely; Gunner: Andrew Fysche.
1513	Master: Thomas Pert.
1514, ?Jan–Feb	Captain: Edw. Bray.
1514	Captain: Sir Henry Shernburne.
1514, March	Master: John Brown.
1514, April–June	Captain: Sir Henry Sherburn/ Sir Harry Sharborne.
1517, Oct–Dec	Keeper: Wm. Mewe, plus 4 men.
1522, June	Lord High Admiral: Thomas Howard, Earl of Surrey; ? status of Fitzwilliam; Master: John Browne.
1524	Shipkeeper: Fadere Conner.

Soldiers, Mariners, Gunners and Others

The numbers of men on board during active service were listed as shown below.

This indicates that the normal active complement was about 185 soldiers, 200 mariners and 20–30 gunners. The 'others' comprised a surgeon, trumpeters and 'servators'. The abnormal number in the summer 1512 entry reflects the carrying of men for the invasion of Gascony. When not on active service, that is 'in

Date	Soldiers	Mariners	Gunners	Others	Total
1512 (summer)	411	206	120	22	729
1512 (October)	?	120	20	20	160
1513	?	200	?	?	200
1513	?	102	6	?	108
1522?	126	244	30	2	400
1524	185	200	20	?	405
1545/6	185	200	30	?	415

ordinary', the *Mary Rose* had a skeleton crew comprising a Keeper and about eight men, the total numbers of men being given as 4, 8, 8 and 17 on various occasions.

The First French War, April 1512–1514

The year 1512 was the first in which the *Mary Rose* saw action at sea. It followed Sir Edward Howard being appointed Lord High Admiral in April, after which he took the new *Mary Rose* as his flagship rather than the old fashioned and much larger *Regent*. He was about 35 years old, and had been knighted while serving in Scotland in 1497 when only 20 years old. His youthful vigour and ambition in 1512 must have appealed to Henry VIII, himself aged only 21, but this ambition was to cause Howard's death in action about a year later. Thomas Sperte was the Master of the *Mary Rose*, and was a remarkable man who had the confidence of the King. He became master of the *Henry Grace à Dieu* and other ships, and was a yeoman of the crown. By letters patent of 10 November 1514 he enjoyed an annuity of £20 a year. In 1517 an exploring expedition was apparently sent out under the command of Thomas Sperte (Oppenheim 1896, 91). Sir Thomas Wyndham was also based in the *Mary Rose* [27].

Howard's duties were set out in a document dated 8 April 1512 [24]. His fleet would carry 5000–6000 men [28, 30] in eighteen ships, the largest of which were the *Regent*, 1000 tons, the *Mary Rose*, 500 tons, and the *Peter Pomegranate*, 400 tons. His task was to sail for three months and return to Southampton having cleared the sea between England and northern Spain of French naval opposition. This would allow a second fleet of troop transport ships to carry an English army of 10–12,000 men to Fuentarabia at the north-east coast of Spain, close to the French border [28].

Howard's fleet set sail in April, and eventually returned to Southampton [26, 27, 28]. By 6 May, Henry VIII wrote that Howard had taken twelve Breton and French ships [30] and, subsequently, Howard followed this up by landing soldiers in Brittany. Over a period of four days they won several battles, slew many enemies, captured many knights and other gentlemen, and burnt the towns and villages for 30 miles (48km)

around [32]. Amongst the towns was Conquet (*Dictionary of National Biography* (*DNB*), Sir Edward Howard).

The complement of the *Mary Rose* suggests how the ship was used [27]. The crew of 206 mariners, led by the Master, Thomas Sperte, controlled the ship, but once an enemy vessel was engaged it was the responsibility of the 20 gunners to disable the enemy and allow the *Mary Rose* to manoeuvre alongside. Once in position, it was up to the 411 soldiers to fight in hand-to-hand battle. Sometimes the soldiers were landed on an enemy shore to attack communities but, to reach the shore, it was necessary for the *Mary Rose* to negotiate the shallows and find an appropriate anchorage. She carried two pilots (or 'lodesmen') for this purpose.

Sir Edward Howard's fleet returned in June 1512 and, by 1 July, Howard had met the King at Southampton [32], no doubt to plan the next stage of the offensive against the French.

Howard's fleet put to sea again in August, probably from Southampton and, on 10 August, in a high wind and a heavy sea, found the French fleet 3 miles (*c.* 5km) off Brest (Fig. 1.7). There are several accounts of what happened next [35, 36, 39], such as a report sent by the Venetian Envoy in England [39]:

'Towards 11am, off Brest, the look-out man of the Admiral's galley discovered some two leagues off in the mouth of the gulf of Brest a number of ships, which proved to be the French fleet. Chase given with extreme joy by the Admiral in his ship of 500 tons [ie. presumably the Mary Rose*] and another of 400, commanded by a valiant knight, called Sir Anthony Ughtred [Antonio Utrect], they leaving the other ships a quarter of a league astern, lest the French, who were in force at anchor and so near shore, should sheer off, as they, however, did. The English Admiral [ie. in the* Mary Rose*] cannoned the French Admiral, compelled him to cut his cables, and put to sea, and with a single shot from a heavy bombard disabled his mast, and killed 300 men, the ship saving itself amongst the rocks. Attack in the meanwhile by the ship of 400 tons on the carrack of Brest, called the* Queen *also the* Cordeliere*, of 400 tons burden, and carrying 400*

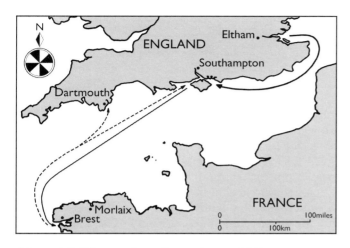

Figure 1.7 The attack on Brest, August 1512

men. The former did not grapple, but in a moment riddled the latter so between wind and water (ie. on the waterline) by shots from six large 'cortos,' that the French could not keep her afloat. The rest of the English fleet coming up, the Regent boarded the carrack with 400 men, and she surrendered, but the powder magazine (containing 300 barrels for the use of the French fleet) blew up instantly, the explosion being so furious, that the Regent, of 800 tons, caught fire, and both ships were burnt together, though 180 of the Regent's men, throwing themselves into the sea, were saved by the ships' boats of the English fleet; of the French only six escaped, and they were made prisoners. The ship of Sir Anthony Ughtred [Antonio Utrect] with 30 men sheered off (se tiro), and during two days the whole of the English fleet remained in this bay of Brest to raise the anchors of the 53 French ships [which had cut their cables].' [39].*

The wrecks of the *Regent* and the *Cordeliere*, when discovered off Brest, are potentially very important archaeological sites from which, in the future, it will be possible to obtain some archaeological information to compare with the *Mary Rose*. Unfortuantely, as they blew up, it is unlikely that much of the ships' structure will have survived.

Sir Anthony Ughtrede is described in the naval accounts of 1512 as having been the late captain of the *Mary James* (*CSP* I–I, 1414), a warship of 260 tons [130], but this ship is not amongst those listed in Sir Edward Howard's fleet [24]. Those who died in the *Regent* included her Captain and Howard's brother-in-law Sir Thomas Knevet, Sir John Carew and 600 soldiers and sailors. On the French side fatalities incuded Monsenior de Clermont, High Admiral of France, and the Seneschal (steward) of the town of Morlaix [36, 39].

On the next day the English landed, burnt 27 French ships and captured five more, captured 800 people and burnt 'many places on land' [39], but stormy weather forced the English fleet to return home

to Dartmouth, with a few ships returning to Southampton for repairs [36].

A curious incident occurred at this time when Jacques Berenghier, a merchant of Lille who had been forced to join the crew of the *Mary John* as a gunner, was court-martialled on board the *Mary Rose* and found guilty of sabotage [37, 38]. It seems that he had overloaded a number of guns by placing in them two stones wrapped in rope, so that the guns would burst when used against the enemy. Moreover, he carried flints for making sparks and also gunpowder loose and not in a horn around his neck. He was sent back to his own ship to be examined and was tortured on the rack to discover if others had been involved, and as a result lost a foot. Thereafter, he was returned to Admiral Howard, and was sentenced to have his ears cropped.

By 14 October the *Mary Rose* was one of several warships moored at Southampton and, following a discussion at Eltham Palace in north Kent (for a description see Thurley 1993) between the King and the ships' masters, including Thomas Sperte of the *Mary Rose*, it was decided that she should winter in the Thames with her sister ship the *Peter Pomegranate* [40], not far from Eltham.

Whilst the *Mary Rose* was moored in the Thames at the start of 1513, and her guns were being repaired [56], there was considerable planning and replanning by the King concerning the manning of the navy during that year [44, 45, 46]. Admiral Sir Edward Howard again chose the *Mary Rose* as his flagship, with 200 soldiers. Thomas Sperte continued as the ship's Master with 200 mariners. For the first time there is a reference to the *Mary Rose* having a bark, a small sailing tender whose Master was called Davison [46]. It is perhaps similar to that shown in the *Anthony Roll* [143]. A vessel named *The Baptist of Harwich* was also assigned to the *Mary Rose* to supply victuals for the men on board [45].

The movement of Admiral Howard's fleet in general, and of the *Mary Rose* in particular, is set out in her expenses between 14 March and 16 July 1513 [53]. On 18 March she lay moored at Woolwich and, next morning, Saturday 19 March, after the King had visited the fleet, she set sail downstream [54, 55]. Howard had just written to Wolsey expressing concern about the need for victuals for the fleet; and he also advised that someone captured in the ship *Marya de Loretta* should 'be well twitched, for I ween he can speak news.' [54].

Off north-east Kent the Admiral raced the fleet, as already described [55], and gave the results in a letter to the King, dated 22 March 1513. He ended his letter requesting the safe arrival of much-needed victuals, but they did not arrive. Fourteen days later, on 5 April, when the fleet was moored at Plymouth, he wrote to Wolsey from his cabin in the *Mary Rose* describing the desperate need of victuals. They had only enough for fifteen days and the *Katharine Fortileza* had no provisions. He knew that there were plenty of victuals at Sandwich, but did not want to leave Plymouth as an enemy fleet was approaching Devon [58]. Howard also mentioned a curious incident about the carpenter of that ship having bored so many holes in her hull that she leaked like a sieve. The textual context implies that his behaviour might have been connected with the lack of victuals!

The absence of victuals was still a problem when Howard's fleet, including the *Mary Rose*, sailed from Plymouth on Sunday 10 April with a strong NNE wind. It arrived off Brest next day, and saw a French fleet of fifteen vessels flee to join 50 more in the harbour, where they were defended by the castle [60]. Brest is situated on the north side of a deep water, west facing inlet open to the Atlantic, and is easily defended. Already, the French King, Louis, had summoned the French Admiral, Pregent de Bidoux, to bring his galleys to defend Brittany against the English [62], but this did not stop the English blockade. Howard landed men close to Brest on 13 April and managed to burn some houses, but was soon opposed by 10,000 French. The French, in turn, blockaded the haven with moored hulks, and Howard considered landing men with a gun to sink them.

A sea battle occurred on Friday, 22 April, in which the French galleys sank 'Master Compton's ship' and crippled a new bark [59]. As the galleys still remained a threat to Howard's fleet he led a group of men in four shallow-draught vessels to attack them on Tuesday, 25 April. This foolhardy escapade met the French vessels, which were heavily defended by guns and crossbows. Howard's vessel pulled alongside the galley commanded by Admiral Bidoux and, with seventeen men, Howard managed to get aboard to secure a cable to its capstan. But the French severed the cable leaving the two vessels drifting apart, and Howard in the hands of his enemies. He was last seen crying out to his men 'Come aboard again! Come aboard again!', but he was attacked by armed men and was 'cast overboard with morris pikes' [63].

The English were filled with sorrow at the death of their Admiral and Admiral Bidoux managed to recover Howard's body. Howard's whistle of office was sent to the French Queen, his clothes to Madame Claud and his body was 'embalmed' while awaiting advice from the French King [62].

The English fleet abandoned the blockade and returned to Plymouth [63], and news of the disaster was sent to King Henry. Lord Thomas Howard, elder brother of Sir Edward, was appointed the new fleet commander and was sent urgently to Plymouth which he reached, weary of riding, on the morning of 7 May. He took up quarters in the *Mary Rose* and, assembling the ship captains, began a post-mortem on why the blockade was abandoned [64]. The reasons were that the English fleet was almost out of victuals, that the French galleys posed a serious threat, and that had the wind turned to the west it would have held them to the French coast and allowed no chance of escape. Lord Thomas Howard concluded that his brother's failed

operation 'was the most dangerful enterprise' he ever heard of.

How the naval ships, including the *Mary Rose*, were intended to be used in conjunction with the army on land is set out in a document written by Henry VIII to Lord Howard and Sir Charles Brandon, now Lord Lisle, and dated 13 May 1513 [68]. Lord Thomas Howard was to take the fleet back to blockade Brest so as to 'distress' the French navy now in Brittany, and Lord Lisle, the chief captain of the enterprise by land, would join the Admiral at Southampton or Plymouth. Lord Howard and Lord Lisle were to work closely together and the King agreed that they could both modify arrangements if necessary. The character of Lord Lisle, however, may have made this difficult, for although being tall, sturdy and valiant, with a tendency to corpulence, he had a strong animal nature, and was not very much restrained at any time by morality, delicacy or gratitude (*DNB*).

This scheme was ill-fated too, for Lord Thomas Howard could not sail his fleet due to adverse winds. When writing to Henry VIII from the *Mary Rose* on 13 May 1513, he described Plymouth as 'the most dangerous haven in England for so many ships ... and when the wind is southwards it is impossible to leave' [69]. With his fleet wind-bound, there was soon trouble amongst the fleet's men and Howard had to construct a pair of gallows at the waterside, where some will 'towter' tomorrow, the 16 May [71]. The *Mary Rose* and the rest of Howard's fleet attempted to leave Plymouth on a south-westerly wind on the 15 May, but it 'blew so rudely' that they had to return [72]. The south-westerly gale increased to such an extent that the fleet was forced to lay out shot anchors, but many anchors and cables were broken, the latter being of the worst stuff that ever man saw [73]. The fleet remained at Plymouth until after 20 May, where Howard in the *Mary Rose* reported that she was 'warping with much pain fro Cat Water to the Sownde.' [78].

By 5 June the fleet had arrived at Southampton [81], and was being loaded with supplies for the intended attack on France [83], some of which were of poor quality [84]. Moreover, some of the men assigned to the new operation had run away, and Hereford gaol was full of them. The King commanded that a number of them should be executed [84].

The ships were at last underway by 14 June but Howard, writing to Wolsey and others from the *Mary Rose* off Quarr Abbey, on the north-east coast of the Isle of Wight next to modern Fishbourne, was clearly frustrated when he explained that 'we are here strong enough to encounter the whole fleet of France, and, had the wind served, had been gone towards Brest ere now' [85].

This intended attack on Brittany seems to have been abandoned for nothing more is heard of it, and the *Mary Rose* was stood down for the winter. During 1513 Edward Bray had been captain of the *Mary Rose* [87],

Rob Symson the Surgeon [89], and John Brerely the Purser [91]. The names of the crew are, as usual, not known, though Andrew Fysche is recorded as being a gunner for he received a payment of 13s. 4d. 'to heal him of his hurts.' [91].

Until now the *Mary Rose* had seen action only in the English Channel and off Brittany, but soon she was to see service off north-east England. In 1513 the Scottish King James IV, who was in an alliance with the French King, issued an ultimatum to Henry demanding that the English army withdraw from France. As Henry ignored this, the Scots invaded England but were defeated at the battle of Flodden on 9 September 1513, and King James was killed.

The naval support for the English force included the *Mary Rose* and, early in 1514, Howard submitted his costs, including that of the wages of the captains of his fleet of fifteen ships. This shows that Edward Bray was still captain of the *Mary Rose*, and that the fleet had been at Hull for four days 'afore they landed at Newcastell toward the Scottish field', before proceeding on to Newcastle for sixteen days [94] (Fig. 1.8).

Figure 1.8 The voyage to Hull and Newcastle, 1513

It is not known where the *Mary Rose* wintered during 1513–1514, though there is the annual list of 'The names of the ships, captains, mariners, soldiers and gunners, which be appointed to be in the King's army by the sea this next year'. Amongst them is the *Mary Rose*, 600 tons [95]. John Brown was appointed to be master [97], and John Brereley to be purser [100].

In April 1514, the *Mary Rose* was again in active service until at least 19 June, with Sir Henry Sherburn

as captain, and with 185 soldiers, 200 mariners and 20 gunners [99, 102]. The plan was to attack the French galleys commanded by 'Prior John' [103, 104] and the French coast near Cherbourg [105].

In May, John Wodlas, from Harwich, was paid for conveying the *Mary Rose* from Harwich to meet the King returning from Calais, and then up the River Thames to Blackwall [101]. It is possible that this payment relates to the return of Henry in October 1513 following his capture of Therouanne and Tournai.

In ordinary, 1515–1520

By July 27 1514, the *Mary Rose* was laid up at a mooring in the River Thames at Blackwall with her sister ship, the *Peter Pomegranate*, and the *Great Elizabeth* [108]. An inventory was made of all those fittings that had to be removed from the *Mary Rose* [106]: her masts, sails, rigging and other things that were to be delivered to John Hopton, comptroller of the King's ships, together with the anchors, cables and the ship's two boats and their masts and fittings. The guns, shot, flags and a few cooking utensils (3 trivets, 1 spit, 1 cob-iron, 1 grid-iron, 1 frying pan, 1 tar kettle, 1 pitch kettle, 1 cook room kettle, etc.) enough for the skeleton crew, were left on board in the custody of John Browne, master, and John Bryarley, purser. It was unusual to leave the guns on board, though the bows, arrows, armour, gunpowder, pikes, etc., were delivered to John Millet and Thomas Elderton [106].

Here we can see the ship being put in reserve, or in naval terminology 'in ordinary', for the foreseeable future. A skeleton crew was sent to live on board who, between 1517 and 1521, comprised four men in the charge of William Mewe [110].

Between late 1514 and early 1522 the *Mary Rose* remained mainly in this state, though maintenance was necessary in 1517 when a wet dock was built at Deptford for five great ships including the *Mary Rose* [109], and in 1518 when John Hopton organised a routine repair and caulking of the *Mary Rose* [111, 112]. In October 1520 it was necessary for seven men to help pump the ship for a day and a night [114].

In June 1520 the *Mary Rose* was briefly returned to active service to take part in an important and colourful occasion with several other warships – her duty being to scour the seas and so guard the passage of Henry VIII when he crossed the Channel to France to meet the French King, Francis I, at the Field of the Cloth of Gold [113] (Figs 1.9, 1.10). The aim of the meeting between the two kings was to find solutions to their differences and so stop further wars.

Second French War, 1522

Two years later war was again declared between England and France following a secret treaty between

Figure 1.9 Embarkation for the Field of the Cloth of Gold, 1520 (The Royal Collection © 2003, Her Majesty Queen Elizabeth II)

the new Holy Roman Emperor, Charles V, and Henry. The initial aim was to attack Paris – English troops, commanded by Suffolk, coming from the north, and Spanish troops from the south. The purpose of the *Mary Rose* and other ships of the English navy was to protect the convoys at the Calais bridgehead, then owned by England.

On 30 May 1522, the *Mary Rose* appears to have been at Dover when the King was present in the port. Initially, she was the flagship of Vice-Admiral Fitzwilliam who noted that, when they tried to set sail

Figure 1.10 Francis I, King of France 1515–1545 (The Bridgeman Art Library TWC 62736)

westwards for Southampton, the wind changed to WSW and blew so hard that he had to sail eastwards and anchor in the Downs until 2 June. When the wind

changed to west by north on 2 June they were able to recommence the voyage, though not so much by being propelled by wind but instead by being carried on the tidal flow. By stopping at every flood when the sea was flowing east, and drifting west with the lowering tide, the ship was able to resume her voyage. But even this failed for the wind soon went back to the SW and the ship had to put back to the Downs, where she was still at anchor on 4 June [115].

Vice-Admiral Fitzwilliam monitored the sailing ability of the ships between Dover and the Downs and concluded in a letter to Henry VIII that the *Henry Grace à Dieu* sailed better than any other ship in the fleet, and weathered them all save the *Mary Rose*, and on a wind it would be hard to chose between them [115]. Also of interest is a hint at how stable a carrack behaved in a strong wind, bearing in mind that the high fore- and sterncastles may well have caused the ships to roll while at anchor. Fitzwilliam tells of how all day, on 3 June, the wind blew 'sore and strainably', and yet the *Henry Grace à Dieu* rode as still and gently at anchor as the best ship in the fleet [115].

Once in the Solent the fleet was ready for the embarkation of the army of 5000 men. Thomas Howard, Earl of Surrey, had joined the *Mary Rose* on 19 June but found that, although the fleet had been supplied with meat, fish and biscuit for two months, they only had beer for one month. Indeed, some of the ships were victualled for only eight days. The Admiral put the problem down to negligence and, on 21 June, when writing to the King from the *Mary Rose*, he was 'doubting much more of the victual than wind.' [116]. On 23 June the fleet, still in need of victuals, was under sail westwards off St Helens, at the east end of the Isle of Wight, with a light north wind [115, 116]. It was bound for Dartmouth, but by 27 June the fleet had only reached Portland because of a contrary wind [119].

The wind must have backed round to the east or north-east soon after, for the *Mary Rose* and the fleet arrived at Dartmouth on the evening of 29 June. As it had taken about two-and-a-half days to travel the 46 nautical miles from Portland to Dartmouth the *Mary Rose* had sailed at an average speed of about 0.76 knots, but this assumes that she sailed both by day and night [120].

Having collected water at Dartmouth on 30 June 1522, the *Mary Rose* led the fleet towards France, and three days later Surrey wrote to Wolsey (Fig. 1.11) from the *Mary Rose* that he had taken the French port of Morlaix, though the fleet was in desperate need of victuals. Many of Fitzwilliam's ships were without meat and fish and the *Mary Rose* had beer for only twelve days and was considering using water [121].

Figure 1.11 Cardinal Thomas Wolsey (by courtesy of the National Portrait Gallery, London)

The fleet returned home and, a month later, on 3 August, the Admiral, Thomas Howard, left for Calais leaving Vice-Admiral Fitzwilliam in charge on the *Mary Rose* at an unspecified port. Fitzwilliam wrote to Wolsey saying that the *Mary Rose* and *Peter Pomegranate* could be laid up as no more great ships would be wanted, unless the French king prepared an army [122].

At mid-summer it was the King's policy to start thinking about where to berth the *Henry Grace à Dieu* for the winter, and Fitzwilliam discussed the matter with the warship masters, including John Browne of the *Mary Rose* and John Clogge of the *Peter Pomegranate*. These two were sent to make soundings in the Camber off Rye, but could find no place fit for her there. All agreed that Portsmouth and Dartmouth were the fittest places [115] and, on 30 June, Thomas Howard recommended to Henry VIII that the fleet winter in the well-protected haven of Dartmouth [120].

In ordinary, 1522–1545

And so it was that, for the rest of the war with France, from 1522 to 1525, the *Mary Rose* was held in reserve. The King still needed a fleet during this period and authorised the construction of a number of warships, as the following list shows [130]:
Ships completed in:

1519	none
1520	*Trinitie Henrye*, 80 tons
1521	none
1522	none
1523	*Maudelen of Depforde*, 120 tons
	The Hulke, 160 tons
	Katerine Barke, 100 tons
	Sweepstake, 65 tons
	Grett Sabra, 50 tons.
	Lessere Sabra, 40 tons.
1524	*Mary Impercall*, 120 tons
1525	*Mary Gylforde*, 160 tons
1526	*Minion*, 180 tons
	Barke of Murlesse (Morlaix), 60 tons
	Swalowe, 60 tons

In 1524 the *Mary Rose* was moored with ten other warships at Portsmouth Harbour, and had a skeleton crew of seventeen men under Fadere Conner as shipkeeper [125]. There are several administrative documents, including payments, relating to the care of the ships and their skeleton crews in 1524 and 1525 [125; 126; 127; 128].

The end of the war was followed by a review of the condition of the fleet in October 1526 [130; 132]. The largest ship, the *Henry Grace à Dieu* was moored at Northfleet, and the *Gabriel Royal* was moored off Erith, the *Sovereign* lay in a dock at Woolwich, and the *Mary Rose* was in a dock at Deptford. The *Mary Rose* required caulking 'from the keel upward, both within and without,' whereas the *Sovereign* must be 'new made' from the keel upward. This latter report is important for the remains of this ship were found under Woolwich Power Station in 1912 (Salisbury 1961, and Chapter 14). Another report in 1526 stated that the *Mary Rose* was good for war but her 'overlop' (ie, Orlop deck), summer castle and decks must be caulked [134]. The *Mary Rose* still had a skeleton crew of eight men on board in November 1526 [133].

The preparations for the repairs began in 1526 when nine acres (4.6 ha) of land were bought at Portsmouth by the King so as to dig out a new dock, to build storehouses and to make 'vices' for winding aground the King's ships. The whole area was to be surrounded by a hedge and ditch, with access gates. The dock was dug in early 1527, the labourers being paid 2d. each tide [135, 137].

The *Mary Rose* was under repair during June and July 1527, and was caulked at her overlop and decks fore and aft inboard and likewise caulked from the keel

Figure 1.12 Thomas Cromwell (by courtesy of the National Portrait Gallery, London)

upwards outboard. Also, her boat was repaired and trimmed. All this required the purchase of 37 feet of planking 5 ins (*c.* 130mm) thick presumably for the hull outboard, 120 ft (36m) of overlop deck planking 2 ins (50mm) thick, 46 ft (13.8m) of squared timber perhaps to replace deck beams and frames, and there were numerous nails of various sizes, including 'overlop nails' and 'scupper nails' to fasten the timbers. The caulking required 6.75 hundredweight (*c.* 340kg) of oakum and eight barrels of tar, with some 'thrums' (sheepskin used in caulking). Curiously, treenails which would be used under the waterline, are not mentioned by the supplier Thomas Jermyn, 'Clerk of our sovereign lord' [136].

Very little is known about the *Mary Rose* from late 1528 until 1539 due to the paucity of documents, and there is some confusion around published statements that the *Mary Rose* was believed to have been 'rebuilt' in 1536 (Oppenheim 1896, 49; McKee 1982, 23; Rule 1983, 21, 27), and Bradford (Bradford 1982, 23, 29) gives both 1536 and1539/40 for her being 'rebuilt'.

No contemporary source for these statements can be found, and there may have been a misunderstanding of a document written by Cromwell in 1536 in which he says that amongst the 'Things done by the King's highness sythyn I came to his service' included 'new made' the *Mary Rose* and six other warships [138]. The interpretation hinges on two things: (1) the meaning of 'new made', and (2) when Cromwell considered that he was in the King's service. The first cannot be resolved as it is not certain what 'new made' included, though a major rebuild seems to be the meaning of the term in relation to the *Sovereign* given in a document in 1526 [130].

The date when Cromwell (Fig. 1.12) considered that he had started on the King's service is uncertain, though in the same manuscript as he refers to the purchase of Hampton Court which occurred in 1529 (Thurley 1993, 50), it is therefore possible that he was involved in organising the repair of the *Mary Rose* the year before. This early date in the service of the King is reasonable for in 1525 he was amongst three men who were commissioned by Wolsey, on behalf of the King, to survey monasteries, and thereafter he was increasingly involved in their dissolution and demolition. In 1531 he was made a privy councillor and, in 1532, he was appointed master of the jewels and master of the King's wards. In 1533 he became Chancellor of the Exchequer, and in 1534 was appointed the King's Secretary and also Master of the Rolls [*DNB*, Cromwell].

The view that the *Mary Rose* was 'new made' in 1536 is not supported by any known document or by any expenditure, and in the light of this it is more likely that it was the repairs of 1527 to which Cromwell was referring in the 1536 manuscript. He may have been inflating his achievements on behalf of the King – a wise thing when remembering the uncertainties of working for Henry VIII. Just four years later Cromwell lost his head on Tower Hill.

Tree-ring dating of timbers in the *Mary Rose* show that repairs certainly occurred around 1535–6, and it is to these that a document of 1539 possibly refers when stating that the *Mary Rose* and other ships were then 'new made' and standing in their docks beside the River Thames, but were without their masts [139].

The years, 1535–1536, were of fundamental change with the Dissolution of the Monasteries just beginning and not receiving popular support, and this led to revolution in England in 1536 and 1537. In 1538 Rome called on all Christians to attack and destroy the English King. Consequently, it would be entirely understandable if the *Mary Rose* and other warships had been strengthened at that time. In 1539 both Francis I, King of France, and the Emperor Charles V of Spain agreed a pact to oppose Henry VIII, and it was as a result of the need for intelligence about England's readiness for war that Francis I received information about English naval strength [140].

Third French War, 1544–1545

The inevitable war was slow to come, and although the English warships were apparently kept armed [141, 142], it was not until 1544 that Henry's troops captured Boulogne. Although Henry was old, sick and tired by then, he still had ambitions in France and required a navy that was up to strength. A programme of warship building ensued as is seen in the list below (Glasgow 1970, 299–307):

Figure 1.14 Sir George Carew who died aboard the Mary Rose (The Bridgeman Art Library WES 32299)

Figure 1.13 Admiral Claud D'Annebault, who attacked Portsmouth in 1545 (The Bridgeman Art Library CND 171321)

c. 1530 Trinity Henry, 250 tons
1531 none
1532 none
1533 none
1534 none
1535 Sweepstake, 300 tons
1536 Lion, 140 tons
1536 none
1537 none
c. 1538 Jennet, 180 tons
1539 none
1540 none
1541 none
1542 Dragon, 140 tons
1543 Pauncey, 450 tons
New Bark, 200 tons
1544 Great Pinnace, 80 tons
Galley Subtyle, large
Swallow, 300 tons
1545 Grand Mistress, 420 tons
Ann Gallant, 450 tons
Greyhound, 200 tons
Falcon, 80 tons
Roo, 80 tons
Saker, 80 tons
Hind, 80 tons
Brigandine, small galley
1546 Bull, 200 tons

Tiger, 200 tons
Hart, 300 tons
Antelope, 300 tons
Phoenix, 70 tons
George, 60 tons

Part of the third naval development programme comprised the acquisition of prizes and the purchase and hire of ships. For instance, around 1545 four vessels of between 400 and 600 tons were bought from the Hanse in Germany.

The pattern shown by this and the previous lists is that there was a concentration on having smaller and more manoeuvrable ships. Throughout the sixteenth century there existed few very large warships like the *Mary Rose*, and it was not until about 1557, during Queen Mary's reign (1553–1558), that a new *Mary Rose* was completed, again of 600 tons and with 300 men (Glasgow 1970, 304).

1545

The record of events surrounding the sinking of the *Mary Rose* fall into four groups:
1. those dating from 1545 before the sinking on 19 July;
2. those dating from 1545 describing the sinking;
3. those sixteenth century documents dating from long after the sinking;
4. those dating from 1545–1547 describing the salvage.

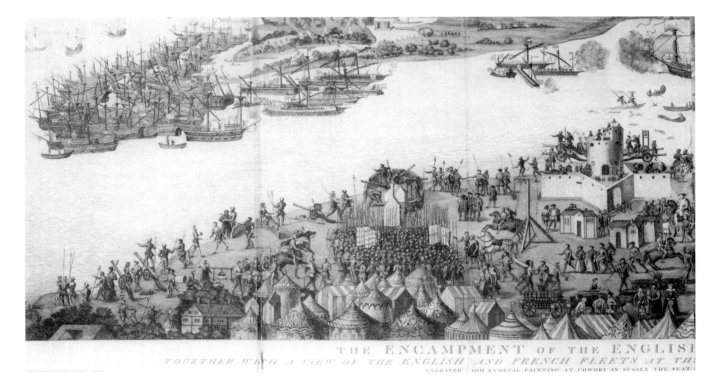

Figure 1.15 The Cowdray Engraving and detail of the sinking of the Mary Rose *(© Society of Antiquaries of London)*

The reason for separating the records under these headings is to identify those that have the integrity of immediacy, and to isolate those of later date that are more likely to include distorted hearsay through re-telling.

1545, *before the sinking of the* Mary Rose

It is not known where the *Mary Rose* wintered in 1544–1545, but on 23 and 24 June 1545 she was in the Downs with other warships ready to join the transports of the army [147]. They were supporting Henry VIII having taken Boulogne in 1544, and were to oppose growing French forces aimed at retaking the town. On 6 July 1545, French warships under the command of Admiral D'Annebault (Fig. 1.13) set sail to attack Portsmouth with a view to reducing the size of the English fleet. As the English anticipated a fleet action, an order of battle at sea was drawn up, in which the *Mary Rose* was placed in the main battle fleet with other warships, and the galleys on the wings [145]. The *Anthony Roll* [143] gives the latest statement of the *Mary Rose* before her loss: 700 tons, and with 185 soldiers, 200 mariners and 30 gunners, and heavily armed, particularly with guns, bows and arrows, and with morris pikes.

By 18 July the *Mary Rose* was moored off Portsmouth with a substantial English fleet ready to oppose the impending French attack. Viscount Lisle had compiled a battle plan for the confrontation with the French [144, 145]. Henry VIII had a banquet on board the *Henry Grace à Dieu*, and with him were Admiral Sir John Dudley, Viscount Lisle, and Sir George Carew (Fig. 1.14) who that day was appointed Vice-Admiral and was serving in the *Mary Rose*. It is said that the master of the *Mary Rose* was a Roger Grenville (McKee 1982, 25), but this remains to be confirmed [172].

1545, *date of the sinking of the* Mary Rose

There has been uncertainty as to when the battle between the French and English fleets occurred and when the *Mary Rose* sank. Early authors (Horsey 1844: *Holinshed Chronicle* 1577; John Stow 1605; Oppenheim 1896, 66) calculated the date as the 20 July, but recent authors (Bradford 1982, 11; McKee 1982, 26–7; Rule 1983, 32) have quoted the correct date of 19 July 1545.

The significant clue is in a letter, dated 24 July 1545, from Van der Delft, the German Emperor's Ambassador, to Charles V [149], for this described the sinking as having occurred on a Sunday. The Julian Calendar was then in use, and I am grateful to Emily Winterburn of the Royal Observatory, Greenwich, for making the calculation (Bear 1989). The correct date of the Sunday is 19 July 1545.

1545, *sinking of the* Mary Rose

The only contemporary account of the sinking of the *Mary Rose* [149] is derived from a survivor of the ship who told Van der Delft that:

FORCES NEAR PORTSMOUTH,
COMMENCEMENT OF THE ACTION BETWEEN THEM ON THE XIX.th OF JULY MDXLV.

'the disaster was caused by their not having closed the lowest row of gun ports on one side of the ship. Having fired the guns on that side, the ship was turning, in order to fire from the other, when the wind caught her sails so strongly as to heel her over, and plunge her open gunports beneath the water, which flooded and sank her.'

Lord Russell wrote to Sir William Paget on 23 July saying that the *Mary Rose* was sunk due to 'great negligence' [148]. The French view, however, was different, for Martin du Bellay, apparently a French eye-witness, claimed that the *Mary Rose* was sunk by gunfire, and out of five or six hundred men only 35 were saved [150] (Fig. 1.15).

Only three years after her loss, an account was published in Hall's *Chronicle* of 1548 [151] which said that the *Mary Rose* was sunk:

'by to much foly … for she was laden with much ordinaunce, and the portes left open, which were low, … so that when the ship should turne, the water entered, and sodainly she sanke.'

The contemporary accounts are all in accord, that she sank due to water entering her lowest gunports which had been left open. They all approximately agree with the *Anthony Roll* [143] figure of her complement of 415 men, Van der Delft saying that there were 500 men; du Bellay, 500–600 men; and Hall, 400 men. The number of survivors is given in two accounts, Van der Delft says that there were 25–30 men; and du Bellay gives 35 men.

Hollingshed's account of 1577, although published 32 years later, accurately reflects the contemporary descriptions:

'One of the King's shippes, called the Marye Rose, was drowned in the myddest of the haven, by reason that she was overladen with ordinaunce, and had the portes lefte open, whiche were very lowe, and the great artillerie unbreeched, so that when the ship shoolde tourne, the water entred, and soddainely she sunke. In hir was Sir George Carewe, knight, and foure hundreth souldioures under his guidyng. There escaped not paste fortie persons of all the number.' [168].

The Chronicle of Charles Wriothesley adds:

'The 20th day of July the Mary Rose, one of the King's great ships, by misfortune by leaving the port lids open, as she turned sank, and all the men that were in her, saving 40, were drowned, which were above 500 persons; Sir George Carew, Knight, Captain, which was drowned; this was done before Portsmouth haven.'

The account by Richard Hooker, written after 1575, in his biography of Sir Peter Carew [168], although very important, should be treated with some caution because, although it tells a good story about the sinking, there is no way that most of what he relates can be checked. Moreover, the one detail that can be checked, his saying that the ship carried 700 men, is clearly at variance with *all* the early accounts of the loss and must be incorrect. He says that:

'Sir George Carewe being entered into his shippe, commaunded everye man to take his place, and the sayles to be hoysed, but the same was noe sonner donne, but that the Marye Roose beganne to heele, that is, to leane one the one syde. Sir Gawen Carewe beinge then in his own shipp, and seeinge the same, called for the master of his shippe, and tolde hyme there of, and asked hyme what it mente? who awensweared, that yf shee did heele, she was lycke to be caste awaye. Then the sayd Sir Gawen, passinge by Marye Roose, called oute to Sir George Carewe, askeinge hyme howe he did? who answered, that he had a sorte of knaves whom he could not rule. And it was not lounge after but that the sayde Mary Roose, thus heelinge more and more, was drowned, with 700 men wiche were in here, whereof very fewe escaped.' [167].

It is appropriate to mention here that the archaeological evidence seems not to agree entirely with the description given by Van der Delft [149] that she heeled over and water entered her open gunports because 'having fired the guns on that side, the ship was turning in order to fire from the other'.

Although the gunports appear to have been open when she sank, the guns that were recovered both in the nineteenth and twentieth centuries, for which there is a record of whether or not they were loaded, were all found loaded. These were originally from both the port and starboard sides and, as they represent a considerable proportion of the guns in the ship, they are likely to be representative of the ship's armament at the time of sinking. They suggest that there was time to reload after firing, and cast doubt on the need for the *Mary Rose* to turn to present the guns on the other ship's side. This would explain why the gunports were left open, in that the ship was *not* trying to turn when she sank. It was the great weight of guns and an unexpected wind that heeled her over (see Chapter 13).

1545, salvage of the Mary Rose

Sir William Paget organised the initial plans to raise the ship only a day or two after her sinking [152], and Charles Brandon, Duke of Suffolk (Fig. 1.16), was put in charge [153]. By 1 August he had a list of equipment

Figure 1.16 Charles Brandon, Duke of Suffolk, responsible for trying to raise the Mary Rose, *1545 (by courtesy of the National Portrait Gallery, London)*

needed: two great hulks, four great hoys, lengths of the greatest cable available, with capstans and pulleys, 60 ballast baskets, and 40 lbs (*c.* 18kg) of tallow. He also wanted 30 of the best Venetian seamen as salvors, and one Venetian carpenter [153]. The aim was to pass cables under the wreck and to attach these to the empty hulks at low tide, so that on a rising tide they would lift the *Mary Rose* and enable her to be transported underwater closer to the shore [154, 155, 156, 157].

Work started on 3 August [155] and, by next day, they had managed to recover some of her sails and yards which were laid out to dry [157]. Also, they tried to pull the wreck more upright on 6 August [157, 158]. They tried again on 8 August and managed to pass cables under the midship area of the hull, where they were found in the recent excavation (see Chapter 13). This is a measure of how nearly they succeeded, but difficulties remained and it was concluded on 9 August that the Italians could not recover the ship. Indeed, they had broken her foremast [159, 160]. References to further efforts at salvage stop after August, though payments to the salvors continued until December 1545, and included the cost of 22 tuns of beer consumed during the salvage work [161, 162, 163, 164]. It seems that within a month or two all hope was lost in raising the ship, though attempts continued until 1549 to salvage as many guns as was possible [165, 166].

Thereafter the *Mary Rose* was abandoned to her sea-bed grave. Coincidentally, the reason for the existence of the ship, the ambition of Henry VIII, faded as a treaty of peace with France was signed in June 1546. Henry died on Friday, 28 January, 1547, aged 55 years.

2. Discovery of the Wreck of the *Mary Rose*, 1836

The wreck of the *Mary Rose* was first seen on 10 June 1836, by Henry Abbinett, a diver employed by five fishermen to disentangle their nets from a seabed obstruction (Bevan 1996, 112). Two other professional divers, John Deane and William Edwards, were called to the site at Spithead by the fishermen, and they recovered an old bronze naval gun with an inscription referring to Henry VIII. It was 12 ft (3.65m) long and the findspot lay about a mile north-east of the wreck of the *Royal George*, which John and his brother Charles Deane had been salvaging (Fig. 2.1).

A month later the *Hampshire Telegraph* of 15 August 1836, reported that some guns had been found by Deane 'resting on some wreck, which was so completely buried in the sand that the diver could find nothing to which he could afix a rope' (Bevan 1996, 111). This shows that, after about 300 years, the site resembled its state when first seen by John Bevan, before the 1970's excavations started: 'The sea bed in the area consists mainly of shingle and slipper limpits on a featureless bed of mud and hard clay' (*ibid.*, 114). During the centuries between 1545 and 1836 all of the exposed hull, mostly the port side and the castle structures, had been eroded away, leaving just the buried hull.

John Deane, born in 1800, and his brother Charles were descended from Sir Anthony Deane (1638–1721), the famous naval architect and Surveyor of the Navy, but they themselves were of humble means and grew up in the maritime community of Deptford on the south bank of the River Thames downstream from London. In 1823 Charles patented a breathing apparatus for use in fires (McKee 1982, 41), and it was this that he developed into an efficient diving helmet more advanced than any others at that time. Charles and John soon became salvors of naval wrecks with contracts from the Admiralty, and so it was during the 1830s that they were working in the Solent salvaging the *Royal George* which had sunk in 1782 (Bradford 1982, 76) (Fig. 2.2). Hollingsworth's *Guide to Portsmouth* (1840) describes Deane's diving dress:

> 'Mr. Deane did not make use of the old-fashioned Diving Bell, but pursued his submarine researches protected by an India-rubber dress, impervious in every part to water, whilst the head is guarded by a metal helmet, having plate-glass in front and on either side to admit light. A constant supply of air is forced down by an air pump on the deck of the vessel above, into a hose communicating with the top of the helmet. The buoyancy of the human body is such that in addition to the ponderous helmet, the diver is obliged to wear leaden shoes mounting in all to near 300 lbs. weight.' (Bevan 1996, 116). (Fig. 2.3)

The involvement of the five fishermen who were the co-discoverers of the *Mary Rose* is described in a letter

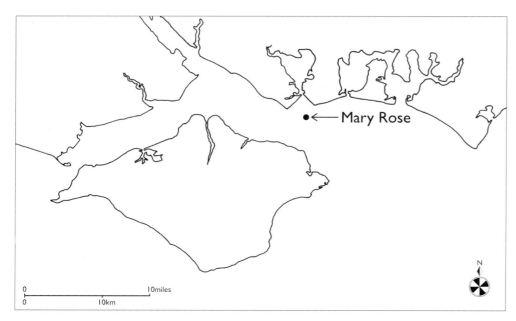

Figure 2.1 Position of the wreck of the Mary Rose

Figure 2.2 Lithograph commissioned by Charles Deane to illustrate his record-breaking dive on the Royal George *in 1832* (Portsmouth Museums & Record Services 913/1974/Photograph by Whitstable Museum)

from John Deane to the Board of Ordnance on 18 July 1836: a gun

> 'was recovered through the instigation of five poor fishermen who had frequently got their lines, etc., entangled in something, but could not find out what it was. That in consequence of getting entangled the 16th June they applied to us to descend and discover what was the cause of their frequent losses, and the obstruction to their daily occupation: that previous to descending, to prevent any disputes, an arrangement was made, that if anything was found, whether of great or trifling value, it should be equally divided between themselves and us, but on going down about half a cables length from the bows of HM ship Pembroke, their line was found to have caught a piece of old timber which was extricated, but on searching in the vicinity, some more old timber was found and the gun in question recovered .' (ibid., 109)

John Deane reported the discovery of the sixteenth century bronze gun to the Civic Officers of Portsmouth who immediately informed the Secretary of the Board

of Ordnance. The Surveyor General accepted the report and on 26 September paid John Deane £220 19s. 0d. Meanwhile, on 19 August the Superintendent of the Royal Military Repository requested 'that the 24-pounder brassd gun of the reigne of Henry VIII, lately recovered at Spithead by Mr. Deane may be deposited with other curiosities of that nature at the Royal Military Repository' at Woolwich (Bevan 1996, 109).

Other objects were soon found, including more guns. The *Hampshire Telegraph*, of 15 August 1836, described them as being:

> ' two extremely handsome brass pieces – one a 42 [pounder] – and the other an 18-pounder, and an iron gun, with part of another of similar construction, greatly corroded. The two latter are objects of great curiosity, and must be of great age; the entire one is 14 feet [4.26m] long; they are constructed of thin iron bars; both were loaded with a stone shot, of about the size of a 32-pounder; the entire one rests on a wooden stock, the half of its circumference being embedded therein its whole length, and it had evidently moved on a slide. The two brass guns were cast in the reign of Henry the Eighth – the largest of which weighed

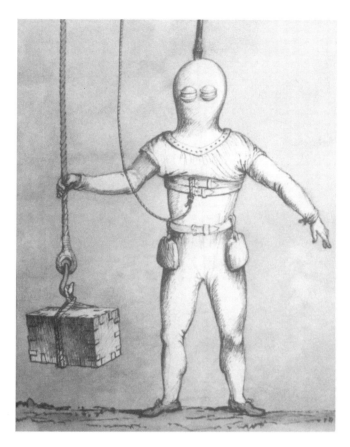

Figure 2.3 Details of a drawing by Simon Goodrich, Chief Mechanist of the Royal Navy (c. 1830) of the Deane brothers with their diving equipment (Science Museum, Science and Society Picture Library)

4,377 lbs (1987kg), decorated with the Royal Arms, and with the Rose and Fleur-de-Lis alternately; the smaller weighing 2,622 lbs (1190kg), with the Rose only, having under it the words (the only that can be deciphered), 'Colveryn Bastard'. These pieces, with the iron-hooped one, were discovered on the same spot, resting on some wreck, which was so completely buried in the sand that the diver could find nothing to which he could afix a rope'. (Bevan 1996, 111)

'they discovered the wreck of a ship at Spithead (supposed to be the Mary Rose, *sunk in the reign of King Henry the Eighth) and requesting to be allowed the privilege of working on her...'* (Bevan 1996, 110)

The identity of the wreck as the *Mary Rose* was soon established for, on 12 August, Admiral Sir Frederick Maitland, who was Admiral Superintendent of Portsmouth Dockyard, was able to refer to it as such. This was quickly made public in the *Nautical Magazine* on 21 August: 'Part of these pieces of ordnance are supposed to have formed the armament of the good ship *Mary Rose*' (*ibid.*).

The discovery generated conflict between the fishermen and the Deanes, and Abinett and the five fishermen decided to become salvors themselves. They petitioned Admiral Maitland who, on 12 August, referred it to Charles Wood, Secretary of the Board of Admiralty, with the comment that:

Four of the fishermen are named on their petition: Henry Richards, William Burnett, Sebastin Redman and John Richards, all of Gosport. Not surprisingly, their version of how the wreck was discovered is rather different from that of Deane. They said that:

'the 16th June 1836 we applied again [to John Deane for salvage help] when we got up another brass gun which is now at Woolwich for inspection and which was got out of some ship sunk there many years ago – and again on the 8th August Instant we got up another brass gun out of the same wreck, and on the 9th Instant we applied again for the vessel which was brought and

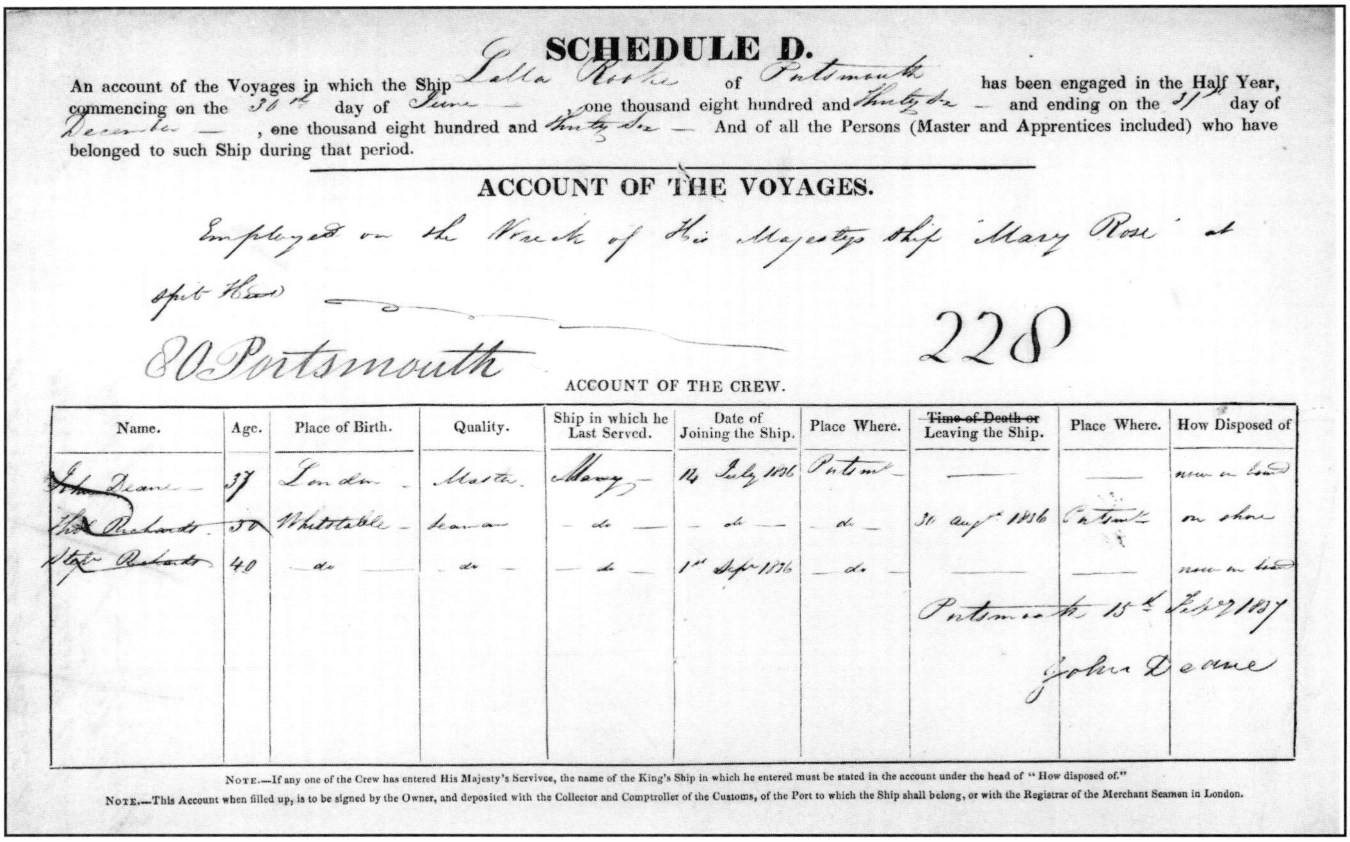

SCHEDULE D.

An account of the Voyages in which the Ship Lalla Rookh of Portsmouth has been engaged in the Half Year, commencing on the 30th day of June, one thousand eight hundred and Thirty Six and ending on the 31st day of December, one thousand eight hundred and Thirty Six. And of all the Persons (Master and Apprentices included) who have belonged to such Ship during that period.

ACCOUNT OF THE VOYAGES.

Employed on the Wreck of His Majesty's Ship 'Mary Rose' at Spit Head

80 Portsmouth 228

ACCOUNT OF THE CREW.

Name.	Age.	Place of Birth.	Quality.	Ship in which he Last Served.	Date of Joining the Ship.	Place Where.	~~Time of Death or~~ Leaving the Ship.	Place Where.	How Disposed of
John Deane	37	London	Master	Mary	14 July 1836	Portsmouth	—	—	now on board
Thos Richards	30	Whitstable	Seaman	do	do	do	30 Augt 1836	Portsmouth	on shore
Stephen Richards	40	do	do	do	1st Sepr 1836	do	—	—	now on board

Portsmouth 15th Feby 1837
John Deane

NOTE.—If any one of the Crew has entered His Majesty's Service, the name of the King's Ship in which he entered must be stated in the account under the head of "How disposed of."

NOTE.—This Account when filled up, is to be signed by the Owner, and deposited with the Collector and Comptroller of the Customs, of the Port to which the Ship shall belong, or with the Registrar of the Merchant Seamen in London.

Figure 2.4 Registration cetificate of John Deane's boat, Lalla Rookh, *during its work on the wreck of the* Mary Rose *in 1836* (Public Record Office BT 98/450 3169)

moored over the wreck. Mr. Deane being then absent from home his man whom Deane left as the Master went down in the diving apparatus and shortly afterwards returned when he stated to your petitioners that he had discovered two more brass guns but were unable to sling them until such time some part of the wreck was removed, which wreck lies in the roadstead in seven fathoms [ie. 42 feet or 12.8m] at low water. That your Petitioners then went to work and removed the same accordingly when the same man who had charge of the vessel said he should not go down to sling the guns on that day that he should let it remain until the next day when your Petitioners all left the vessel and came ashore to Gosport – when to our great surprise the next morning we found that on the evening of the same day (9th) during our absence the master of the vessel went down in his diving apparatus and got up another gun, and on the evening of the 10th we went onboard of the vessel again according to Agreement when the Master informed your Petitioners that as he had got up the gun himself he could do without further assistance from your Petitioners, and he did not consider we had any claim to it whatsoever. Your Petitioners therefore most humbly beg that as we first discovered the wreck your Lordships will take our case into consideration and allow us your Petitioners to have some indulgence as you have been pleased to allow Mr John Deane and Mr Henry Abbinett.'. (Bevan 1996, 110–11)

Sir Frederick Maitland decided on 19 August to prohibit further salvage work until the fishermen and Deane had reached an agreement.

The argument was not resolved, and on 1 September 1836, John Deane wrote to the Admiralty a very full account of the discovery:

'On or about the 10th June of the present year, five fishermen who are in the habit of using graplines, and sweeplines, and who with many other fishermen etc, etc, of Portsmouth and Gosport, for years past, could at any time catch their sweep lines fast at a particular spot at Spithead, by appointment, went off with Hy Abbinett who has one of our Diving Apparatus, to descend and discover, what it was they were fast to. On Abbinett's man going down, he discovered it to be a piece of old wood, he disentangled their lines and came up. On 16th June, by express appointment with the same fishermen we went off to the same place at Spithead with them and previous to my leaving the deck of our vessel to make the descent we agreed that whatever it might turn out to be, should be equally divided between themselves and my party. That on my descending I also found it to be a piece of wood, when I

entangled their lines and they went away but on minutely examining and searching about I found a gun deeply embedded in the clay, which we got up, the fishermen returning and assisting in raising it. Immediately on the recovery of the same (which but for my own exertions and perseverance might not have been found by me, any more than the other person who went down) they desired to be paid the half part of the gun, at their own valuation, which I could not consent to do, stating to them it must be delivered up to the Ordnance Department to await the decision of the Honble Board upon it, but I agreed to, and did, advance them £25. From that time up to the present I have frequently received a great deal of unpleasant language from them, for not paying them half the value of the gun, according to the agreement which I could not consider myself authorised to do, until the decision of the Honble Board of Ordnance, which I did not receive until 2 days ago. I humbly beg leave to state to your Lordships that we did not go near the place again from that day (16th June) until 8th August. From 8th August and during my temporary absence from Portsmouth my party have recovered two more copper and 2 iron guns from about the same place. On two occasions, while getting up 1 copper and 1 iron gun, the fishermen were onboard the vessel and assisted, but in my absence from home no agreement could be made as to the amount of their share, and in the seven tides, the descents made to recover the other copper and iron guns the fishermen did not assist, not being in attendance on board.' (Bevan 1996, 112)

The matter was supposedly resolved by 7th September as John Deane and the fishermen had discussed the matter with Sir Frederick Maitland and Admiral Sir Philip Durham, Commander-in-Chief of Portsmouth Dockyard, and agreed their salvage claims.

On 5th September, however, Henry Abbinett wrote to the Admiralty staking his claim in the wreck to the *Mary Rose*:

'I beg leave to state to your Lordships, that in June last, my attention was called by fishermen to a wreck laying in the anchorage at Spithead, and on my diving down to examine the same, I found her to be so encompassed by weeds that I considered it quite impossible to do anything effectually with her at the time and thought it would be most prudent to wait till a strong SE wind had broken up the weeds and cleared away the ground.' (Bevan 1996, 113)

He went on to say that Deane was, in effect, an interloper and:

'I do most humbly hope and pray that your Lordships will grant me permission to work upon her in some manner and on the same terms as Mr. Deane is now doing and which is also the wish of the men who first discovered her.' (ibid., 114)

The Admiralty did not accept Abbinett's claim, but did accept the solution agreed between the fishermen and Deane, and accordingly gave Deane the exclusive salvage rights on the basis that he shared equally the salvage value of the guns jointly recovered, and that the fishermen received one-third of the value of the other guns and any future finds that Deane recovered (Bevan 1996, 113). With this exclusive salvage permission John Deane was able to continue work in his cutter, the *Lalla Rookh*, which he had purchased earlier that year (Fig. 2.4). According to her Board of Trade registration certificate of 1836, she was 'Employed on the Wreck of His Majesty's Ship *Mary Rose* at Spithead' (ibid., 114).

There was considerable public interest in the four guns that had been recovered, and a poster with drawings of three of them, plus one gun from the *Royal George*, was commissioned by Admiral Durham in 1836 (Fig. 2.5). Deane himself had watercolour drawings of the guns specially made with a view to their eventual publication in John Deane's *Cabinet of Submarine Recoveries, Relics and Antiquities* (Fig. 2.6). A fragment of one wrought iron gun was given to the museum of

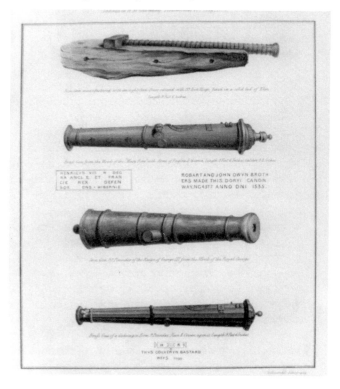

Figure 2.5 Three guns from the Mary Rose *and one from the* Royal George *recovered by John Deane and William Edwards, 1836* (Portsmouth Museums & Record Services 239/1946/Photograph by Whitstable Museum)

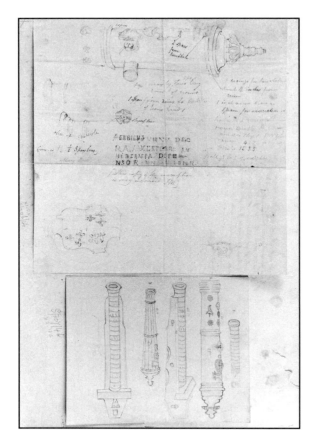

Figure 2.6 Pencil sketches and notes on the Mary Rose *guns used for planning John Deane's* Cabinet of Submarine Recoveries, Relics and Antiquities *(Portsmouth Museums & Record Services 307/1945/ Photograph by Whitstable Museum)*

the Portsmouth and Portsea Literary and Philosophical Society on 2 September.

That same month Major General Millar, Colonel Sir Alexander Dickson and Major Dundas reported to the Admiralty on the significance of the discoveries, and most importantly, in view of what was to occur about 150 years later, concluded that:

> 'the Mary Rose *was lost at Spithead and the ship never was weighed up … It may fairly be presumed, therefore, if the wreck the guns were laying on could be dispersed to some degree, that more guns and other articles of an interesting character might be discovered and weighed.'* (Bevan 1996, 114)

That there were other objects is shown by drawings in Deane's collection for these included pieces of iron guns, portions of rope, bronze sheaves from rigging blocks, and even human bones (*ibid.*, plate 22). Unfortunately the book of Deane's 'submarine recoveries' was never published, though some of the excellent watercolour drawings do survive in Portsmouth City Museums and Record Services.

John Deane stopped salvaging the *Mary Rose* in 1836, but returned to the site in 1840 when he used explosives to open up the seabed (Bevan 1996, 169). He requested the Ordnance Board 'the grant of a few old condemned bomb shell (13in./330mm) for the purpose of exploding gunpowder in continuation of our operations on the wreck of the *Mary Rose* at Spithead'. He was given 'six unserviceable 13in. shells' (*ibid.*, 171). Deane had already used 13in. shells on the wreck of the *Royal George* in 1839, and evidently found them useful.

The usual method of exposing a wreck was described by Colonel C. W. Pasley of the Royal Engineers:

> '*Mr. John Deane invariably descends himself, and our usual course is first to go down and survey, and select out the best situation to place the powder in, so as to have the most powerful effect in the destruction of the object. We then haul the Cask or Cylinder of powder down and secure it in the desired spot, and afterwards fire it with a quick fuze through an Indian rubber or leaden tube, and we find 50lbs or 60lbs of powder placed in a proper position, amazingly destructive under water.'* (Bevan 1996, 136)

Such fuses were unreliable, however, and in 1839–40 both Deane and Pasley were experimenting with 'firing gunpowder in deep water, and in a rapid tideway, by the Voltaic battery' (*ibid.*, 155). On the *Mary Rose* Deane used 'a voltaic battery of 4 cells … their wires in pairs with rope wound round them and lashed together' (*ibid.*, 166).

John Deane himself said in 1841 that for efficiency he preferred 'a small portion of powder confined in a bomb shell, and sunk some distance in the earth near the object of research, to a much larger quantity of powder deposited in a cylinder placed on the surface' (Bevan 1996, 188).

Horsey, in 1844, described the result of Deane's method of salvage in 1840:

> '*Mr. Deane, with spade, shovel, etc., then excavated a portion of the sand, etc., and fired a charge of gunpowder, and found on descending again that he had got into the hold of the unfortunate ship, having made a crater of large dimensions by this explosion.'* (Horsey 1844)

The recent archaeological survey of the *Mary Rose* disclosed about 40 fragments of those bombs, their scatter showing that the main working area was in the middle of the ship in sectors H6, O6, O7 and M6, and confirming that Deane did indeed expose part of the Hold around the mast step (Fig. 2.7). The bombs have cast iron shells 42–55mm thick, and fragments of at least three bombs have been identified so far. Others may be identified when the remaining fragments have

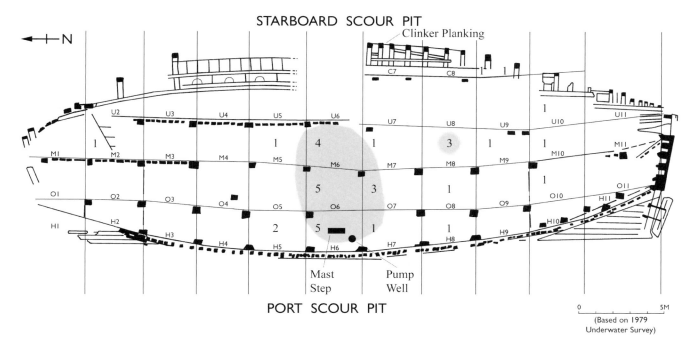

STARBOARD SCOUR PIT

Clinker Planking

Mast Step

Pump Well

PORT SCOUR PIT

0   5M
(Based on 1979
Underwater Survey)

Figure 2.7 Distribution of Deane bomb fragments and main areas of bomb damage

been conserved. Two joining fragments (80A0348; 80A0696) of one bomb, originally 13 inches (330mm) in diameter, have a fuse hole 45mm in diameter, and a secondary hole 11mm in diameter, passing through most of the shell to hold a lifting handle (Fig. 2.8). Each bomb originally required several men to lift it, judging from the weight of these two fragments which were found in sectors M5 and M6. One was a surface find, but the other lay in the Tudor deposit context 101, where it had been driven by the force of the explosion.

Another possible type of underwater explosive device, though this is far from certain, was feature 4 found in sector M5 (Fig. 2.9). It was an oval shaped depression about 850mm long, 450mm wide and 180mm deep in layer 10, and it had traces of a 'black sooty metallic' lining, and small patches of a 'sooty black stain' within its outline. It could also have been a corroded powder ladle (Site Notebook: TB1/80/05-06/001-173/ 1980 Trench 5/6, pp. 84, 85, 142–6).

Publicity so inflated the value of even the smaller finds from the *Mary Rose*, including pieces of wood from the hull structure, that they ended up in local shops. In December 1840 one shop was selling a piece of *Mary Rose* wood about 6ins [152mm] square for 5s, and a bow was priced at £1 10s. (Bevan 1996, 167). Almost all of these objects have ben lost, though a particularly fine German stoneware jug with a bearded face, recovered from the *Mary Rose* around 1840 is now in the Victoria and Albert Museum.

The wood from the *Mary Rose* and the *Royal George* was carved into chairs, tables, work boxes, walking sticks, sword sticks, riding crops, ink stands, guns, carved sailors, book covers and other items.

The main discoveries of 1840 were listed by John Deane and William Edwards in a letter dated 5

September to the Board of Ordnance. They included an inscribed brass 24 pounder gun 11ft. 6ins [3.5m] long, four wrought iron 32 pounders from 6ft [1.8m] to 8ft [2.4m] long each containing powder and stone shot, seven or eight smaller guns, swivels and parts, a human skull, two archers bows, and a small quantity of old

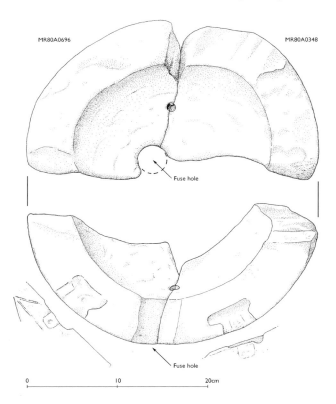

MR80A0696   MR80A0348

Fuse hole

Fuse hole

0   10   20cm

Figure 2.8 Fragment of one of Deane's cast iron bombs.
Scale 1:4

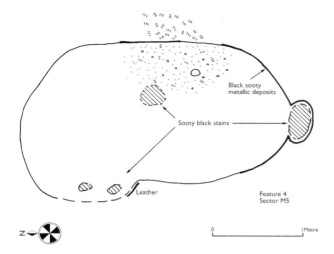

Figure 2.9 Feature 4, M5

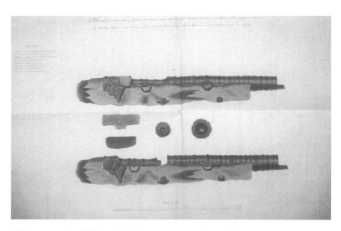

Figure 2.10 Wrought iron gun and carriage recovered by John Deane during his second excavation of the Mary Rose *in 1840* (© Royal Institution of Cornwall)

timber (Fig. 2.10). The *Portsmouth Independent* of 10 October 1840, reported that 'the brass piece is very beautiful, and was found to contain an iron shot, two wads, and about two quarts of gunpowder.' The newspaper added that:

> *'the iron guns are of a most antique and rude construction, being formed of wrought iron bars, secured throughout with strong iron hoops. They vary from two to eight feet [0.6–2.4m] in length – two of them rest on thick beds of elm, which form their carriages, some of these contain powder and stone shot as large as our present 42–pounders.'* (Bevan 1996, 169)

The guns were shipped to the Office of Ordnance at Woolwich in October 1840 and some were preserved at Woolwich and at the Tower of London (*ibid.*, 170).

In total, Deane salvaged four bronze guns and nineteen parts of wrought iron guns from the *Mary Rose* in 1836 and 1840. Also there were eight 'warrior's bows' (McKee 1973, 338). Bevan (1996, 169–70) has suggested that as at least some of the guns were from the destroyed port side of the ship, they were the counterpart weapons to those found on the starboard side in the 1970s.

The main structural discovery in 1840, however, was believed to be the lower part of the main mast. It is described in the *Portsmouth Independent* of 10 October, 1840:

> *'The piece of the mast is fifteen feet long [4.5m], and, at the partners [ie. at deck level], is nearly as large as that of a 75 gun ship. The centre is a fine piece of solid oak, and the whole is in the highest state of preservation.'* (Bevan 1996, 169)

Unfortunately no part of the mast has survived. However, the clue to its diameter is that it was 'nearly as large as that of a 75 gun ship'. There was no 75 gun

ship in the early nineteenth century, but the diameter of a 74 gun ship was 37ins [0.93m] (Falconer 1815, 266). From this it seems that the mast of the *Mary Rose* was about 36ins [0.91m] in diameter. The part of the mast, described as 'a fine piece of solid English Oak' (Bevan 1996, 172), was amongst a collection of miscellaneous artefacts from the *Mary Rose* that were auctioned by Deane at Portsmouth 1840. The collection included:

> *'the heel of the mast (oak) sold for £30; stone and iron shot from 20s (shillings) to 30s each; common glass bottles from 10s to 15s; Warrior's bows from 10s to 15s; iron ring of antique cannon, leaden shot, curious old padlock, part of stock of matchlock gun, brass sheaves.'* (Bevan 1996, 172)

In addition to the mast, a pump was also found in 1840 (*ibid.*, 186), but details are lacking. As the bomb fragments and Horsey's comment in 1844 show that Deane had opened up the Hold in the area of the mast step, it is possible that both the mast and the pump were removed by them. Margaret Rule, however, has stated that what Horsey wrote:

> *'cannot be true. Either Horsey misunderstood what he was told or Deane was exaggerating. The hard shelly clay which underlies the mobile upper sediments and seals the Tudor levels is unbroken by either crater or spade.'* (Rule 1983, 47)

The hard shelly layer represents the erosion horizon between the stable Tudor deposits containing the wreck and the unstable overlying recent layers. But for Deane to have recovered fragile objects, such as the long bows, he must have penetrated into the stable Tudor deposits with his explosives.

Another clue to where Deane undertook salvage is given in the newspaper report of 10 October 1840, which adds that 'It may be interesting to the naval architect of the present day to learn that so large a ship as the *Mary Rose* was clinch built, as this mode of building is now entirely confined to boats and small craft' (Bevan 1996, 169). Since the Sterncastle is the only part of the hull structure that was clinker built, this must refer to salvage work in that area.

Whilst Deane was salvaging the *Mary Rose* in 1840, a Colonel C. W. Pasley of the Royal Engineers was demolishing the nearby wrecks of the *Royal George* and *Edgar* by means of explosives and a giant rake. Although there are passing references in later books in the Royal Engineers' library saying that Pasley had extended his destruction to the wreck of the *Mary Rose* in 1843–4, this is highly unlikely. One reference (Porter 1889, 27) states that:

> 'The Mary Rose lay at the bottom of the sea off Spithead until the year 1843 when Colonel Pasley RE, having succeeded in removing the wreck of the Royal George, destroyed the remains of the Mary Rose also after it had lain sub-merged for nearly three hundred years.'

Two other references to the destruction by Pasley in 1844, are quoted by McKee but the sources not attributed (McKee 1973, 181–2; 1982, 42).

John Rhodes, Curator of the Royal Engineers Museum, Chatham, has kindly investigated this matter and found that two earlier publications have no reference to Pasley having worked on the *Mary Rose* site and cast doubt on the reliability of the 1889 reference. One is the *History of the Royal Sappers & Miners*, vol. 1, by T. W. J. Connolly (ed. 1855); and the other is Colburn's *United Service Magazine*, September 1844, which, although having an article about the *Mary Rose*, entitled 'The *Mary Rose* and the French Historians', only refers to Deane's discoveries. Moreover, John Bevan has checked the Pasley letters and diaries for 1843–4 preserved in the British Library (*Pasley Papers* vol. xxx, Add MS 41990) and found no reference to Pasley having even dived on the *Mary Rose*. Indeed, none of Pasley's papers or published works in the library of the Royal Engineers Museum refer to the *Mary Rose*, nor did his son-in-law, Sir Henry Tyler, mention her in his manuscript *Life of Pasley* or in his obituary to him published in the *Professional Papers of the Corps of Royal Engineers*, vol. xii, new series 1863. If one adds to this the fact that no objects are known to exist that were recovered from the *Mary Rose* by Pasley, either in the Royal Engineers Museum at Chatham or elsewhere, the conclusion must be that Pasley had no connection with the wreck and that some writers confused the separate salvage operations by Deane and Pasley in the same general area and at about the same time.

The Admiralty had been very much involved in Deane's salvage of the *Mary Rose*, as it had in the demolition and salvage by Col. Pasley of the wrecks of the *Royal George* and *Edgar*. In particular it was concerned to ensure the removal of these wrecks as hazards to shipping. Consequently the Hydrographic Department ensured that the positions of all three were charted by Commander Sheringham in 1841, though the discovery of the position of the *Mary Rose* on this chart was not to be recognised until 1966 when Alexander McKee found it. This, in turn, led to the discovery of the wreck on the seabed, and opened the way to her entire excavation and recovery.

A curious post-script to this first phase of salvage is recorded in a letter from A. Hillhouse (of Beale's Wharf, Southwark) to the Duke of Wellington in 1841, now in Southampton University Library (Wellington MSS., 2/81/107). The letter reads:

> 'To his Grace the Duke of Wellington
>
> At a moment when so many valuable relics of antiquity and trophies of British valour have been irrecoverably lost to the nation, I trust I shall stand excused of the liberty I take in informing Your Grace of the fact, that the anchor of the "Mary Rose" (whose cannon in the Tower and carved memorial at Greenwich Hospital have both disappeared by fire) having been raised and purchased by a Jew is either arrived at, or on its way to Sheffield probably to be converted into five times its weight of unauthentic trifles.
>
> Not knowing whom to address I ventured trespassing on Your Grace's known promptitude should it appear desirable to rescue so interesting a relic from its probable fate.
>
> The proprietors of Beals Wharf, Southwark, to whom it was consigned for transporting to Sheffield can doubtless furnish the necessary particulars.
>
> November 17th 1841.
> Most respectfully,
> Your Grace's
> Obedient servant,
>
> A. Hillhouse'.

3. Rediscovery and First Survey of the *Mary Rose*, 1965–1978

The search for the *Mary Rose*, 1965–1971

It was Alexander McKee, historian, journalist and amateur diver, who had the inspiration, ambition and leadership to rediscover the *Mary Rose* in 1971, though he had provisionally identified the site in 1967. On 2 January 1965, he invited a group of amateur divers, mainly from the Southsea branch of the British Sub-Aqua Club, to join him on a project to investigate twelve historic shipwreck sites in the Solent. These included the *Royal George* sunk in 1782, the *Boyne* sunk in 1795, and the *Mary Rose* sunk in 1545. Those who were initially involved in what he called 'Project Solent Ships' were Alan Lee, John Baldry, Roger Hale, John Towse and R. W. Wells (McKee 1982, 43), but soon the team was enlarged to include others. A detailed account of the early stage in the discovery of the *Mary Rose* is set out by McKee (1968; 1982).

McKee's aim was:

> 'to locate some of the more important of the historic wrecks, starting with the Royal George … we are not thinking in terms of an excavation, because present methods are too primitive and might damage the remains, but merely of an inspection and assessment of the problems.' (1968, 196)

He added that 'good care was taken to see that the diving teams taking part in Project *Solent Ships* had a range of knowledge which, when combined, at least eliminated the possibility of embarrassing errors'.

> 'The most pressing requirement was for conservation, as some materials will deteriorate markedly within a very short time of being removed from the water, and on almost every occasion we managed to have a professional conservation expert actually in the boat, so that conservation began on site. This was Mrs. Margaret Rule, an archaeologist in charge of on-site conservation at the current land "dig" at Fishbourne. But the role of Mrs. Rule went well beyond this. As a professional archaeologist, she could follow each step we made, check it, and argue it out.' (McKee 1968, 200–1)

McKee was not the only team leader looking for the *Mary Rose* at that time. As its potential historical and archaeological importance was so great, it was also the objective of Lieut-Cdr Alan Bax RN, working with the support of the Committee for Nautical Archaeology in London (*ibid.*, 221–3). The CNA was a group of academics and others who were concerned that the discovery of historic shipwrecks in British territorial waters by amateur divers might lead to their destruction, as had occurred in other parts of the world. The CNA was set up in 1964, only months before McKee began searching for the *Mary Rose*, following the discovery of a Roman shipwreck in the River Thames at Blackfriars, City of London (Marsden 1994, 33–95). With George Naish of the National Maritime Museum as Chairman, and Peter Marsden of the Guildhall Museum, City of London, as its first Secretary, it was anxious to monitor discoveries by amateur diving groups and to give them advice. It was also keen to lobby Parliament requesting that significant underwater wrecks should be given adequate protection as historic monuments. At that time, ships and shipwrecks were excluded from legal protection as historical monuments due to their having been once mobile structures and therefore in law 'chattels'. In certain cases members of the CNA, with the support of the Committee as a whole, considered that it was necessary to head off archaeologically unqualified diving teams looking for very important historic wrecks by becoming involved themselves. The *Mary Rose*, the Dutch East Indiaman *Amsterdam* sunk off Hastings in 1749, and the Royal yacht *Mary* sunk off Anglesey in 1675 were all on this early priority list (Marsden 1972; 1986a, 198–202; 1986b, 179–83).

In 1965 McKee and Bax had different views regarding where the *Mary Rose* was to be found, and both led diving groups to search separate areas of the Solent, but without success. The problem was that the sixteenth century record of the sinking, and especially the evidence of the Cowdray engraving, were not sufficiently precise. In February 1966 both groups were brought together by Joan du Plat Taylor, a maritime archaeologist and a future Secretary of the CNA, at a meeting in Guildford to consider the historical evidence. They concluded that, as the wreck could not be seen on the seabed, and the sixteenth century records did not show where it lay, the only solution was to visit the archives of the Hydrographic Department of the Navy to examine nineteenth century charts which might plot the site. Bax set up the visit for 10 May but was unable to attend himself, so it fell to McKee and

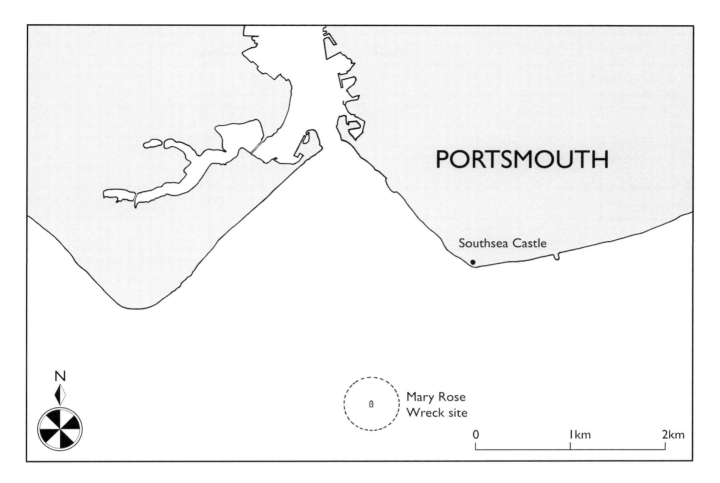

Figure 3.1 The exact position of the wreck of the Mary Rose

John Towse to be the first to examine a chart by Commander Sheringham of 1841 which gave the positions of the *Royal George, Edgar* and *Mary Rose*. This was the much-needed breakthrough, though they subsequently found that the chart positions did not quite match modern charts. 'Bax settled the matter by asking the Hydrographer of the Navy to transfer the position from the old chart to the current one, using a station pointer. This corrected position was exactly on the edge of the scour mark' which McKee had already located by diving in 'his' area (McKee 1968, 222–3) (Fig. 3.1). The position of the *Mary Rose*, marked by a red cross, lay at the edge of Spit Sand in 6 fathoms (11m) of water at low tide (Rule 1983, 51).

Although McKee found that his group had been looking in the right area, he concluded that:

'Our long detective work had proved accurate, but without Bax's help we would never have obtained access to the chart, so we could hardly act dog-in-the-manger ... We should have to co-operate. CNA neatly solved the situation by making Mrs Rule director of the project, with Bax and myself as representatives of S & TG [Scientific & Technical Group] and Southsea Branch [both of the British Sub-Aqua Club] respectively.' (1968, 223)

McKee was Director of Excavations until 1978 (McKee 1982, 92).

Now that the location of the *Mary Rose* site was known, it was only a matter of time before the wreck itself would be found. Consequently, McKee decided to gain additional archaeological help in interpreting evidence of the wreck by involving Joan du Plat Taylor and Peter Throckmorton. The latter was an American maritime archaeologist working on wreck sites in the Mediterranean, and both made a significant contribution (McKee 1968, 236) in support of Margaret Rule whose considerable archaeological expertise at that time was restricted to land sites. In 1971 Margaret Rule learnt to dive and so began to take archaeological responsibility for work on the seabed (Rule 1983, 59–60).

When McKee and Towse first dived in the expected wreck area on 14 May 1966, they found that there was no ship to be seen. Instead the seabed comprised a soft mud with 'occasional eroded lumps of clay upstanding from it, beds of slipper limpet shells in layer-lines as if sorted by wave action, and now and then, quite wide pools of sand' (McKee 1982, 55).

McKee's underwater search had started in April the previous year, when he and his diving colleagues explored the site of the *Royal George* which he thought might lie close to the *Mary Rose*. Their technique was to dive in pairs and swim around the seabed looking for clues. In 1966 McKee and Margot Varese, a project volunteer, dived and found a mound and hollow in the seabed a considerable distance away from the *Royal George*, and he thought that these might be a scour-pit caused by an old buried shipwreck (*ibid.*, 58–9). The site coincided with the charted location of the *Mary Rose*.

Defining the nature of the suspected wreck site more closely was made possible by Professor Harold Edgerton's company EG&G International, which ran a sonar profiler and side-scan sonar across it in 1967 and 1968 (Fig. 3.2). These located a buried 'feature' in the seabed (McKee 1968, 235, 244–5), and strengthened McKee's belief that this may be the *Mary Rose*. All that remained was to carry out a pilot excavation to recover objects, and so check whether or not they were of sixteenth century date. But first, it was considered necessary to try to protect the site from possible interference by treasure hunters (*ibid.*, 248).

Legal protection for the wreck site

The CNA was well aware that the Ancient Monuments legislation in England at that time could not be applied to protect underwater archaeological sites. Consequently, it was necessary to work with others to persuade the government to create legislation that would give adequate protection to historic shipwrecks, such as the *Mary Rose*, *Amsterdam* and *Mary*. The awful

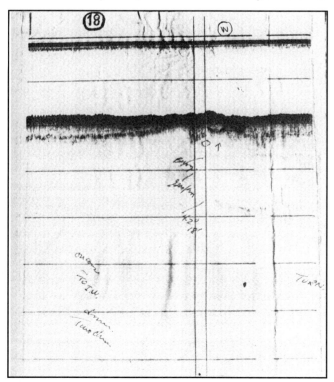

Figure 3.2 1978 sonar image of the wreck site

reality at that time was that once the *Mary Rose* had been discovered, another diving group could mount a salvage operation on the wreck and, with an uncontrolled grab, as happened to another British historic wreck in the Goodwin Sands in more recent years, could salvage the wreck. Indeed, mechanical excavators were also used, within the law, by treasure hunters on the eighteenth century wreck of the *Amsterdam* at Hastings in 1969 and 1974. Contesting these activities in the courts would have been beyond McKee's means, and in any case the salvage law, as was then embodied in the *Merchant Shipping Act* 1894, would have required that the salvaged goods were auctioned off to the highest bidder for the benefit of the salvor and the Crown (McKee 1982, 48). This had already been the fate of antiquities from other historic shipwreck sites in Britain, most notably the warship *Association* sunk off the Isles of Scilly in 1707.

It is to McKee and his team's credit that they did not choose the normal path of wreck salvage that was then practised and that the law encouraged, but instead they chose to treat the *Mary Rose* as part of Britain's heritage that must not be violated. It is fair to say that each member of the team could have become personally wealthy by selling off the discoveries as was obligatory under the salvage law. Although it is said that the gift to the nation of the Saxon treasure in the Sutton Hoo ship by its owner was one of the greatest examples of public munificence, it is fair to say that this is paralleled by McKee and his team in respect of the *Mary Rose* and by others with regard to some other historic shipwrecks.

It is not generally known that the conflict with salvage law continued for years during and after the total excavation of the *Mary Rose*, for the Receiver of Wreck tried to insist that the personal property in the wreck, including the Barber-surgeon's chest of equipment and the gold coins, should be sold for the benefit of the Crown and to pay both the Receiver's and salvor's costs, if it was not claimed by the modern descendants of its original owners. The Mary Rose Trust had the right to buy them, but was reminded that the Receiver had the right to instruct Customs officers to enter the Mary Rose museum to seize the offending objects. These contentious matters, which also related to other important historic wrecks, particularly the *Amsterdam* (1749) and two medieval rudders salvaged off East Sussex, are now settled, but it is important to appreciate that they were real and difficult issues then, and that the future direction of the project that McKee had started was decided in 1966–7.

The CNA had taken legal advice and suggested that McKee's group should establish itself as a formal organisation that could act as a body rather than as individuals. Thus the 'Mary Rose (1967) Committee' was formed 'to find, excavate, raise and preserve for all time such remains of the ship *Mary Rose* as may be of historical or archaeological interest' (McKee 1968,

Figure 3.3 The four original members of the Mary Rose (1967) Committee signing a lease to the seabed where the wreck was believed to lie in 1967. Margaret Rule, Commander Alan Bax, W.O.B. Majer and Alexander McKee (Photo: G. Mudle)

248; Rule 1983, 54). The members of the Committee comprised: Alexander McKee, Lieutenant Commander Alan Bax RN (CNA) and W.O.B (Bill) Majer (a trustee of the Society for Nautical Research), and Mrs Margaret Rule, a professional archaeologist and in time herself Secretary of the CNA (Fig. 3.3).

At its first meeting, in November 1967, the Mary Rose (1967) Committee decided to apply to the Crown Estate Commissioners for a lease of 1200 square feet (334 square metres) of the seabed where the suspected wreck lay, in the hope that this would stop others 'occupying' the property and undertaking any salvage. A leasing arrangement helped, as did the uncertain rights of the Committee as 'salvor in possession' of the wreck under the 1894 *Merchant Shipping Act*, to protect the *Mary Rose* from interlopers and treasure hunters. But had any other potential salvor challenged the Committee's 'rights' in a court of law there was considerable doubt about whether the validity of the arrangements would have been upheld. Although the members of both the Mary Rose (1967) Committee and the CNA privately knew the great weakness of the site's protection, they continued the bluff by always presenting a confident public face. The best protection of all was secrecy. Margaret Rule wrote that when the diving team went to the site in the fishing boat:

'Relocation on the site at the beginning of each diving day was done by means of line-of-sight

transects to shore marks 1 to 3 miles [1.6–4.8km] away and, as McKee usually observed one set of marks and I observed the other, most people on board had no idea why we stopped when we did!' (Rule 1983, 55)

There was great relief therefore when the site was formerly designated as protected under the new *Protection of Wrecks Act* 1973 and it became illegal for anyone to interfere with it without a licence (McKee 1968, 248).

Discovery of the *Mary Rose*, 1971

Between 1969 and 1971 the team worked to find the structure of the suspected wreck. They spent the summer of 1969 using water jets and a crane-grab dredger to dig a seabed trench 11.5m long, 1.5m wide and up to 2m deep (McKee 1982, 73–6). By October they were able to probe down into the underlying deposits with the aid of an air-lift supplied by the Royal Engineers Diving School at Marchwood, near Southampton. No wreck structure was found and work resumed in May 1970 on the trench which had 'only slightly filled with soil' during the winter. This was probed and small excavations were carried out on suspected contacts. McKee described a significant discovery on 30 May:

'some five feet [1.5m] of timber about a foot wide was exposed there, both ends continuing into the faces of the excavation ... The last diver had dug down beside the timber and then excavated underneath, so that I could see plainly that it was a plank, not a beam, a number of treenail holes showing where it had been pegged to a ship's frames'.

This was the first contact with the *Mary Rose*, though the plank was not attached to a wreck and so was lifted (McKee 1982, 81–2).

Further excavation was undertaken in August, firstly by crane-grab dredger for two days, followed by five days by the Royal Engineers divers. The grab removed the overburden, revealing a clay layer from which were raised two more pieces of ship's timber, part of a 'fashion piece' and a large cleat. However, the first dateable evidence that this was the *Mary Rose* occurred when McKee used the grab to dig deeply into a nearby area and:

'at 12.20 a very large concreted object appeared, so big that it was held between the jaws of the grab. ...We managed to get ropes round and so lowered it to the deck ... There was a slight bump as it touched the deck and about three inches of the concretion broke off, exposing a triple ring of grey metal. The crew looked totally disbelieving. "You don't mean to tell us that's a gun!" they said. But by God it was!' (McKee 1982, 85)

The gun was quickly sent to Portsmouth City Museum where it was cleaned and conserved by Chris O'Shea. It proved to be a sixteenth century built-up wrought iron gun 2.28m long with a bore of 95mm, and of a type that Deane had found in the *Mary Rose* in 1836. It showed that they were almost certainly on the *Mary Rose* site and that it was only a matter of time before the structure of the ship itself would be found.

The discovery of the gun gained the interest of the Royal family, business and industry, and the Royal Navy declared the site a 'prohibited area' for their surface vessels and allowed the team to mark it off with full-size mooring buoys (McKee 1982, 86).

The structure of the *Mary Rose* was first seen by Percy Ackland on 5 May 1971, after it was exposed by winter scour. He was seriously ill during the dive, but later recorded the occasion of the discovery:

'Mac [McKee] said he would like the end of the excavation dug last season buoyed, as that was where we aimed for today. I attached a length of line to a buoy and coiled it up so it would release without snags. By this time we were on site and Tony [Glover] had anchored up. I finished kitting up and Mrs Rule, who was doubling up as log-keeper, acknowledged my departure. ... Visibility was a gloomy three to four feet [0.9–1.2m]. ... I

headed S.W. for about 80 feet [24.4m], when I noticed a change in the bottom. I swam back and found a ledge. I swam along the ledge and found a fragment of timber. I felt around it. It was not attached to anything. I moved ahead and saw an indistinct dark object. I moved towards it. It looked like a frame. IT WAS A FRAME! Eroded at the top like a pyramid about two inches by ten inches [50–250mm]. Six inches [150mm] away was another one, and beyond that yet another. I moved along, noticing they ran north to south; I found more frames – only this time with some planking attached. I touched it, half to reassure myself it was real and half to check the width of the planking which was about four inches. I swam along all the frames visible above the seabed. This must be the Mary Rose.' (McKee 1982, 88–9)

In all, a 20.1m length of framing belonging to the port side of the ship near the stern was surveyed that day, and loose objects were recovered. Most were of recent date, but some were undoubtedly of the sixteenth century, such as stone moulds for casting lead shot found by Reg Cloudsdale and a pewter flagon found by Percy Ackland (McKee *ibid.*, 90–1). A deep trench was next dug on what was believed to be the outboard side of the hull. This showed that the tops of the frames were badly eroded, but below 1.5m there was planking, initially thin and distorted but below that in excellent condition.

Site survey and trial excavation, 1971–1978

During 1971 the task of uncovering and recording the outline of the *Mary Rose* was divided between Alexander McKee and Margaret Rule. McKee led a diving team of members of the Southsea and Southampton branches of the British Sub-Aqua Club to uncover the ship timbers using an airlift, and Rule in a separate boat led a team from the Naval Air Command Sub-Aqua Club and the Chichester Branch of the BSAC to survey the uncovered remains (Rule 1983, 60), usually in a visibility of about 1m.

The priority of the 1972 season was to map the extent of the surviving top of the remains of the wreck. Although the year was plagued with poor diving weather, and 59 out of 97 diving operations were cancelled, the top of the hull was uncovered and traced for a considerable extent. Moreover, many sixteenth century objects were found, including a wooden comb, two spinning bobbins, a thimble, the wooden handle of a 'kidney dagger', an inscribed wooden bowl, and yet another wrought iron gun which this time was on its timber bed. Amongst the finds were many human bones.

By the end of that year the team had found that although the hull normally had carvel planking, at its south-eastern part there was also some clinker planking which later proved to be part of the Sterncastle. The different methods of hull construction could be seen on each side of the wreck, and the slope of the frames showed that the hull lay at an angle in the seabed.

By 1973 two groups were officially involved with the ship: the Mary Rose (1967) Committee, which that year became a registered charity (Rule 1983, 67) and which administered the project, and the Mary Rose Special Branch of the British Sub-Aqua Club (previously called the Mary Rose Association). The official support of the Lord Mayor of Portsmouth gave the project significant encouragement, and in 1973 and 1974 the Committee included representatives of both the City of Portsmouth and Hampshire County Council, the National Maritime Museum, the Maritime Trust, the BSAC, the BBC *Chronicle* programme, and the Commander in Chief, Naval Home Command (Rule 1983, 67). Many people and companies generously supported the team. John Barber, for example, kindly supplied the *Roger Grenville* (Fig. 3.4) and the *Curlew* dive boats, and Volvo donated the engines.

Figure 3.4 The catamaran Roger Grenville, *used as the dive ship from June 1971 till the arrival of the* Sleipner *in 1979* (Photo Ref.: 80.1067)

One of the objectives of the 1973 investigation had been to establish the angle that the ship lay in the seabed, for only then would it possible to plan a full excavation. It was not until August 1975, however, that the sternpost was identified by Morrie Young and the angle of heel established as 60 degrees (Rule 1983, 67).

Other important developments occurred during this phase of the project. 1973 saw the wrecks of the *Mary Rose*, the *Amsterdam* (1749) and the *Grace Dieu* (1439) designated as protected historic wreck sites of national importance under the new *Protection of Wrecks Act* 1973. And on 30 July 1974 the project received a Royal seal of approval when HRH Prince Charles dived on the *Mary Rose* and examined the hull. He was the first member of the Royal family to visit the ship since Henry VIII in 1545, and as a result gained considerable public support for the project in funds, equipment and expertise.

Significant objects were recovered, such as two gunport lids found in the scourpit where they had fallen from the eroded port side (Rule 1983, 69).

By 1977, the surveyed outline of the hull had reached sufficiently forward to show that the bow had not survived in an intact state. However, a major trench across the surviving forward end of the ship identified the Orlop and Main decks, and showed that much of the starboard interior of the ship was intact with objects still in place where they had fallen in 1545 when the ship heeled over and sank (*ibid.*, 72).

By the end of 1978, then, the wreck had been identified as the *Mary Rose* on circumstantial evidence, and almost the entire outline of the hull had been mapped (Fig. 3.5) showing that she lay aligned north–south with her bow to the north. Trenches had revealed that the ship was heeled at an angle of 60 degrees to starboard, and that her stern was buried deeper than her bow.

Planning the future

As the excavation progressed it became increasingly clear that decisions should be made concerning whether or not to excavate the ship completely. If this was to occur it would be necessary to establish a Mary Rose Museum and a more professional organisation with an effective legal status. On becoming Director of Museums for Portsmouth, Richard Harrison joined the Committee, was elected Chairman at the end of 1976 and led the way in encouraging the Committee to consider these longer term issues (see Chapter 6).

The form of the future management of the project was eventually agreed, and in November 1978 the 1967 Committee appointed a Steering Committee to move things forward. The members were: Councillor Sotnick (Chairman), Alexander Flinder, Sean McGrail (National Maritime Museum), Richard Harrison, Margaret Rule and John Reid.

The implications of the decision to proceed with a plan to excavate the inside of the ship over a three year period were considerable. The establishment of a Mary Rose Trust was necessary to provide an organisational framework that could attract substantial financial support and, once the Trust was created, one of its first decisions was to request the Department of Trade and Industry to transfer to the Trust the licence to survey, excavate and recover the *Mary Rose* under the *Protection of Wrecks Act* 1973.

Planning and executing this major archaeological excavation required key staff to be appointed; the provision of a substantial diving platform; developing resources ashore to receive finds and provide storage; and creating a drawing office, photographic studio and a suitable area for the treatment and conservation of finds. Crucial to the thinking behind the excavation plan was a commitment to transfer the principles of archaeological investigation of sites on land to the

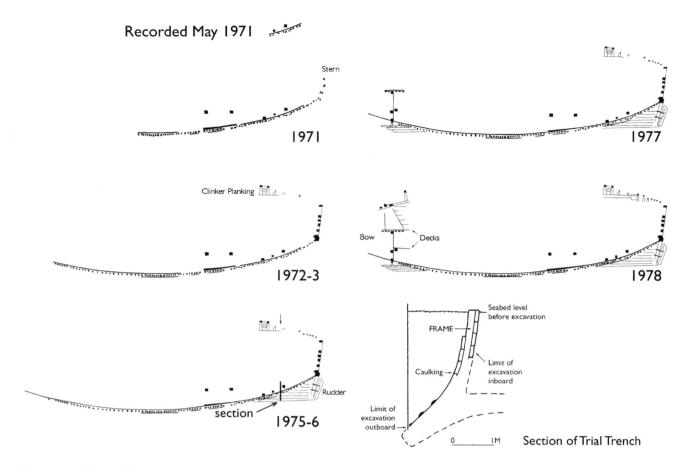

Recorded May 1971

Stern

1971

Clinker Planking

1972-3

section

Rudder

1975-6

1977

Bow

Decks

1978

Seabed level
before excavation

FRAME

Caulking

Limit of
excavation
inboard

Limit of
excavation
outboard

0   IM   Section of Trial Trench

Figure 3.5 Plan of the wreck as exposed, 1971–78

underwater environment. No other underwater archaeology project had been attempted on such a large scale.

Staffing

One of the first steps taken by the Trust was to appoint Margaret Rule as Archaeological Director. She in turn recruited a core team of archaeologists and divers to carry out the excavation and supervise not only the large teams of volunteer divers, but also finds staff, draughtspersons and conservators. By the end of 1979 sixteen people, together with the crew of the salvage vessel *Sleipner*, had been employed.

In those early days the team included Keith Muckleroy, Adrian Barak and members of the Aston University Diving Club. In time Jon Adams and Andrew Fielding joined the dive team, followed by others, including Barry Andrian (later Burden), Christopher Dobbs, Alexzandra Hildred, Berit Mortlock, Bob Stewart and Christopher Underwood.

On-site base

The scale of the excavation was daunting, and Portsmouth City Council helped by promoting a work

experience programme at Portsmouth Museum to assist in documenting the finds during the excavation seasons 1971–1977. This established a finds procedure for the 1978 season.

A substantial diving platform was required which would provide substantial working space and remain on site all season. During their visit to the *Vasa*, a seventeenth century warship recovered from Stockholm Harbour in 1961, the Trust directors had learnt that the salvage vessel *Sleipner*, then docked in Gothenburg, was for sale. Built in 1943 to recover submarines, she had a keel length of 43m, as well as substantial on-board accommodation. *Sleipner* had also been used in the recovery of the *Vasa*. Following a detailed survey carried out by British Petroleum, *Sleipner* was purchased from the Neptune Salvage Company on behalf of the Trust by Portsmouth City Council, towed from Gothenburg, fitted out for her new role at Marchwood, near Southampton and moored on site early in April 1979.

Onshore accommodation

The Trust inherited a licence to use storage space in the Block Mills in the Portsmouth Naval Base. The damp, cool conditions in a basement were ideal for the storage of waterlogged ship's timbers. Moreover, the City

Council also provided accommodation in a three-storey building in Bishop Street, Old Portsmouth and in a house in Old Commercial Road. Additional temporary office accommodation was obtained free of charge in buildings on the site of the redundant power station in Old Portsmouth.

The need was also for a single 100 square metres building in the longer term, and towards the end of 1979 the Trust was offered rent free the two-storey Bond Store, owned by Whitbreads, in Warblington Street, Old Portsmouth, close to the harbour. It was fitted out and served the Trust well until 1986 when the Trust moved to the present accommodation in the Naval Base.

Conservation

Facilities for the conservation of the very large numbers of vulnerable organic and metal artefacts recovered from the site was essential, and during 1979 action was taken in three directions:

- A contract with the Portsmouth City Museum Conservation staff ensured that a certain amount of conservation work would be undertaken on behalf of the Trust. Their laboratory was particularly well equipped to conserve large metal objects, such as guns, and also to freeze-dry organic artefacts. Facilities were also provided in the Bond Store for conservation, and by 1980 the Trust was employing four conservators.

- The National Maritime Museum agreed to investigate the conservation requirements of the ship.

- As many artefacts would present special conservation problems, a three year grant from the Leverhulme Trust financed a research team to investigate these. Moreover, an Advisory Committee, chaired by Sèan McGrail (National Maritime Museum), was appointed in December 1979 to support the conservation programme.

There was no precident in British underwater archaeology for establishing the backup facilities that were created for the *Mary Rose*, but experience showed that they would be essential to the success of all major underwater projects. Details of the still continuing programme of conservation of the hull and its contents can be found in Volume 5 of this series.

4. Excavating and Recording the *Mary Rose*

This chapter summarises the highly complex operation of excavating and recording the *Mary Rose* whilst in the seabed and is mainly based on archive records by Jon Adams. As this can only be a summary, readers requiring more detail will have to refer to the archives of the Mary Rose Trust. This chapter does not include the post-excavation archaeological research work leading to publication.

Strategy

Following the first sight of the ship by Percy Ackland in 1971, the team was initially faced with an enigmatic series of frames sandwiched by planking. With so little visible, it was impossible to identify what part of the hull was revealed: fore or aft, or port or starboard. Nearby timbers merely confused the situation, and could mean that the wreck was broken into large pieces. The first task, therefore, was to follow the timbers to reveal the complete run of frames. In the following year the south end was found to lead into the stern structure, including the transom timbers and diagonal planking. The north–south alignment of the wreck was thus established and the large square timbers were shown to be deck beams, although their angle was still puzzling.

From this point, the excavation strategy was to cut exploratory trenches to answer specific questions, and until the nature and general condition of the wreck was better understood these were to be confined to areas outboard. Moreover, large numbers of organic and metal artifacts requiring specialist conservation were not expected outboard. The aims of this phase (1972–1976) were to determine:

- the degree of structural coherence,
- the overall extent of the site and the depth of the stratified remains and surface sediments,
- the exact orientation of the ship,
- the nature and density of any material outboard but adjacent to the hull.

Underwater excavation consisted of two distinct procedures each with its associated tools. First, there was digging with trowels, brushes or by hand to reveal archaeological material; and secondly, there was the removal of 'spoil' - the unwanted sediments loosened in the process.

The equipment each excavator took underwater was carried in a plastic string bag of the sort that was common in bargain-basement stores at the time. In it was a trowel and any other excavation tool likely to be needed, such as a paintbrush. A few sealable plastic bags were to contain small finds, although many, including sediment samples, required more secure packaging in plastic boxes. Large or very fragile items often had containers specially made for them. All excavators were expected to record the finds they recovered, once their removal had been agreed by the supervisor. Standard survey equipment was a drawing board fitted with sheets of drafting film, a pencil, tape measure and perhaps a folding straight rule. In periods of low visibility torches were carried or, from 1980, worn on helmets.

Appalling weather severely curtailed the 1973 season and, partly as a result, there was a slight hiatus in 1974. Initially it was decided to concentrate on uncovering the outboard areas, partly to avoid finding many objects which would require conservation, for at that stage conservation facilities were extremely limited. Momentum was restored in 1975-6 when the major task was to cut a trench to define the stern structure. In 1976 it reached down to the keel, 4m below seabed, probably the deepest underwater archaeological trench that had been dug up to that time. It established the angle of heel of 60 degrees to starboard, thus making sense of the deck beams, and the true extent of the surviving structure. As the north side of the trench was studied in section, its strata provided the first real insight into the site formation processes.

In 1977 a trench was excavated outboard at the bow on the port side, and, as well as clarifying the mechanisms of the site's formation, it also showed that the hull at the scarf between the keel and stempos‗ was on the same alignment as was the stern and therefore that the ship had not broken up or been badly twisted or 'hogged'. As well as establishing the cohesion of the keel it showed that the keel sloped upwards towards the bow at a rise of about 4 degrees. Sufficient was now known to justify moving the excavation inboard.

The first trench was excavated across the hull from port to starboard in 1978, and although rather less than half of the hull survived, it established that, as with the keel, the structure was coherent rather than a collection of fractured sections. On this basis the 1967 Committee held meetings of invited observers to con-

TRENCH GRIDS 1975-8

starboard scour

CASTLE

UPPER

MAIN

ORLOP

HOLD

port scour

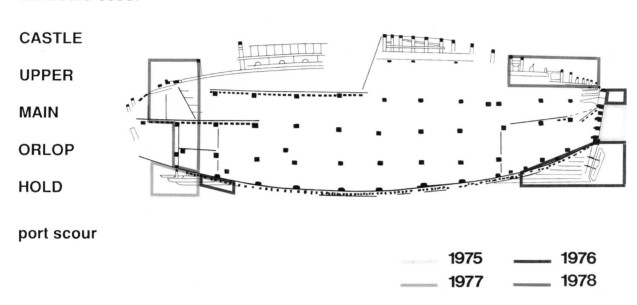

	1975		1976
	1977		1978

TRENCH GRIDS 1979

starboard scour

CASTLE

UPPER

MAIN

ORLOP

HOLD

port scour

metres

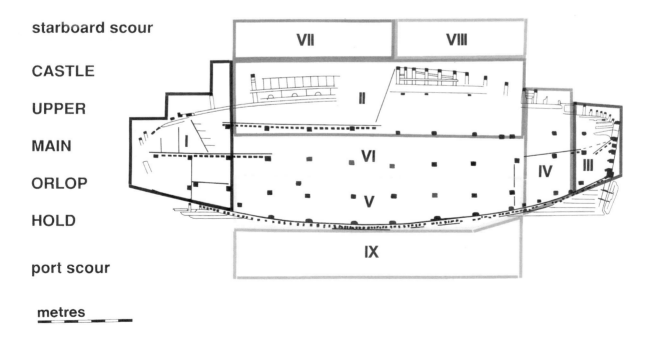

Figure 4.1 Trench grids 1975–79

sider the results of the excavation so far. They sought answers to two questions: was the hull sufficiently well preserved to justify full excavation? And if so, was it necessary to set up a trust to look at how the ship might be fully excavated and raised? The decision was then taken to form a charitable company with limited liability, to be known as the Mary Rose Trust, and to re-launch the project aiming at total excavation and, if possible, raising the hull.

From 1979 onwards, following the formation of the Trust, the strategy was to replace individual trenches (Fig. 4.1)with a more open-area excavation (Fig. 4.10) and initially remove the modern objects and strata. This took the form of 12 parallel trenches, each about 3m wide whose sides were determined by the position of deck beams, crossing the ship from east to west, and extending far enough outboard to include the areas of scour around the hull.

Within the ship, the sides of the trenches were made to coincide with the exposed ends of the major deck beams, and as each trench was dug the sloping timbers of each deck were found crossing it. This enabled the finds from each deck and trench to be located in a sector. Trench 3, for example, crossed the Hold and that sector was designated H3. It also crossed between the Orlop and Main decks, the sector between being designated O3. Thereafter it crossed between the Main and Upper decks, the sector being designated M3, and so on for the Upper deck.

The dive records gave more precise positions of objects within each sector, but until they are processed and plotted in relation to the ship within each sector, the system of recording the location of finds by deck and sector remains the basis for interpreting the contents of the ship.

Team structure and policy

The decision to form the Trust in 1979 enabled a professional excavation team with many volunteers to be established. Opening up the whole site would be a monumental task, exposing large amounts of archaeological material, including the ship, to erosive environmental forces. It was essential that if the ship was to be excavated and raised, the work had to be completed quickly (Rule 1982, 72).

This meant that both the length of the excavation season and the number of people required were vastly increased. This progress was reflected by the changing diving vessels. Prior to 1971, an interested local fisherman named Tony Glover offered his boat, a converted, formerly *Queen Mary,* lifeboat, and took Alex McKee and his team out to the site, mainly at week-ends and odd days, for only the cost of his fuel. In 1971, the wooden-hulled, though engineless, catamaran *Roger Grenville,* so named after a supposed captain of the *Mary Rose,* was donated to the Mary Rose 1967 Committee by local business man John

Barber, and became the main diving platform right through until 1979. Initially, Tony Glover used his boat to tow *Roger Grenville* out to the site, saw her moored up safely before going about his fishing for the day, and returned in the evening to tow her back to Portsmouth Harbour. At a later date, *Roger Grenville* was given a set of engines, courtesy of Volvo. From 1979, with the formation of the Mary Rose Trust, the ex-Royal Naval Lifting vessel, used in the salvage of the Swedish warship *Vasa* and rechristened *Sleipner* by her Swedish owners, was purchased by the Trust and moored each season permanently over the site of the *Mary Rose*, with personnel being ferried back and forth by small tenders (Fig. 4.2). Seasonal length varied, but in general, diving operations went from a team of twelve working a four month season, to around 50 people working for nine months, sometimes around the clock. This did not include either the 500 amateur divers, or the additional personnel required to run the shore base and conservation laboratory, all of whom brought the total to around 70.

Figure 4.2 The salvage vessel Sleipner *(Photo ref.: 80.0639)*

The existing diving team, comprising Rule, Fielding, Adams, Barak and Andrian, was enlarged in 1979 by Dobbs, Hildred, Mortlock, Stewart, Underwood and Yorke. Keith Muckleroy had joined the staff at the National Maritime Museum, Greenwich, although he still paid regular visits including some for extended periods. The team was also enlarged with the addition of Debbie Fulford (Draughtsperson), Andrew Elkerton (Finds), and Ian Oxley, together with finds supervisor Adele Wilkes and three finds assistants who were responsible for receiving, documenting, packaging and transporting finds back ashore to the conservation staff. The Leverhulme Trust also funded a conservation scientist, John Harvey.

This large team worked very well in terms of its organization, and supervised the work of the amateur divers using a rota. The staff worked two days aboard the diving barge *Sleipner* and spent every third day ashore, sometimes resting. With Rule keeping up a break-neck pace of direction, fund-raising and other commitments, it meant that at any one time there were only five or six supervisors on board managing up to 45 volunteers. The professionals, skilled at archaeological work, found they were doing less archaeology and more marshalling their teams in and out of the water twice a day.

Moreover, as the minimum period for volunteers was only nine days, it was found that just as they began to get useful, they left and the next group would arrive. Happily, this situation did not last long, and soon the minimum period for a new team member was increased to fourteen days.

A pool of 'staff divers' soon began to develop, as some of those who had arrived for nine days became hooked by the work and volunteered to stay on indefinitely. These tended to be the people who had a natural flare for the tasks involved, so their status was formalised and those who were obviously gifted and reliable were invited to stay permanently. Other measures included giving priority to those volunteers who had been before and who had a proven capability. Where entirely new people were involved, priority was given to those who were able to commit themselves for longer periods. As this process continued, a new class of team member emerged who combined some of the skills of archaeology with those of diving: the 'archaeological diver'. These people were not archaeologically trained, yet they became highly skilled in both excavation and the associated task of recording. They also built up an intimate knowledge of the site and many became key members of the team for the rest of the project.

By 1981 the number of archaeological divers had virtually doubled, and it was found that the overall size of the team could be reduced, as the core team was diving for longer and getting more done. This enabled the staff to achieve a much better division between doing some of the work themselves and teaching others. Overall the speed of work increased to a good standard.

Organisation of work

A minimum of two archaeological supervisors were placed in control of specific trenches, and working with them were one or more staff divers and a group of volunteers. The latter would be a balance between more experienced 'returnees' and novices. By working in a designated trench, they gained familiarity with the area and so increased the overall efficiency and standard of work. The supervisors were responsible for the documentation of work in their trenches, under the direction of Rule and Fielding. All records were in a written form as there were no computers on the salvage barge except for processing DSM results by modem to Cambridge University. Finds records were later transferred from finds cards to computers ashore.

From late 1979 onwards, a volunteer was required to participate for a minimum of fourteen days, whilst the staff divers worked the same two-days-on, one-day-off shift as the archaeological supervisors. As diving regularly carried on until after 8pm and started before 6am, the staff and divers on the last shift stayed on board *Sleipner* overnight.

The staff in charge of each pair of trenches also worked staggered shifts so that at least one archaeological supervisor and one staff diver were always present. Both supervisors were present on one day in three, and discussed developments and aims of the forthcoming work. Margaret Rule staggered her shifts with Andrew Fielding, and both made regular inspections of all trenches and discussed the progress and priorities of each with the supervisors concerned and the overall progress with the two Deputy Directors (A. Fielding and J. Adams). Regular team meetings ensured that the overall progress was relayed throughout the team as a whole, although the pace of the project and the shift system did not allow everyone to be present at any one time.

Diving management and safety

Until the end of 1979 all underwater work was carried out using scuba (self-contained underwater breathing apparatus), and as most of the team were sports divers, the operation was managed using a system that everybody was familiar with. Prior to 1979 the archaeological director had delegated the day-to-day running of the diving and its safety to a diving officer (A. Barak), but from 1979 the much larger team meant that responsibility was divided between two Diving Officers: C. Underwood and R. Yorke, Barak having become one of the archaeological supervisors.

Since the system was designed around scuba diving, various primary directives were established for on-site conduct, initially, as a set of Mary Rose Special Branch diving rules, and subsequently as a comprehensive Code of Practice. The first involved communication, and although archaeologists may work alone, they were required not to dive alone unless on a lifeline, or using surface-supplied air. This regime ensured that people worked at their allotted tasks in adjacent parts of the site where they were in visual or audible contact with one another.

In view of the number of dives involved, it was decided that decompression diving would not be routinely carried out. This decision was taken both for safety and logistical reasons. Due to the varied nature of the tasks it would have been inefficient to run all dives in shifts, as managing decompression for several divers, all on different schedules, would have been impossible. Diving practice not involving decompression procedures was also safer and more akin to procedures then in general use by amateur divers.

Because the *Mary Rose* site was a mile (1.6km) offshore and in an area of busy shipping it was not practical for the divers to be dropped from a boat and

Figure 4.3 Some of the excavation documentation aboard Sleipner. *In the picture are (left to right) Ted Clamp, Jon Adams, Barrie Burden, Faye Kert, Colin McKewan and Stuart Vine* (Photo ref.: 81.5953)

recovered at the end of their dive. Instead, the vessel *Sleipner*, moored over the site, gave secure diver access to the site, and also served as a machinery platform, site office, finds centre and a hotel with catering facilities and sleeping accommodation (Fig. 4.3).

The strong current and low underwater visibility made it necessary for divers to make their way to and from the site down shotlines and via a grid of scaffolding on the seabed. It was strictly forbidden to return to the surface away from the shotline unless in difficulties, and if a diver did appear on the surface it was assumed to be an emergency until determined otherwise. Despite all this, there was still one terrible accident, and most sadly even an immediate response to the emergency did not save diving volunteer Louise Mulford who tragically died during the 1980 season (Rule 1982, 100-1).

As the project developed so the system of dive management was modified, because more and more tasks required equipment and techniques beyond those taught within sport-diver training schedules. The most immediate of these was the lifting of heavy objects such as guns, parts of the ship's structure, and fragile archaeological material. Consequently, the decision was taken to transfer various tasks to team members qualified to use surface-supplied diving equipment.

The revised management system of 1980 replaced the two Diving Officers with three Chief Divers (variously B. Burden, P. Berchtold, T. Clamp, P. Dobbs and N. Blair), whose shifts overlapped so that each was in primary control for one day, assisting on another and ashore for the third. Of the two diving officers, R. Yorke temporarily returned to commercial diving, while Chris Underwood took over responsibility for dismantling the ship's structure and recovering heavy objects such as guns. The latter was done using surface supply, as were some excavation tasks such as excavating underneath the overhanging Sterncastle.

Prior to commencing any diving operation various conditions had to be met and certain procedures carried out. The Chief Diver first ascertained that it was safe to dive in the prevailing or imminent conditions, the most important of these being:

- sea-state, affecting how safely people could enter and exit the water and how effectively the safety boat could be launched in an emergency;
- tidal strength, affecting the safety of anyone who lost direct contact with the grid or shotlines;
- underwater visibility, restricting the range of tasks that could be carried out and requiring more experienced personnel; and
- cold, especially in the days when drysuits were rare, was a factor that might curtail a dive, especially a repeat dive, as well as reduce the efficiency of the diver concerned.

If judged safe the following procedures were carried out:
- An 'Alpha' flag, denoting that diving operations were taking place from the vessel, was raised to alert other sea users in the vicinity.
- The safety boat was at immediate readiness to recover any diver who had surfaced free of the shotline and was in danger of being carried away by the tide. This was a rigid-hulled inflatable suspended on a davit and capable of being deployed in less than 60 seconds. Regular drills were carried out to ensure that the engine was operational and only approved personnel could act as coxswain.
- A log-keeper was appointed to record divers in and out of the water, and as this required considerable concentration, shifts were restricted to two-hours. The only verbal communication permitted with the log-keeper was task-related, ie.: name, trench, air supply, etc.
- A standby diver was stationed in immediate readiness by the dive ladder, and although one of the more onerous tasks, its importance required that only experienced team members, with a detailed knowledge of the site, could qualify.

Volunteers provided their own equipment, and certification was checked when they first came on board. Most important was that air cylinders were within the stipulated test period and that there was nothing irregular about their equipment (for instance, home-made or adapted items were prohibited).

To run this number of dives necessitated filling up to 100 air cylinders per day. From 1980 onwards, a dual compressor system was installed on board *Sleipner*, capable of pumping a large air storage bank from which the diving cylinders were filled. Only nominated personnel were allowed to operate the system.

This diving system worked well, but at periods of maximum intensity, when ten or more divers might be in the water at the same time, even this system came under strain. A dive rota board was developed that displayed all the vital information that chief divers, archaeological supervisors and team members needed. It displayed the order in which divers were to work in their respective trenches, determined by the supervisors prior to the shift. Name-tags were double sided, coloured white on one and red on the other. When displaying the diver's name in red it indicated that the person was in the water. As the board also displayed time in hours the chief diver could see at a glance how many divers were in the water, where on the site they were working and how long they had been in. Divers could also see exactly where they fitted into the rota and so judge when to get ready (Fig. 4.4).

From mid-1979 onwards, supervisors were supplied with diving equipment thereby ensuring that everyone's equipment was of a common safety standard. All supervisors used a regulator fitted with an 'octopus' rig which is an additional hose to facilitate air sharing.

Figure 4.4 HRH Prince Charles being prepared for diving assisted by Jon Adams (left) (Photo ref.: 82. 7253)

Diver recall

On some occasions divers needed to be recalled from the seabed, perhaps at the end of a shift or if the weather was worsening. The routine recall was accomplished by hammering on the dive ladder with a series of pre-arranged signals, while emergency recall was a thunder-flash, though this was rarely used. The hammered signals were acoustic versions of diving rope signals. Four blows on the ladder meant finish work and come up. Continuous blows meant come up immediately. The noise carried to all parts of the site and in most circumstances divers heard it easily. Should a diver not hear the recall, perhaps because of working with an airlift, other divers on the way back would alert them. In the case of a general recall, a staff diver was

ready to do a circuit and hurry up or assist any divers reacting slowly.

Supervisors and staff divers usually did repeat dives and often approached the end of their 'no-stop' time, in which case a pre-arranged signal in 'bells' was given some minutes before this occurred. These were pairs of hammer blows, and it was surprisingly easy to distinguish high numbers: nine bells for someone working in trench nine, seven bells for trench seven, etc.

When monitoring divers, it became a procedure for each supervisor or staff diver to go in with a list of divers, checking that they were in their allotted stations whilst on their way to their own trench. In order to regularise such inspections, the interval between such checks was no more than 20 minutes and these inspections would be logged. Dive schedules were overlapped to achieve this routine, otherwise a staff diver was sent in specifically to do one. These routine checks were helped by having each diver's initials written in white rubber paint on the underside of their fins. Checks could therefore be carried out without descending right down into the trench to recognise them. This would have disturbed the loose sediments as the divers generally worked head down, with their feet and fins resting on the grid system so as not to damage archaeological material or disturb the silt, which would cause a deterioration in visibility.

Diver training

A diver training scheme for new members existed from the beginning of the project, and after 1979 a careful induction of all new team members occurred on board the barge *Sleipner*. All volunteers received an illustrated introductory talk on the project's aims and state of play, usually from Margaret Rule or from one of the deputy directors. They were then introduced to the diving regime by one of the chief divers, followed by the archaeological supervisor, to whom they had been allocated, carrying out their own trench-specific briefing, often making use of video. This was followed by an introductory tour dive around the site with one of the staff divers or supervisors, the emphasis being on navigation around the grid and its location tags. This was often all that could be done on day one, especially considering the amount of information that had to be absorbed.

The second dive was an introduction to airlifting and excavation procedure, after a careful briefing on the surface about how the equipment was used. The standard induction period for a new team member averaged four days, for, although allocated tasks were kept simple, recording skills had to be acquired as well as finds procedure and log-writing. In many ways what the supervisors tried to impart during this period anticipated the syllabus of the Nautical Archaeology Society's Training Programme established years later.

Underwater work

All underwater work was affected by the tidal currents, the depth of water, by spring and neap tide runs, working times and weather. There was a 'tidal rose', used by the supervisors to calculate tidal current strengths, the direction and duration of which changed with spring and neap tides.

The tasks carried out on the site fell into one of four categories: excavation; recording (including structural survey, photography and video); removal and recovery of objects; general maintenance. Excavation and recording were usually carried out as individual tasks by staff and volunteers alike, while the recovery of objects and maintenance work often involved teams of divers working together.

Briefing

A detailed briefing from the supervisor preceded all dives (Fig. 4.5), whilst at the end of their dive the excavators and surveyors usually left the water before their replacement went in. This allowed the supervisor to debrief them and thus take account of the situation in briefing the next person.

Figure 4.5 Diver briefing (Photo ref.: 80.0549)

Record documentation

At the end of a dive all divers wrote a log, detailing their work, on pro-forma sheets that were serial numbered and placed in the archived trench files (Fig. 4.6). These log sheets recorded details of the precise location and feature worked on, preferably with sketches. Any objects recovered were listed with their finds numbers, together with context descriptions and survey data.

These detailed logged records comprised a primary site documentation, although supervisors also wrote in trench books and kept day journals in which they collated their understanding of the material being revealed (Fig. 4.7). The journals collectively helped the director to assess progress across the whole site and to review the allocation of tasks and staff.

```
        Site Director's Book
         |            |
  Trench Book    Supervisor's Book
     |                |
     Volunteer's Dive Log
```

Excavation

A primary aim of the *Mary Rose* excavations was, and always had been, to uncover and record the archaeological features with as much control as one would expect on land. A second aim was that the excavation would be stratigraphic.

A general flaw of much early underwater excavation on other sites was that this distinction was not recognised, and various suction devices, such as airlifts and suction-dredges, were used to do the digging into the seabed, resulting in the indiscriminate sucking of sediment and any finds in it to the surface. This earlier technique unfortunately negated two of the biggest advantages of underwater sites and shipwrecks in particular – the superior preservation of organic materials, and the relationship between objects and their contexts of use. Organic material and other fragile objects often disintegrate on their way up the airlift, and if such objects are only first noticed on the surface their exact relationships and hence much of their significance may be lost.

Early attempts to excavate on the *Mary Rose* site had been carried out with a water jet provided by the Fire Brigade (McKee 1973), but as excavation began in earnest, the *Mary Rose* team designed and built their own equipment. The tool chosen was the airlift, a suction device originally developed for industrial purposes which had already been adapted for use on archaeological sites elsewhere (Dean *et al.* 1992, 308-9). The early *Mary Rose* airlifts were ingenious, well designed and fabricated to a high standard, but they were not suited to the more delicate, precision work that was increasingly required from 1975 onwards. Each generation of airlift thus became easier to control and both simpler and lighter (Fig. 4.8).

As the excavation team became larger and more airlifts were needed on site, a better method of getting the air to the seabed was required than having an individual hose from the surface to each airlift. The first improvement was to run a hose to a take-off point on the seabed from which three airlifts could be powered and this was then increased two points, one for the bow and one for the stern. Finally for the 1980 and 1981 seasons a manifold supplied by a wide-diameter hose, was run down the length of the wreck outboard and up to ten airlifts could be attached each side using quick-release 'chicago' couplings.

81/9/819

U9 F110

NAME _SCRIVENER_ DATE _13-8-81_ TIME _3-15_ TO _3-50_

U/W VIS.	U/W CURRENT	SURFACE UPRIGHTS	WEED
3m	W		

OBJECTIVES DSM and Sketch Box in Upper Deck between Trench 8 and Trench 9.

RESULTS

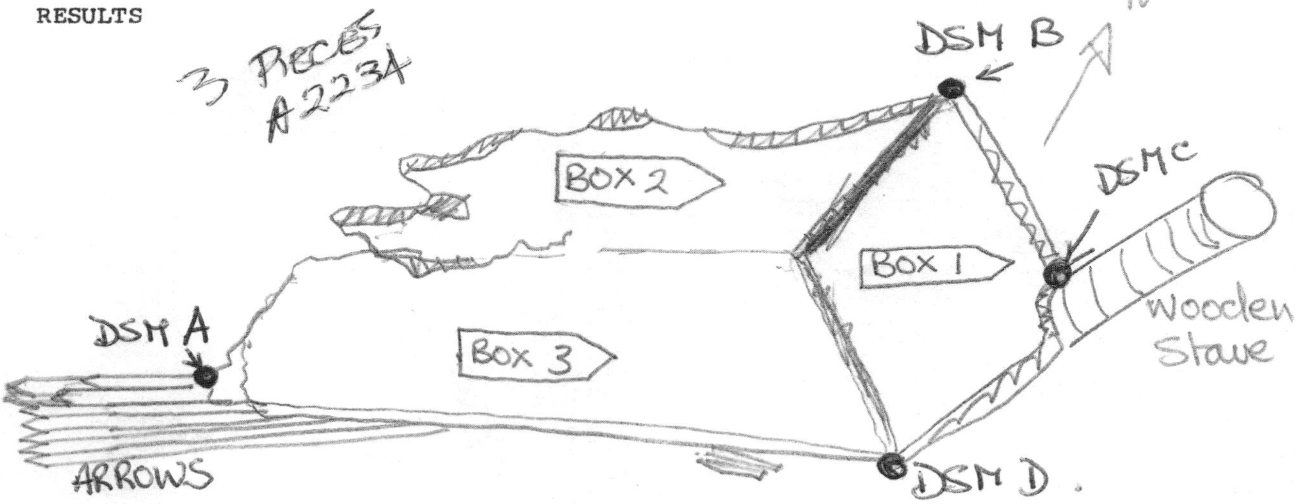

3 PIECES
A2234

BOX 2

BOX 1

BOX 3

DSM A

ARROWS

DSM B

DSM C

Wooden Stave

DSM D

N

FINDS (DESCRIPTION, position, number in finds index)

DSM Points		489N	490N	480W	S19W
	A	2·80	3·08	1·24	2·74
	B	3·50	3·81	1·56	2·14
	C	3·46	3·71	1·70	2·24
	D	3·40	3·67	1·64	2·45

DRAWINGS (Description and number in finds index)

81A 2099
OTHER PARTS 81A 2234 Recovered not a direct measurement
BY BRYAN/FREEMAN NOT LOGGED only a good approximation

PHOTOGRAPHS (Description and number in finds index)
MERELY REFERRED BACK TO
THIS LOG AMS 24/9/87

Figure 4.6 Example of a dive log (81/9/819)

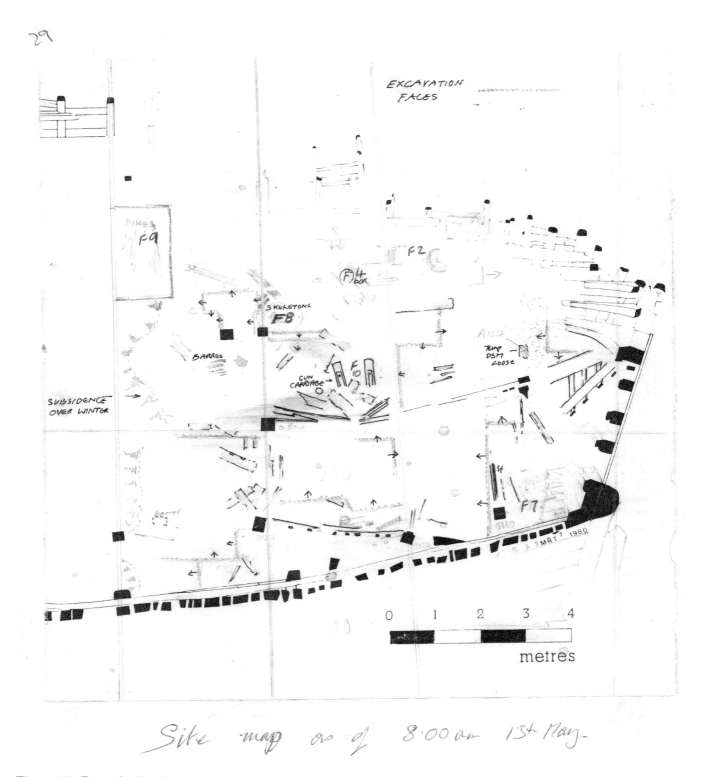

Figure 4.7 Example of a site map

A mode of excavation now became standard in which excavators rested themselves and their airlifts not on the seabed but on the grid around the trench. This also enabled the excavators to position themselves over the features being dug. Once at work, it became accepted practice sometimes to remove fins to avoid damage to fragile material. With their feet on the grid, excavators would hover over the trench, only touching the deposits with the selected tool, an ability that gravity denies to land diggers. As the trenches got deeper, the grid system was extended downwards, additional grid bars providing optimum access and support for the excavator. These various configurations were christened trapezes due to the instability of the prototypes rigged out of rope and scaffold, but in their later form were stable and effective. The components

Figure 4.8. Divers using airlifts, watched by a friendly cuttlefish (Mary Rose Trust)

for the grid itself were generously supplied by British Gas through David Price and comprised one inch (25mm) diameter steel gas pipe, coated with bright yellow polyethylene which was not only strong enough to support divers but also was visible in the murky waters of the site. Prior to that, scaffold poles were kindly supplied by SGB Scaffold.

A further refinement was practiced in these deeper trenches, in which the increase in the airlift's buoyancy was utilised when the intake was partially obstructed. By holding the airlift by the rim, buoyancy could be adjusted simply by opening one's fingers into the water flow, thereby enabling the excavator to lower and raise themselves in archaeologically sensitive areas of the trench. For this reason, writers who have designated airlifts as the tool for heavy work and the suction-dredge for delicate work are mistaken. Both can be used extremely delicately, allowing control over the rate at which archaeological material is revealed. A useful maxim is that excavators should know what is going up the pipe, otherwise they are excavating too fast or without proper control. Used in this way, the airlift not only kept the visibility clear but constituted the all-in-one equivalent of the land excavator's dustpan, brush, bucket, wheelbarrow and conveyor-belt.

Airlifts and dredges could also incorporate the land excavator's sieve, although on the *Mary Rose* site the decision was taken to do without them because they were judged to be unnecessary. The reason was that the airlift was not to be used as a digging tool, but instead to remove excavated spoil. Consequently, all objects

should have been seen and recovered by the excavator. It could not be claimed that small items never went up the airlift, but rather that the number of objects recorded *in situ* and safely recovered without a scratch considerably exceeded what would have been possible using any alternative procedure.

Survey

As the structure of the ship was of great complexity, it was recorded by surveyors under the overall control of Andrew Fielding, using drawing boards and drafting film, tapes and rulers, as well as equipment to install new datums, including plumb-bobs and bubble-tubes. Site photography was mostly undertaken by the archaeological supervisors, and was mainly carried out at slack water, when excavation was suspended to avoid spoil landing back on excavated areas. A slight tide run helped keep sediment moving. Photography was also done as near to mid-day as possible to maximize the amount of surface light reaching the sea-bed.

Recording techniques

Nails were used to attach identification numbers to the tops of frames from 1971, and until 1980 the primary survey datums were 6 in. (150mm) nails hammered into the tops of major timbers, particularly the deck beams. While local accuracy was achieved with tape measures, the site plan inevitably suffered from a compound error as it grew to encompass a large area of 45m x 25m. In 1979 the primary datums were surveyed with a Partridge Rangemeter lent by Sonardyne International Ltd (Rule 1982), which gave an accuracy of ±100mm for any point on the site. This solved the problem of compound error and provided a basis over which the individual surveys of higher local accuracy could be assembled.

The positions of new timbers or objects could then be fixed by triangulation measurements from the primary datums. Ideally a third measurement would be used as a check, and a straight rule or a plumb-bob provided the depth below datum. Sections were drawn as on land sites, by establishing a horizontal datum line related to the primary datums, and the strata were plotted by measuring their offset distances from the datum line.

Planning-frames were tried particularly on flat surfaces (Fig. 4.9), but the highly three-dimensional nature of much of the site, the generally low visibility and other problems such as weed made their use difficult. Tracing some timber joints onto film was also carried out, though throughout the recording process underwater parallax through the face mask could be a problem.

Simple triangulation was satisfactory while the trenches were relatively shallow, but by 1979 many trenches had exceeded 2m in depth and in the following year this was doubled, then tripled. As the

Figure 4.9 Diver using a planning frame (Photo ref.: 80.0094)

starboard side was reached, more and more well-preserved Tudor material was revealed, making the archaeological recording more difficult. Accurate recording demanded extra time and increasing mid-water gymnastic skills by the diver, whilst low visibility (usually less than the depth of the trench), weed, and the proximity of other workers made this harder.

Direct Survey Method

It was felt that taking direct measurements at an angle from datums to an object would be far easier than the conventional horizontal and vertical measurements, but at the time the team knew of no mathematical way of calculating the positions of the points. In fact the problem had already been solved in other archaeological situations, notably in Sweden by the engineer Eliz Lundin (Lundin 1973) and by workers on the wreck of the frigate *Lossen* in Norway (Anderson 1969). But the *Mary Rose* team was not aware of this and, instead, proceeded on a course of similar development. Nick Rule, a staff member who was then also a student of computer science at Cambridge University, made it his mission to solve the problem. He established various ways of locating a three-dimensional position, one using simple geometry, though this was too time consuming for routine use, and another involving vector maths.

Details of this process have been covered in detail elsewhere (Rule 1989; 1995; Adams and Rule 1990) so only a summary is needed here. In principle, if the XYZ co-ordinates of three datums are known, the measured distances from them to a new unknown position can be used to calculate its 3D position relative to the datums. The Norwegian method does exactly this and relies on three high quality measurements. The difference in Rule's method was that he assumed that in the *Mary Rose* conditions mistakes would be made in taking measurement, so he built in a means of checking by stipulating that measurements should be taken from four points. This gave four answers, one for each combination of three datums, and these could be averaged to provide a best guess, and the disparity between the answers would give an indication of the quality of the survey.

This technique was known as the Direct Survey Method (DSM), partly to distinguish it from other techniques then in use, and Rule wrote a computer programme to do the calculations. The method began to be tested in 1980, and as early results were impressive, the decision was made to install a new array of datums throughout the hull to record artefact positions as a routine. The new datums were placed not on top of the ship's timbers, but on their sides to give direct lines of site to everywhere within the hull. The datums were small plastic hooks that held the zero end of the tape, and the surveyor simply attached a tape to the four most convenient datums within the trench and recorded the distances to objects in tabular form. Typically, up to 30 objects would be recorded at the same time, and even in low visibility this was far easier, quicker and more accurate than horizontal trilateration. Not all objects were recorded this way however, for if an object was immediately adjacent to a structural element or something else that had already been surveyed then a record was made on the dive log to this effect, together with its layer number.

DSM came into its own for objects or complex assemblages that did not lie in such convenient relationships, though it should be admitted that not all DSM measurements were processed at the time, partly because of the lack of computer facilities. Consequently, the distribution of most finds has yet to be plotted out relative to the ship.

The next version of the DSM programme incorporated the 'least squares' algorithm in order to refine the 'fit' between the observed measurements and the computed position. It was this version that was subsequently used on the eighteenth-century Dutch East Indiaman *Amsterdam* wrecked at Hastings in 1749 (Marsden 1985; Adams 1986), and the programme has been continuously updated ever since.

Survey grids

Prior to 1979, when isolated trenches were being surveyed, it was found that the grid was unstable and could be dislocated by anchors or trawls. Moreover, it had a tendency to creep downwards into the sediments over time even when anchored on concrete sinkers. This problem was compounded if the temporary grids were used to anchor downlines or airlifts. Consequently, once the main site plan was established in 1979, and with more of the ship's structure becoming exposed on a daily basis, the grid ceased to have a value for survey, but was still vital both for site navigation, and for divers to lie on whilst excavating. Instead the major deck beams formed natural grid squares, and from then on all recording was related directly to them (Fig. 4.10).

Structural survey

Structural recording was usually carried out by Fielding and Adams and by other divers when the programme demanded. This essential and time-consuming activity enabled the team to gain an

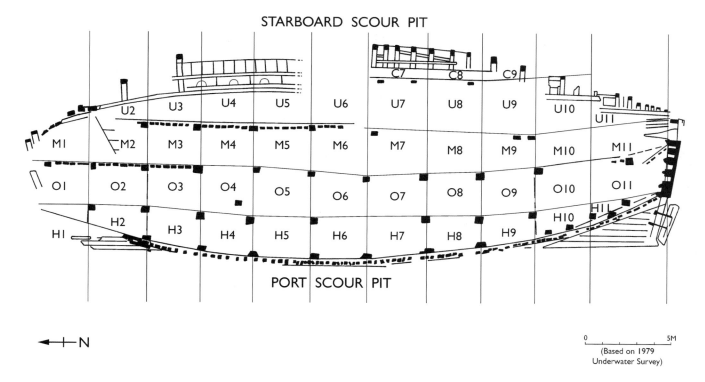

STARBOARD SCOUR PIT

C7　　　C8　　　C9

U2　U3　　U4　　U5　　U6　　U7　　U8　　U9　　U10　　U11

M1　　M2　　M3　　M4　　M5　　M6　　M7　　M8　　M9　　M10　　M11

O1　　O2　　O3　　O4　　O5　　O6　　O7　　O8　　O9　　O10　　O11

H1　　H2　　H3　　H4　　H5　　H6　　H7　　H8　　H9　　H10　　H11

PORT SCOUR PIT

←—N

0   5M

(Based on 1979
Underwater Survey)

Figure 4.10 The trench nomenclature adopted in 1979

understanding of the hull, establish which areas needed reinforcing and provided accurate hull profiles for the construction of the cradle that would eventually support the ship when raised. It should be remembered that the final go-ahead for the salvage of the hull was not given until July 1982, the alternative being to devote the rest of the season to hull recording and backfilling.

Existing DSM datums already in place, together with others added around the ship for the specific task, were utilised in the structural survey as a three-dimensional control. Lines running between the DSM datums were the basis of offset measurements to specific points on the ship's structure, such as to the edges of timbers, to seams and to fastenings. These were called 'site points', and many were marked with mapping pins or small tags to ensure that multiple measurements were all taken to precisely the same point. Important points along the line of a profile or section were checked by trilateration. Measurements were also taken directly between site points, and the angles of faces were taken with an inclinometer.

Before the days of dive computers, depth gauges were not sufficiently accurate for recording depths. In sheltered waters, measurements could be taken directly from the surface, but tidal changes and rough water made this difficult on the *Mary Rose* site. Bubble-tubes were used instead: these simple lengths of transparent plastic hose partially filled with air, used the fact that the interface between air and water at either end of the bubble will be at the same level. The relative depth of

points could therefore be established by measuring their height above or depth below the interface.

Working drawings of surveys were made on board *Sleipner*, at a scale of 1:10 or 1:20 and these contributed to the site drawings and to the isometric made up in the drawing office ashore.

Finds recovery

Artefacts revealed during the course of a shift were treated in a number of ways. The norm was that they remained in place until the supervisor had decided on an appropriate course of action. This might involve further excavation to reveal more of an assemblage that could then be recorded on video or in other ways. If finds were relatively robust they could be recorded and raised in a suitable container by the excavator, but if fragile they might be left for the supervisor or the next diver who would come equipped with a suitable container. As the riskiest time for an object was when it was lifted out of the water, wherever possible artefacts were placed in containers underwater and sealed. In order to minimise damage, an object was often recovered with a quantity of its surrounding sediment, which also provided valuable environmental information.

Typical for such treatment were the sixteenth century chests that contained personal possessions, longbows, arrows, etc. Had these been lifted directly into air they would have disintegrated from the weight of objects or sediment inside. Although the wood panels often looked perfect, the wood and the fastenings were normally heavily degraded.

Each lifting crate was lined with heavy-gauge polythene, weighted, lowered into the water and placed next to the object to be recovered. The object was then carefully lifted and transferred into the crate. The polythene was wrapped over and the lid secured, and the whole package was hoisted on deck by *Sleipner*'s crane. The result was that once on the surface, without the constraints of short dive times, the excavation and recording of the contents of chests could be much more thorough than was practical on the seabed (see *AMR* Vol. 5 for further details).

Objects that were large and heavy were a problem, and were sometimes lifted on a lorry body submerged for the task before being sent to the holding pond at Eastney Pumping Station. The most obvious were the guns, and large parts of the ship's dismantled structure. More unusual tasks included using explosive charges to fracture the large volume of iron concretion that was bonded to the hull. Excavation under the overhanging sterncastle was also an experience, both because of the stunning mass of *in situ* rigging and because of the structure looming overhead.

The gun lifts were quite complex as many were still at their stations protruding through the gun ports. During the capsize, some had tilted forward and were rammed against the upper edge of their ports, and could not simply be stropped and lifted out vertically. They had to be supported as they were excavated or they would have fallen over. In this mode they were extracted at an angle so that the lifting dolphins on the guns did not get caught on the edges of the gunports. As some guns were still on their carriages, these too had to be rigged in such a way as to avoid damage, particularly as gun carriages of the period had not survived elsewhere, and therefore were of the utmost importance and required great care in handling.

The guns and their carriages were rigged using nylon strops padded with sponge to avoid any compression marks. A five ton capacity tirfor (a pulling device that can be used at various angles) was rigged so that the wire passed at a steep angle to the stern of *Sleipner*, and the Master, Sam Dooley, had to position

Figure 4.11 Raising a gun (Photo ref.: 80.0882)

the vessel just back from the gun. This angle gave the lateral pull needed to remove the gun from the port. A crane hook was lowered and connected to the main strops, and over the communication system, the divers would give him the all clear to tension the lifting wire. Once the lifting strops were tight the tirfor applied tension pulling the gun out of the port. The lift and the tension were gradually increased until the gun began to free itself slowly, like extracting a tooth. These operations required two divers with good quality communications, a diving supervisor familiar with the technique of lifting heavy objects, a barge skipper in charge of the salvage vessel, and an alert crane operator with a light touch and in direct communication with both the barge skipper (Fig. 4.11, right) and the diving supervisor. Two divers were needed, as they had continually to monitor the state of the lifting rig, the gun and the ship's structure from which it was being removed, all at the same time.

On arrival at the surface, finds became the responsibility of the finds assistants who logged each object and allocated a finds number. Numbers were entered on the dive logs after each dive, and the unique number of the dive log itself was cross-referenced with the finds record card. These cards and dive logs still form the primary record for the archive, and the secondary record in the computer system provides the necessary searching and listing tools.

5. Raising the *Mary Rose*
Wendell Lewis

There were several reasons why it was decided to raise the *Mary Rose* at the completion of the underwater excavation. They included the aim of creating a museum that would allow this unique ship and her contents to be displayed and her story told. Raising her would also enable a full record of the ship's structure to be made including the underside, for that was almost impossible underwater. Although raising her was always part of the vision for the Mary Rose Trust, the final decision to raise the *Mary Rose* was not made by Trustees until 14 January 1982 and even then a number of cut-off dates were built into the programme when the operation could be cancelled and the site back-filled.

There were huge difficulties in the way, however, for the ship was a relatively fragile and complex structure and had no transverse strength. In water its remains weighed about 45 tonnes, but when taken out of the water it would weigh six to seven times more and could collapse under its own weight if left unsupported. On the plus side, the hull was generally held together by oak treenails, still tightly driven into their peg holes so individual joints remained sound. By contrast, had she been held together with iron bolts, these would have corroded during their long immersion in the sea and would not have been reliable during a modern salvage attempt.

The only possible comparable precedent for such a salvage operation was with the Swedish warship *Vasa*, sunk in Stockholm harbour in 1628, and raised in 1961 for preservation in a special museum. But it soon became clear that both the physical and practical circumstances of the *Mary Rose* and the *Vasa* were entirely different, and that direct comparisons would not always be appropriate. On the one hand the Swedish Government and the Swedish National Museum had taken the initiative and led the recovery operation, the preservation and the display of the *Vasa*, thereby ensuring that the project succeeded. On the other hand the *Mary Rose* project had to be entirely self-sufficient and was led by a charitable trust with no statutory government funding. There was valuable support in kind from some government related bodies such as the Science Museum, and the Ministry of Defence in the form of the Royal Engineers, but most support was from industry, businesses and many individuals both at home and abroad.

Moreover, the situation of the sunken *Vasa* was entirely different from that of the *Mary Rose*. The former was almost complete and was found standing upright in tideless, calm cold fresh water on the safe harbour bottom in Stockholm at a depth of 32m. She had considerable internal transverse strength that enabled the engineers to dig tunnels using water jets and pass lifting wires under her hull. Once these were attached to submersible pontoons which were slowly raised by pumping out their ballast water, the ship was eased from the bed of the harbour in stages, whilst still containing much of her content. She was brought underwater to shallows where she was strengthened with mild steel bolts and bracing rods, her damaged stern was repaired, and her gunports were sealed. She was then raised to the surface by seven hydraulic jacks until she could be pumped out, her final 'voyage' being to float into a dry dock on her own keel. This operation took 20 months to complete.

In contrast, only about one-third of the *Mary Rose* remained, lying heeled over onto her starboard side, and completely buried in the seabed mud. Moreover, she was in comparatively shallow water at a depth of only 12m, and in a tidal sea where the *Teredo* 'shipworm' and other marine organisms could quickly attack exposed timbers.

In September 1978 a seminar was held to consider possible methods of raising the *Mary Rose*, and it was in that year that John Reid, an engineer, joined the team already working on the project. His responsibility was to co-ordinate the work of a group of consultants who, with the archaeologists Margaret Rule and Andrew Fielding, prepared an initial recovery plan. Four submissions were considered in February 1980 for the recovery of the hull. They were offered by Mr M. Hazell of McAlpine and Sons Ltd, Mr C. Ward of Clive Ward and Associates, Mr A.C. Crothall who was a marine consultant in conjunction with Mr J. Grace. A variation of the latter proposal was offered by Mr J. Grace of R.J. Crocker and Partners. These submissions were adjudicated by a panel consisting of Professor G. Goodrich of Southampton University, Captain A.D. Marshall of the Salvage Association and Mr M. Pugsley from HM Naval Base, Portsmouth. The panel decided in favour of the submission offered by Mr J. Grace of R. J. Crocker and Partners. By this time many varied proposals had been received by the Trust including the

Figure 5.1 The Hull Salvage Recovery Team, 1981. From left to right: John Grace, Cdr Joe Evans, Wendell Lewis, Peter Pawlyn, Geoffrey Ashworth and Capt Jonathan Brannan

construction of a cofferdam; the use of air bags or other smaller buoyant vessels (ping pong balls, cork floats, etc); pontoons; and, finally, pumping brine into the sea-bed which, when frozen, would rise to the surface complete with the remains of the hull!

There were also a number of theoretical alternatives for carrying out the excavation. It could be done underwater in the current location, or alternatively in air after raising the hull and contents together. Another possibility was for the hull and contents to be transferred underwater to a more protected and shallower site where the excavation could be carried out in more controlled circumstances than in the open sea. However, the most practical alternative was that the hull be emptied of its contents before recovery, partly because there was a serious risk of the hull collapsing. The shallow water at the narrow entrance would also have precluded bringing the ship into Portsmouth Harbour whilst still submerged.

Eventually it was decided that, having emptied the ship of its contents underwater, it could then be stiffened with steel braces and frames, and finally to lift the ship by floating sheerlegs holding the ends of nylon strops passing under the hull. As the ship reached the surface it would then be pumped out and lifted onto a steel support cradle on a barge for transportation ashore. It was agreed to ask the team of consultants already involved, including importantly John Grace and Peter Pawlyn, to study how best to transfer the hull to a support cradle underwater. This would ensure that the load, and therefore the chance of damage, would be much less. In February 1980, the Trustee Board decided that the recovery of the ship should be targeted for 1982.

In 1981, the Trust appointed a Hull Salvage Recovery Team with Wendell Lewis as Project Manager. He had 25 years experience as a Royal Artillery Technical Staff Officer in the Ministry of Defence and, since 1977, had been consultant to R.J. Crocker and Partners, Civil Engineering Consultants. The rest of the Recovery Team (Fig. 5.1) comprised John Grace, an associate partner with R.J. Crocker and Partners; Peter Pawlyn, a heavy lift consultant and Managing Director of Branchglen; Commander Joe Evans R.N. (Retd), salvage advisor; Captain Jonathan Brannam, Royal Engineers Project Officer; Geoffrey Ashworth,

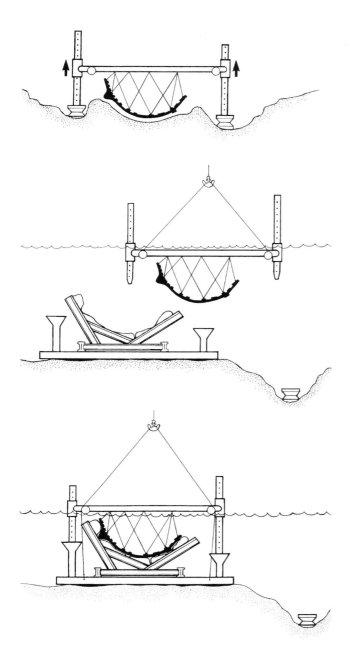

Figure 5.2 Diagrammatic explanation of the process of lifting the hull out of the seabed and onto the cradle

Quantity Surveyor of Monk Dunstone and Associates; and Richard Harrison, Chief Executive Officer and Margaret Rule, Director of Archaeology at the Mary Rose Trust.

A team of professional divers, qualified to 'offshore' standards was recruited from those who had worked for the Mary Rose Trust since 1979, and they were placed under the leadership of Jonathan Adams and Christopher Underwood. They would be responsible for supervising all the delicate work on the hull, including the positioning of internal stiffening braces. They would also be responsible for further archaeological work underwater, including the excavation of important deposits outside and beneath

the hull, as well as under the fragile Sterncastle, where some standing rigging was still attached to the hull.

Another team of divers, from the Royal Engineers, would undertake the heavy engineering aspects of the salvage under the command of Captain Jonathan Brannam, an army inspector of diving at the Royal Engineers Diving Establishment (REDE), Marchwood, beside Southampton Water. A contract was agreed between the Mary Rose Trust and the Royal Engineers in which responsibilities were apportioned, and, as with all Armed Services contracts, it contained a standard clause covering the need for top priority to be given to tasks in the national interest. At that stage, who could have envisaged a Falklands War? This event placed enormous pressures on REDE in their efforts to meet both requirements and it was regrettable that some experienced RE divers who had by then become familiar with the *Mary Rose* tasks had to be replaced by less experienced though very enthusiastic personnel.

Both teams would use surface demand diving equipment with hard-wire communication links to the Dive Control Centre on the surface ship *Sleipner*, whose Master, Sam Dooley, played a significant part in the excavation and recovery operations.

The writer became Director of Salvage and Recovery for the Mary Rose Trust in January 1982, and Margaret Rule, having directed the final intense programme of archaeological diving by June 1982, was appointed by the Trust to have executive responsibility for the recovery programme. Richard Harrison concentrated on organising the events on the day of recovery, the shore-based activities and ultimately the housing and display of the ship once ashore. Principals meetings were held at intervals considered necessary to agree and apportion tasks. These were attended by the Deputy Executive Director, Margaret Rule; the Commanding Officer of the Royal Engineers Diving Establishment, Lt. Col. Peter Chitty R.E.; the Senior Partner of the Consulting Engineers, Mr R.J. Crocker; and the Director of Salvage and Recovery, Wendell Lewis.

In mid 1982, the detailed concept for the recovery was altered (Fig. 5.2) and this caused an enormous increase in the workload for both the recovery team and for those designing and fabricating the lifting components. This placed huge additional demands on all concerned, especially the designer John Grace and the prime contractor Babcock Construction Ltd, whose response was exemplary in every respect. Only an industrial giant of their capabilities could have accommodated the rapid changes in remit without significant slippages to the programme. A redeployment of effort soon became necessary and discussions with the Chief Executive and Trustees brought about the welcomed change. Most obvious was the expansion of the Hull Salvage Recovery Team to include several members of staff who had been for many years associated with the Trust. Worthy of special mention was the appointment of Adrian Barak as the

Figure 5.3 A series of sketches to show the method of attachment of the lifting gear

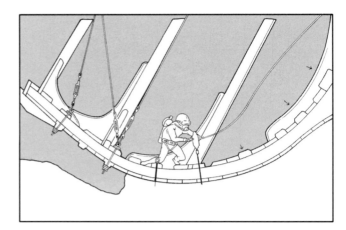

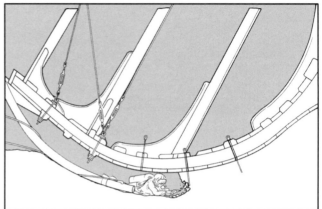

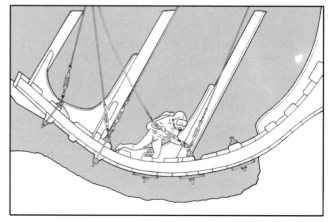

writer's deputy and the inclusion into the Recovery Team of both the Diving Superintendents, Jonathan Adams and Christopher Underwood.

In March 1982, the salvage vessel *Sleipner* had a dive control centre and dive platform installed, to a design of Jonathan Adams and Christopher Underwood, which was fabricated by Fabweld of Portchester. This included a decompression chamber and other diving equipment loaned by Comex Houlder whose specialist expertise was invaluable throughout.

In earlier discussions, it had been made clear that specialist heavy lifting equipment would be needed, so the Mary Rose Trust decided to avail themselves of the crane barge *Tog Mor* which was loaned by Howard Doris Ltd. This most generous gesture was made by the Chairman of that company Mr A.J. Granville. Exploratory discussions had by then been established with the Marine Divisional Manager, Captain John Gray, with whom the recovery team formed a very close working relationship throughout the entire project. *Tog Mor*, capable of lifting 900 tonnes, was commissioned in 1981 and was one of the most up-to-date marine crane barges available at that time. Its characteristics, especially the control of the load under difficult conditions, proved ideal for this project and its Master, John Suddes, remained dedicated to the project throughout.

The basic plan for lifting the *Mary Rose* hull was quite simple but its execution was filled with problems for there was no precedent to work to. An agreed concept was submitted to the Mary Rose Trust Executive Committee in January 1982. Before this date, very close liaison had been established between the designers of the main lifting components and the manufacturer Babcock Construction Ltd, and on 16 December 1981, Sir John King (later Lord King), Chairman of Babcock International Ltd, visited the project in Portsmouth. The two major components, the underwater lifting frame (ULF) and the cradle, were designed by John Grace using the surveys of the hull made underwater by Andrew Fielding and his team. They were fabricated by Babcock, at their Wolverhampton, Gravesend and Retford factories by teams managed by Mr M.W. Cockell, Mr J.O. Ormston and Mr A.A. Macpherson respectively, under the direction of Mr P.R. McAinsh, Managing Director of Babcock Power Ltd. The strength and quality of both the ULF and the cradle was later submitted to tests carried out by teams of inspectors from the quality assurance departments within the manufacturers premises, and independently by the Royal Arsenal, Inspectorate of Armaments Division. These confirmed that they met the high standards used in the quality assurance programmes normally applied to the most sophisticated weaponry, including nuclear devices, supplied to the Ministry of Defence.

The decision to attempt the lift was made by the Executive Committee on 14 January 1982. It had been preceded by years of debated contributions from several sources. These included engineers both civil and military, archaeologists, many of whom had been involved for more than ten years, and most importantly from Alexander McKee and Margaret Rule without whose persistence and dedication the hull would not have been raised.

In June, the scheme to attempt a lift, using an internal framework and the nylon strops previously mentioned, was changed in favour of lifting the ship from the seabed and transferring her, suspended beneath an Underwater Lifting Frame (ULF), itself supported on four legs. This was to be constructed from steel mainly supplied by EAL Tubes Ltd. The ULF and ship would then be lowered into a large cradle lined with conformable airbags, lying near-by on the seabed. The cradle with the *Mary Rose* lying in it would then be lifted to the surface and lowered onto a barge that would carry the entire package into Portsmouth Harbour.

In March 1982, work began clearing the wreck of winter accumulations of silt and debris and the Mary Rose Trust salvage team undertook the tunnelling, drilling, plate fixing and wire attaching needed for lifting the hull (Fig. 5.3). Meanwhile, the Royal Engineer divers began digging pits to accommodate the feet of the ULF. The ULF was launched at Hythe, a United States Services Logistics Base on Southampton Water, on 31 March. It was tested for stability by the Royal Engineers and was brought by barge to the wreck site and lowered to the seabed on 16 June, some two months late due to slippage in the barge modification programme. Concurrently, and in recognition of the contract to which *Tog Mor* was committed with a leading oil company in west Africa, a warning was received that the crane *Tog Mor* might not be available if a lift attempt occurred very late in the year. The writer therefore liased with Roger Wilson of Smit International (UK) at the Baltic Exchange, and with Captain W. Moerkerk, Managing Director of that company, who visited the project in Portsmouth on 15 July. Captain Moerkerk offered the services of his company to continue the recovery in the event of *Tog Mor* not being available. This offer was a great comfort to the Trust Directors and even though never implemented, great credit should be recorded to Smit International for their keen interest, encouragement and for their willingness to help should it have been necessary. Very recently the writer learned of the congratulatory greetings from Smit International to Captain Gray at Howard Doris which concluded with 'we understand you received one pound sterling for the job – we would have done it for one Dutch guilder!!'.

The decision to lift the hull from above, using suspension wires attached to eyebolts fastened through the hull, introduced extra strength to the hull via the bolts and backing plates, particularly where original iron fastenings had corroded away. The Mary Rose Trust divers would attach over 150 eyebolts, together with neoprene liners and marine plywood spreader plates both inside and outside the hull (Fig. 5.4). One or more steel wires would be attached to the eyebolts on the inside of the hull using a bottle screw that allowed the tension to be adjusted, and these wires would then be attached to the ULF above so that once the lift began, the hull would be suspended. By tunnelling under the ship and drilling holes through the hull, it was possible to insert the steel bolts, position

Figure 5.4 A trial version of the bolt assembly with backing plate and pads (Photo.: Wendell Lewis)

their backing plates outboard and then attach the lifting wires to the ULF. Hydraulic jacks were fixed to the legs of the ULF so that the hull could be lifted from the seabed by jacking the frame up the four legs. This measure of control was absolutely vital to overcome the enormous suction generated by the seabed mud and silts. Once free, the hull would then be transferred to a cradle situated on the seabed nearby, complete with its conformable rubber mattress of bags supplied by Dunlop Ltd (Fig. 5.5). Some of these were to be filled with water and later, at the surface, the remainder filled with air, the water having been dumped. The bolts, by then protruding from the outer surface of the hull, would be cropped by the Royal Engineer divers before the transfer and their ends covered with nylon caps to stop them puncturing the bags.

In June, the four pits excavated in the seabed to house the legs of the ULF were finished and this allowed the ULF to be installed above the hull on 16 June. Meanwhile another archaeological team supervised by Andrew Fielding, Adrian Barak, Barrie Burden, and Alexzandra Hildred, completed the excavation inside the hull except the brick galley structure. This team worked on a night shift to avoid overcrowding on the seabed during this intense programme when the two salvage teams were working on the hull during the day. The Mary Rose Salvage Diving Team subsequently carried out a rescue excavation on the galley and completed the sensitive excavation of the rigging that had been discovered beneath the overhanging Sterncastle. This programme was carried out in tandem with their salvage work on the hull.

The ship was now almost fully exposed and isolated on the seabed. Speed was vital if the exposed timbers were to be saved from further deterioration. At this stage the Trust Directors decided to seek an independent overview of the whole project and appointed Nobel Denton and Associates Ltd, marine consultants and ocean engineers, to this task and the closest possible liaison was subsequently maintained throughout the project.

Releasing the ship from the suction of the seabed was a potential major problem although undercutting the hull to position the salvage bolts alleviated some of the effect. It was recommended by several contractors experienced in dealing with similar problems, some from North Sea oil and gas rigs, that a 'peeling' technique should be used for the initial detachment. In the event, a system of hydraulic jacks was deployed and operated by Bygwik Telford. Bill Summers, Managing Director of the company, directed the whole operation in the presence of the majority of the Recovery Team.

Figure 5.5 The lifting cradle with its cushions (Photo refs: (top) Wendell Lewis; (bottom), 82.7372)

Figure 5.6 The first of several tense moments during the raising of the hull: the ULF breaks the surface (Photo ref.: 82.7072)

The installation of the cradle on the seabed was completed on 29 September using special additional sling guides to the design of Offshore Design Engineering Ltd, in conjunction with Babcock Power. The cradle was located a few metres south-west of the ULF, together with its cushion of rubber bags. A system of acoustic position-fixing devices was deployed by Sonardyne to monitor the movement of the hull during its transfer to the cradle, a technique that was considered to be much safer than divers manning legs during the transfer.

This crucial operation was dogged with additional difficulties, particularly as the Falklands War occurred and had become the top priority for the Royal Engineer divers. Some personnel had been deployed elsewhere and, together with other difficulties and poor weather, the positioning of the cradle on the seabed had been delayed. This was dangerously close to the onset of autumn gales, and it was clear that the ship could not possibly survive intact and unprotected throughout the winter storms. Hence there was much anxiety about the ability to complete the raising of the hull in 1982.

The ULF with the ship attached was raised by jacks located on its four legs, each on an inverted cone placed at the bottom of a pit dug down to solid clay. The final part of the jacking operation began around midnight on 30 September by a team including Jonathan Adams, Christopher Underwood, Christopher Dobbs, Adrian Barak, Margaret Rule, David Burden and Royal Engineer divers under Captain Jonathan Brannam. The jacks were operated by Bill Summers. The large number of suspension wires ensured that the load did not exceed three tonnes on any one of them and an additional advantage of the suspension wires was that monitoring their tension during the jacking lift could be used as a method of checking that the hull was being raised evenly off the seabed. It was Christopher Dobbs who had the privilege of reporting to the control room on *Sleipner* that the hull had been safely detached from the seabed in one piece at 03:25 on 1 October and the film of the hull gently moving underwater was shown

Figure 5.7 The Mary Rose *herself emerges from the Solent, safely padded by the cushions of the lifting cradle* (Photo ref.: 82.7127)

on the national television programme *News at Ten*. This was considered to be a crucial point during the whole operation for it had been feared that the ship might suffer severe damage.

The transfer occurred about a week later at the end of spring tides. There were many complex calculations to make and these were undertaken by Nigel Kelland and David Lewes of Sonardyne. Jim Clark, on loan from British Airways, looked after the communications systems, and Jonathan Brannam, of the Royal Engineers, co-operated closely with Mary Rose Trust divers to achieve this delicate operation. At 08:25 on 9 October, the great crane on *Tog Mor* lifted the ULF with the *Mary Rose* suspended beneath it on polypropylene strops. The total lifted weight was 94 tonnes underwater, but when in air this would increase to 272 tonnes of ship and 72 tonnes of ULF. It was intended that the four steel legs of the ULF would dock into stabbing guides on the cradle but whilst underwater one leg, at the north-east corner of the ULF, was accidentally bent and docking proved to be a major difficulty (Fig. 5.6). In the end it could only be achieved by the Mary Rose Trust and Royal Engineer divers manning the four legs to describe the situation through their hardwire communications. Only three legs could be docked as the north-east leg was bent in a southerly direction indicating that it had failed to clear the seabed when the ULF was first moved north during the transfer. After some debate it was decided that the offending leg had to be removed underwater, so that corner of the ULF had to be suspended from an extra fly-hook from the *Tog Mor* crane.

During these activities, the project was visited on several occasions by HRH The Prince of Wales who had shown a continuous keen interest in the project since his first dive on the site in 1975. In the latter stages of the lift programme several meetings were held on *Sleipner* in which HRH played a most significant part when he insisted we took certain decisions. No one disagreed (!) and with renewed energy, but after many sleepless nights, the final lift began at 08:06 on 11 October, one day later than expected. A fleet of boats,

yachts and pleasure craft had encircled the site to be close to the action whilst in marquees on Southsea Common, Arthur Rogers, the Trust's Press Officer, co-ordinated a throng of the world's press. The BBC Outside Broadcast Unit relayed the pictures from the Solent through this encampment and then out to 60 million viewers world-wide.

At 09:03 the *Mary Rose* began to break the surface. At that time it was noticeable that the south-east corner surfaced first, and on close inspection by the writer it was revealed that the main south-east lifting sling had, during the night and in pitch black water, been incorrectly slung. This caused almost the entire load to be distributed between the south-east and north-west corners of the ULF and cradle. The steel ropes and equipment supplied by Martin Black Ropes of Scotland and British Ropes, together with the anchor shackles supplied by The Steel Company of Forth Worth, Texas, USA, were clearly of the highest quality attainable as they withstood the additional strains and distortions. It also speaks well for the design and construction of the ULF and cradle that they coped with such a gross distortion of weight distribution. This incorrect sling positioning later caused a sudden slippage of the ULF sleeve down the leg at the south-east corner of the structure. Fortunately this error caused no damage to the hull, and the transoms of the ULF then adopted their correct horizontal attitude (Figs 5.7, 5.8).

Figure 5.8 The Mary Rose *is gently lowered by the lifting vessel* Tog Mor *onto the waiting barge* TOW1 (Photo Ref.: 82.7175)

Figure 5.9 The Mary Rose being transferred from TOW1 to GW73 (Photo ref.: 82.8080)

Figure 5.10 Margaret Rule witnesses completion of the transfer of the hull to the barge as the Mary Rose finally arrives at the dockyard – only 437 years late! (Photo ref.: 86.0308)

That moment of slippage was described as follows by Margaret Rule:

'An unforgettable crunch was heard at the south-east corner of the ULF as a tubular pin used to restrain the leg had given way, and the sheath or collar which connected the ULF to the leg had slipped by more than a metre. All hearts stopped but no damage had been done to the ship. The lift continued and by teatime the whole package was safely on the barge. No-one felt entirely safe, champagne went un-drunk and celebration cakes were uncut. Until we were safely into harbour no-one was happy'. (Rule 1983, 227)

Once raised it was necessary to free the ULF from its slings and allow its legs to rest in the cradle sockets. But as there were only three legs, one being missing, a fourth leg was quickly constructed and welded in place by Mary Rose Trust divers. This new leg was of steel supplied by Howard Doris (Tog Mor's parent company) and was approved by the representative of Lloyds Underwriters.

The barge TOW1, carrying her precious cargo, received a tremendous welcome into Portsmouth Harbour at 21:50 on 11 October 1982. Meanwhile the writer, as Director of Recovery aboard TOW1, signalled the Port Admiral for permission to enter the harbour after a rather long commission of 437 years.

The barge was moored to an anchor buoy pending transfer of the hull to a smaller barge in No. 1 Basin, prior to being docked in No. 3 Dry Dock. To achieve this transfer, the hull was winched across a steel bridge between the two barges on a series of modular hydraulic bogies incorporating 192 wheels. The work was carried out by ITM (Offshore) Ltd from Middlesborough, who had to ensure that the Mary Rose hull was placed with great accuracy on Wimpey's barge GW73, the ballasting of the two barges being carefully controlled to compensate for the shift in load (Fig. 5.9). The hull was finally brought 'home' into No. 3 Dry

Dock alongside HMS Victory at noon on 8 December (Fig. 5.10). During the whole of this period and whilst a spandrel building was being constructed over the dock, the hull was sprayed with cold water to stop any damage from the timbers drying out.

The raising and subsequent bringing into the dry dock marked the successful completion of an enormous task for a number of teams who had been close to the project. However it was the start of a new phase of work for another team of staff and volunteers. An around-the-clock watch was kept on the hull as Andrew Fielding, Adrian Barak and their team rigged up temporary spray systems and coverings for the hull (Fig. 5.11). This ensured that the timbers did not dry out before the cocoon of the shiphall was built around her and more permanent arrangements made. Generators, pumps, compressors, sprays and other plant needed to be set up and the now redundant ULF had to be removed from its precarious position above the cradle and hull. One era had ended, and a new era was just starting.

This project owes its success to the dogged determination of a small army of professionals and amateurs world-wide, in addition to those already mentioned here. Within the staff of the Mary Rose Trust and directly connected with the raising activities were many procurement and administrative staff. With this in mind the name of Jim Lovegrove should be recorded, as he contributed enormously in many ways, not only as the Finance Officer of the Trust but also with his success in procuring barges for a variety of purposes from Wimpey Marine at Great Yarmouth and Otto Wolf in Cuxhaven. These activities brought him into close liaison with Captain Arthur King of Alexander Towing Co Ltd, who was responsible for those activities. The writer is acutely aware of the pride Jim felt at being aboard one of the towing tugs (Victoria and Brockenhurst) that evening with Otto Wolf and others, as the barge TOW1 carried her precious cargo, the Mary Rose, into Portsmouth Harbour. Regrettably

Figure 5.11 *The hull, under continuous water spray, lying in dry dock awaiting construction of the shiphall* (Mary Rose Trust)

Figure 5.12 *Wendell Lewis holding a scale model of the lifting cradle* (Photo: Mrs K. Lewis)

the writer (Fig. 5.12) finds it impossible when reporting the events of the recovery operation to credit by name all those to whom an enormous debt is owed by the project overall. For these omissions, the sincerest apologies are offered.

The success of this pioneering recovery operation was partly due to innovation and flexibility, as well as to a determination to succeed by everyone involved. But to quote, with due humility, another former professional soldier, this was only 'the end of the beginning' and it was, for the recovery team an enormous privilege to have played some part in this successful operation. Henceforth, it was urgently necessary to create an entirely new museum to house the ship and her contents, in which they would be preserved, exhibited and have their story told.

6. Creating the *Mary Rose* Tudor Ship Museum

Richard Harrison

Soon after the discovery of the *Mary Rose* it became very clear that there was a need to develop a longer term strategy. This was underlined by the growing evidence that a substantial part of the hull was intact and that the ship was a 'time capsule' of Tudor life. The involvement of Portsmouth City Council was essential from an early stage, and Richard Harrison, as Director of Museums for Portsmouth City Council, joined the Mary Rose (1967) Committee in 1975 as the Committee's Vice-Chairman and subsequently Chairman.

This led to two studies in 1978, the first to assess the results of the excavations and the:

- historical importance of the ship and her contents; and the second to examine the
- feasibility of recovering the hull. Implicit in the positive outcome of both these studies
- was the need to establish a facility in Portsmouth to receive the hull and its
- contents so as to ensure their long-term preservation and allow public access.

These were subsequently recognised in the Memorandum of Association of the Mary Rose Trust

> 'The words Mary Rose mean the various remains of the ship lying at longitude 01 degrees, 06 minutes, 10 seconds west, latitude 50 degrees, 45 minutes, 48 seconds north, known (or believed to be) the Mary Rose built by Henry VIII and any part, or parts of her and all that was in, or connected with her'.

The objects for which the Trust is established are:

'A. *To find, record, excavate, raise and bring ashore, preserve, publish, report on and display for all time in Portsmouth the* Mary Rose.
B. *To establish, equip and maintain a museum or museums in Portsmouth to house the* Mary Rose *and related or associated material.*
C. *To promote and develop interest, research and knowledge relating to:*
   (i). *the* Mary Rose *and all matters relating to or associated with her, and without prejudice to the foregoing her place in maritime, naval, military and social history and her excavation, and display, and*
   (ii). *all matters relating to underwater cultural heritage, wherever located.*
   All for the education and benefit of the Nation'.

These recognised that the project provided a challenge rare in the museum world: the creation of new museum capable of responding to the latest thinking in museum philosophy and which met the highest possible professional standards.

In order to respond to this challenge a certain number of criteria were identified. The first was to create an appropriate organisation and staff structure. This was met by the establishment of the Mary Rose Trust in January 1979 as a charitable company limited by guarantee and the recruitment of Trustees with a wide range of skills and experience. This included not only local businessmen and politicians but also a number of individuals representing national maritime, archaeological and museum interests. Notable amongst these was the appointment of Sir Eric Drake, the then recently retired Chairman of BP. HRH The Prince of Wales agreed to be the Trust's President.

An Executive Committee of Trustees was appointed to deal with policy issues on a regular basis. It was also recognised at an early stage that the finances of such an ambitious programme required careful management and a small Finance Sub-Committee was appointed to advise the officers and authorise expenditure.

The Company Secretary was Ronald Tweed, Portsmouth's City Council's City Secretary. This was an important appointment as it not only committed the City Council to supporting the project but also eased access to various resources within the Council, notably Secretariat, Planning, Estates and Engineers.

Lloyds Bank Ltd was appointed Bankers and provided invaluable support particularly when cash flow became a major problem. The Portsmouth office of Thornton Baker was appointed Auditor, and John McMillan, a senior partner, provided invaluable financial advice to the Trustees throughout the project. Others were appointed to provide specialist advice, from the National Maritime and Science Museums, as well as Portsmouth City Council and the Royal Navy.

The senior staff structure comprised: an Executive Director, Richard Harrison – initially seconded part time from the City Council; an Archaeological Director, Margaret Rule; and a Director of Recovery and Planning, John Reid – seconded from IBM.

Figure 6.1 Illustrating artefacts (Photo ref.: 91.0010)

Figure 6.2 Conserving objects: a wooden bowl about to enter the freeze-drier (Photo ref.: 85.4002)

preferably in a location suitable for the longer term development of a museum.

A major press conference was held at the London headquarters of BP on 31 January 1979 to launch the Trust and the original three year excavation programme.

The Eastney museum proposal

As part of the on-going discussions on the future of the project during 1978, it was recognised that three key issues needed to be addressed if a museum building was to be ready to receive the ship when it was recovered:

- The site, preferably in Portsmouth City Council ownership, would need to be immediately available and provide a suitable location for a substantial museum development likely to attract a large number of visitors.
- To have a building within which such a large vulnerable object as the ship could be worked on and conserved using the latest techniques within a carefully controlled environment.
- A building design which not only met the complex requirements for preserving the ship and its contents, but also which would be a major new tourist attraction incorporating all the academic, museological and interpretive features demanded by a modern museum. It was also felt important that the design should be appropriate for a city of Portsmouth's significance and maritime tradition.

In order to manage and support the work being undertaken, a Site Development Group was set up consisting of Councillor Sotnick (Chairman), Alex Flinder, Seán McGrail and Alex McKee, together with three Trust Directors and representatives of the relevant City Council Departments.

Richard Harrison was subsequently appointed full time to the post of Executive Director as the Trustees recognised the longer term objective of developing a major new museum. Initially John Reid also took administrative responsibilities, but on his retirement in 1980 he was replaced in this administrative role by Jim Lovegrove who came to the Trust from Barclays Bank. As the project moved forward a team was appointed to manage the recovery of the hull (Chapter 5).

The second criterion was to respond to the decision to minimise the deterioration of the hull and its contents by completing the excavation in three years (later revised to four), and by finding accommodation in which to receive, store, record and conserve the finds as they came ashore (Figs 6.1, 6.2). Initially, the Trust staff had to work from a variety of buildings spread around Portsmouth, including an office at the Charles Dickens Museum and a temporary archaeological workshop set up in Bishop Street. Clearly this was not ideal and after a long search and thanks to the generosity of Whitbreads, these facilities were provided in a redundant Bond Store in Old Portsmouth, which because of its previous use was ideal for the purpose.

The third criterion was to have a building ready to receive the ship immediately after it was raised –

The first issue outlined above required an exhaustive assessment to be made of potential locations within the densely developed City of Portsmouth. Due to the good offices of the Lord Mayor's Mary Rose Support Committee, this survey was undertaken in 1978 by the City's Planning Officer, Ken Webb to criteria provided by Richard Harrison. As part of the preparation for this study, visits were paid by Richard Harrison, Margaret Rule, John Reid and Ken Webb to the *Vasa* in Stockholm and to the medieval Bremen Cog in Bremerhaven. Twenty-four potential sites were considered, most of which failed to meet one or other of the criteria. Eventually a short list of four was identified of which only one, that at Eastney, could realistically be available in the timescale. An empty, featureless, exposed site at the eastern end of the sea-front, it had the support of the City Council in that it would take some of the visitor pressure off Portsea and the Old Town. However, it would clearly present a major challenge to any architect. In considering the options John Reid also had to commission a study to show that it was feasible to bring the hull ashore over the beach.

In the context of subsequent events it is interesting to note that Lord Mountbatten, who by this time was taking a considerable interest in the project, argued very strongly for finding a site in the historic Naval Dockyard close to HMS *Victory*. However, the Ministry of Defence (MoD) indicated that nothing could be made available in the timescale, let alone for a decision to be reached as to whether such an intrusion into the Dockyard would be acceptable.

The decision to develop the museum on the Eastney site further underlined the importance of selecting a distinguished design team. With advice from the Royal Institute of British Architects, seventeen architectural practices were approached from which a short list of four made presentations to the Trust's Executive Committee at the end of 1979. The selected team were: Architect, Ahrends Burton and Koralek; Structural Engineer, F.J. Samuelly and Partners; Services Engineer, Zisman Bowyer and Partners; Quantity Surveyors, Monk Dunstone Mahon and Sears; Landscape Architects, Landesign Group. It was also felt important to include a museum designer in the team, an unusual step at that time, and Robin Wade and Partners was appointed.

It was agreed in the first instance that a long-term overall strategy be prepared for the museum site. Richard Harrison, in consultation with colleagues and Trustees, prepared a detailed brief. This led to the preparation of a development plan which Peter Ahrends described as

'not being intended to be a building design but rather a proposal which embodies in a zoned three-dimensional form the ideas laid down and developed in the brief. The programme of conservation for the hull is likely to extend over a period of at least ten years. The problem is not to design now in detail what a completed building will look like but rather to lay down a planned framework which can be developed in time to respond to the conditions surrounding the growth of the museum.'

Further work on the Development Plan was overshadowed by concerns about the cost of having a building in which to put the ship when it came ashore in 1982, whilst at the same time funding the recovery programme. Detailed plans were, therefore, prepared for a Phase I building which incorporated sophisticated proposals for handling and giving access to the hull and providing an appropriate environment. It was in this context that the decision paid off to appoint only the best. The work that went into the various engineering requirements of the building in terms of its structure, handling and access equipment as well as environmental control, was of the highest order, much of which was not negated by subsequent decisions. Phase I at a cost of £1.053 millions was approved on 1 January 1981.

Management of the Trust

Following the recovery of the ship, members of the Executive Committee took the initiative in reviewing the management structure of the Trust, taking into account the change in emphasis from being primarily an archaeological project to becoming a museum and major tourist attraction, and all that implied in museological and business management terms.

As a result, changes did occur and were influenced by two factors:

- A view that in future the management of the Trust and the functions of the Mary Rose Development Trust should be managed by one chief officer in view of the changed priorities from exclusively fund raising to including revenue generation.
- That, in view of his museum experience, the Executive Director, Richard Harrison, should be able to focus all of his time onto the establishment of the museum.

It was decided to appoint a Chief Executive with overall responsibility for the Trust's affairs, and in view of the move into the Dockyard there was some merit in appointing a recently retired serving officer as Chief Executive. From a number of applicants, Captain Charles Douds RN was appointed in May 1983; Richard Harrison was appointed Museum Director with responsibility for establishing the museum and its day-to-day management; Margaret Rule became Research Director with responsibility for the management of the ship, the collections and the on-going research programme; Jim Lovegrove became

Finance Director and David Evans was Director of Fund Raising. The existing publicity and public relations department was retained, responsible directly to the Chief Executive. Sir Eric Drake took the opportunity of retiring as Chairman and was replaced by Lord Caldecote.

The historic dockyard: shiphall

In January 1982, the Trust made the final decision to proceed with the recovery of the hull, and in March of the same year the decision was also taken to consider the feasibility of taking the ship into the Dockyard as a temporary measure. Two factors lay behind this decision:

1. The *Defence Review* of 1981 revealed that as a result of reductions in the size and role of the Royal Navy it was likely that some of the older buildings and structures in the Dockyard would become redundant.
2. Increasing concern that the Trust would have considerable difficulty in finding the very substantial sums involved in raising the hull at the same time as paying for the Phase I building at Eastney.

The possibility of parts of the Historic Dockyard, over and above those storehouses occupied by the growing Royal Naval Museum, becoming redundant together with the continuing public interest in HMS *Victory* also led the Portsmouth City Council at this time to express an interest in developing public access to the Dockyard.

Throughout the project the Royal Navy had been represented on the Trust by the Flag Officer, Portsmouth, who at this crucial moment in time was Rear-Admiral (subsequently Vice-Admiral) Tony Tippet. He was particularly supportive of the Trust, and took the initiative in investigating the availability of a dry dock to house the hull, and subsequently in finding

a building in which to locate a major display about the *Mary Rose* and its contents.

Coincidently, Trust staff had been given details of a relatively new temporary building structure being manufactured and marketed by Spandrel Orbital Structures Ltd. Very popular with the organisers of golf tournaments, it combined lightness with strength and ease of erection, and was initially considered as an alternative to the Phase I building at Eastney.

Following the decision by the MoD to make No. 3 Dock available to the Trust on a two year lease, it became clear that a Spandrel orbital structure was an excellent solution. It would provide a roof over the dock within which work on the hull could be carried out in suitable environmental conditions whilst allowing access by the public. The negotiations in implementing this decision were lengthy and difficult involving as they did the MoD, the Historic Buildings and Monuments Commission (now English Heritage: the dock being a Scheduled Ancient Monument) and the Planning Authority.

In due course the ship was transferred from the lifting barge *TOW1* to the smaller barge on which the hull was placed in the dry dock (Fig. 6.3). There the archaeological team began the process of clearing out mud from the ship, maintaining sprays of water and wrapping exposed timbers in protective material to stop the ship drying out, and even maintaining nightwatchmen to prevent timbers being stolen. These difficult tasks were led by Andrew Fielding, and included Mark Jones, Doug Barnett, Paul Chisholm, Ian Oxley and John Buglass.

Following the successful recovery of the hull on October 11 1982, work was put in hand as quickly as possible to fit out the dock. This involved not only erecting the Spandrel building over the dock (Fig. 6.4) but also providing all the insulation, lighting, spraying, access and environmental equipment necessary to conserve the ship and provide access for Trust staff. All the mechanical and electrical engineering work was designed and installed by Zisman Bowyer based on the work done for the Eastney project who, along with

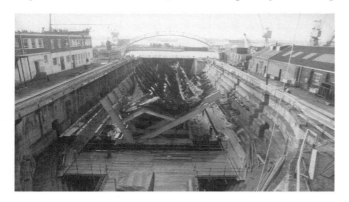

Figure 6.3 The hull in dry dock before construction of the shiphall (Photo ref.: 83.8002)

Figure 6.4 The shiphall under construction (Photo ref.: 83.8011)

Robin Wade from the original design team, agreed to continue to work on the project. Public access was considered important: entrance doors into the dock were provided through an airlock and a bridge was built over the dock from which the ship could be observed. A small interpretive display about the *Mary Rose*, designed by Robin Wade, was provided under cover, together with a temporary ticket office (subsequently replaced by a more permanent structure).

Considerable thought was given as to how best to manage the anticipated large numbers of visitors, recognising that they could only be let into the shiphall in small numbers at any one time. A Visitor Services Manager was appointed (at the time this was seen as an innovative approach to visitor management in the museum world) and a system devised, using volunteer guides and crowd barriers, to manage the queue and admission in groups to the shiphall. The volunteers gave a short talk on the viewing bridge using a public address system. The shiphall (Fig. 6.5) was first opened to the public on 4 October 1983, and between then and the opening of the exhibition in the following July there were over 200,000 visitors.

Figure 6.5 The completed shiphall with HMS Victory *in the foreground* (Photo ref.: 84.6503)

When the plan to house the ship in a dry dock in the Dockyard was conceived, it was envisaged that at some point in the conservation and reconstruction process the ship would be turned through 60 degrees, almost back to an even keel. Not only would this improve the visitor experience but more importantly it would enable the hull to be better supported, and would facilitate the reinstatement of the timbers removed during the excavation. By 1984 it was also clear that the barge on which the cradle rested was deteriorating and needed to be replaced.

The main contractors were Taylor Woodrow and the subcontractors, Bygwik Telford, Spencer Thetis Wharf and Ocean Marine and Technical Services, working under the day-to-day management of Captain John Cook, the Trust's Project Co-ordinator. The operation was in four distinct phases and took place between December 1984 and July 1985:

1. With jacking towers installed to support the cradle, the barge on which the *Mary Rose* was dry-docked, was cut away and removed.
2. The cradle was jacked down 2.2m to rest on a series of brick-built plinths on the dock floor.
3. Jacks and shoes were installed to slide the cradle sideways and up the wall of the dock until it rested at an angle of about 30 degrees. Then vertical jacks were installed to control the lowering of the port side.
4. A further jacking operation completed the rotation of the hull, and the cradle was secured into its final, almost vertical position (Fig. 6.6).

Figure 6.6 After 440 years the hull of the Mary Rose *stands upright once more* (Photo ref.: 85.8083)

The final operation was completed on July 19 – the 440th anniversary of the sinking of the ship.

It was recognised that the lowering and turning of the hull would reduce the impact of the view from the original viewing bridge, but it did provide the opportunity to build viewing facilities along the south side of the dock (Fig. 6.7). Two galleries were constructed one above the other with a cross-over in the middle. Four groups of 40 people, entering and exiting through two air-locks built into the side of the Spandral orbital structure, could view the hull at the same time, each having a high and low level view. The established techniques of visitor management and

Figure 6.7 The viewing gallery in the shiphall in 1994 (Photo ref.: 94.1041)

Figure 6.8 No. 5 Boathouse stripped out ready for the creation of the new museum (Photo ref.: 83.6612)

interpretation were maintained, as groups of visitors were escorted by volunteer guides using a personal address system operating through a number of loudspeakers.

Historic dockyard: exhibition hall and shop

As work progressed on the shiphall it became increasingly clear that the MoD supported a vision which saw the greater part of the Historic Dockyard being opened to the public. This had the support of the Portsmouth City Council and other tourism agencies and it became inevitable that the Trust would see the Dockyard as a permanent home for the Mary Rose Tudor Ship Museum. This led to an urgent search for a suitable building as close to the shiphall as possible, in which to house a major exhibition and shop.

There was also a need to consider the financial implications of developing the museum in the Historic Dockyard. It was clear that, in addition to raising the capital to establish the museum, the longer term revenue implications of managing a major new museum had to be considered, as well as funding the care of the collections and the on-going conservation and research programmes. The very considerable public interest in the project and the popularity of HMS *Victory* as a visitor attraction, backed by consultation with specialists in the field, encouraged the Trust to project visitor numbers in the region of 350,000. If these could be achieved, admission income together with the profits of the Mary Rose Shop would go a long way to providing the income needed to support all aspects of the Trust's revenue (but not capital) needs. This optimism was subsequently shown to be correct. It should be stressed that this forecast was based on a commitment to using the best interpretive techniques available and for the displays to be informative, educational, stimulating and enjoyable for visitors of all ages.

In the event, the only building that the MoD was prepared to make available in a reasonable timescale was No. 5 Boathouse close to Victory Gate. This 150 year old building with its even older annexe provided an ideal space, but it was in a poor state of preservation and was not designed for public access. Robin Wade was asked to prepare a detailed design for its conversion and, in view of the need to carry out extensive restoration of the timber framed and timber clad structure, to insulate it and strengthen the floor (Fig. 6.8). He recommended the appointment of an architect, Andris Berzin, who had worked on this type of conversion before together with a structural engineer, Jim Tyne, experienced in timber framed building.

Trust staff prepared a brief for the exhibition with Robin Wade and established a number of key criteria:

- In view of the fragile nature of most of the artefacts from the ship it was essential that humidity and temperature levels be kept within tight parameters – even tighter than those normally recommended for most fragile museum objects.
- It was necessary to present the story of the *Mary Rose* in the context of Tudor period history.
- Whilst it was necessary to interpret key features of the design of the ship and its armament, it was also important that the artefacts should reflect everyday life on board the ship and should largely be allowed to speak for themselves.
- The design of the exhibition should be based on a one and a half hour visit and that any text should not take more than an hour to read in total. With these factors in mind a short introductory audio-visual programme was envisaged.
- The interpretation of the story of the *Mary Rose* and any text used in the exhibition should be at a level accessible to a 12 year old.

Zisman Bowyer solved the environmental control specification within a single skinned timber building by

Figure 6.9 The audio-visual theatre (Photo ref.: 84.6522)

Figure 6.10 Inside the museum (Photo ref. 03.323)

providing it direct into each of the display cases. This placed considerable constraint on the exhibition designer but was the only solution in the circumstances. In order to provide sufficient contextual material, mainly through pictures, the Trust employed an art historian to trawl through possible sources. A twelve minute introductory audio-visual programme using film and slide became a feature of the exhibition and was housed in a self-contained theatre which doubled up as a lecture theatre (Fig. 6.9).

A copy writer, Sally Rousham, was employed to write all the text, based on information supplied by the archaeologists. This proved to be a considerable challenge but was well worth the effort. Drawings for a part-reconstruction of two of the decks of the ship, a diorama of an underwater scene showing two divers at work on the hull and a reconstruction of the Barber Surgeon's cabin were provided by Andrew Fielding, based on the data produced during the underwater surveys.

In order to gain maximum financial benefit from the 1984 tourist season, Trustees felt it was essential that the exhibition be open by July. Only after lengthy negotiations with the MoD, English Heritage and the Planners was final approval given to go ahead in November 1983. Brazier and Son Ltd of Southampton won the contract for the conversion of the building and subsequently were appointed main contractors for the display work. They had first come to the Trust's attention as one of the bidders for the Phase I building at Eastney. The initial restoration of the building's timber frame and the need to strengthen the floor to carry the weight of large numbers of people caused a great deal of concern as considerably more rot was uncovered that expected. However the contractors responded well to the challenge and the exhibition was opened by HRH the Prince of Wales on 9 July 1984.

With the opening of the exhibition, in addition to engaging ticketing and security staff, two professional appointments were made – a museum assistant to be responsible for the collections on display, and a display

technician responsible for the maintenance of the displays. Volunteers continued to man the shiphall and also played a part in 'meeting and greeting' visitors to the exhibition. The provision of an education service to schools and other bodies was recognised at the outset as an important function of the museum, but at the time, apart from informal help, little was possible on any scale until more funding was forthcoming.

The public response to the opening of both the shiphall and exhibition was much as had been predicted. However 1985 was the first year in which visitor figures for a complete calendar year could be computed. Because of the limitations on throughput in the shiphall, separate tickets were necessary. Consequently, it was impossible to monitor precisely the extent to which people visited both the shiphall and exhibition. Visitors to the shiphall totalled 321,000 and to the exhibition 235,000. This represents a best guess of 340,000 individual admissions, which was in line with initial predictions and put the Mary Rose Museum in the top ten most-visited museums in the UK (Figs 6.10, 6.11).

Fund raising

The fund raising programme of the Mary Rose Project was one of the most successful of its kind at the time, £4 million being raised in cash and kind between 1979 and 1982 to fund the excavation and recovery of the ship.

It was clear from the two seminars organised by the 1967 Committee in 1978 that in order to achieve the excavation and recovery of the ship, and establish a museum in the timescale envisaged, very considerable funding would be required. On the recommendation of other organisations involved in major fund raising, a leading fund raising consultancy – the Wells Organisation – was approached for advice. This led to their seconding a member of their staff, Robin Brown,

Figure 6.11 The front of the museum (Mary Rose Trust)

who initiated a fund raising campaign that led to the creation of the Mary Rose Development Trust and the setting of a £3 million target (subsequently increased to £4 million). Charles Tidbury (later Sir Charles), Chairman of Whitbread, became its first Chairman and in August 1980 Ian Dahl (initially seconded from Marks and Spencer where he was a senior manager) was appointed Director of Fund Raising. The MRDT was entirely independent of the MRT and had the sole objective of raising funds for the Mary Rose Project.

Crucial to getting the fund raising campaign off to a good start was obtaining a number of substantial 'lead' contributions. Portsmouth City Council and Hampshire County Council led the way, but the most important early contributions were those from the business sector, including contributions 'in kind' from BP and in cash donations from IBM and Whitbread. Perhaps the most innovative aspect of the fund raising campaign was the creation of the Court of the Mary Rose based in the City of London which became something of an exclusive club for the 'great and the good' of the City. This was established in 1980 with membership being granted on making a contribution to the project. This was mirrored by similar Courts in Portsmouth and Southampton and the eventual setting up of the Society for the Archaeological Study of the Mary Rose Inc. in the USA (a name acceptable to United States Revenue for tax deduction purposes).

Whilst seeking contributions in cash or kind from the business sector, those government agencies able to help such as the National Heritage Memorial Fund, were key to the fund raising strategy. Contributions from charitable trusts and fund raising events also played an important part.

Evidence of the scale and success of the fund raising strategy can be illustrated by taking the results of one years activities – by the end of 1980, 84 companies, charitable trusts and other organisations had contributed £1.2 million in services, cash and goods in kind.

The support of the Prince of Wales was invaluable in raising the funds needed to complete the project

successfully and on programme. Not only did he support fund raising events but also his personal support was demonstrated by his regular visits to the site. It has been estimated that his involvement was probably worth 50% of the sum raised. In this context the support of Lord Mountbatten, until his tragic death, was also important – he gave the impression that the project was one of his favourite subjects of conversation, and undoubtedly he encouraged the Prince of Wales initially to support the project.

Following the raising of the ship, Ian Dahl returned to Marks and Spencer, and David Evans, recruited from Nabisco Brands Incorporated, replaced him. As part of the reorganisation that took place in May 1983 the Development Trust was placed in 'cold storage' and David Evans became part of the Trust staff as Fund Raising Director. The administration of the Trust, the ongoing work of the archaeological team, the conservation of the hull and artefacts, the building of the shiphall, the conversion of No. 5 Boathouse continued to put considerable pressure on fundraising. Nevertheless substantial support continued to be forthcoming, a further £2.5 million being raised by the end of 1985. By this time, however, the Mary Rose Museum was also making a considerable contribution to Trust funds – over £500,000 in 1985 from ticket sales.

Public relations and publicity

In the period prior to the establishment of the Mary Rose Trust, BP had played an important part in obtaining valuable publicity for the project. This was recognised by the Trustees as the public awareness of the project was considered important from a fund-raising point of view.

To assist with this, Lt Commander Peter Whitlock was recruited in 1979 on his retirement from the Royal Navy as Captain of HMS *Victory*. His great knowledge of maritime history and experience in dealing with the media was invaluable. Subsequently this vital work was supported by Arthur Rogers, seconded initially from the Portsmouth Evening News as their contribution to the Trust. He later joined the staff and played an important part in keeping the project in the public eye.

One of Peter Whitlock's major contributions to the Trust's public relations policy was the Bulletin, the first edition of which was published in May 1979. Thereafter it appeared on an as-and-when required basis and it remains a valuable testimony to the day-to-day activities and achievements of the Trust. One of the key media initiatives was a contract with BBC *Chronicle* to film all the critical moments in the excavation and recovery of the ship. This led to four documentaries and what was the longest outside broadcast to date on the days of the recovery.

An exhibition about the *Mary Rose* in Southsea Castle had opened in 1975 and played an important part in informing visitors to Portsmouth about the project. But with the start of the programme to excavate the ship fully it was felt that this needed to be expanded and brought up to date. The City Council made three rooms in Southsea Castle available for this purpose and a new much larger exhibition designed by Richard Daynes opened in May 1980. Until the opening of the shiphall this was the major focal point for those wishing to know more about the *Mary Rose*.

Another by-product of the Trust's public relations policy was the creation of the Mary Rose Information Group. Public interest in the project inevitably led to a huge demand for lectures. Initially staff responded as best they could but on the initiative of one of the Trustees, Lord Cathcart, together with the involvement of Peter Whitlock, the Information Group was established leading to the recruitment of over 100 volunteer lecturers across the country. They remain an important resource of the Trust.

In 1983, following the publication of a major article about the *Mary Rose* in the *National Geographic Magazine*, the Trust was invited to mount an exhibition in Explorer's Hall in Washington. This was opened on 11 October 1984, the second anniversary of the recovery of the ship. It created a great deal of interest and supported the efforts of the Society for the Archaeological Study of the Mary Rose to raise funds in the USA. It also encouraged Dr Armand Hammer (President of Occidental Oil) and acquaintance of Prince Charles to play a bigger role in its affairs. As a result the Hammer Foundation took over the National Geographical Society Exhibition, redisplayed it for touring purposes and circulated it to a number of major museums in the USA over the next two years.

Mary Rose Trading Company

Establishing a separate trading company was one of the recommendations from the 1967 Committee to the Trust when it was established, for this would enhance the value of the project in public relation and fund raising terms. It also formed part of the subsequent recommendation to set up the Trust as a charitable company limited by guarantee. This was accepted, and in 1979 the Mary Rose Trading Company was established with its own Board of Directors, Councillor Wyn Sutcliffe as its Chairman and Richard Harrison as Managing Director. During this time, a range of exclusive *Mary Rose* souvenirs was developed, many of which are still available. From 1979–83 the Trading Company ran a small shop at Southsea Castle managed initially by Hazel Harrison and staffed by volunteers. Although in these early days the turnover was modest, the shop did make a useful contribution to Trust funds. Subsequently the Trading Company was managed

under the guidance of Ian Dahl (Director of the Mary Rose Development Trust) who, with his Marks and Spencer experience, expanded the range of goods for sale and initiated a mail order business.

When the decision was reached to use No. 5 Boathouse for the exhibition, the shop moved from Southsea Castle and occupied part of the building until restoration work began. Out of these small beginnings grew the highly successful shop in the Dockyard that makes a very substantial contribution to the funding of the Trust. In the first year that the shiphall was open the Trading Company covenanted £58,000 to the Trust doubling to £116,000 in 1987.

The Mary Rose Society

When the formation of the Mary Rose Trust was under consideration it was suggested by a number of supporters, notably Ken Webb, Portsmouth City Planning Officer, that it might be appropriate from the outset to establish a 'Friends' organisation that could be a focus for community support and an 'umbrella' for the many volunteers it was hoped to involve in the project. The Society was formed in 1978 under Ken Webb's chairmanship, and continues to flourish as a support organisation for the Trust with several hundred members.

Fund raising for the Trust was a primary consideration and over the years the Society has raised substantial sums for the project. The image of the project in Portsmouth in 1978 was mixed, and the Society saw, as one of its roles, the promotion of the project locally. Thanks to the gift of a large towing caravan and the commitment of a retired Vice-Admiral, Sir Charles Darlington, the Society was able to respond by taking the caravan with its small display and shop to many venues in and around Portsmouth. The caravan was subsequently replaced by an exhibition bus, managed by the Public Relation and Publicity Department of the Trust.

It is intended that this chapter should describe the creation of the museum up to the time the ship was lifted upright in 1985. Much has happened since, and nowadays the Mary Rose Trust is looking forward to the future form of the museum. This includes completing the conservation of the hull using polyethylene glycol, and developing plans for the new museum, and, ideally, complete it in time for the 500th anniversary of the building of the *Mary Rose*. And finally, a priority is to complete the analysis and publication of the archaeological and historical research arising from the excavation. All of these will facilitate an updated exhibition and the already highly successful programmes of public education.

7. Monitoring the *Mary Rose* Site

After the *Mary Rose* was raised in 1982, there remained an elongated north–south pit in the seabed, bounded on the east and west by mounds of spoil and the remains of equipment from the excavation, including a sunken diving platform.

Although the main archaeological deposits were removed there are others that still require investigation in the future. The wreck site therefore still retains much information on the ship's rigging, armament, collapsed Forecastle, and traces of the aborted efforts made in 1545 to raise the vessel. As it is important to ensure that these vital deposits are not eroded away, it has been necessary to ensure that the integrity of the site is carefully monitored as well as remaining protected under the *Protection of Wrecks Act* 1973.

The archaeological deposits lie mainly in two areas: in the scourpit around the former location of the *Mary Rose*, and within the area of the collapsed Forecastle. Some artefacts that fell from the masts and bowsprit may lie scattered beyond those two areas. In particular the large grappling hook, shown in the Anthony Roll as hanging from the end of the bowsprit, might have survived in the seabed.

The site monitoring has been managed by Alexzandra Hildred of the Mary Rose Trust, the purpose being to assess the groundlines, grids and other equipment abandoned on the seabed; to assess the erosion and infill of the hull pit; to check for unauthorised human interference; and to examine archaeologically sensitive areas, particularly un-excavated parts of the scourpit and the collapsed Forecastle, and either to recover or bury archaeological objects under sandbags. The government's Archae-ological Diving Unit (ADU) also checks the site periodically, and checks the government's buoy that marks it as a protected historic shipwreck.

The site of the *Mary Rose* is unfortunately well known as an excellent fishing ground, and damage to the site by fishing was noted as early as 1986. This has resulted in abandoned lobster pots, and abundant fishing lines and fishhooks that have become tangled in the seabed equipment. Fishing on the wreck site has particularly damaged the few groundlines and regularly disrupts attempts to rationalise the site. The popularity of the site is such that in 1990 the team even saw fishing boats tied to the protective buoys, and a survey by the ADU in September 2002 disclosed clear scour marks of trawling in the seabed. Fortunately, there is no evidence of unauthorised diver activity and the site's protection under the *Protection of Wrecks Act* 1973 is respected.

The excavation grid of pipes was removed prior to lifting the ship in 1982 and its elements were stockpiled along the sides of the hull depression, but by 1990 many of these had become scattered by fishing and most have since been removed. East of the hull depression lie the remains of the 1973 sunken diving platform measuring 8x6m. Other structures include the partial remains of the air manifold used for the airlifts.

The site has attracted some surprising modern detritus: a chair, a dog kennel, a boat cabin and, most surprising, human cremation caskets, one of which was found in 1990 in the hull pit and another in 1991 beside the starboard shotline. Alexzandra Hildred reported to the Mary Rose Trust that 'This begs the question as to whether the site is being chosen for this purpose'. However, she also concluded that:

> *'They can be used as indicators of movement, infill, buildup of corrosion products (over brass name plates) and wood deterioration. To date neither has been moved from the positions in which they were observed by us'.*

The hull depression is only slowly filling-in and in 2002 was much in evidence. In 1990 it was 3.5m deep, with a silt infill that ranged from 0.10m to 1.0m in thickness. There was some erosion around its sides, and erosion and infill monitors were established to check on the processes. These were lengths of pipe driven into the seabed both vertically and horizontally, and measurements were taken periodically of the level of the seabed relative to the ends of the pipes.

The hull pit has maintained itself during the 20 years since the raising, even though it lies north–south across the east–west tidal flow and it was expected to have filled with silt more quickly than it has. However, divers have noted that there was a strong north–south current in the hull pit, and this might prevent excessive silt deposition. By 1991 there was a marked decrease in the steepness of the north and south ends of the hull pit, and by 1997 erosion had exposed artefacts to the east of the area where the Sterncastle had been situated, and these were surveyed and removed. In contrast, the important Forecastle area was well covered with new sediments by 1998.

The modern environment has been examined, and most areas of the site were found to have been colonised by marine life, including slipper limpet (*Crepidula*), crabs and lobsters. They suggest that the seabed is fairly stable. Also, the site was one of three in the Solent where the colonisation of exposed and buried wood by *Limnoria* has been studied. Water samples have been taken for various purposes, including to monitor the amount of sewage around the site. Core samples of silts have also been taken, as have temperature readings at specific locations. By 1991 the most sensitive area was found to be around the former Sterncastle for this was actively eroding, aided by crabs and lobsters burrowing into its steep face.

When the excavation ended, it was recognised that substantial unexcavated deposits with Tudor artefacts and hull structure remained in the seabed. Also, a few excavated objects still remain stored to the east of the site. These include the upper rail of the waist (a particularly significant timber), parts of two gun carriages, part of an iron gun, and a cache of rope.

Many objects have been raised since 1982, including breech chambers for large wrought iron guns, a cast iron hailshot gun, portions of wrought iron guns, swivel guns, shot and rope, galley bricks and concretions formed around groups of objects. The largest concretion weighed about a ton.

Traces of the salvage of 1545 remain in the form of thick cables which have been noted at locations in the hull pit, and they require archaeological examination in the future.

In order to define the extent of the archaeological remains, a probed survey to a depth of 1.0m was undertaken at 0.10m intervals in 1990 to see if sub-surface obstructions could be found east of the ship. Nothing was found.

Understanding the formation of the site is crucial to locating further ship's structure and objects, and towards that end a geophysical survey was carried out by the University of Southampton in November 1994, twelve years after the ship was raised (Quinn *et al.* 1997).

A seismic reflection survey with a 'Chirp' digital sub-bottom sonar profiling system was used, and this gave a better vertical resolution through the seabed than was obtained from traditional sonar systems. A grid of 29 seismic profiles showed both the pit, measuring about 50m long by 20m wide, that formerly contained the *Mary Rose*, and around it the horizontal stratigraphy of the local geology of clays and sands. When the grid was plotted out it enabled a contour map of the seabed around the wreck to be reconstructed.

The sonar sections located two anomalies, one extending about 50m long and 20m wide west from the site of the ship's bow, and another slightly narrower extending west of the site of the ship's stern. These followed the westward peak tidal flow and are interpreted as erosion hollows caused by the ship soon after it sank. These were later filled with alluvial material as the exposed port side of the ship collapsed and was eroded away. It is likely that these erosion hollows might contain objects and timbers from the ship. The sonar profiles did not identify any scourpit on the east side of the wreck into which the bowcastle might have collapsed.

In September 2002, almost twenty years after the ship was raised, the ADU examined the site using Reson Multibeam Sonar (Plate 14), and clearly showed both the pit that once contained the ship and traces of former archaeological activity around it. In particular the old diving platform was clearly seen on the east side of the wreck.

The monitoring programme shows that the site is reasonably stable, with periodic episodes of erosion to the east of the former site of the sterncastle. At a future date it will be necessary to undertake a detailed archaeological survey of the site to establish the full extent of remaining archaeological deposits, before undertaking a full excavation to recover the considerable remaining parts of the *Mary Rose*. Until then it will be essential to continue the monitoring programme.

8. The *Mary Rose* Site and Environment Today

K. Collins and J. Mallinson

Location, water depth, shipping

The Solent, where the *Mary Rose* sank, is in a region which includes Southampton Water, several shallow estuaries, and the extensive Portsmouth, Langstone and Chichester Harbours. It is the only major sheltered channel in European waters between an island, the Isle of Wight, and a mainland, and is the largest estuarine system on the southern coast of the United Kingdom. Surprisingly, considering its economic and recreational importance, it includes internationally important marine nature conservation areas. As a major international shipping area, the Solent has a long history of receiving alien species, such as the slipper limpet, *Crepidula fornicata*, introduced at the end of the nineteenth century and now so widespread as to be characteristic of the region (Collins and Ansell 2000).

Much of the area to the east and west of the Isle of Wight is less than 20m deep (Fig. 8.1). Large shipping traffic enters the Solent through the Nab Channel (dredged to 13m) from the east then passes through the Solent, much of which exceeds 20m in depth. Another dredged channel is maintained to the west of this, leading through Southampton Water to Southampton Docks. Yet another dredged (9m) channel leads into Portsmouth Harbour from the Spithead, East Solent.

Currents, tides, salinity

The tides of the Solent are some of the most complex in the world, a distinctive feature being that Southampton has a double high water and a short ebb flow (Webber 1980; Sharples 2000). The tidal characteristics of the English Channel control the Solent, and the average tidal range increases markedly from the west (1.2m in Christchurch Bay) to the east (3.0m in Southampton and Portsmouth). The water moves from east to west commencing at about 2 hours before high water at Portsmouth, and for a while even when the ebb is running fast the tide is still rising. In the narrows off Hurst Castle the maximum tidal stream at springs is 4.5 knots.

Differing periods of slack water and changing tidal velocities enable mud to accumulate on the seabed and have contributed to the preservation of the *Mary Rose*.

Seabed geology and sediments

The area in which the *Mary Rose* sank has an interesting geological history that ensured the survival of the wreck. The ship lay in soft yielding Eocene clays that allowed it to sink into the seabed, assisted by the scouring action of the tides below the surface.

The reason for the survival of the ship is that the Solent lies in a geological basin between east–west lines of hills, the Purbeck–Wight Chalk Ridge to the south and the Portsdown Anticline to the north (Figs 8.1 and 8.2). The Upper Chalk underlies the whole area, dipping gently from the north then rising almost vertically in the Isle of Wight and forming the cliffs at its eastern and western (Needles) ends (Chatwin 1960; West 1980; Velegrakis 2000).

At the end of the Cretaceous period the Solent region lay beneath an extensive sea in which the chalk was deposited as calcareous plates from planktonic algae. After gentle uplift, erosion and gentle down-warping a smaller shallower sea was formed over south-east England in which Eocene marine clays, Reading Beds and London Clay, were formed, the latter some 50 million years ago. These were deposited in a warmer climate than at present, as is indicated by the remains of palm trees. Subsequently, the Bracklesham Beds and the Barton Group, comprising mixtures of clay and sand, were laid down in river and coastal environments.

By the late Eocene–early Oligocene periods, the basin was almost filled with sediment (Headon, Osborne and Bembridge formations) and became a shallow lagoon environment reminiscent of the Florida cypress swamps. Subsequent uplift and folding formed the anticlines on the Isle of Wight, and this was followed by erosion leaving a gap of several millions of years without any geological record.

As the climate fluctuated during the recent glaciations so the sea-level rose and fell several times leaving widespread Pleistocene gravels on a series of terraces above and below the current sea-level around the Solent. The existing local rivers were established in approximately their current positions by then. The sea-level was considerably lower during the last Ice Age which ended about 10,000 BC and the English Channel was dry. A major 'Solent River' then flowed eastward across the present Poole and Christchurch

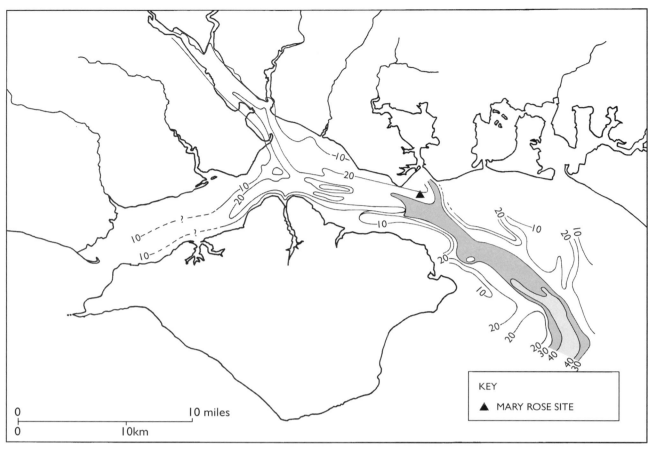

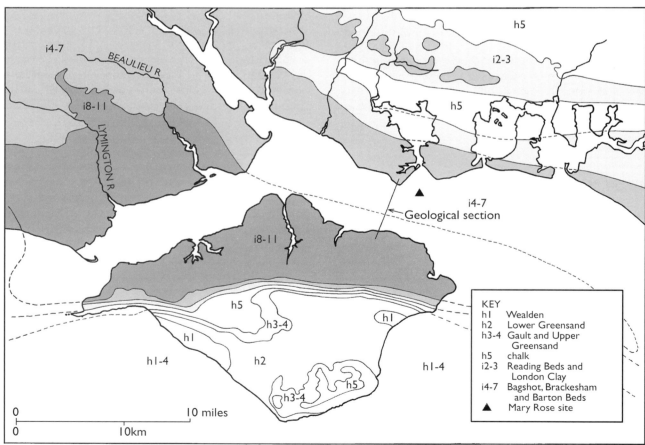

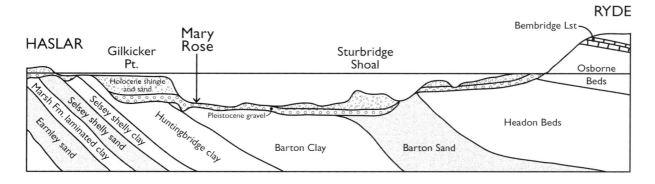

Figure 8.2 Geological section through the east Solent (see Fig. 8.1 for position) showing the eroded Solent river, solid geology, recent infill and equivalent position of the Mary Rose site (after West 1980)

Bays through the Solent, and the Rivers Piddle, Frome, Sour Avon, Test and Itchen were its tributaries. Its course has been established from seismic profiling and boreholes (Velegrakis *et al.* 1999; West 1980; Dyer 1975) which show that from the east of the Isle of Wight it swung south-west down the English Channel to join the River Seine off the Le Havre region. On the *Mary Rose* site it cut down into the soft Eocene sands and clays to a depth of 46m below Ordnance Datum and the wreck itself lay within its alluvial fill.

As the sea-level rose after the last Ice Age, the Pleistocene valleys, including the Solent River, were flooded thereby forming the Solent, Southampton Water and Spithead, as well as the Portsmouth, Langstone and Chichester Harbours. Subsequently extensive deposits of marine shingle were deposited on the seabed, and reached 21m in thickness under Horse Sand Fort outside Portsmouth Harbour. Elsewhere, fine silts and muds were formed in the sheltered harbours and in the Solent, including on the *Mary Rose* site, and led to the preservation of the wreck (Fig. 8.3).

Marine life

The Solent region contains a wide diversity of marine habitats, from exposed rock on the coast of the Isle of Wight to sheltered muds in the extensive shallow harbours at Portsmouth, Langstone and Chichester. There are mixtures of sand and gravel on the seabed, often with shell, and extensive areas of pure cobble in the East Solent towards Selsey Bill (Collins & Mallinson 1983; Collins *et al.* 1989). The anemones *Anemonia viridis*, *Urticina felina*, *Cereus pedunculatus* and *Cerianthus lloydii* are commonly found there. Where conditions are siltier *Cerianthus lloydii* is more typical. The sand and gravels support the sand mason worm *Lanice conchilega* and, where finer sediments are associated with the gravel, there occurs the peacock worm, *Sabella* sp. The slipper limpet, *Crepidula fornicata*, is a characteristic species of the Solent region and its shells can form a hard layer in areas of soft sediments, as on the *Mary Rose* wreck site. Exposed gravels are often colonised by tubeworms such as *Pomatoceros triqueter*, and by barnacles (*Balanus* spp.).

Areas of clean sand extend across Bracklesham Bay from Whitecliff Bay on the Isle of Wight. This sand is very mobile with ripples inshore and deep waves in the tidal mainstream. The burrowing worms *Lanice conchilega* and *Arenicola marina* are found in the more stable areas together with hermit crabs, *Pagurus* spp., and gastropods such as *Hinia reticulata* and *Buccinum undatum*. A number of species, including the anemones, *Urticina felina* and *Cereus pedunculatus*, require some underlying stone or hard stratum for attachment.

The muds and silts of the Solent region contain a rich marine life dominated by polychaete worms and small molluscs. North of Bembridge in St Helen's Road, there is a unique area of fine, deep, soft mud without any hard strata which supports a large population of the echiurid worm *Maxmuelleria lankesteri* with the amphipod *Ampelisca diadema* and the bivalve mollusc *Nucula nitidosa*.

The slipper limpets (*Crepidula fornicata*) on the surface of much of the Solent mud provide attachment for other organisms, including hydroids (*Kirchenpaueria pinnata* and *Hydrallmania falcata*), and sponges (*Halichondria* spp. and *Suberites* spp.). A number of small crab species (*Pisidia longicornis*, *Macropodia rostrata* and *Pagurus bernhardus*) are found in the cover provided by the slipper limpet shells, together with bottom living fish such as dragonets (*Callyonimus lyra*), sole (*Solea solea*) and pogge (*Agonus cataphratus*). There are also patches of oysters (*Ostrea edulis*) (Fig. 8.4).

Whilst natural rocky areas are mostly limited to the Isle of Wight, there are also extensive man-made structures in the region, particularly a string of forts built on the seabed across the eastern Solent, and these

Figure 8.1 Position of the Mary Rose wreck site in relation to (top) depth of the seabed and (bottom) geology

are populated by a variety of rock-favouring species (Dixon and Moore 1987).

The excavation of the *Mary Rose* provided a temporary habitat for gribble (Collins and Mallinson 1984), and whilst exposed some of the wood began to be degraded by isopods such as gribble (*Limnoria* sp.) and the boring bivalve mollusc 'shipworm' (*Teredo navalis*). The rapid colonisation by ascidians (such as *Ciona intestinalis* and *Botryllus schlosseri*) may have afforded limited protection (Eltringham and Hockley 1958).

Alien species

As the Solent region is a major international waterway it has a long history of receiving alien species through fouling of ships hulls and as larvae in ballast waters (Eno *et al.* 1997; Thorp 1980; Collins and Mallinson 2000). For example, the slipper limpet, *Crepidula fornicata*, is considered to have been introduced with American oysters at the end of the nineteenth century, and as it occurred in the erosion layer over the *Mary Rose* it is an important dating indicator for the

deposition of some 'recent' deposits over the wreck. *Crepidula* and the ascidian, *Styela clava* (introduced in the 1950s) are now both so widespread as to be characteristic of the region (Barnes *et al.* 1973). Other recent notable introductions have been Japanese seaweed, *Sargassum muticum* (Farnham *et al.* 1973) and the kelp, *Undaria pinnatifida* (Fletcher and Manfredi 1995).

Conclusions: conditions contributing to the preservation of the *Mary Rose*

It was the geological history of the area in which the *Mary Rose* sank that mainly determined how well the ship was preserved. That history included the formation of the Hampshire basin, filled it with soft sediments which were subsequently eroded to a great depth by the Solent River and its tributaries during the low sea-level of past glaciations. The subsequent flooding of these valleys in the 10,000 years since the last glaciation has led to the creation of natural sheltered harbours, including Portsmouth, a home of the British fleet. The clay seabed of the *Mary Rose* wreck site is relatively

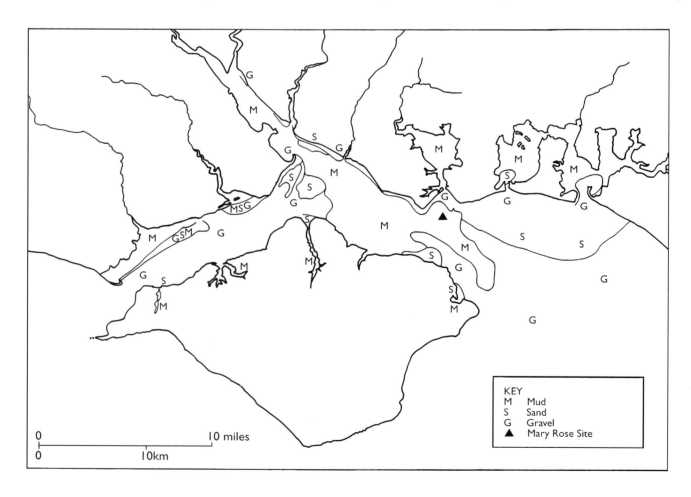

Figure 8.3 Distribution of surface sediment types in the Solent (after Dyer 1980))

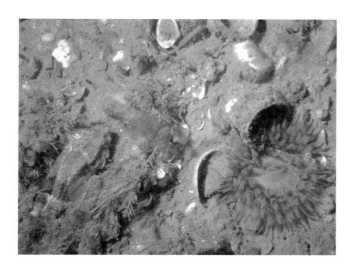

Figure 8.4 The seabed in the area of the Mary Rose *wreck site (240mm across) showing typical mud with slipper limpet shells and small stones providing attachment for a dahlia anemone (lower right), hydroids, worms and algae (centre to left). A well-camoflaged bottom-living fish, a pogge, lies to the lower left*

deep due to the infill of the erosion by the Solent River, and to its position, sheltered by the Isle of Wight, has been protected from destructive wave action.

The position of the Solent beside the centre of the English Channel, and its morphology creates a unique tidal regime which causes the deposition of soft sediments. These sediments are organicly rich, resulting in anoxic conditions which provide the perfect conditions for the preservation of the ship and its artefacts. The ship site is on soft yielding clays which allowed it to sink, assisted by the scouring action of the tides below the surface. If the ship had sunk in the Western Solent or even a few hundred metres to the north, onto hard flint gravels, it would have been unlikely to have been preserved to the remarkable extent that it was. Microbial action and wood-boring organisms would have weakened the structure, which would have then been dispersed by the tidal currents.

9. Stratigraphy of the *Mary Rose* Wreck Site

The following account is derived from the post-excavation study of the site by Jon Adams, and is based upon his experience both of the site and of the many excavation records, particularly dive logs, supervisors' reports, plans and section drawings. He subsequently rationalised the complex numbering system that developed as the excavation proceeded.

The marine environment created problems of interpretation that are not normally found on land, primarily due to the strata in and around the wreck being naturally deposited underwater. For example, when the 'straw' (deposits 21, 49, 50) was found it was not always immediately clear whether it was plant material originally in the ship, possibly used as bedding, or if it was eelgrass deposited naturally.

It was possible to draw sections underwater and to combine these with a detailed record of the stratigraphy in different parts of the wreck as the excavation proceeded. The overall stratigraphical picture, therefore, is represented in true section drawings (Fig. 9.2), and as a stratigraphical matrix (Fig. 9.4). The position of drawn sections is shown in Figure 9.1.

Eighty separate 'deposits', mainly layers, were recorded, including concretions and sediments within containers. But with several supervisors at work at any one time duplication of allocated deposit numbers sometimes occurred, so that, for example, deposit 22 became variously known as deposit 22, 46, 47 and 69. After studying all the supervisors' records it was possible for Adams to rationalise the original deposit

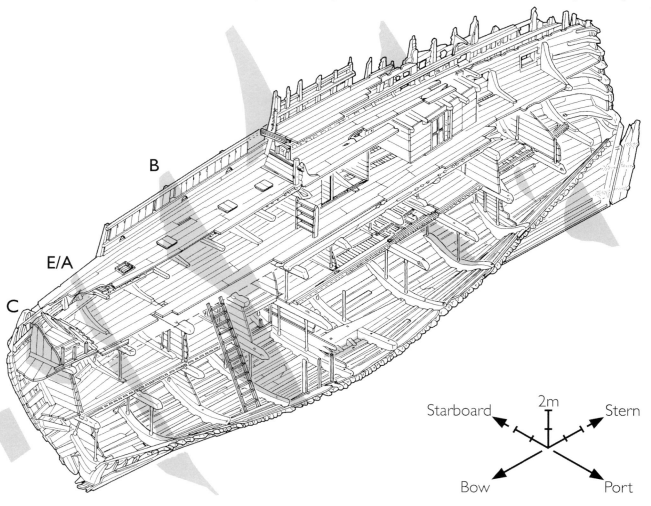

Figure 9.1 Position of drawn sections

list and combine all of those that were duplicated. Rather than continue the old numbering system he felt that it was better to start again for the purpose of publication.

In this publication, therefore, the original excavation deposit numbers are given as 'deposits' 1–69, and, so as to avoid confusion, the new rationalised numbering is given as 'contexts' 200–230. The following is the final list of all the contexts which were sediment layers that are believed to be the same deposit. Former deposit numbers are also given. Sediments within boxes or chests have been omitted. In addition various stratified deposits have been added that were not numbered at the time. This has reduced the final number of contexts to 30 and includes the underlying geological 'bedrock' of clay.

Summary description of deposits and their interpretation

The 30 separate contexts found on the *Mary Rose* site fell into four groups:

- Recent deposits overlying the entire wreck (contexts 200–210)
- Tudor deposits within the ship (contexts 211–220)
- Tudor deposits in a scourpit immediately around the wreck (contexts 221–229)
- Deposits pre-dating the wreck (context 230)

A 'Hard Grey Shelly Layer' (context 209) formed the top of the stable seabed and separated the Tudor deposits from the modern. There is some uncertainty about whether or not the gastropod *Crepidula fornicata*, which had been introduced into British waters with oysters from America in 1880 (Hancock 1969), occurred in context 209, though it was certainly in some overlying deposits which must therefore date from after 1880. It is possible, however, that the Shelly Layer at the point where a sample of the shells was taken was disturbed recently, perhaps by trawling, and allowed the introduction of *Crepidula*.

After the ship had heeled over and sunk to the seabed in 1545, she penetrated the upper alluvial sediments and came to rest on an underlying firm clay (context 230). The ship was four degrees down at the stern and heeled to starboard by 58 degrees, and because it was buried in alluvium, much of the starboard side was ultimately preserved.

Initially the ship was proud of the seabed and formed a massive barrier to the tidal flow, resulting in the formation of a large scourpit around the hull. The heeling action had caused a general collapse of moveable objects towards the starboard side within the ship, and once underwater an initial sorting of items occurred, depending on weight and buoyancy. Much of this floating material was at first confined in the wreck

by the decks, cabins and anti-boarding netting, but on becoming waterlogged it settled back to become assimilated into the rapidly accumulating sediments that dropped out of suspension within the hull (contexts 216–218). The deposits inboard had built up so rapidly that the hull timbers and the organic objects were soon protected from many biological and erosive forces.

Initial salvage in 1545 had succeeded in retrieving some of the uppermost guns mainly from the port side, which lay closest to the surface of the sea, as well as some of the masts, spars and rigging. During the excavation, traces were found of two lifting cables that had been passed under the ship during the attempted salvage operation.

The biological and mechanical erosion of the hull began as soon as the ship sank. The lighter fastenings began to fail and some of the now waterlogged timbers from the upper part of the ship began to collapse. Some fell inboard, others fell into the scourpit, and yet more were carried away by the currents. During this process the interior or the ship ceased to be sealed, with the result that weed and coarser particles of alluvium entered the hull and settled on top of the initial fine silts (contexts 211–215).

As the process of decay continued, the hull became progressively less of a barrier to tidal flow thereby allowing the water to flow through the structure rather than around it. Scour action was consequently reduced outside the wreck and sediments began to be deposited in the scourpits (contexts 221–228). During the sixteenth century the wreck formed an ideal marine habitat that was heavily colonised by oysters and other organisms until the ship became completely buried.

After the collapsed and partly eroded wreck was buried, silts and rubbish began to accumulate over it. These upper layers (contexts 201–208) were more mobile and from time to time were partly eroded away, as in 1836 when local fishermen caught their nets on the wreck, and in 1971 when the wreck was rediscovered. The base level of this mobile deposit was the 'Hard Grey Shelly Layer' (context 209) which overlay the Tudor deposits.

From the eighteenth century onwards, bottles, fishing gear and general anchorage rubbish, including coal and boiler clinker from the age of steam, collected over the site and was assimilated into the most recent deposits over the 'Hard Grey Shelly Layer'.

Description of stratigraphic contexts

Recent deposits
Context 200 (formerly deposit 1)
Backfill resulting from previous excavation, including the gravel that was dumped on the site at the end of the 1977 season to protect it. Due to prevailing tides, the spoil jettisoned from the airlifts during excavation built

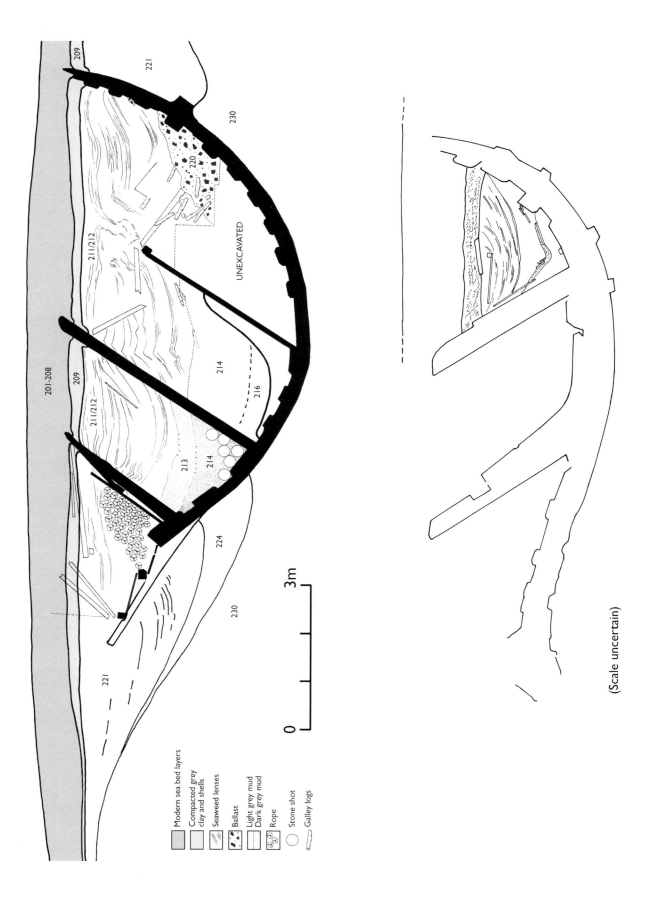

201-208

209

211/212

211/212

213

214

214

216

UNEXCAVATED

209

221

230

220

230

224

221

0   3m

Modern sea bed layers

Compacted grey
clay and shells

Seaweed lenses

Ballast

Light grey mud
Dark grey mud

Rope

Stone shot

Galley logs

(Scale uncertain)

Figure 9.2 (upper) Schematic Section B; (lower) Section C (see Fig. 9.1 for positions)

up two shallow mounds, each parallel to and on either side of the ship. This created several new layers which are grouped here as one.

Context 201 (previously part of deposit 2)
The modern seabed deposits prior to excavation. Soft silty clay, easily wafted into suspension, contained many shells, mostly slipper limpet (*Crepidula fornicata*). Total thickness 50–100mm. Occurred over whole site although the density of *Crepidula* varied. Waves, formed due to sediment transport patterns, were evident on side-scan sonar traces. In the depressions there were often accumulations of coarser material.

Lying on or within this context was modern anchorage rubbish such as rope, wood, tin cans, bottles, etc. The density of shells and areas of coarser material formed a crust, though heavier objects sank through into the softer sediments below.

Context 202 (previously part of deposit 2)
A layer of soft clay below the surface crust of *Crepidula* shells. Dark grey to ochre in colour, soft and sticky in texture. Thickness 50–200mm. Occurred over the whole site. Inclusions as in context 20. Below context 201; above context 203.

Context 203 (not previously designated)
Gravel with some sand in well defined layers like a well-worn gravel path. Coarse grained material resistant to movement, residual after a period of scouring. Similar deposits were detected in other localised areas at various depths, but the most substantial and extensive area was found over sectors O/M3, O/M/U4, M/U5. Thickness 20mm. Below context 202; above context 204.

Context 204 (not previously defined)
Erosion interface between gravel context 203 and the sediment below. Below context 203; above 205.

Context 205 (formerly deposit 2)
Clay, very dark grey, oily in texture over the whole site. When it was first found it was almost black but after a period of exposure the content oxidised and became khaki/ochre in colour. Contained some *Crepidula* and various modern objects such as cans, pottery and other general anchorage rubbish. Burrows due to worm activity were common. Thickness 200–300mm. Below context 204; above context 206.

Context 206 (formerly part of deposit 2, not previously defined)
Consolidated silty clay around a densely packed layer of *Crepidula* shells. A former seabed, possibly overwhelmed by a period of rapid sedimentation. A similar context was found in several different parts of the site, including at the bow and in the starboard scourpit, but it is not known if it was the same former seabed. It may represent a number of former seabed surfaces covered during rapid shifts in sediment. Thickness 60–80mm. Below context 205; above context 207.

Context 207 (formerly deposit 3)
Silty clay, similar to context 202, though more compact and of a slightly lighter mid-grey colour. Often mottled with darker patches and had burrows due to worm activity. Inclusions were *Crepidula* and other shells (*Spisula* spp) with some oyster. Objects within it included boiler clinker, coal, animal bone, ceramics, glass and clay pipes. Extended over the whole site. Thickness 200–300mm. Below context 206; above contexts 208, 209, 212.

Context 208 (formerly deposit 5)
Thin lenses of sand and gravel at the base of context 207. May be similar to context 203. Seemed to be fairly localised over the port bow. Thickness 50–60mm. Below context 207.

Context 209 (formerly deposit 6)
A very hard compacted clay containing a mass of shells, called the 'Hard Grey Shelly Layer'. It extended over most of the site and was generally light to mid-grey in colour and 100–150mm thick. In some areas it was considerably thicker, either as infill within a scour or other disturbance, or over some parts of the scourpits, notably at the bow. In those areas it comprised several laminae, verging from almost pure shell fragments, to bands of compacted silty clay ranging in colour from very light grey to dark greys and browns.

A similar range of objects was found within it as occurred in context 207, including lead fishing weights, clay pipes (Fig. 9.3) iron concretion, leather and eroded wood, some of which is Tudor. It sealed much of the ship's structure, and extended downwards around the eroded ends of deck beams and other timbers as a result of scour action. The layer extended outboard across the scourpits, though it became less distinct towards the perimeters. Below contexts 207, 208; above context 210.

A selection of shells from this context was examined by Norman Tebble, of the Natural History Museum, who reported:

'that the animals in the "Shell Layer" were principally a few species of bivalve mollusc and some gastropods which preyed upon them. Spisula was the most commonly identified genus and the particular species S. subtruncata is noted for frequently occurring in large numbers. Nucula species are also commonly found offshore in soft sediments. Amongst the gastropods are two shells of Crepidula fornicata. *These were introduced into Essex waters with oysters imported from America in 1880 (Hancock 1969), and they may not have*

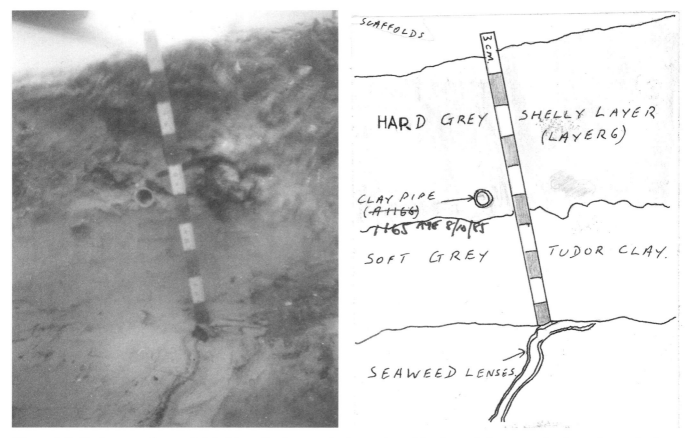

Figure 9.3 Underwater (hence slightly blurred) photograph of a section with schematic interpretation from site notebook TB1 79/5/101 dated 2 October 1979

arrived in the Solent until after 1900. The only other gastropods present are the generally carnivorous whelk, Buccinum undatum, *of which only one small shell was present, and the pyramidellid* Turbonilla *which parasitizes the polychaetes* Audouinia *and* Amphitrite. *This and the presence of the many mud, or muddy sand dwelling bivalves, suggests that the substrate was soft and organic enough for these worms although we cannot be certain which shells may have perhaps been carried to the site by currents'.*

There is uncertainty as to whether or not the *Crepidula* shells are from this shell layer or from immediately above, and the excavated samples require careful analysis in the future.

Context 210
Erosion interface between context 209 and the deposits below. Below context 209.

Deposits inside the ship
Context 211 (formerly deposit 10)
Soft light grey clay, often creamy texture like potters clay. Within it were laminae of organic matter most of which was eelgrass (*Zostera* spp). These laminae varied

in thickness and indicate the cyclical nature of deposition under environmental influences. Found throughout the ship to a depth of several metres in places. Below context 210; above contexts 212, 213, 214.

Context 212 (formerly deposit 13)
Organic (eelgrass) lens resulting from a greater than normal influx, presumably associated with the progressive collapse of partition planking. It could be seen as a phase within the continuing deposition of context 211 and in that sense could he omitted as separate context. Within 211; above 214.

Context 213 (formerly deposits 47 and 69)
Rubbery thixotropic clay (ie., a thick emulsion of material that becomes temporarily liquid when disturbed). Similar to context 216 (see below). Below context 211; above context 214.

Context 214 (formerly deposits 14 and 17)
Smooth grey clay deposited prior to the final collapse of the partition planking, therefore the amount of organic and coarse material is much less than in context 211. Although the constituent materials of the sediments appeared very similar, a transition occurred with the collapse of the planks and subsequent influx of weed. A

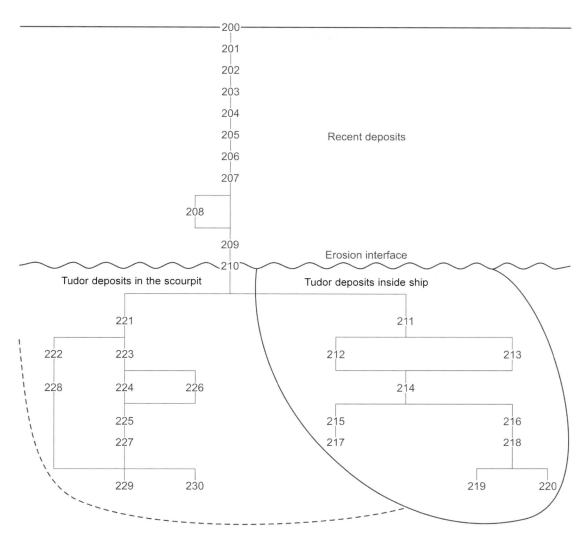

200

201

202

203

204

205   Recent deposits

206

207

208

209

210   Erosion interface

Tudor deposits in the scourpit   Tudor deposits inside ship

221   211

222   223   212   213

228   224   226   214

225   215   216

227   217   218

229   230   219   220

Figure 9.4 Simplified site matrix

similar change could be seen throughout the ship, from the clean deposit of context 213 to that of context 211, incorporating laminae of eelgrass in increasing density and thickness. In some cases there was a definite interface as in area M1, while in others the change was more gradual. Below contexts 211, 212, 213; above contexts 215, 216, 217, 218, 219, 220.

Context 215 (formerly deposit 15)
An organic deposit similar to context 212, but possibly the straw fill of a mattress that, after the ship sank, floated and remained buoyant while a small amount of silt was deposited at the junction of the deck and the starboard side (context 217). The now sodden mattress settled back over this primary silt, together with a certain amount of weed (*Zostera*) and the collapsing, light softwood, lining planks of a cabin. Below context 214; above context 217.

Context 216 (formerly deposits 22, 46, 47, 69)
Rubbery thixotropic silt, light to mid-grey in colour, with a fine grain and very compact. Very resistant to

impact but yielded under steady pressure to become semi-liquid. If exposed in section, it would flow out and re-settle horizontally. Below context 214; above contexts 218, 219.

Context 217 (formerly deposit 16)
Soft unconsolidated silty clay, dark grey in colour probably due to a high organic content. This covered objects that had slipped to the side of the ship during capsize. Below context 215.

Context 218 (formerly deposit 20)
Very soft, light grey clay. This was the initial deposit in various recesses of the ship's structure where it was not subsequently compacted or contaminated. It was differentiated from context 217 by its lack of organic inclusions and its stickier texture. Below contexts 214, 216; above contexts 219, 220.

Context 219 (formerly deposit 25)
Sand on board prior to sinking. Found overlying the port side ceiling planking. The outer few millimetres

were stained mid to dark grey and the lower 3–4mm were still yellow–brown. The layer was 10–15mm thick. Below context 213; above the ship.

Context 220 (formerly deposit 18)
Shingle ballast placed in the ship, which when the ship heeled over spread across the lower starboard side, sealing various objects. Below contexts 213, 215; above the ship.

Scourpit deposits outside the ship
Context 221 (formerly deposit 11)
Equivalent to inboard context 211 but deposited in the outboard filling of the scourpits. Similar colour and texture and also included laminae of eelgrass, but due to the relative exposure of the scourpits there were more inclusions of oyster shells and collapsed ship timbers. This layer comprised the bulk of the scourpit fill and, like context 211, was several metres thick in places and occurred around the whole ship. Below context 210; above contexts 222, 223, 224, 225, 226, 227.

Context 222 (not previously defined)
Layer of shell fragments and coarse sediment marking a period of equilibrium in the scourpit infill. Similar phenomenon to context 203, heavy particles collecting at the lowest point of the scour trench during a period or periods of heavy scour. Sealed by resumption of sedimentation. Below context 221; above context 228.

Context 223 (formerly deposit 68)
Thick lenses of mature oyster shell collected in the scourpit, perhaps after a storm had dislodged them from degraded timbers. Below context 221; above context 224.

Context 224 (formerly deposit 12)
Soft grey clay equivalent to context 214 inboard. Below contexts 221, 223; above contexts 225, 226, 229, 230.

Context 225 (formerly 58)
Soft silty clay under the Sterncastle within which was densely packed eelgrass matted around the collapsed shrouds and associated rigging. The high concentration of organic material gave this layer a dark, almost black appearance when first exposed, though as in other instances, this oxidised and turned a similar grey to the clay context 224 above it. Below context 224; above context 227.

Context 226 (formerly deposit 61)
Very soft light grey clay containing young oyster shells. An early deposit laid down after the silt layer, context 227, and at the same time as context 225, was deposited behind the chainwale, away from the weed-festooned shrouds and other rigging. Like similar deposits inboard, it remained clean and uncompacted. Below context 224; above context 227.

Context 227 (formerly deposit 60)
Similar silt to contexts 213 and 216 but deposited outboard. Below context 225; above contexts 229, 230.

Context 228
The primary, soft clay infill in the bow scourpit was probably deposited after a partial settling of part of the bow structure, thereby marginally reducing the scour action. There appears to have been a further period of equilibrium after which the shell layer (context 222) was deposited. It was also the infill of a disturbance in the scourpit deposits under the Sterncastle. Below context 222; above contexts 229, 230.

Context 229
Erosion interface at the base of the scourpit.

Context 230 (formerly deposits 19 and 67)
Seabed deposits predating the wreck. These were of light hard grey natural clay with some horizontal layering.

Discussion

Geological deposits

The seabed appears to have comprised a geology either of London Clay or of a redeposited London Clay (context 230) into which the *Mary Rose* sank in 1545.

Formation of the scourpit

The ship was lying approximately north–south and at a heeled angle of 58 degrees, thereby forming a considerable barrier to the east–west tidal flow. Deep pits were scoured around the hull and varied considerably in size. These were first seen during the excavation of the outboard stern trench in 1975–6, where the effect of the ship coming to rest on the seabed was to create a wave of hard natural clay along the port side of the keel. This was subsequently seen continuing along the stern section of the port side but progressively reduced towards the bow, as if the stern had hit the seabed first.

When excavation commenced in the outboard bow trenches, the scourpit was found to have undercut the keel. The scourpit was deepest at the bow, and extended as a crescent-shaped basin around the bow, linking up the scourpit on the port and starboard sides (Fig. 9.5). Along the port side, the scourpit narrowed from approximately 5m down to 4m along the main body of the ship widening again around the stern. Under the

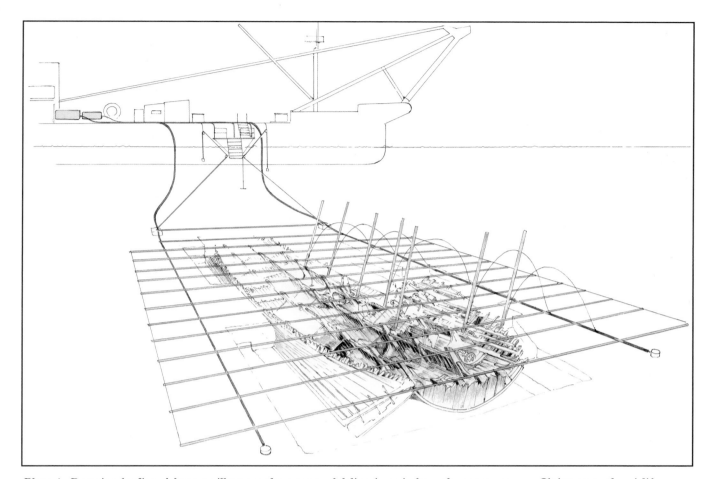

Plate 1 Drawing by Jon Adams to illustrate the system of delivering air from the compressor on Sleipner to the airlifts on the seabed. The yellow pipes mark the excavation zones in the wreck.

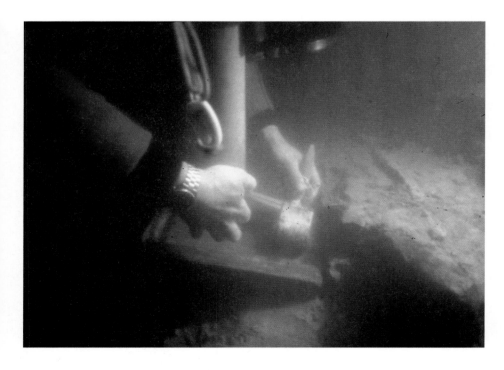

Plate 2 Diver using airlift and brush

Plate 3 (above) Investigating the wheel of a gun carriage

Plate 4 (above) Margaret Rule under the Sterncastle, looking through an open gunport

Plate 5 (below) Margaret Rule examining a box of longbows, looking for evidence of any nock ends or bowstrings

Plate 6 (below) Adrian Barak surveying the hull after recovery

Plate 7 *Recovery of an iron swivel gun*

Plate 8 *11 October, 1982* Tog Mor *lifts the hull clear of the water*

Plate 10 *(below) One of the ornate bronze guns*

Plate 9 *8 December 1982, The* Mary Rose *completes her final voyage, to her new home beside HMS* Victory *in HM Naval Base, Portsmouth*

Plate 11 Detail of ship's timbers, the hull lying in the cradle on the day of recovery – looking aft, Main and Upper decks. Compare with Plate 16 of the same area now

Plate 12 Working on the ship in full protective clothing while under spray. After rotation of the hull. View, looking forward, of the Main and Upper decks

Plate 13 Display case in the museum with scale model of the hull lying in the cradle before rotation to the upright position

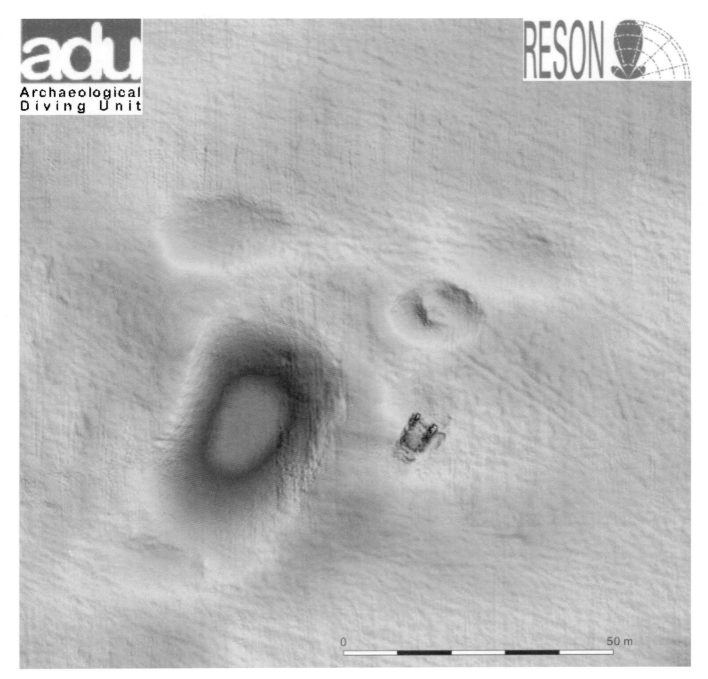

0   50 m

Plate 14 Bathymetry of the Mary Rose *wreck site undertaken in 2002 using Multibeam Sonar. North is to the top. False colours: the deep pit (blue) is where the ship lay, and the feature to its right is a sunken diving boat. The score marks on the seabed are caused by trawling across the site* (Courtesy of the Archaeological Diving Unit and Reson Offshore Ltd)

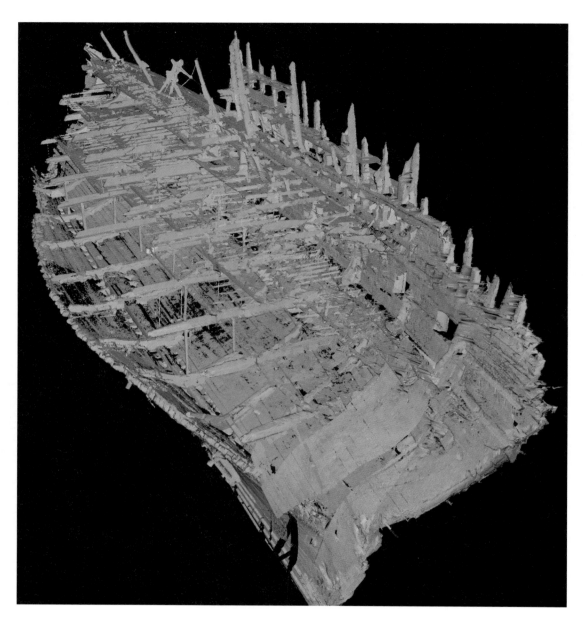

Plate 17 General view of the Mary Rose *in the shiphall, taken in 1994*

Plate 18 Many items of standing and running rigging were recovered

Plate 19 A huge collection of carpenters' tools was recovered, many items stored away in chests in one of the cabins.

Plate 20 (right) wooden objects, such as this tankard and plate, as well as ship's timbers, survived in remarkable condition

Plate 21 (left) A selection of the many thousands of objects recovered from the wreck that tell us so much about the everyday lives of the crew of the Mary Rose

Plate 22 Two of the golden 'Angels' (coins)

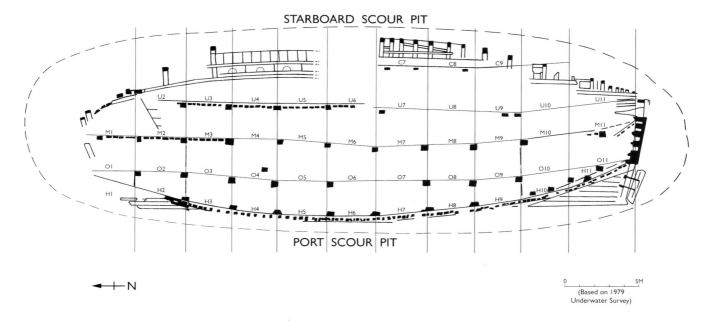

STARBOARD SCOUR PIT

PORT SCOUR PIT

N

0   5M

(Based on 1979
Underwater Survey)

Figure 9.5 Diagrammatic view of the scourpit

Sterncastle it was much wider, extending at least 8m outboard. It may well have been even wider but circumstances limited excavation and the extent of this trench could not be reached in the time available. Consequently, future site excavation could determine the shape of the scourpit in greater detail.

Excavation of the starboard scourpit under the Sterncastle began in 1981, where it was obviously different from that under the bow. The pit, about 3.5m deep, seemed to have been scoured relatively quickly, reaching down to the main deck gunports. However, unlike the bow scourpit, it seemed to have silted up quickly for the hull planking had remained pristine and the standing and running rigging had survived.

Salvage 1545

Attempts to salvage and raise the ship were carried out in the weeks immediately after sinking in 1545. But as the scour action was forming pits under the ship, and weed was accumulating on the standing rigging still attached to the heads of the masts, the task of salvage was becoming more and more difficult. The failure to raise the ship may have been due to its rapid burial in the seabed.

The rigging was no doubt cut in preparation for the salvage of the masts, which would account for it lying on the newly deposited sand on the floor of the scourpit, where it was soon covered by silt. Some destruction of the upper Sterncastle may have occurred around this time as this would account for the change in the action of the sea from scouring to the deposition

of clays within the scourpit. Above the collapsed shrouds were lenses of seaweed very similar to those seen inboard. This deposition probably occurred soon after the collapse of the rigging, as the condition of the outer hull of the castle structure was in a relatively good condition and had no trace of gribble (*Limnoria*).

In the sand layer at the bottom of the scourpit were found two large cables, each about 100mm in diameter, that appeared to be associated with the attempted salvage in 1545. They were found running straight down under the ship, and could not have fallen into the scourpit in that configuration. Their location at the forward end of the Sterncastle, close to the middle of the ship, indicates a considerable achievement in dragging them so far.

Deposition in the scourpit

Once the ship's structure had begun to collapse it slowly ceased making such a strong scouring action in the seabed, and deposition occurred within both the scourpit and the ship. The coarseness of the silt deposits, and the location of the layers that contained collapsed ship structure reflect the process by which the wreck was assimilated into the seabed.

The earliest deposit in the scourpit was a fine clean clay or sand, which had accumulated up to the keel. When this was removed it was found that the keel-stem scarf joint had sprung, the clay preserving the surfaces of the joint in a perfect condition. The cause of the spring in the scarf may have been the gradual collapse of the bow castle, for relatively uneroded timbers that had fallen from the forecastle at an early stage were found in this clay. Had the whole of the bow structure collapsed into the scourpit at this point, scour action would have been reduced abruptly and the pit would have infilled very quickly. Near the level of the keel were several thin layers of shell and coarse sediment, indicating subsequent short-lived bases of the scourpit. Clay had been deposited above these, together with an increased incidence of lenses of seaweed.

The initial sandy layer (context 227) was about 0.75m thick in the bottom of the scourpit, and tapered up the scour slope to only 30–40mm thick at mean seabed level. During excavation it had to be cut with a trowel or a water-jet as it was extremely compact. It was very resistant to sudden force but would 'give' or flow slowly under constant pressure. In this way it was 'thixotropic', since once disturbed it became almost fluid, and yet when settled it would re-compact. Any exposed edge or face would begin flowing and after a few hours would leave a considerable undercut beneath the layer above. In this way it was identical to deposits (contexts 213 and 216) found inboard.

This layer included laminae of various thickness from fine to coarse, indicating the cyclical nature of its deposition. The coarser material might have been deposited during rough weather, when heavier particles would be carried in suspension, followed by the finer material deposited in calmer weather and during neap tides. At its base was a concentration of very coarse sand or grit which verged on gravel, and also shell fragments. The fill of the pit indicates that the power of the scour action was reducing and that increasingly fine particles were able to consolidate after deposition rather than be washed out.

The lowest laminae had a high sand content and did not appear so black when first exposed. They contained much of the rigging associated with the Sterncastle, and isolated blocks and deadeyes were found higher up in the next layer. Both rope and blocks were found tightly matted with eelgrass which made the task of following them relatively easy once it was realised that it was easy to peel away the overlying clay-impregnated eelgrass mat in layers, revealing the rope and cable. As more of this layer was exposed, it became apparent that its formation was directly associated with the rigging. It seems as though the whole rigging assemblage had acted as a net, trapping weed as occurred to the modern datum lines during the excavation. Indeed, the large volume of weed was one of the limitations on survey during certain times of the year, or after storms when there was an abundance of it in the water.

Oyster shells in the silts also reflected the speed of the infill of the scourpit. Oyster spat were evidently adhering to the exterior of the ship's structure within a short period of the sinking, but as they needed a firm surface on which to grow together with clean flowing water they did not colonise the interior of the hull. The outer hull and exposed parts of decking and upper structure on the other hand offered an ideal site for a time and in many areas the oysters had reached a considerable size (70–80mm diameter). In time they were either smothered by accumulating sediment, or the timber to which they adhered finally degraded due to biological attack thereby causing the oyster to fall.

At a fairly early stage it was considered that the size of oysters might offer a means of dating the rate of deposition, but as their rate of growth is affected by many factors, such as temperature, light level, current, water and turbidity, this was decided to be an uncertain method of determining the rate of deposition. However, a rough guide could be obtained from the incidence, size and location of oysters. At the Sterncastle scourpit there were just a few adhering to the hull planking, but the number gradually increased higher up. Most were very small and none appears to have reached a great age. But as clays were deposited, there was an increasing number of mature oysters often found in layers, suggesting the passage of storms where large numbers might have been washed off the higher timbers of the hull. Further aft some collapsed timbers were found with oysters adhering to what had been their outer side when *in situ*.

There was an increasing amount of collapsed structural timber together with objects from the ship in the upper levels of the scourpit. Considerable attention was paid to the orientation of these timbers as many were very eroded on one surface and pristine on another, signifying exposure '*in situ*' for a period prior to collapse, at which point erosion had ceased.

Differential erosion was seen on the '*in situ*' hull planks, such as where the seam covering pieces of the hull bottom had protected the surface of the plank beneath, whereas between the covering pieces the surface of the planking was furrowed by erosion. However, this differential erosion around the seam covering laths could have occurred before the ship sank.

It was clear from the random orientation and partly eroded state of the ship's timbers that their location and condition was the result of a gradual process of degradation and collapse rather than the wholesale sudden collapse of a large section of the upper hull. The general state of preservation of the timbers improved the deeper they lay below the seabed, showing that they had been exposed for a shorter time.

Deposition inside the ship

The well preserved condition of the hull and organic materials within the ship show that the deposits inboard had built up rapidly enough to protect at least the lower 5m of hull and contents. Initially the hull was a relatively sealed structure that protected a large body of water from the effects of swell, tidal flow and coarse sediment (Fig. 9.6). Fine estuarine silts and clays are characteristic of the Solent, and would have gained access through deck hatches, companionways and gunports to be deposited within the ship. As a result, much of the initial deposition was of a fine clay. But as the ship's structure began to collapse, so the variability in the rate of deposition and the nature of the material being deposited changed. One of the first signs in the sediment was the gradual increase in organic matter seen as fine bands or laminae, similar to varves in a lake bed, reflecting cyclic patterns. In general the higher the deposits, the coarser these bands or lenses became. Much of this material was eelgrass and increasing amounts of it were carried into the hull on fast tide runs, possibly at spring tides and in rough weather. It settled and was subsequently sealed under light silts and clay presumably deposited in the slack-water of neap tides and calm weather.

In many places within the hull, the thickness of the laminae increased rapidly from fine bands only just discernable underwater, to layers over a centimetre thick. This marked influx of material may correspond to the first major collapse of the upper structure and hull planking, and the beginning of the main infilling of the scourpit.

Drawn sections of strata were only recorded at selected positions, the main one being in a trench cut across the ship in 1980 (Fig. 9.1, section B) at the junction of sectors 4 and 5, one metre north of the beams H, O, M, and U40, its aim being to assess the integrity of the hull. This allowed the sedimentation outboard and inboard to be seen in relation to each other. There was much less collapsed ship structure inboard than occurred in the outboard scourpit. Although the less compact upper silts were stepped back as a precaution against collapse, the lower levels proved very stable and were able to hold a vertical section for a period of weeks.

As excavation proceeded downwards, the various changes in colour, texture and constituent materials in the deposit became apparent, with the interfaces between them being particularly distinct. Due to the stability of the sides of the trench, the opportunity was taken to record the deposit in standing section across the entire width of the ship to a depth of 2.5m below the seabed. This section, while not reaching the bottom of the Orlop and Main deck areas, did reach the ballast in the Hold, enabling the complete sequence of deposition to be seen there. A similar section across the ship was cut further forward in sector 2 and revealed similar upper deposits (not illustrated).

In section A the interface between the Hard Grey Shelly Layer (context 209) and the soft clay beneath was not as distinct as it was over most of the site. The hard shelly material was less compact.

The detailed analysis of the stratigraphy has been limited to certain areas described below. The stratigraphy of other areas, such as the Orlop deck and much of the Main deck, still requires study.

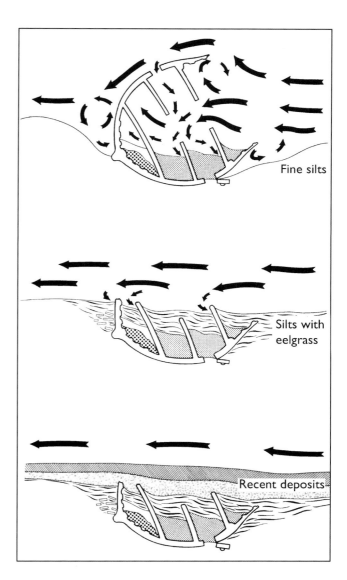

Figure 9.6 Sequence of erosion and burial of the wreck

Hold

Initially the restricted passage of water through the Hold after the sinking, resulted in the first deposit over the ballast being a clean light grey clay (Fig. 9.2, section B). Section A displayed a typical sequence of deposits: A fine soft clay (context 214) had inclusions of very fine laminae of compressed organic material, indicating the cyclic nature of deposition. In general the clay appeared almost sterile. Above this the laminae of weed were more regular and much thicker and lenticular in shape, occurring in regular groups 40–60mm thick. This change suggests that the structural collapse of the ship had begun to permit the access of a greater quantity of organic material. It is equivalent to the initial stage of collapse recorded in the 1978 Pilot's cabin section (Fig. 9.2, Section C, context 12).

Main deck, Pilot's cabin (sector M1–2)

A section was cut through the deposits in the Pilot's cabin in sector M1 on the Main deck (Fig. 9.2, Section

C). As it was a small area, excavation could continue down to the junction of the Main deck and the starboard side. Since this cabin was a relatively well sealed compartment within the hull, the initial deposit was a very fine dark creamy clay, the dark colour being due to its high organic content. It had accumulated over various objects that were in extremely good condition, indicating that they were sealed very quickly. Some were probably already in or near this position: others, like a small stave built container, had fallen against the side of the ship during the capsize and had come apart. This layer was eventually sealed by collapsed partition planking. With the collapse of the cabin partitions it was possible for alluvium to be deposited at a faster rate. Initially a quantity of seaweed and straw settled over the planking, which in turn was compressed by the now rapidly accumulating clay. The clay continued to be deposited with fine seaweed lenses and contained some objects, though not as many as in the primary layer. This light clay was typical of much of the infill inboard. The good condition of the objects within it and the structure that it covered indicated that it too was deposited very rapidly.

Upper deck

Due to the density of objects on the Upper deck there was no point at which deposits could be followed continuously down to the junction of the deck and starboard side. Collapsed timbers, guns 'in situ', an anchor and cable, together with a large number smaller objects meant that the nature of the deposits had to be recorded in a cumulative manner.

The initial deposit was a layer of silt or rubbery sand, followed by the typical soft grey clay (contexts 211 and 214) which accounted for the whole of the deposit between the objects. Along much of the Upper deck there was virtually no sandy layer, the clay having been deposited directly over the junction between the deck and starboard side. Both types of sediment seem to have been incorporated into the concretion forming around iron objects.

Recent deposits over the site

At the level of the upper collapsed timbers, the nature of the scourpit filling became harder, until it contained a large amount of broken shell as well as a high density of complete oyster shells. Around the port bow this was thicker and dark coloured. Within it was a mixture of objects both Tudor and recent, such as clay pipes, seventeenth and eighteenth century bottles etc., together with a large number of very eroded collapsed timbers. The top of this layer approximated to just below the uppermost surviving integral structure of the ship. It represented the top of the permanent seabed, above which deposits were in a mobile state and were deposited and eroded away from time to time.

At the time of the excavation there was an overlying deposit of soft dark organic clay containing modern anchorage detritus such as boiler clinker, animal bones, coal, glass and pottery. Although present over both scourpits, it was found to be progressively less distinct further away from the hull. It contained eroded Tudor objects, indicating they had been exposed from time to time, as well as post-Tudor material in varying states of preservation.

Localised scour action had occurred around the ends of major timbers such as deck beams, and hard shelly material had filled the pits scoured into the softer clay. At some point this process had ceased and above the shelly layer and surviving ship's timbers there had accumulated a deposit of dark soft organic clay, in some places almost a metre thick under the modern seabed.

10. Identity of the Wreck as the *Mary Rose*

Nothing has been found in the wreck stating that the ship was the *Mary Rose*, nevertheless the evidence from documents, from the ship itself and from its contents, all reflect its identity beyond doubt.

One alternative means of identifying any sunken ship is to find in it the possessions of someone who was known to have been on board. Pewter plates with the owner's initials 'GC' were found in the ship and could have belonged to Vice-Admiral Sir George Carew, but this cannot be proven. Of greater value are other pewter plates found with the coat of arms of the Lord High Admiral, John Dudley, Viscount Lord Lisle KG. Although he was certainly present at the sea battle of 1545, he is known to have been in his flagship, the *Henry Grace à Dieu*, when the *Mary Rose* sank, and as his own ship survived, the wreck in which his plates were found cannot be the *Henry Grace à Dieu*. Why his plates were in another ship is unknown.

The identity of the wreck as the *Mary Rose*, therefore, relies entirely upon a very substantial quantity of circumstantial evidence. The date and nature both of the ship and its contents are vital clues, and care must be taken to ensure that the dating evidence is from completely sealed archaeological deposits, particularly chests of goods, within the wreck, and not from deposits that might have been disturbed. It is possible that later objects on the seabed might have been introduced into the uppermost seabed deposits and so suggest a false date, and therefore an incorrect identification. It is also salutary to remember that objects of seventeenth, eighteenth, nineteenth and twentieth century date as well as of the sixteenth century, were found on the wreck site. But by carefully recording the strata in the wreck it has been possible to show that the objects in the wreck are all of the sixteenth century.

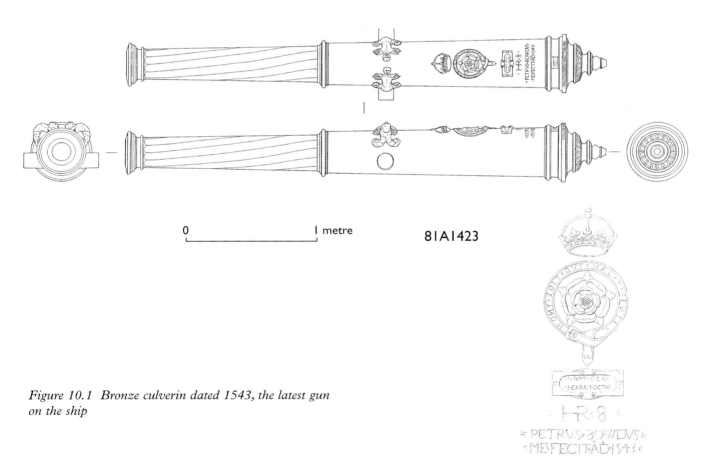

Figure 10.1 Bronze culverin dated 1543, the latest gun on the ship

Figure 10.2 Gold Angel of Henry VIII's third issue - introduced in April 1545 (Photo ref.: 85.0100)

The evidence to identify the ship is derived from the following sources:

1. Historical evidence

Although contemporary written records show that the *Mary Rose* had sunk in 1545 between England and the Isle of Wight, the Cowdray engraving, shows that the sinking occurred off Southsea Castle in the area of the wreck.

2. The Deane discoveries

Guns believed to be from the *Mary Rose* were found in 1836 by Deane, and the location was marked on a chart by the hydrographer, and it was this chart that led McKee to rediscover the wreck site. Consequently the guns and other objects recovered by Deane can join the finds from the twentieth century excavations in

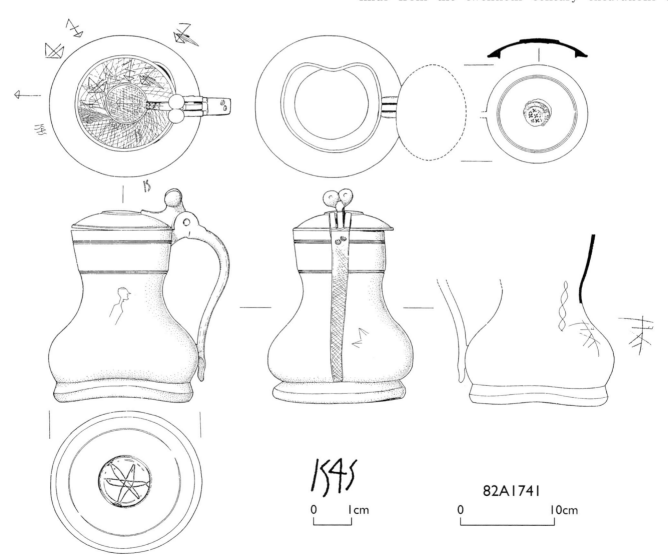

Figure 10.3 Pewter tankard with the date 1545 engraved on the lid

assessing the identity of the ship since they are from the same wreck.

3. The wreck is of a sixteenth century warship

The archaeological evidence shows that the wreck was of a heavily armed warship, with inscribed guns referring to Henry VIII. As the *Mary Rose* was the only warship of his fleet to sink in the Solent, the wreck must be of that ship. This is confirmed by the guns being dated not later than 1542. These include the bronze guns made by John and Robert Owen in 1537 and 1542, and by Peter Baude in 1543 (Fig. 10.1). Therefore, on this evidence alone the loss of the ship could not have occurred before 1543, and is further confirmation that the wreck is the *Mary Rose*, as no dates occur which are later than her sinking in 1545.

The guns found in the wreck, although incomplete in total number, closely match the list of guns in the *Mary Rose* described in the *Anthony Roll* inventory of 1546. Alternative ships also listed in the inventory with similar guns, such as the *Henry Grace à Dieu* and the *Jesus*, continued in service after the loss of the *Mary Rose* and were not sunk in the Solent. The content of guns alone, therefore, provides convincing evidence that the wreck was the *Mary Rose*.

It is possible that the bronze guns were reused in a later ship, though the wrought iron guns were already old-fashioned and were unlikely to be reused later. Consequently, it is important to note that there are other dated objects from the wreck that confirm that it is of Henry VIII's reign. These include many cast iron shot stamped with the initial 'H', thought to refer to Henry VIII. Three archers' leather bracers from the wreck are embossed with the royal arms and garter, and in the four corners there are the Tudor Rose and the Fleur-de-lys of Henry VIII, as well as the pomegranate and castle badges of Catherine of Aragon.

4. Tree-ring dates

Tree-ring dating helps to confirm the identification, for of the 41 ship timbers dated by this method, none is later than 1540 after which the sinking must have occurred (Dobbs and Bridge 2000).

5. Dateable objects from secure contexts

The date of the wreck is reflected by the overwhelming quantity of objects found which date from the first half of the sixteenth century. Of special importance are those items which were recovered from absolutely sealed deposits, including wooden chests, for these show that the sinking must have occurred on or after the date of the latest dated object. For example, three coins, half sovereigns, of Henry VIII, third period (1544–1547), issued from April 1545, were found with a wooden chest on the Orlop deck in O10 (Fig. 10.2). A seal or religious icon dated '1542' was found in a pouch in a chest on the Main deck in M8 (81A4262). But most important is the latest dateable object from

Figure 10.4 The ship's bell, made in 1510, the year in which the Mary Rose *was probably commissioned* (Photo ref.: 82.0368)

the wreck – a pewter flagon (82A1741) with a graffito date '1545' (Fig. 10.3). It was found in a sealed deposit on the Orlop deck in sector O8. Collectively these give a cut-off date in 1545 and show that the ship must have sunk in 1545 or soon after.

6. Dateable objects from less secure contexts

Other dateable objects were recovered from less enclosed but secure deposits on the wreck site, including a ship's bell, with an inscription date of 'MCCCCCX' (ie. 1510) (Fig. 10.4). The bell was found outside the ship in the starboard side scourpit, sector 11. Its date concurs with the known period of building the *Mary Rose*.

7. No other possible wreck

Although wrecks of later warships are known to exist in the Solent, such as the *Royal George* sunk in 1782, the only English warship known to have been sunk there during the sixteenth century is the *Mary Rose*.

Conclusion

The circumstantial evidence shows that the wreck is of an English warship of Henry VIII's navy that had sunk in 1545 or soon after. As the only documented warship loss in that area during the sixteenth century is the *Mary Rose* there is no doubt that the wreck is of that ship.

11. Description of the *Mary Rose*

Extent of the evidence

The purposes of recording the remains of the *Mary Rose* are to reconstruct what the ship was like in 1545; to assess how she was built and repaired; to estimate her performance and stability; to understand how she was used; and to establish why and how she sank. These are considered in further detail in *AMR* Vol. 2 and only a summary description of the remains of the vessel is included here.

Since only about one-third of the ship's structure was found there will always remain considerable gaps in knowledge of what the vessel was like and, therefore, alternative reconstructions are always possible. The bow and bow- or Forecastle are entirely missing (though collapsed parts of their structure may still lie buried in the bow scourpit). As it is not possible to complete a detailed record of the ship until all the deck, cabin and other structures, removed during the excavation, are eventually conserved and replaced, the description given here must remain provisional.

A considerable amount of detail of the ship has been recorded both underwater and in the museum by many people including A. Fielding, J. Adams, C. McKewan, and A. Barak, and more recently brought together and described by A. Fielding, C. Dobbs, S. Vine and D. McElvogue in archive drawings and reports, and it is upon their excellent work that this summary chapter is based.

Dendrochronological, or tree-ring, dates from the oak ship timbers need a little explanation. Each is given here as the last date present in the sample and not as the actual felling date because in almost every case the latest annual growth ring, identified by the presence of the bark, is absent, since it was cut away by the shipwright or is eroded away. In some cases the latest date is in the heartwood and so the felling date can be very many years later, and in others it is in the sapwood, and so the felling date can be more accurately estimated. It is also possible that a few timbers were reused from other ships, in which case the date will not have a particular value. Reused timbers can usually be recognised, however, since they contain fastening holes and cut features that do not relate to the *Mary Rose*. In many cases the tree-ring dates are years later than 1512 and must relate to repairs to the ship.

Shape of the hull

Eleven provisional sections or profiles drawn by Andrew Fielding across the ship were intended to create an interim set of drawings that represent the shape of the ship as found. The conventional form of the drawings used by naval architects are termed 'body plan', 'waterlines' and 'buttock lines', and are collectively known as the ship's 'lines'. They represent the hydrodynamic shape of the hull below the waterline, and show how well the ship was designed for speed through the water.

There were difficulties in recording the transverse sections as they were completed independent of each other, and not to a common longitudinal vertical axis of the ship, and it was necessary to joggle them relative to each other to make a best fit for the entire ship. The problems arose because access to the ship in the museum for recording was very difficult and restricted while the ship initially lay at an angle of about 60 degrees, and was being sprayed with chilled water. Subsequently, when the ship was upright, it was being sprayed with PEG (polyethylene-glycol) and access to the hull remained restricted.

By February 2002, technology for recording had advanced enormously and it was then possible to record the shape and structure of the ship very accurately using the Cyra Laser scan, in one day, relative to various horizontal and vertical datums. Much detailed recording work in the ship has been undertaken by D. McElvogue (eg, Fig. 11.1), which, when added to the earlier work by Fielding, makes it possible to compile an accurate detailed description of the ship, including its shape as exists in the museum. This will be published in *AMR* Vol. 2.

Clear evidence of the ship having been distorted has been identified, particularly in its forward half, and this will need to be quantified and adjusted at least on paper to arrive at the hull's original shape. Already it is clear that above the ship's waterline the hull narrowed upwards to give a 'tumblehome', and therefore bringing the centre of gravity towards the ship's central axis. This important aspect of stability compensated for the weight of heavy guns, men and equipment on the decks, which would have raised the ship's centre of gravity and given the vessel less stability.

The ship's original waterline has not yet been established, but for the purpose of this publication is

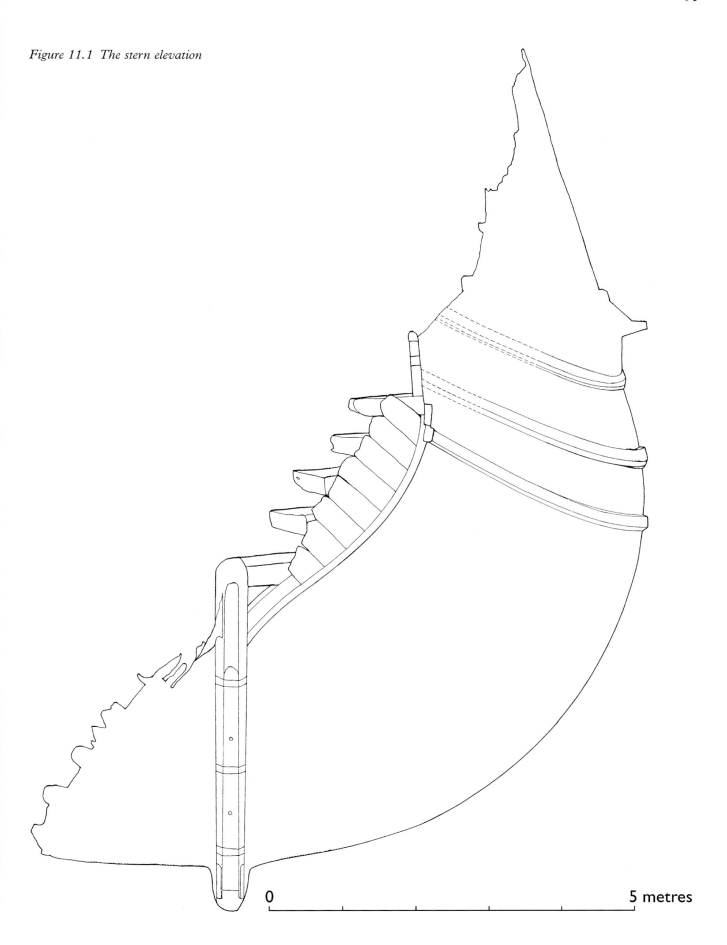

Figure 11.1 The stern elevation

0   5 metres

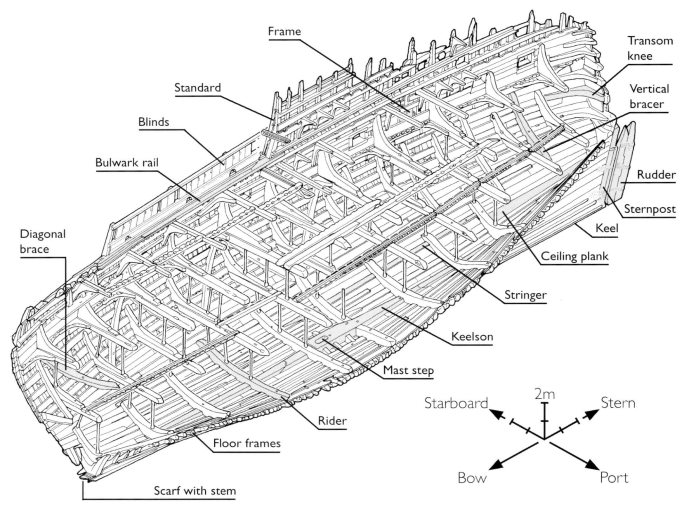

Figure 11.2 The main constructional features of the ship

assumed to be just below the lowest wale outboard amidships. This would give the ship a draft of about 4.5m at that point, but how valid this is requires checking.

Construction of the ship

The construction of a ship gives it strength, and is entirely different from the 'shape' as a key factor in describing a vessel. As the *Mary Rose* could have been built to its same shape in various ways, its actual construction is a reflection of the state of shipbuilding technology at the time. It is fair to say that large warships like the *Mary Rose* were the most complex dynamic structures built at that time, for they had to be strong enough to withstand the enormous stresses of rough weather and battle at sea and, being propelled by sail in many weather conditions, they had to be stable. They also had to be home to hundreds of men for long periods at a time. As a result the *Mary Rose*, like other ships, had these essential features: being watertight,

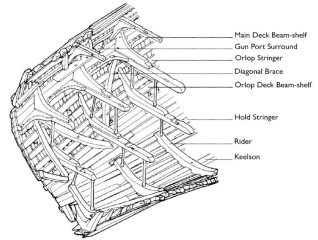

being stable, being strong and being capable of propulsion and manoeuvre.

It is against these characteristics that a description of the *Mary Rose* is best undertaken, defining factors that made the vessel successful for so long, and identifying other factors that could have led to her sinking in 1545. The main constructional elements and areas of the ship are shown in Figures 11.2 and 11.3.

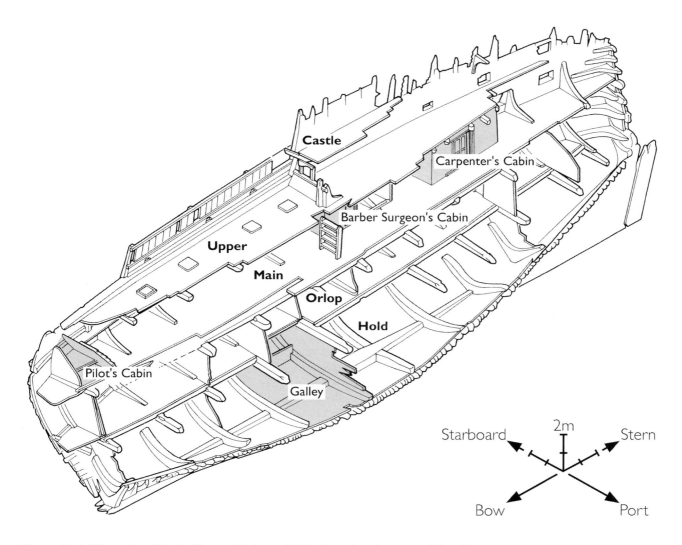

Figure 11.3 The decks (Castle, Upper, Main and Orlop) and main areas of the ship

The keel

The keel is the main longitudinal timber of the ship, and defines its central axis. It is almost complete and comprises three sections of timber, elm and oak, scarfed together to give an overall surviving length of 31.17m and a width of between 0.32 and 0.40m. The lower end of the sternpost is scarfed into one end, leaving a skeg extension just beyond and, although the extreme forward end is missing, it cannot have been much longer since at that point there exists part of the scarf with the inboard 'apron' timber of the stem.

A number of bolts exist along the lower part of both sides of the keel, many of which appear to fasten a timber cladding. Some have no clear purpose, and it is just possible that they were part of an attachment to hold a false keel that is now missing. This would explain the single vertical treenail in the underside of the keel 2.5m from the stern, which otherwise has no known purpose, though a number of other treenails would be expected. The purpose of a false keel, a kind of lower keel timber below the main keel, was to protect the

main keel if the ship ran aground. It would also increase the depth of the keel and so reduce 'leeway' (sideways movement of the ship). As false keels existed in British warships of the seventeenth and eighteenth centuries for practical reasons, it is possible that this feature existed in large warships of the sixteenth century, like the *Mary Rose*.

Hogging and distortion of the keel

The keel is not straight, but is arched upwards ('hogged') by between 0.25 and 0.60m relative to its ends, and in plan it bends up to 0.25m to starboard. It is not clear if this deformation occurred during the construction or the usage of the ship, or if it is the result of pressure after the sinking. However, experience on other historic shipwrecks has shown that, in the past, little attempt was made for precision in shipbuilding, so that timbers need not be exactly straight, and opposite sides of a hull need not be an exact mirror image of each other.

The frames

Numerous frames are fastened across the top of the keel and establish the shape of the hull from the keel to the gunwale at upper deck level. The outer and inner planking of the hull is attached to the frames by treenails.

Each frame comprises a number of futtocks, or short lengths of timber, sometimes scarfed together endways. The scarfing pattern seems to show considerable disunity with little attempt at lining up frame or futtock edges so that the line of a frame can be followed from the bottom to the gunwale.

The frames over the keel are termed 'floor-timbers', and they vary from 0.25 to 0.50m wide, and they are over 0.20m deep. They are spaced with gaps between of roughly 0.30–0.50m, and have limber holes, to allow the bilge water to flow to the lowest part of the ship's Hold.

Since the ceiling or inner planking obscures most of the framing in the bottom, it is difficult to reconstruct the framing pattern. On the port side, however, the erosion line shows a mostly continuous wall of frames, both floor-timbers and futtocks, without significant gaps between.

The outer planking

The outboard planking of the ship up to the Upper deck is of carvel laid oak 10cm thick, adzed on its outboard face, and this is secured to the frames by treenails. A run of horizontal planks forms what is called a 'strake'. At each butt joint both plank ends are fastened by nails to the frame behind. These joints are staggered so that none lies next to another thereby causing a weakness in the hull. The ends of the planks at the stern are fastened into a rabbet in the sternpost usually with two nails. The treenails that fasten the outer planks to the frames are up to a metre long.

The seams between the outer planks are all caulked, but the materials have yet to be identified. Close to the keel are four seams that are partly covered by laths, semicircular in section and fastened to the hull planking by small iron nails. Each lath is about 140mm wide and 30mm thick, and overlies a caulking of hair and tar. They are probably to prevent leaking seams and are a distinctive feature of the *Mary Rose*.

Three narrow wales, extra-thick longitudinal timbers between the outboard planks, are situated in the upper part of the hull, and gave strength to the ship above the waterline, and also protected the planking from damage when running alongside a quay or another ship. Two of the wales lie immediately above and below the lower deck gunports and reinforce the hull at those openings.

At an early stage in the investigation of the *Mary Rose* it was thought that the ship might have been originally built with overlapping clinker planking outboard, and was subsequently rebuilt with carvel planks to give a smooth exterior. Rule noted that frames at the Main deck level on the starboard quarter had been adzed as if to remove the notches which originally housed clinker planking and that, as it was not possible to remove all trace of the notches without weakening the frames, a shipwright had inserted a fillet of wood to accommodate the gap (Rule 1983, 21). Subsequent examination, however, has not been able to confirm this and suggests that the main part of the hull was never built with clinker planking.

The outboard face of the planking below the waterline is not covered by sheathing to protect the hull from marine borers such as *Teredo*, such as occurred in some later warships. This suggests that the hull was protected in another way. In medieval times the underwater planking of a ship was often coated with pine tar. By the seventeenth century ships were coated with a 'white stuff', a mixture of whale oil, rosin (ie. pine resin) and brimstone (ie. sulphur) which turned white on contact with water. The *Anthony Roll* picture of the ship shows a dark surface below the bottom wale and suggests that the *Mary Rose* had some such coating. This is also suggested by a picture of several English warships escorting Henry VIII from Dover in 1520 to the Field of the Cloth of Gold to meet Francis I of France. Five ships are clearly shown with a whitish hull from the waterline downward. Whether or not the hull of the *Mary Rose* still retains traces of an outboard coating is not known, though it is just possible that traces have survived under the laths and where the cradle supports for the ship have been held fast against the outer face of the hull, and have protected the timber surfaces from water and chemical spray.

The inboard planking

There are two thicknesses of longitudinal oak planks attached to the frames inside the ship: the standard ceiling planks, and the much thicker stringers (see below), all of which not only protected the inboard surface of the hull from damage, but also helped fasten the frames in position and gave longitudinal strength to the vessel. The ceiling planks vary in length from over 9m to a mere 0.30mm, and from 75mm to 0.50m in width, and are 60–80mm in thickness.

Stringers

Five oak stringers, extra-thick inboard planks, are fastened to the intact starboard side of the hold, and there are three more surviving on the incomplete port side. As those on opposite sides of the bottom are of similar construction and distance from the centerline it is possible to reconstruct the entire hull below the Orlop deck. At a higher level are yet more stringers up to the Upper deck level. The hold stringers vary

Figure 11.4 Detail of the mast step (Photo ref.: 94. 1045)

between 0.23 and 0.26m in width, between 0.13 and 0.17m in thickness, and are fastened to the frames with treenails.

Keelson

The keelson is another longitudinal strengthening inboard timber overlying both the frames and the keel to which it was fastened by iron bolts. Part of its purpose was to spread the weight of the main mast over a considerable length of the ship's bottom. It is complete, 20.96m long, and comprises three oak timbers, fastened together by horizontal diagonal scarf joints. Its underside is rebated to fit over the frames.

The main mast-step

The mast-step (Fig. 11.4) is a rectangular socket 0.70m long, 0.34m wide and 0.16m deep, cut into the top of the keelson where it is at its greatest width of 0.80m. On either side of the keelson are three timbers that buttress the step against the first stringer on either side of the keelson, and hold the mast-step in place. Limber boards that could be removed to clean and inspect the bottom, lie on either side of the keelson at the mast-step.

There are three shallow rebates in the top of the keelson just aft of the mast-step. Another rebate lies some distance aft, just forward of rider 7. These might have held stanchions at some time.

Riders

Riders are massive curved transverse timbers lying across the keel line within the hold, which give additional support to the hull bottom. They are like an extra group of inner frames, but are more substantial and fewer in number than the frames.

Nine riders were found in the wreck, though that nearest the bow (R1) was removed during the excavation and has yet to be replaced. The riders are numbered from bow to stern.

Rider 5 is typical, being 0.36m wide by up to 0.44m thick, and is fastened to the stringers by six bolts. Rider 6, in contrast, does not pass over the keel, but instead has two separate arms that butt up against either side of the keelson. Three bolts fasten the starboard side, two of which are over stringers and one over a ceiling plank.

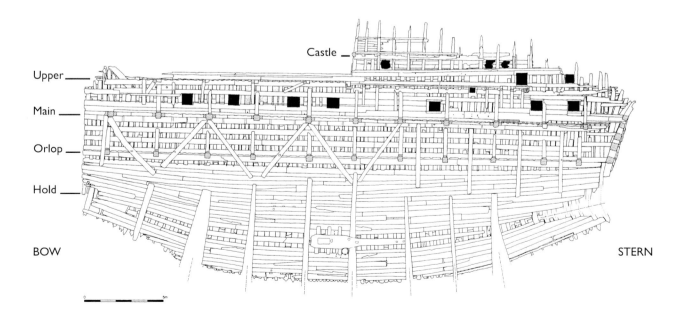

Figure 11.5 Projected internal view of the hull (scale approximate)

Figure 11.6 Inboard view of the stern (Photo ref.: 93.1016)

It is certain that at least some of the riders were added to the ship some time after her construction but it is not clear if they were replacements of earlier riders. However, as the upper surface of each rider has fixings for stanchions supporting the decks above, it is clear that one function of the riders was to support the weight above.

Braces

Substantial timber braces, strengthening the side of the hull at the waterline, are attached to the starboard side of the ship inboard, mainly at Orlop deck level. Twelve were found, but that nearest the bow was removed during the excavation and has not yet been replaced.

The braces, curved to the rounded shape of the hull, are between 3.07m and 4.16m long, 0.215–0.295m wide, and from 0.28–0.36m thick. Their lower ends mostly rest on a stringer below the Orlop deck. All braces are finely adzed and have chamfered edges.

There are two forms of brace: vertical and diagonal (Fig. 11.5). The lower ends of the latter follow-on from near the ends of the riders in the ship's bottom, whereas the vertical braces do not follow-on the line of the bottom riders. The braces are fastened to the hull by treenails and iron bolts, the varying use of fastenings suggesting that they were re-fastened at some stage.

The stern

The hold of the ship narrows from amidships aft to form a sharp narrow stern below the waterline, and includes a solid complex of timbers forming the 'deadwood' foreward of the sternpost. Above the waterline the stern has a flat transom with diagonal planking outboard, though only the starboard side has survived and that is heavily eroded (Fig. 11.6).

The surviving upper part of the stern is shaped by a pair of nearly vertical curving 'fashion pieces', which give the shape to each corner of the ship. Horizontal knees fastened to transom beams brace the starboard corner of the ship.

Outboard, below the lowest wale, each 'fashion piece' is rebated on its leading edge to accept the butt ends of the outboard carvel hull planking, and on its after edge to accept the diagonal transom planking.

The Sterncastle

Only the forward part of the Sterncastle on the starboard side has survived. It lies above the Upper deck, and has a lighter construction than the main body of the ship. Only some frames extended upwards into the castle beyond the gunwale at the Upper deck, and these are of smaller dimension than the frames below. The outboard planking of the castle was attached by iron nails to the notched outboard faces of the castle frames to form overlapping weatherboarding. Since rivets did not fasten the planks to each other, as occurs in true clinker boat planking, the term 'clinker' is probably not appropriate to describe this overlapping construction.

The interior of the ship

The Hold

The Hold is the bottom of the ship below the Orlop deck (Figs 11.5 and 11.7) and it was a dark and damp place. It lay well below the waterline and had a headroom of 1.75m amidships. Its main functions were to contain the ballast that helped to give the ship stability, to provide a storage for barrels of tar and spare cables, and to contain the galley where the food was cooked for the ship's complement.

The ballast
The ship's ballast was of well-rounded but broken flints, originally washed out of the nearby chalk hills during various ice ages and deposited in gravel beds

Figure 11.7 The interior of the vessel looking aft (Photo ref.: 93.1009)

probably in the Portsmouth or Southampton areas. It included cockle, winkle and oyster shells indicating that it was obtained from beach deposits. Several fresh leaves were also found.

The extent of the ballast, together with its volume and weight, has yet to be plotted out and calculated, though it is clear that when the ship heeled over the ballast shifted to the starboard side.

Transverse partitions

A number of transverse partitions existed in the hold, dividing it into sections at riders 1, 3, 5 and 9, though it is not clear if there was a further partition at rider 2. They were of planks about 30mm thick that were fixed to the stanchions and partition supports on the riders.

The galley

The galley area lay immediately forward of the main mast in the widest part of the Hold at sector H5, and was surrounded by timber partitioning on three sides, 1.98m fore-and-aft, by 4.15m transverse, which enclosed two brick ovens (Fig. 11.8). Access to the

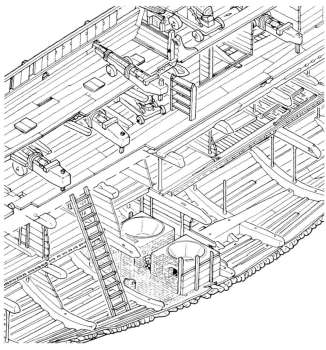

Figure 11.8 Isometric reconstruction including the galley

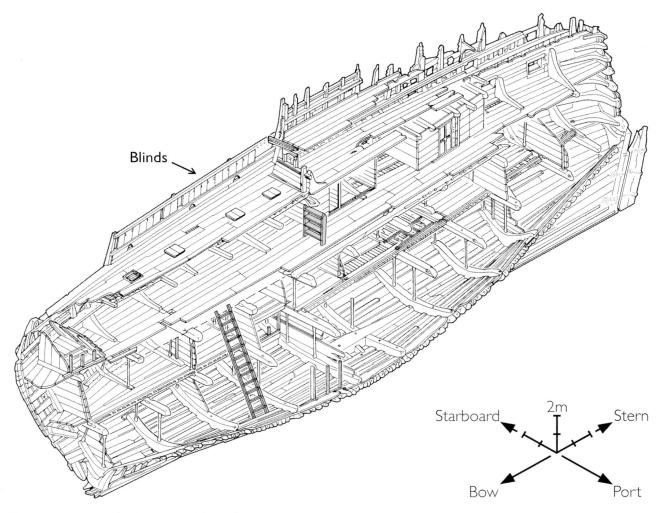

Blinds

Starboard   2m   Stern

Bow   Port

Figure 11.9 Isometric showing positions of companionways and blinds

galley was by ladder down from the Orlop deck into area H4. A working area lay just forward of the ovens in sector H4 and included a store of logs for the fires. This has all been studied by Christopher Dobbs who excavated, recorded and reconstructed the ovens.

Only a small part of one oven was found intact, the remaining brick structures having collapsed when the ship heeled over and sank. The intact structure was built of bricks and lime mortar, and survived only on the starboard side of the ship. The bricks formed part of a circular firebox beneath a dished upper structure that, together with two iron cross-bars, originally supported a large brass cauldron. The brickwork stood nearly a metre high and matched the shape of a cauldron 1.45m wide at the rim, 0.63m deep with a full capacity of 600 litres. The front of the hearth probably had an arched opening, one end of which was recorded *in situ*, and it is conjectured that the entire opening was about 0.70m wide and 0.50m high. The hearth was built on a floor of bricks set in a layer of mortar 100mm thick. This in turn overlay the gravel ballast, which was about 0.44m at its maximum thickness. The surface of the brick floor lay just above the top of rider R5.

The presence of two cauldrons amongst the collapsed brickwork, the extent of the partitioned area, and the size of the surviving brick hearth, all indicate that there had once been a port side hearth, though of smaller capacity since its cauldron was 1.34m across the rim, 0.535m deep and had a capacity of 360 litres.

Above the galley were traces of a plank-lined ventilation shaft that extended upwards through the orlop deck and perhaps beyond.

Assuming that the partly surviving brick hearth on the starboard side of the galley was built central to its circular 'fire-box' then it is conjectured that the hearth structure was originally 1.62m wide.

A third copper alloy cauldron (81A2340), that was free-standing and with lug handles, was also found in the galley. Although in a poor condition it seems to have been oval, with diameters of 0.66m and 0.756m, and a height of 0.458m.

A three-legged bronze cooking pot was found at the entrance to the starboard furnace, and a similar iron pot was nearby. Five ceramic and one iron cooking pots were found in the galley area, and show that food was also prepared in smaller quantities than the major

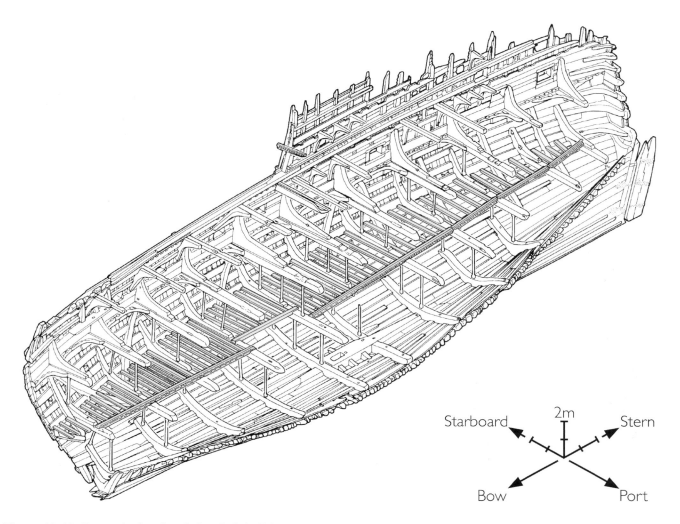

Starboard   2m   Stern

Bow   Port

Figure 11.10 Isometric showing Orlop deck half beams and carlings

brews in the two large cauldrons. Artefacts closely associated with the use of the galley include bellows, ladles, a bread trough, ash boxes and shovels.

Access from the Hold to the Orlop deck

A substantial but moveable ladder was found loose, and evidently extended upwards from the Hold in the area between riders 3 and 4, through the Orlop deck to the Main deck (Fig. 11.9). Judging from the angle of its foot, this ladder had an incline of 65 degrees. It is not clear to what the ladder was fastened, but it is likely that it rested against the Main deck carlings. If so, its lower end would have been situated between the first and second stringers in the hold. The ladder was of beech, 0.65m wide, and had twelve surviving steps each with a rise of 0.40m. It is estimated to have been *c.* 5m long.

The Orlop deck

The Orlop deck is the lowest deck in the ship, and was primarily a storage area for everything from rigging to officers' chests. Compared with the other decks, which supported the artillery and contained living quarters, it is lightly constructed, with comparatively thin planking and relatively few nails fastening the planks to the half-beams. The planks are perfectly cut to fit around the braces and between the knees, and against the side of the hull.

Deck clamp

The 'clamp' is a substantial longitudinal run of timbers, 0.40m wide and 90–160mm thick, which helped support the ends of the deck beams, and is treenailed to the inboard face of the frames. It comprises five sections of timber scarfed together, and extends throughout the surviving length of the ship's side.

Deck beams

The Orlop deck beams are single timbers originally stretching across the hull. They average 0.30m wide and 0.285m thick, and are chamfered on both lower edges. Their outboard ends are housed in the deck clamp and are fastened to rising knees by iron bolts. There is a considerable amount of sapwood on some beams.

Rising knees

A rising knee is bolted to the upper face of each deck beam, and attaches the beam to the side of the ship by bolts. Each knee is cut from a single piece of timber grown to shape and is rebated to fit around the starboard side stringers, though its whole length protrudes above the deck planking. The dimensions of the knees vary considerably, from 1.20–2.75m long, 1.15–1.68m high, 0.31–0.50m thick, and 0.19–0.30m wide. Five, possibly six, of the Orlop knees are incised with large Roman numerals.

Eight of the knees have provided dendrochronological dates, the latest date in the samples being 1474 (ORK70), 1474 (ORK40), 1494 (ORK50), and 1497 (ORK60) indicating that these were probably part of the original construction. Latest dates from other knees are 1523 (ORK10), 1511 (ORK20), 1514 (ORK100), and 1524 (ORK1) and show that these were installed during refits (Dobbs and Bridge 2000).

Figure 11.11 Orlop deck half beams (Photo ref.: 87. 1048)

Half beams and carlings

Half-beams and carlings fill the area between the main beams, their purpose being to support the deck planks to which they were nailed. They are of oak with an average width of 134mm and a thickness of 108mm.

Small shelves house the outboard ends of the half-beams at the side of the ship, to which they are fastened usually with two nails, and the inboard ends are fastened to carlings (Figs 11.10 and 11.11). Tool marks on some half-beams show that they were sawn, though others have been partially dressed by adze. Four of the Orlop deck half beams are inscribed with carpenter's marks.

Deck planks

The Orlop deck planks (Fig. 11.12) are lightly constructed, averaging 25mm thick and are mostly of

Figure 11.12 Orlop and Main deck planks (Photo ref.: 93.1022)

elm. They are flat-sawn and appear to be relatively new when the ship sank, displaying very fresh saw marks on both their upper and lower surfaces. A number of planks had been trimmed by adze at their long edges to ensure an even deck surface with adjacent planks.

The planks are shaped to fit around the vertical and diagonal braces at the side of the ship, and short planks are laid between the knees, with longer planks over the main part of the deck. Instead of relying upon a uniform pattern of narrow stealer planks to compensate for the longitudinal curve of the hull, the majority of the planks are shaped to the curve of the ship's side. However, a few sharply angled stealer planks also exist. The Orlop deck planks are generally fastened to the half beams with fewer nails than are the planks of the other decks.

Deck partitions

The Orlop deck was divided into a series of transverse compartments by light feather-edge planking fastened to upright stanchions and battens at deck beams O30, O40, O50 (Fig. 11.13), O90 and O100. Above the galley there was an open ventilation well through the Orlop deck that was surrounded by partitions.

Access from one partitioned area of the deck to the next was presumably via a central gangway, and although the means of access through the partitions had not survived, that at O30 possibly includes the side of a doorway.

Deck companionways

Companionways are ladders or stairs giving access between decks, and two were found that linked the Orlop deck to the Main deck above (Fig. 11.9). They are more accurately described as moveable ladders, for they were not fixed to the ship. They appear to have been associated with a system of central hatches.

One of the movable ladders was found in sector O4, and rose from the Hold in sector H4 through the Orlop deck and extended upwards to the Main deck between beams. The other ladder gave access from the Orlop deck to the Main deck in sector O8, and was found loose in sector M8 with one end across the M70 deck

Figure 11.13 Stanchion on the Orlop deck illustrating a sliding mortice (Photo ref.: 91.1061)

Figure 11.14 Orlop deck half beams (Photo ref.: 87. 1031)

beam. Its cheeks, of a coniferous wood, are *c.* 2.54m long, *c.* 75mm wide and *c.* 100mm thick, and it has semicircular oak steps, *c.* 75mm wide, with a rise of 0.50m.

Hatches and hatch covers

A series of hatches occupied at least part of the centreline of the Orlop deck, but as they lay close to or beyond the line of erosion they are imperfectly preserved (Fig. 11.14). The complete system of hatches and their covers has yet to be studied fully.

Each hatch cover consisted of five or six oak planks nailed to three half beams. Holes at two of the diagonally opposed corners of the hatch were perhaps for lifting rings. Some of the Orlop deck hatches have a spattering of pitch and grit on them, possibly to act as a non-slip surface since their seams are not caulked.

The Orlop deck hatches are marked with Roman numerals and a circle, starting at II at the stern and progressing towards the main mast (number I has not been found). Hatches forward of the mast are not numbered.

The Main deck

The Main deck was where the heaviest guns and some cabins were located, consequently its structure is very substantial and is supported by lodging knees, double carlings and thickened beam shelves.

This is also the lowest waterproofed deck, for the planking is caulked and waterways are cut through the midships rising knees and led to scupper holes (see below) through the hull. The Upper deck above steps

down from the ship's waist amidships to the area beneath the Sterncastle. Because of this, the distance between Main deck and the Upper deck varies. Forward of the Sterncastle, there is a minimum clearance of 1.75m from the Main deck surface to the Upper deck half-beams; but below the Sterncastle, where the deck is somewhat differently constructed, the clearance to the Upper deck beams is between 1.65m and 1.83m.

The side of the hull

The side of the ship is heavily constructed to accord with this being a fighting deck with guns and gunports. Its frames are somewhat irregularly spaced, and often have gaps large enough to accommodate another frame. No inboard ceiling planks are attached to the frames, except under the Sterncastle. However, there are substantial longitudinal stringers inboard, and wales outboard to give the hull strength above and below the gunports. The three wales run from stem to stern outboard following the rising sheer of the deck. Three scuppers, fitted with simple leather valves about 0.50m long, drained water from the Main deck, and show that the waterline lay below.

Gunports: Seven gunports exist in the surviving part of the starboard side of the ship at the Main deck, each being fitted with a lid. Each lid was constructed of extremely heavy oak boards, fastened by massive iron bolts and fitted with large iron straps to hinges attached to the chamfered edge of the upper wale outboard. A heavy iron ring on the inside of the lid allowed it to be held shut within the recessed port opening. The method of fastening the gunports open is not clear.

The deck

Deck clamp: The main deck beams are rebated into a very substantial deck clamp composed of seven sections of timber secured to the hull by treenails.

Deck beams: The Main deck beams are 0.30–0.40m square, and, with the exception of M60, they may have been single pieces of timber spanning the width of the hull. M60, the longest beam in the ship, had at least two sections of timber, jointed with locking scarfs.

The deck beams are firmly secured to the hull, not only by resting in the deck clamp, but also by being fastened to rising and lodging knees which are themselves fastened to the deck beams with clench bolts of considerable length.

With the exception of deck beams at Ml0 and Ml10, which are eroded, and M100, which is missing, all the deck beams have stepped rebates on their fore and aft faces for fore-and-aft carlings.

An interesting feature of the Main deck beam at M40 is its offset position relative to the stern of the O40 deck beam below. This causes the Orlop deck stanchions to lean aft at a rather alarming angle. Careful inspection indicates that the beam was deliberately installed in this manner, possibly because it was a replacement as it gave a dendrochronological date of 1535 (it included the bark). In contrast other beams have returned dates from the original construction phase, M70 having produced a date after 1443, M60 after 1452 and M90 after 1465.

Rising knees: The rising knees of the Main deck are similar to those of the Orlop deck though more massive (Fig. 11.15). They are of oak, varying from 1.42–3m long, 1.20–1.87m high, 0.52–0.90m thick, and 0.20–0.37m wide. They are bolted to the deck beams below and are bolted and treenailed to the hull. One of the major differences between the Main and Orlop deck rising knees is the stepping of their inboard ends which allows for a greater area of uninterrupted planking on the Main deck.

The knees at M30, M40, M50, M60 and M70, have waterway holes 70–100mm square cut through their widths at deck level. The absence of these waterways through other knees towards the bow and stern is probably due to less water entering the area covered by the castles and to the increased height of the Main deck gunports above the waterline at the stern. The knees at M60, M80 and M90 also contain rebates for partitions.

Some knees were replacements, judging from the dendrochronological dating, the latest year in the samples being 1525 (knee at M10), 1526 (knee at M30) and 1528 (knee at M80).

Lodging knees: These horizontal knees gave a substantial extra reinforcement to the side of each deck beam, for they are fastened to the hull with both treenails and bolts, and to the deck beams with bolts (Fig. 11.15). The lodging knees vary considerably in size, from

Figure 11.15 Main deck lodging and rising knees (Photo ref.: 91.1034)

1.48–2.40m long, 0.30–0.60m thick, and 1.40–2.40m high.

Carlings: Carlings, the fore-and-aft timbers that in some cases formed one side of a central row of hatchways or gratings, exist on the main deck and are 0.29–0.30m wide and 0.215–0.35m thick, and sit in single-stepped rebates in the deck beams, similar to those on the Orlop deck.

Further aft, in sectors M8 and M9, there are long, shallow rebates in the inboard face of the carlings, perhaps to house the step for the mizzen mast. Most of the outboard half-beam rebates in the M8–M9 carling are angled to lock the half beams firmly in place, and would provide extra stiffening in an area where the forces imposed by a mast would affect the structure.

Half-beams and shelves: The half-beams in sectors M7–M9 and Ml1–Ml2 are more massive than those of the Orlop deck, perhaps to support the heavier deck and its guns. They are 160–190mm wide and 100–150mm thick. There are between five and eight half-beams per sector, except in M9 which contains eleven.

Deck planks: The Main deck planks are of oak and about 70mm thick. They vary considerably in size, the maximum width being around 0.50m and the greatest length being 7.33m (Fig. 11.16).

A ridge, 60–160mm wide and 40mm high, extends at least from sectors M3 to M8 on the inner edge of the inboard deck planks and acted as a coaming, preventing water from penetrating down to the deck and hold below.

The deck planks are secured to the half-beams by iron nails whose heads are countersunk and plugged with pitch, although this may be an accidental by-product of caulking the seams. The seams are filled with a mixture of hair and pitch, with additional pitch being

Figure 11.16 Main and Upper deck planking looking aft (Photo ref.: 93.1050)

poured along the top of the seams, often covering a considerable portion of the deck planks.

Cabins

Three cabins were discovered on this deck against the starboard side of the hull, and they have been named after their most likely occupants, judging from the artefacts found in each. They are known as the Pilot's, Barber-surgeon's and Carpenter's cabins (see Fig. 11.3 for location in the ship).

Other cabins no doubt existed on the port side of this deck, and although that part of the ship was completely eroded, a careful study of the distribution of artefacts may in the future suggest concentrations of related types that will reflect the furnishing of the conjectured cabins.

The Carpenter's cabin: This cabin lay under the Sterncastle, and had three wall partitions, two extending inboard from the starboard side, and the third linking them fore-aft. The maximum dimension of the cabin was 2.30m wide by 4.20m long, and the wall planks, 20mm thick, were fastened to upright posts. At least two of the planks had marks showing that they were reused from a previous structure.

The fore-aft wall had a horizontal sill beam nailed to the deck planks, and seven vertical posts. Originally the wall had a sliding door closer to the stern end of the cabin, but at some stage the cabin was extended and the doorway became central. Originally, the aft wall had been located against the rear face of the rising knee at M90, but in the extension process it was moved about 0.90m aft.

The sliding door had two vertical planks chamfered together on an external oak frame with vertical and horizontal cross battens. It rested in two oak runners, approximately 1.84m in length, one above the door and the other below. Nail holes in the horizontal central door batten suggest the location of a handle, and a small wedge, between the bottom of the door and the runner, was presumably used to keep the door closed.

Two beds, one on either side of the doorway, lay in the cabin. The aft bed was approximately 1.22m from bow to stern and 1.30m across. It was fashioned to fit around the knees and must have been constructed after the cabin was extended. This bed was made from three planks with a raised shelf on its forward edge to secure the bedding of grass or hay. The planks sat on a rail attached to the starboard side, and on another rail, which was fastened to the inboard partition supports. The forward bed had only one plank *in situ* when it was excavated, but it was presumably constructed in a similar way to the after bed. Again, it appears to have had a covering of hay or grass.

A small ventilation port had been cut through the side of the ship at the Upper deck clamp, and was fitted with an external opening lid, hinged at the side. A semicircular recess was cut into the underside of the chainwale to allow the lid to be swung outboard.

The Barber-surgeon's cabin: This lay a little forward of the Carpenter's cabin, in an area of the ship that was damaged during the sinking process. This resulted in the fragmentation of some of its wall planking, and as a result some aspects of the cabin's reconstruction are conjectural.

The cabin had three timber partition walls forming two separate cabin areas, each approximately 1.9m long by 2.3m wide, the one nearer the bow containing the Barber-surgeon's chest and equipment. Because of the damage, it is not possible to define either the inboard wall, or establish if the cabin had doors or just openings. The only well-preserved part of this cabin was the forward athwartship partition, whose planks were 25mm thick.

The Pilot's cabin: This small cabin was situated near the bow, directly beneath the M2 companionway that lead from the Main to the Upper deck. The cabin had a maximum width of 2.59m (the length of the sill beam supporting the companionway) and a length of 1.73m.

The sloping overlapping planking backing of the M2 companionway that formed the aft wall of the cabin, is the only part of the cabin that has so far been surveyed and reconstructed on paper. The inboard fore-and-aft wall comprised a number of upright supports resting in a sill beam, stretching upwards either to the companionway or to the underside of the Upper deck planking. Since both the supports and the planking had collapsed it is difficult to reconstruct their precise arrangement. The forward wall also had a sill beam and several upright supports and planks.

A crudely constructed bed, of four transverse planks with their inboard ends resting on a longitudinal sill beam, dominated the interior of this cabin. The bed was approximately 1.73m long and 1.39m wide. A chest containing a gimballed compass lay in the area between the bed and the inboard longitudinal sill beam. A pair of dividers in a case was found nearby and it is the presence of these navigational instruments that have lead to the belief that the cabin was used by the Pilot (but see *AMR* Vol. 4, chapter 7 for further discussion).

Companionways and hatches

Two companionways giving access to the Upper deck were found in sectors M2 and M6, and another, found in sectors H4–M4, was an upward extension of the ladder from the Hold through the Orlop and Main decks (Fig. 11.10).

M2 companionway: This was fastened to the sloping after face of the Pilot's cabin partitioning at an angle of 70 degrees, and gave access to the Upper deck and presumably to the Forecastle. Unfortunately the upper end of the companionway is missing, so its original height is unknown. Its four surviving steps, each with a straight back and a bowed front, are about.1.15m long, up to c. 0.25m wide, and have a rise of approximately 0.30m.

M6 companionway: This gave access from the Main to the Upper deck just forward of the Sterncastle. It was angled at 70 degrees, and the four surviving steps, with a rise of about 0.37m, are 1.06m long and 0.23–0.29m wide. The steps were rectangular, not bowed like those in the M2 companionway.

Hatches and hatch covers: Knowledge of the hatch distribution on the Main deck relies on a certain amount of extrapolation, since much of the central area of the deck was completely eroded. Hatches once existed along the centreline of the deck, parts having been recovered from sectors M3, M7/8, M9, M10 and M11. Surviving parts of hatch-covers were found covered by pitch.

The Upper deck

This was both a gun deck and a fighting platform for the archers and other troops. The area in the waist was open to the sky between the Fore- and Sterncastles, and at the time of the sinking was covered by anti-boarding netting. It has a lighter construction than the Main deck, no doubt reflecting its lighter loading, and was constructed on two levels, separated at the junction of the waist and the Sterncastle, the waist being 0.27m higher than the deck level under the Sterncastle. There is a clearance of 1.72m between the Upper and Sterncastle decks, and considerable structural differences between the two sections of deck.

The side of the hull

The waist: The gunwale lay just above the upper deck in the open ship's waist, and above it was a screen of poplar boards, or 'blinds', at waist height supported by oak standards and rails. Being light in weight and non-splintering, the blinds were ideally suited to protect the gunners and archers. During action, alternate blinds could be removed to provide openings.

Two oak rails and four uprights supported the blinds, and below them are two lines of permanent horizontal boards that are fixed between the gunwale and the lower rail. The upper board is pierced by a semicircular hole for a deck gun.

The Sterncastle: Inboard planking that obscured the light framing and the outboard lapboard of the side of the ship under the Sterncastle was removed before the start of the conservation process. However, an inboard stringer and an outboard wale continues the gunwale line aft. This leaves a space near the stern for a gunport to be positioned just above the Upper deck but below the stringer.

The top of the main frames is capped by a thick gunwale, and this rebates around each timber that extends upwards into the castle.

The Forecastle: A substantial timber, angled forwards in the side of the hull, marks the commencement of the Forecastle which was otherwise destroyed, or had collapsed into the scourpit where it may still remain.

The deck

Deck clamps: The ends of the Upper deck beams are slotted into a timber clamp in two areas: in the waist, and under the Sterncastle. The clamp is lighter in construction than those of the Orlop and Main decks, and averages 0.32m high, but only c. 95mm thick at its widest point. The clamp under the Sterncastle is interrupted by a 0.50m cut-out for a small port in the Carpenter's cabin.

Deck beams: The Upper deck beams in the waist, forward of the Sterncastle, are similar in form and function to those of the Orlop and Main decks in that they are regularly spaced and support carlings to house the ends of half-beams (Fig. 11.17). They are 0.21–0.31m wide and 0.19–0.26m thick. Their surviving lengths across the ship vary from 2.0–3.5m. In contrast, the Upper deck beams under the Sterncastle are smaller: 0.17–0.21m wide, 0.17–0.20m thick, and survive to lengths of 2.1–3.7m. The ends of the deck beams are set in rebates in the deck clamp, and are secured to hanging knees with a single clench bolt.

Only one beam (U30) has produced a dendrochronology date, the latest ring in the sample being 1520, showing that it was a repair. The hanging knee beside it has provided a date of 1517, suggesting

Figure 11.17 Details of Upper deck beams (Photo ref: 93.1022)

that they were installed at the same time. As the U40 deck beam is of a coniferous wood, possibly spruce, rather than oak, and is slightly larger in section than the other Upper deck beams, it too is likely to be a replacement.

The deck construction under the Sterncastle is different from that in the waist, as the deck beams are closely spaced, about one metre apart, and have no rebates for carlings on their surviving lengths. A cluster of four deck beams set closely together on the border of U9/10, may have been to help take the weight of the gun in M10, or to help brace the mizzen mast.

There are no stanchion rebates in the surviving beams, so any vertical support for the Sterncastle deck was evidently closer to the centre of the ship where evidence for the rebates has not survived.

Deck knees: The Upper deck beams are also attached to the hull by hanging knees, leaving the deck surface free of obstructions. The knees are bolted and treenailed to the side of the ship and fastened to the deck beams with a single countersunk bolt. The knees in the ship's waist are all fastened to the forward side of the deck beams, while those under the Sterncastle are attached either to the forward or aft faces.

Two knees (UHK20 and UHK50) in the forward part of the ship are fastened to the hull with their lower arms angled towards the bow. For the latter this was probably to allow it to be bolted to the hull since there is no frame for it to be attached directly below the upper arm. Although the latter knee looks like a modification, tree-ring dating has given a date of 1474, suggesting that it is part of the original construction. There is some evidence of possible modification in the U9/U10 area, the knees here having unused treenail holes in them, suggesting that either the knees were re-used or that the hull behind them has been altered.

Deck carlings and half-beams: Carlings, 0.21–0.25m wide, 0.16–0.21m thick and 2.7–3.3m long, have only been found in the waist of the ship. There are half-beam rebates on both the port and starboard sides of the carlings, as well as on the surviving half-beams. It is highly probable, therefore, that there was a second set of carlings on each side of the centreline of the ship, perhaps to accommodate hatches or gratings.

There are two sets of surviving half-beams: one stretches between the starboard side and the carlings, and the other is housed on the inboard rebates of those carlings and would have extended to a second line of carlings closer to the centerline of the ship.

The half-beams appear to be either a modification or a replacement to the Upper deck for two reasons. First, they are fashioned from a variety of wood types, oak, poplar and a coniferous wood, possibly spruce. Secondly, a number of them have part of their outboard ends cut away to allow them to fit the rebates in the deck clamp.

Deck planks: The surface of the Upper deck is uninterrupted by rising knees, unlike the the Orlop and Main decks below. The planks are 45mm thick on average and either butt end-to-end or are keyed together with lap joints. They are caulked in the same way as the Main deck planks.

There are significant differences between the construction of the deck in the ship's waist and beneath the Sterncastle. The planks in the waist have a closely spaced pattern of nails to fasten them to the half-beams, usually two or three nails per plank per half beam. The stern planks, in contrast, have a more widely spaced pattern of nails fastening them to the deck beams, with two nail holes per beam being normal.

The way the planks are laid against the side of the vessel varies between the forward and aft halves of the ship. While both sets of planks are curved to fit against the hull, those under the Sterncastle have a 50mm high waterway rebated into them, whereas those in the waist are simply chamfered to fit against the hull.

Companionway: Traces of a companionway were found on the Upper deck in the U10 area, and comprised one almost complete oak cheek *c.* 2.14m long, 0.20m wide and 80mm thick, with rebates for six steps with a rise height of 0.30m.

Hatches: Although no remaining structure of the Upper deck exists close to the centerline of the ship, there is evidence that hatches had existed since pieces were displaced when the ship sank. These have been found in sectors U3, U5 and possibly U6.

Ventilation hatches: Four small square ventilation hatches exist in the waist of the Upper deck, directly above the guns on the Main deck below (Fig. 11.18). These would have vented smoke and fumes from the

Figure 11.18 The Upper deck planking with ventilation hatches, view looking aft. The gap between the edge of the planks and the side of the ship is due to the distortion of the hull near the bow (Photo ref.: 93.1026.2)

guns as well as provide ventilation and a little light for the Main deck. The hatches are about 0.60m square, each with coaming timbers nailed to the deck surface, and expose the half-beams below. Where gaps in the half-beams were thought to be dangerously wide in U3 and U4, small beams were nailed to the underside of the deck planks to prevent objects and possibly people falling through. There are no ventilation hatches above the guns in the area covered by the Sterncastle.

Companionway hatches: The only surviving companionway hatch is in sector U6, its size, deduced from the width of the companionway below, probably being about 1.26m wide, and perhaps 0.60m long. A small plank, forming a type of coaming on the

starboard side of the hatch, is nailed to the half-beams and the 'daille' (a timber watercourse) and does not protrude above the level of the surrounding deck planks.

Removing waste water from the ship: Waste water from the bilge was pumped up from a 'pump-well' just aft of the main mast-step in the lowest part of the ship, and was discharged overboard at the starboard side from an open trough-shaped deck beam or 'daille', at the forward edge of the Sterncastle on the Upper deck.

The pump itself was probably salvaged in 1840, but during the recent excavation there was also found a spare section of pump shaft in a storage compartment on the Orlop deck that shows what it was like.

The Sterncastle

The Sterncastle was of a much lighter construction than the body of the ship, because the main frames and the carvel planking of the hull terminate just above the Upper deck. Only a few side frames extend upwards through rebates in the gunwale to form the almost vertical side of the Sterncastle.

Although the gunwale is pierced with holes between each frame to support the stirrups of swivel guns, many of these positions were planked over during the life of the ship, possibly when heavier guns were added. Openings in the planks show where gunports were located.

Only a small portion of the castle structure has survived at the forward end of the Sterncastle, and it consists of light overlapping weatherboarding, about 0.25m wide and 30mm thick, not caulked, but fastened internally to rebated frames. The planks are supported externally by a series of standards and knees which are fashioned to fit over the wales and are secured to the frames by nails and treenails.

The resulting castle structure was strong and lightweight and would have been a shield against most contemporary low-velocity missiles. An examination of the superstructure shows no damage which can be attributed to battle, although it had undergone a series of modifications during the career of the ship.

Only the edge of the Sterncastle deck remained, one uneroded plank being 45mm thick. The deck was supported by beams resting in a timber deck clamp, 0.36m high and 70mm thick, and by a series of hanging knees, four of which survive. The castle deck was identical in construction to the after part of the Upper deck, and included a waterway 40mm high on the plank next to the starboard side.

The upper ends of the castle frames have eroded away, so that no part of the top of the castle has survived. Andrew Fielding has speculated that it may not have extend much higher, as 'evidence existed in the form of rails, rebates and dimensions to correlate blinds found stored in the hold with the inter-framing gaps and the sheer of the deck'. This suggests that the upper castle had ogival cut-outs that provided ports for soldiers using handguns, hailshot pieces and swivel guns. This has yet to be studied.

A very small portion of the forward corner of the Sterncastle has survived, and includes a support beam decorated with a carved ropework design.

The Forecastle

Although the Forecastle had not survived, an upward sloping timber at the forward end of the starboard side is believed to be part of the aft support of the castle. Adjacent to this was the companionway at the forward end of the Main deck, which led to the Upper deck, and, most likely, to the Forecastle itself. It was the counterpart to the companionway that marked the forward end of the Sterncastle.

Propulsion

The *Mary Rose* was propelled by sail, as shown by the inventory of 1514 [106] and the *Anthony Roll* of 1546 [143]. She had four masts: the *foremast*, the *main mast*, the *mizzen mast*, and the *bonaventure mizzen mast* as well as a *bowsprit*. None of the masts or yards has survived.

Many clues to the masts and rig were found but have yet to be assessed fully. These include a chainwale, chains and deadeyes on the starboard side of the ship, a store of pulley blocks and deadeyes, portions of mast partners (boards with curving edges that were set around the masts as they passed through the decks), a parrel from the rigging store on the Orlop deck for a mast with a diameter of 0.50m, and a small fighting top for a mast 0.30 in diameter.

Bowsprit

The bowsprit is shown in the Anthony Roll, but no trace of it has been found.

Foremast

No trace of this mast was found or clues to its location.

Main mast

Although the main mast is missing, its step, a rectangular socket 0.70m by 0.35m and 0.13m deep, was found cut into the keelson and once held the tenon at the foot of the mast (Fig. 11.4). The foot of the mast was therefore at least 0.70m in diameter, but as the keelson at this point is only 0.80m wide, and as the foot of the mast is unlikely to have oversailed its sides where it would be unsupported, it seems likely that the foot of the mast was not more than 0.80m wide.

The discovery, by Deane in 1840, of a length of timber believed to be part of the main mast is also important, for fragments of the bombs that he used to help salvage the ship were found concentrated in the vicinity of the mast-step and show that Deane was working in that area.

The mast fragment was described as being a single piece of oak 15ft long (4.5m), and 'nearly as large as that of a 75 gun ship'. Although there was no 75-gun ship in the early nineteenth century, the diameter for the mast of a 74-gun ship was 37 ins (0.94m) (Falconer 1815, 266). Consequently, the mast from the *Mary Rose* site could well have been 0.70–0.80m in diameter.

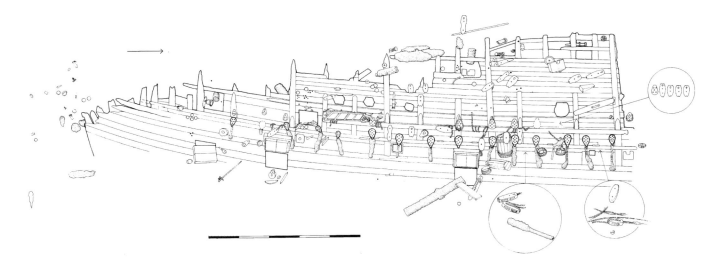

Figure 11.19 Distribution of the rigging fittings as discovered under the hull (starboard side, stern to left)

The rigging of the main mast was originally attached to the hull by means of the iron chains and deadeyes discovered on the starboard side. The lower end of each shroud, or rope supporting the main mast, was originally attached to an upper deadeye in which are holes for a thin rope or lanyard that attached it to a lower deadeye near the chain-wale. The lanyard allowed the distance between the deadeyes to be altered thereby enabling the shroud to be tightened or loosened. Each lower deadeye was, in turn, attached to an iron chain whose lower end was fastened to the side of the ship between the Upper and Main deck levels (Fig. 11.19). Although only portions of chain had survived, at one point an entire chain remained with seven links of iron, each about 175mm long, the lowest being attached to a large ringbolt in the wale above the gunports.

The chain-wale is a timber shelf that ran the length of the Sterncastle. It is 0.60m wide and 70mm thick, and was fastened outboard by standards and knees. Its purpose was to spread the load of the mast shrouds, and to prevent them chafing against the side of the ship.

A timber rail, for tying off running rigging, lies just above the lower deadeyes, and is attached to the knees holding the outboard standards to the top of the chain-wale. This rail is situated in the forward part of the Sterncastle immediately abaft of the main mast, but as it terminates in front of a gunport on the Upper deck it is likely that it mostly served the main mast. Portions of rope, 25mm in diameter, were found looped around it.

Mizzen mast

No trace of the mizzen mast has survived, though rebates in the inboard face of a carling in sectors M8 and M9 might have housed its step, particularly as the half-beams there were angled to provide a stiffening of the deck as if to support a mast.

The shrouds of the mizzen mast were undoubtedly attached to the chain-wale on the starboard side, for

that wale extended to the stern, and in the area outboard of M8 and M9 there were found deadeyes that once held the mizzen shrouds.

Bonaventure mast

No trace of the bonaventure mizzen was found.

Fighting top

The *Anthony Roll* shows that each mast had fighting 'tops', and, although none had survived from the masts themselves, a complete spare top was found stored in the forward part of the Orlop deck. It was very small and may have been intended to fit near the top of a mast.

The top has a base diameter of 0.72m, a rim diameter of 1.45m, a height of 0.60m. There is a rectangular slot of 0.30 x 0.35m for the mast. The top presumably rested on cross-trees attached to the mast.

Rigging fittings

Five basic types of rigging element were found in and around the *Mary Rose*: single pulley blocks, double pulley blocks, deadeyes, thimbles and parrels. Many were found in a rigging store on the Orlop deck.

Blocks

Not all pulley blocks were used in the rigging for they had other purposes, particularly connected with lifting heavy weights and with restraining guns.

Single pulley blocks had a 'shell' or case carved from a single piece of ash or elm, and had an ash or elm sheave (ie. wheel) that rotated on a wood pin.

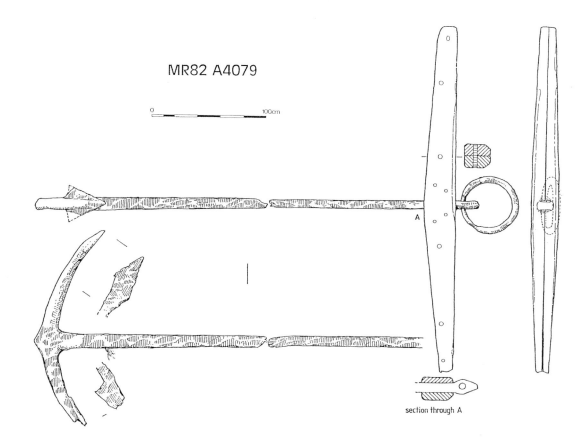

MR82 A4079

section through A

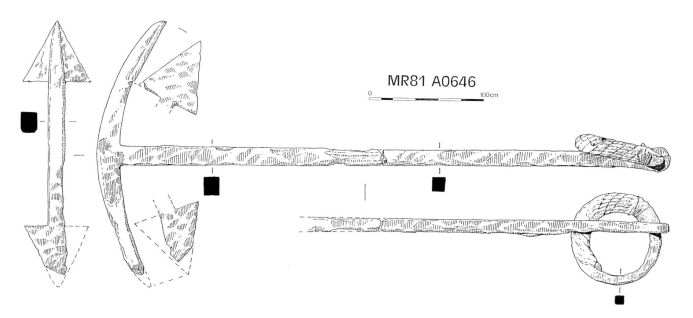

MR81 A0646

Figure 11.20 Two anchors recovered from the Mary Rose

Double sheave blocks had two wood sheaves either side-by-side or end-to-end.

Deadeyes

Pear-shaped deadeyes were found both at the chain-wale on the starboard side of the ship, and as spares in the rigging store. The latter varied in size from small (80 x 160mm) to large (230 x 360mm). Each had three holes for the lanyard that enabled the distance between pairs of deadeyes to be adjusted.

Thimbles

Thimbles are pear-shaped wooden rings grooved on the outside for the eye of a rope, and have a large hole in the middle. Some thimbles have up to three smaller holes in addition to the large hole.

Parrels

Parrels are wooden fittings, comprising ribs and wheels (trucks) with holes in their centres, through which ropes were threaded. Their purpose was to ease the movement of the yards around the mast when they were braced to the wind. A complete set, with seven ribs and 29 trucks, was found in the rigging store, still mounted on their ropes 20mm in diameter. They had been carefully folded, and when extended measured 0.8 x 0.9m. The edges and outer faces of the ribs had a cream paint.

Steering

It is important to recognise that the *Mary Rose* was steered both by manipulating the sails, and by turning the rudder. The lower 4.60m of the rudder was found attached by three iron pintles to iron gudgeons on the sternpost. The rudder is built from two oak timbers, each about 0.25m thick and 0.50–0.60m wide, that are fastened edgeways, presumably by bolts, to form a rudder blade about 1.10m wide at its base.

The forward edge of the rudder, triangular in shape to give a turning angle, has been partly cut away to accommodate iron pintles. The forward corner of the bottom of the rudder is cut at an angle to allow for the skeg end of the keel that projected beyond the bottom of the sternpost. No evidence was found to show how the rudder was steered.

Mooring

Anchors

Three wrought iron anchors were found in the archaeological excavation, two just outside the ship under the bow on the starboard side, and the other on the Upper deck in the ship's waist.

The largest lay in the waist on the starboard side of the Upper deck (81A0646; Fig. 11.20) and, although perhaps belonging to the *Mary Rose*, it is difficult to understand how it could have found its way onto that deck unless it was a spare stored there. Its location suggests that it might be from another ship, perhaps one of those involved in the attempt to salvage the *Mary Rose* in 1545, and was caught in the wreck soon after the sinking. It was found concreted to an iron breech-loading gun, thus indicating that it should date from about 1545, and is 4.96m long, with both arms

2.34m long, ending in triangular flukes 0.60m wide. The stock had not survived.

The other two anchors were found outboard at the starboard bow immediately under the heeled ship in about the position that the *Anthony Roll* shows the *Mary Rose*'s anchor. One of these is 4.22m long, and although only one arm is complete, and has triangular flukes 0.46m wide, it shows that the total length of both arms was 2.2m. The wooden stock is missing.

The other anchor (82A4079; Fig. 11.20) is also incomplete, and as its shank is broken its length is uncertain. The surviving length of the shank is 3.85m, and the total length of both arms was about 2m. The incomplete remains of a triangular shaped fluke also survived. The wooden stock, 3.10m long, survives and comprises two squared timbers fastened together with treenails.

Ropes and cables

Within the ship were found coils of thick cable that were probably used for mooring. The coils were found on the Upper deck in the waist and on the Orlop deck. No certain trace was found of a capstan or winch to haul in the mooring ropes and anchors.

Protective superstructure

The *Anthony Roll* depicts the upper decks of the *Mary Rose* with a covering of anti-boarding netting. Traces of the netting and what are thought to be its timber supports were found, the supports comprising joists which originally fitted into rebates in the uppermost rail of the starboard side above the blinds. The rebates suggest that the netting was horizontal, and not angled upwards to the centreline of the ship as shown in the *Anthony Roll*.

Reconstructing the ship

Although only about one third of the ship had survived, it is because the vessel lay on its starboard side that sufficient of the hull remained to make it possible to reconstruct much of the ship. This will be considered in *AMR* Vol. 2. Areas of uncertainty are those parts for which nothing remained, particularly the Forecastle. Much collapsed ship's structure is believed to remain in the scourpits in the seabed, and future excavations will undoubtedly address how the uncertain areas might be reconstructed.

12. Contents of the ship

Although this is the first published summary of the contents of the ship as found, it is selective because the detailed study of the archaeological records for each sector has yet to be undertaken. The aim of this chapter is to give an impression of the type of contents found in each zone of each deck, and it concludes with a general summary of two particularly important groups of objects – the human remains, and the armament of guns. The former has been published in a popular account (Stirland 2000) with a more detailed report available in *AMR* Vol. 4, and the latter is described in *AMR* Vol. 3.

Over nineteen thousand objects were found in and around the ship, and it is their relationship to the vessel and to each other as found that provides clues to understanding the state and use of the ship in 1545. Amongst the questions yet to be examined in detail are:

1. the process of wrecking,
2. reconstructing the original location of the people and objects within the ship immediately before the sinking,
3. determining the operational and social use of the ship.

The distribution of objects as found can suggest what activity was undertaken in each area. This is not straightforward, however, for many items were redistributed from other areas of the ship during the process of sinking and in the subsequent collapse of the port side.

In identifying which objects were indigenous to each sector it is necessary to look for (a) groups of items that had a common use, for such groups may have kept together, particularly bearing in mind that some sections of the hull were somewhat sealed by partitions; and (b) to look for single heavy objects, such as guns, which mostly cannot have travelled very far.

The layering of objects one above another against the starboard side of the ship is another valuable clue to where they were situated in each sector, for when the ship capsized they were thrown over, and objects from the port side probably fell on top of those nearer the starboard side. Other objects fell vertically downwards as the decks broke up. Many, however, remained floating within the ship for some time and were able to drift some distance. The logs for the galley ovens are a good example for they managed to drift throughout the ship, even though they were stored close to the galley where most were found.

There is a difficulty in how to illustrate the concentrations of the objects massed against the starboard side in a way that is meaningful. As the vessel was heeled at about 60 degrees, any horizontal plans of objects 'as found' in each sector would actually be an arbitrary oblique section between decks and therefore would not convey the sequence of collapse to the side. Furthermore, some objects, particularly barrels, had burst open in 1545 making it sometimes difficult to know what, if anything, in the surrounding mass of objects were their contents.

The huge task of preparing detailed drawings that show where each object was found in the ship has hardly been started. Nevertheless, an important first stage record has been completed which gives their location by deck and sector. This makes it possible to compile a provisional description and interpretation of the contents of the ship. Figure 12.1 gives an indicaton of the main storage areas of the ship.

The following selective account of the contents of the *Mary Rose* seeks to suggest how areas of the ship were used. These aspects are further explored in *AMR* Vol. 4 where the many categories of artefacts are described and discussed in detail. The description is by deck, which is subdivided into 'areas', each of which was originally enclosed by partitions, and by 'sectors' whose limits are defined by the deck beams.

Hold

The Hold was primarily the storage and cooking area in the bottom of the ship. Traditionally the hold of a warship was for storage, particularly of heavy items, and the number of barrels in most areas confirms that. Because it was below the waterline it would have been damp, dark and, except near the galley, rather cold. As the sides of the hull curved upwards to the underside of the Orlop deck it was difficult to move around between the stored equipment and supplies, particularly as stanchions and partitions restricted the crew's movement.

When the ship heeled over to starboard and sank, much of the contents of the Hold collapsed over to the starboard side. The gravel ballast slumped with such force that some Orlop deck planks were displaced upwards, thereby enabling items from above that deck to fall into the Hold; added to which most of the galley collapsed in a mass of brick and mortar rubble.

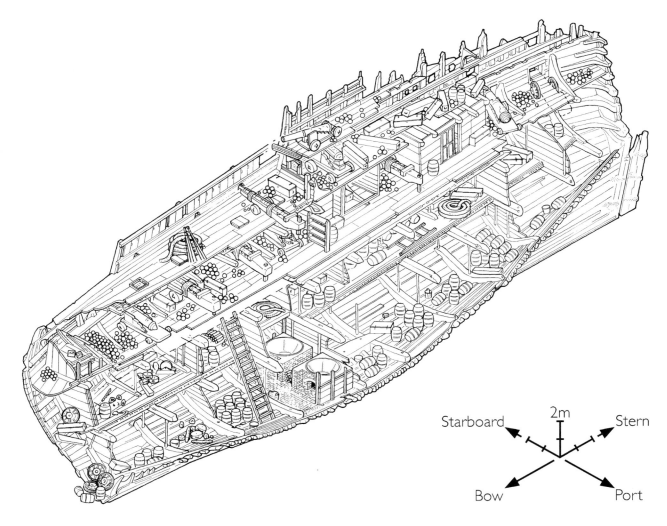

Figure 12.1 Isometric view showing partially conjectured areas of stowage

Substantial parts of nineteen human skeletons were found in the Hold, six in the galley and thirteen in storage areas. Seven more were at the junction of the Hold and the Orlop deck so their original location remains unknown. The remains of so many men in the storage areas needs explanation for it is unlikely that the crew had living quarters there or that so many worked there. It is also unlikely that many bodies would have floated into those enclosed spaces. The skeletons therefore suggest that the men had been ordered to collect equipment from the stores and were caught by the sinking.

Ballast

The lowest part of the Hold contained the ship's ballast that extended aft from sector H2 to H9.

The ballast was of well-rounded but broken flint gravel. Inclusions of cockle, winkle and oyster shells show that it was obtained from beach deposits, probably near Portsmouth. Several fresh leaves, one of oak from sector H6, found amongst the ballast could

suggest that the *Mary Rose* was ballasted in summer. The ballast would stay permanently in the Hold with only minor additions and subtractions according to major changes in the ship's loading, such as the size of the guns or the numbers of crew.

Area divisions of the Hold

The Hold was divided into seven areas, limited by transverse partitions, each of which had a separate function:

Area 1 is sector H1; storage.
Area 2 is sector H2; storage (2 skeletons, plus 1 in H2–H3).
Area 3 is sector H3; storage (1 skeleton).
Area 4 is sectors H4 and H5; galley (6 skeletons).
Area 5 is sector H6; mast and bilge pump, with storage.
Area 6 is sectors H7, H8 and H9; storage (9 skeletons).
Area 7 is sectors H10 and H11; storage?

Area 1, sector H1 – storage of barrels

The bow end of the Hold, designated as sector H1, is where the ship began narrowing towards the bow but has mostly been lost to erosion. A hard grey shelly clay covered this area which was exposed to scouring and damage following the collapse of the Forecastle. Consequently, most of the content of this sector was disturbed.

Three barrels indicated that the area was used for storage. Two lay together on the starboard side, and in one was a fine black sediment that may have been gunpowder. Other items included gun carriage parts. Most objects were badly damaged from gribble and some may have been derived from now missing higher decks.

Area 2, sector H2 – storage of barrels

This was also a storage area, to which access may have been through a hatch in the Orlop deck above. Four barrels were found, three of which were tucked hard under the Orlop deck, lying on their sides in a port–starboard alignment. Three contained pitch or tar. Other items found include tools, such as a mallet, shovel, wedge and chopping block.

Substantial parts of two human skeletons were found in the aft part of the area, and with them were traces of straw and sacking. Various personal possessions were associated with the skeletons, including leather clothing, shoes, a kidney dagger handle, lace ends, a strap, two silver coins and a paternoster or rosary.

Area 3, sector H3 – storage of rigging

This was a storage area, probably for rigging fittings, with access presumed to be through a hatch in the Orlop deck above. It was defined by transverse timber partitions.

Rigging fittings lay against the underside of the Orlop deck, and included a parrel ball, parrel rib, pulley blocks and thimbles (rings forming the eye of a rope). Also there was a wooden mallet. There did not appear to be any order to the scatter so it was not possible to conjecture their pattern of storage, although the heaviest items were closest to the starboard side.

A small cauldron, found concreted to deck beam O20, was used for melting tar and in its filling was found a perfectly preserved iron nail.

Other ship's fittings may have drifted from elsewhere in the vessel after the sinking. These include the companionway, presumably from sector 4, that gave access from the Hold to the Orlop deck, a tabletop, and four logs that had probably drifted in from the galley fuel store.

One fairly complete human skeleton was found, together with another at the junction of sectors H2 and H3. One was articulated from head to femur, though his lower legs were missing, indicating that he was probably in the Hold when the ship sank and that the decomposition of the body was only partial before being buried in silt. There was no significant trace of clothing, apart from shoes, or personal possessions associated with the skeleton.

Area 4, sectors H4, H5 – the galley

This was the galley where food was prepared. Originally two brick ovens were built across the bottom of the Hold on either side of the keelson in sector H5. The cooks had access to them from the forward working area, sector H4, where a ladder or companionway extended down from the Main deck to the Hold.

The ovens had collapsed when the ship capsized, but the forward corner of one oven on the starboard side, built of bricks and lime mortar, had survived under the brick rubble. With it was a brass cauldron, and on the Orlop deck in O5 was another cauldron where it had been thrown with some brick rubble. The two cauldrons indicate that originally there were two ovens.

A large ventilation opening existed in the Orlop deck above the hearths, but there was no trace of a hood to contain the smoke.

Fuel for the ovens was of carefully cut logs, 0.80–1.24m long, which were found mostly in sectors H4 and H5 (162 logs) in the Hold, and in sectors O4 and O5 on the Orlop deck (438 logs). Their average length of about one metre enabled them to fit into the

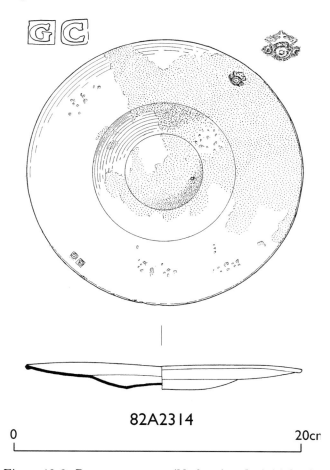

82A2314

0   20cr

Figure 12.2 Pewter saucer possibly bearing the initials of George Carew

hearths. A light scatter of other logs for the galley hearth was found throughout the ship where they had drifted after the sinking, making a total of 763 that were recovered.

Serving cooked food to the crew, officers and gentlemen, must have involved carrying food up the ladder to the upper decks. A bucket, of copper alloy, found in the galley may have been used for this purpose. It had lug handles and, although in a poor condition, seems to have had an oval shape with diameters of 660mm and 756mm, and a height of 458mm. Parts of eight ceramic cooking pots were also found.

Tableware for the crew to use was also stored in the galley, and comprised 60 wooden plates and 37 wooden dishes (Fig. 12.3).

Figure 12.3 Tableware and personal items (Photo ref.: 86.0242)

In addition there was pewter tableware probably belonging to Vice-Admiral Sir George Carew, comprising fourteen pewter plates, twelve of which were inscribed 'GC' and were found in sector H4 (Fig. 12.2). Three more 'GC' inscribed plates were found in sector H5, and eleven in sector O4 on the Orlop deck, with one more in each of sectors O5 and O6. There had been much disturbance to objects in sectors H4–O4, and it would be helpful to understand where and how the tableware was originally stored.

Other pewter plates, with the arms of Admiral Sir John Dudley, Viscount Lisle, were also found in sector H4, and on the Orlop deck above (Fig. 12.4). Their presence is puzzling for Admiral Dudley had entertained both Henry VIII and Vice-Admiral Sir George Carew to a banquet on board his ship *Henry Grace à Dieu* just before the French fleet arrived (see Chapter 1). It is curious that some of Viscount Lisle's tableware should be returned to the *Mary Rose* after the banquet.

Food and drink was stowed in and near the galley, several barrels being found in sector H4. They lay smashed beneath the pile of logs on the starboard side, suggesting that the fuel logs had been stored on the port side and had collapsed onto the barrels when the ship heeled over. As all but one of the barrels was found

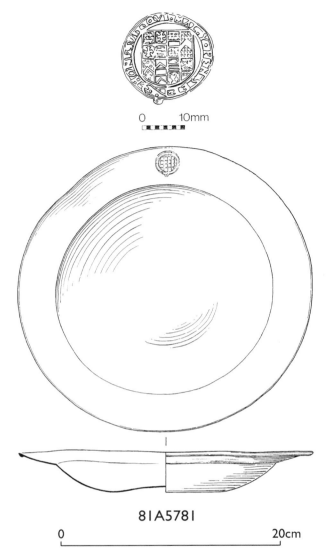

81A5781

Figure 12.4 Pewter platter bearing the arms of Viscount Lisle

empty they may have held drink, such as beer or water, or soluble dry goods such as flour used in cooking.

The bones of six nearly complete human skeletons were found scattered in the galley, some interspersed amongst the logs. These men were perhaps involved in cooking, and one may have been Nicholas[?] Cooper, a cook. His name 'Ny Coep, coek' is inscribed on a wooden bowl from sector U8 on the Upper deck, and 'Ny Cop' is on a tankard lid from the Carpenter's cabin on the Main deck.

A stool was the only item of furniture found in H4, but a possible hammock, of sacking with much cordage and line, lay in sector H5. The imprint of the sacking was seen in the clay in which the sacking was entombed, and the outline of its edge included wooden toggles.

Area 5, sector H6

This area immediately aft of the galley originally contained the foot of the main mast, and adjacent to it was the pump well for the bilge water. This area appeared to be an enclosed compartment with both transverse partitions running completely across the ship. If correctly understood, any access would have been from the Orlop deck above.

Five barrels were found showing that this was also a storage area, though their original contents are not known. Two baskets were also found, one with fruit, but they may have drifted from the galley, together with a musical fiddle and its case which could have dropped down from the Orlop deck.

Area 6, sectors H7, H8 and H9 – storage of barrels

This was the main storage area of the Hold, and was enclosed fore and aft by transverse partitions. Access to it was probably through a hatch in the Orlop deck above H7 or H8. This is suggested by the pattern of logs caught within the area and by the presence of a ladder on the Orlop deck in sector O8. Just as there was a concentration of logs around the hatches in sectors H4/5 and O4/5, so there was a small concentration of 6–16 logs per sector at H6/7/8, O8 and M7 suggesting that hatches existed through the decks were there too. This was quite different from the general scatter of under five logs per sector throughout the rest of the ship.

A hatch there would also explain the concentration of nine fairly complete skeletons in sectors H7, H8 and H9, and the presence of personal objects (shoes, daggers, aiglets or metal lace ends, combs, and a tabor pipe and drum) some of which were presumably derived from the individuals who died there.

About nineteen barrels of various sizes were found in this area, but their content has yet to be established. There was otherwise a basket, two chests (one containing arrows that may have fallen from the Orlop deck), buckets, shovels and two gallon-size serving tankards.

Area 7, sectors H10, H11

This was a narrow stowage area at the stern in which were found three barrels, one containing candles. Also, there were lanterns and baskets, one with fish.

Orlop deck

Area divisions of the Orlop deck

The orlop deck was separated by transverse partitions into eight areas, all of which were used for the storage of various items:

Area 1 is sector O1, gun equipment
Area 2 is sectors O2, O3, rigging store
(2 skeletons, plus one at O3–O4)
Area 3 is sector O4, galley store (5 skeletons)
Area 4 is sector O5, cable store
Area 5 is sector O6, food store (2 skeletons)

Area 6 is sectors O7, O8, O9, weapons store (11 skeletons)
Area 7 is sector O10, food store (1 skeleton)
Area 8 is sector O11, O12, lighting store.

Area 1, sector O1

This badly damaged area at the forward end of the ship contained many items related to the guns, including many tampions in a barrel, and gun carriage wheels, axles and trucks. Otherwise there were two barrels and an open-topped storage chest.

Area 2, sectors O2 and O3

Sector O3 was a heavy rigging store, and sector O2 a lighter rigging store with a sail. The two sectors were not separated by partitioning. As rigging elements were also found in sector H3 of the Hold directly below, some may have fallen from the Orlop deck.

A substantial coil of cable was found in sector O3, together with thinner line and some blocks, and in sector O2 there was also much tangled rope. The cable was probably stored in the centre of the deck as there was a trace of wooden supports to keep it in place. It was tarred to itself and to the deck, but was found spread as an untidy, slumped coil down the length of the deck.

One of the most important finds in sector O3 was a complete parrel assemblage of seven ribs and 30 trucks. One truck lay in sector O2. This assemblage was found against the starboard side between O2 and O3, and a decorative panel lay above it. The parrel ribs were painted, possibly yellow, and showed signs of scorching on the back or flat edge, thus indicating wear. Other signs of wear were two broken ropes linking the ribs and trucks together, suggesting that the assemblage was awaiting repair.

The remains of a sail was found mainly in O2 in large masses that were too fragile to separate underwater so were recovered by being cut into blocks. Each block was raised in a plastic crate, but unfortunately after seven blocks were recovered it became difficult to proceed as decorative panels and other objects impeded progress. The fragile material precluded any hope of entire recovery, and it was hoped that after conservation the fragments of the sail could be pieced together. The most important source of information to the size and shape of the sail is contained in its edges and cringles if ever they can be revealed.

A store of 28 decorative panels for the ship existed in this area (Fig. 12.5). Their precise purpose is unclear, but they appear to have been part of the ship's removable upper structure.

A grindstone lay in the forward part of sector O3 beneath a large wooden buoy or fender, and adjacent to it was a wicker basket and a wooden block. The entire group was covered by a cable and a decorative panel. On the east side of the grindstone was an oblong concretion which may have been part of its mechanism.

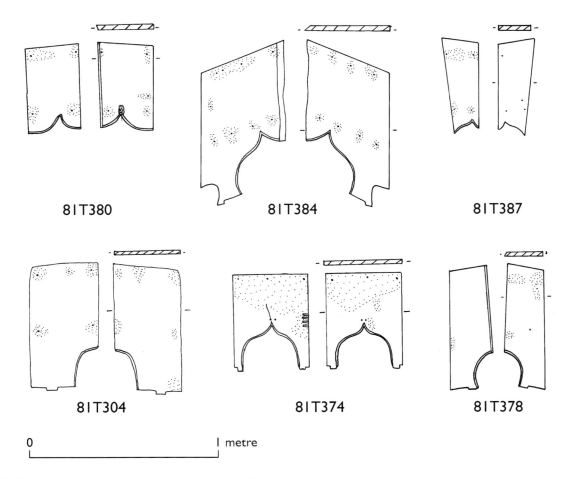

81T380   81T384   81T387

81T304   81T374   81T378

0   1 metre

Figure 12.5 Decorative panels recovered from sector O2

Weapon furniture was found, including a gun-shield, tampions, and a longbow. Other items may have been personal possessions and included kidney daggers, combs and a tinder box.

A considerable amount of clothing, textiles and leather was recovered mostly from the western part of O3. The garments include a jerkin (Fig. 12.7) and shoes. A coarsely woven sack with shoes, some in pairs, was found at the aft end of O3 pinned to the partition by a cable, some barrels and miscellaneous timbers that had shifted when the ship sank. There were also a large number of small personal items, including a 'call'. Two fairly complete human skeletons were found here.

Area 3, sector O4

Access to this compartment from the Hold was by a companionway the top of which was exposed leaning against the starboard side of the hatch and extending down into the Hold. It was fractured in two places, probably by the weight of hundred of logs and several barrels falling against it. One break was in the Hold at the Orlop deck and the other was about two-thirds of the way up to the Main deck.

This compartment provided storage for logs, 389 of which were found, that were used in the galley hearths in the Hold. There was little pattern to suggest how they were originally stowed.

The capsize of the ship and its impact on the sea-bed caused a huge upwards surge of materials from the Hold into sector O4. These include many bricks from the collapsed galley hearth that were thrown into sectors O4 and O5. Burnt ash and an overturned ash-box with a rope handle were also found against the starboard side.

It is not clear if food was stored in O4 as well as in H4 below, but many animal bones were found unevenly distributed near plates and a basket. A worn chopping block, presumably from the galley, was also found in sector O4.

Eleven pewter plates, inscribed with the initials 'GC', were found in sector O4 and must be part of the larger collection of similarly inscribed pewter tableware found in the Hold (Fig. 12.6). They had no obvious container, and as they lay on and between the starboard stringers and frames it is likely that they were thrown from the Hold to the Orlop deck as the ship sank. Other objects included a wooden dish and three wooden plates, again part of the wooden tableware mostly found in the Hold.

Several barrels were found, one having collapsed against the O3 bulkhead. Another was smashed so that the pieces were distributed amongst logs and between stringers in the aft part of sector O4. A wicker basket was found next to a mallet, and a net, perhaps a

Figure 12.6 Pewter platters and saucers
(Photo ref.: 83.0129)

hammock, was also found, but little had survived. A complete staved bucket contained a yellow–white substance.

One personal chest was found in O4 buried under logs, the contents suggesting that it was owned by a man of status (shoes, combs, a silver coin, beads, a cowrie shell, shot mould, swords and a scabbard, leather flask). A compartment in a false bottom contained only a bronze pin, and might just possibly have held the pages of a document or even a keepsake treasured by the owner.

Sector O4 contained the remains of men trapped amongst a collapsed mass of firewood and planking. They were evidently caught here whilst trying to escape from the sinking ship. Five fairly complete human skeletons were found though their bones were somewhat randomly distributed. Clothing held parts of some skeletons together, for example two shoes contained foot bones but were not associated with the rest of the skeleton. Another skeleton was 'wearing' a jerkin, and personal artefacts nearby included a powder flask, a comb, and a globe-encased sundial. A thimble ring was found with the phalanges of a hand.

Area 4, sector O5
A large ventilation hatch lay in the deck of this partitioned area above the ovens in the Hold. Brick rubble and a cauldron from the collapsed galley had been thrown into this sector, including an ash box with a rope handle.

Other finds include 49 logs, a pewter plate inscribed 'GC' and a wooden dish, plate and bowl. These are all clearly overspills from the main groups of objects in sectors O4, H4 and H5. A coil of cable, stored on the starboard side, was propped to keep its shape.

Area 5, sector O6
Barrels of beef suggest that this was a food storage area. Other finds include wooden bowls, a dish, a serving tankard, a pewter plate inscribed 'GC', 15 logs, parts of a personal chest, one basket and a bucket and shovel. This partitioned area contained substantial parts of two human skeletons.

Area 6, sectors O7, O8 and O9
Access to this area from the Hold and the Main deck was probably at sector O8, judging from the concentration of firewood logs that had drifted there.

This was a weapons and food store, particularly in sectors O8 and O9. The stores include arrow chests and a longbow chest. Some longbows were loose, and some chests of arrows had been opened and partly used. Other weapons-related objects include linstocks and a shot gauge. In O7 was found a large part of a broken gun carriage, the rest of which was found upside down on top of a gun in U7 on the Upper deck.

A cable was stored in this area, with barrels in O7, O8 and O9. One contained beef and another fish. A personal chest in O9 contained high status possessions, including a peppermill, mittens and flasks.

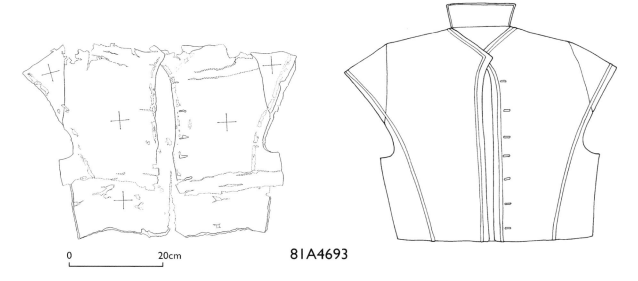

0   20cm   81A4693

Figure 12.7 Example of a leather jerkin (left) as found; (right) reconstructed

The fairly complete skeletons of 11 men were found here, six in O7, four in O8 and one in O9. They presumably account for the quantity of personal possessions and clothing fittings, including many pairs of shoes (Fig. 12.8).

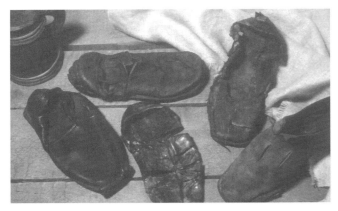

Figure 12.8 Selection of leather shoes (Mary Rose Trust)

Area 7, sector O10

This storage area contained barrels of beef and fruit, as well as other barrels and four baskets. Storage included gun-shields and lanterns. One of three chests was associated with gold and silver coins. There was one fairly complete skeleton.

Area 8, sectors O11 and O12

Three barrels, one containing tallow, were stored here. Otherwise, a variety of objects was found, including lanterns, a sounding weight, hand weapons, a syringe, a balance and a tiny barrel.

Main deck

The function of the Main deck was to support the ship's main armament of carriage-mounted guns, at least seven of which were on each side of the vessel. Cabins relating to the Pilot, the Barber-surgeon and the Carpenter(s) lay against the starboard side. There were few hand weapons compared with the deck above, suggesting that there was little room for anyone other than the gun crews during battle. This may explain why relatively few human skeletons were found on this deck.

A central range of hatches was sealed with covers, one of which, in sector M11, was similar to others excavated in sectors U9, O8, O9 and H9. It was found sitting upright between the Main deck and two gun carriage wheels, suggesting that when the ship capsized it fell out and landed there.

Sectors M2–M3 and M5–M6 were used as areas for the storage of shot, each close to access to the castles as well as to the Main deck guns. A series of shot gauges, found in M5, supports this view. Along the starboard side were the gunports with their lids hinged open, whilst loose in the upper silts were gunport lids from the broken-up port side.

M1

This was a largely disturbed area just forward of the Pilot's cabin.

M2

A cabin in M2 may have been occupied by the Pilot, as a few navigation items were found there (but see *AMR*, Vol. 4, chapter 7) (Fig. 12.9). A personal chest contained a pouch, a compass, aiglets and a knife sheath. About 450 shot were found here, with 164 more at the junction of sectors M2 and M3. Outside the cabin were two fairly complete skeletons.

M3

A bronze culverin gun made by Petrus Bowdus in 1543 lay by a gunport on the starboard side. It is believed that the matching gun originally from the port side was recovered by Deane on 27 August 1840. It was a brass culverin made by Arcanus in 1542, and appears to have been loaded.

About 68 shot were found in this sector with other objects, including a bucket and shovel. Four fairly complete human skeletons were found, plus two more at the junction of sectors M3 and M4.

Figure 12.9 Navigation instruments (Photo ref.: 85.0236)

M4

An iron gun was found at the M4 gunport, and 52 shot in this sector. A personal chest contained a pewter flask, books, a balance case, clothing and a candle-snuffer (Fig. 12.10).

M5

An iron gun was situated at the M5 gunport, and 66 shot nearby. Other items of gun equipment included shot gauges, rams, powder ladles, as well as a leather bucket and shovel. Miscellaneous other finds included barrels and a 'caulking' bowl. One fairly complete human skeleton lay here.

M6

A bronze cannon dated 1535 by 'PB', presumably Petrus Bowdus, was found at the M6 starboard gunport. Its counterpart on the port side, believed to be a brass cannon royal made by R. and J. Owen in 1535, was recovered by Deane on 8 August 1836.

Figure 12.10 A selection of personal objects including a book and writing equipment (Photo ref.: 86.0024)

Figure 12.11 The Barber-surgeon's chest (Mary Rose Trust)

About 377 shot were found in sector M6, with a basket, a barrel, a trestle, buckets and a shovel. Three fairly complete human skeletons were also found.

M7

A cabin, believed to have been occupied by the Barber-surgeon, was situated on the starboard side of the deck. The main associated find was a chest containing medical materials including stoneware jugs, pottery and glass bottles, wooden canisters, a bleeding bowl, bandages, a shaving bowl, a pewter canister, razors, a syringe, a wooden feeding bottle, an ear scoop, a money pouch, and many wooden handles thought to be the remains of medical tools (Fig. 12.11).

Other chests were found in this sector, one containing fishing gear, knives, a cooking pot, a flask, a bowl, and a comb. Otherwise there was found a cooking pot and barrels, two of which contained beef bones, and some shot. At the junction of sectors M7 and M8 was a fairly complete human skeleton, and an anchor stock.

M8

A loaded iron gun was in this sector, and beside it were its chamber and wedges. Its wooden carriage was damaged, the gun having fallen out of its carriage. The gunport lid was found hinged back in an open position as were the port lids in sector M4 and M5, and perhaps those in M3 and M6.

A personal chest had smashed against a wheel of the M8 gun carriage so that the chest's underside was broken. The chest contained some remarkable finds, including a carved ivory plaque, a leather pouch containing what was possibly a seal, as well as silver coins, shoes, a knife sheath and a whetstone. One fairly complete human skeleton lay in this sector.

M9

A cabin on the starboard side contained a considerable number of tools indicating that it was probably occupied by the ship's Carpenter(s). There was also a wooden gallon serving tankard, some shot and a handgun. The almost complete skeleton of a small dog,

about 470mm high at the shoulder, possibly a female mongrel, was also found.

Personal chests were found both in the cabin and outside. Several contained high status objects, such as books, an inkpot, pewter plates, a sundial and case, silver coins, rings, and calls. Also there was clothing, whetstones, a fishing float, knives and gaming dice. This concentration of chests suggests that some may have been derived from a cabin or cabins in the destroyed port side of the ship opposite the M9 cabin.

Three of the chests had contrasting contents. One was found upright on the deck, its upper end having been damaged. In it was a variety of personal items including a finely-carved bone manicure set, a razor, a comb and a wooden rule. Beneath the chest and perhaps associated with it were the wooden beads of an almost complete rosary or paternoster (Fig. 12.12).

Another chest lay across the forward end of the first and above the third, and contained the handles of carpenter's tools. A fourth chest, at the forward end of M9, also had carpenter's tools inside. As they lay close to the M9 cabin in which was found another box of carpenter's tools, it is possible that they were related.

M10

A large loaded bronze demi-cannon, made by Robert and John Owen in 1542, was found projecting through the M10 starboard gunport. This gunport had suffered more wear from the gun than had other main deck gunports. The gunport, measuring 790x620mm, had a greenish deposit engrained in the wood caused by the rubbing action of the gun.

The gun's port side counterpart, a brass demi-cannon made by Arcanis in 1542, was recovered by Deane on 16 June 1836. Otherwise 21 shot and three chests were found, one a store chest. One fairly complete human skeleton was found.

M11

Fragments of an iron gun were found with unassociated spoked wheels and an axle heavily concreted against the starboard side. These fragments are identified as pieces

Figure 12.12 Personal items (Photo. ref.: 83.0165)

of an iron gun found by Deane in August 1836. Seventeen shot were also found.

M12
Eighteen shot were found, with a swivel gun that had fallen from above.

Upper Deck

The Upper deck was a fighting area primarily furnished with guns. It originally comprised three zones: the area beneath the Forecastle which had been almost completely destroyed; the open ship's waist in sectors U3 to U6; and the area beneath the Sterncastle in sectors U7 to U11.

The only fairly complete human skeletons were found under the Sterncastle, and as these comprised the greatest concentration in the entire ship it is likely that they were overwhelmed when ready for action against the enemy. The men were caught as the ship capsized.

Area 1, below the Forecastle

Although the Upper deck in this area was completely destroyed, the broken and scattered remains of gun carriages and other items under the Forecastle presumably represent traces of ordnance from the Upper and Forecastle decks.

Area 2, the open waist (U3–U6)

The central portion of the Upper deck was the open ship's waist, and many of the objects originally there would have been dispersed in the weeks following the sinking. Initially, the men were trapped under the anti-boarding netting that was spread over the waist. Traces of the netting was found in sectors U3 to U6, but as it was in a very fragile state only samples were recovered.

A number of staff hand weapons were found in U3. Bills were found in U4 with a stone shot. A gunport showed that formerly a gun had been positioned here. A coil of cable lay on the deck, as did two decorative panels. In U5 was found four shot, a sounding weight and a basket, but no gun to match the gunport while, in U6, a wrought iron gun lay on its wooden carriage. Nearby were a few shot, a basket and a chest. An anchor was found lying across the sector.

Area 3, below the Sterncastle (U7–11)

The stern area of the Upper deck, between sectors U7 and U11 carried guns, and was an accommodation area for the crew or officers. This is suggested by 29 human skeletons, a quantity of personal possessions mainly in chests and also a large numbers of 'everyday' items such as tableware (flagons, pottery, spoons, wooden bowls and plates) and small kegs with lids and buckets and brushes. Personal items include fishing gear, games, jewellery, combs, coins, musical instruments and many shoes. The violence of capsizing is reflected by their smashed condition against the starboard side in sectors U9 and U11.

The Upper deck was certainly a fighting area as is reflected by the archery and hand fighting equipment (Figs 12.13, 12.14). These include a large number of staff weapons from sector U9 many of which lay in a small area below two chests of longbows and two of arrows (Fig. 12.13). They have been identified as some of the 150 pikes and 150 bills listed in the *Anthony Roll* inventory. The pikes were up to five deep in sector U9. Many of the arrows had been badly broken by the collapse of barrels, chests and people lying on top of them. Archery accessories found include arrow spacers, wristguards and quivers all of leather.

Two guns were found in position on the Upper deck and others were found outboard. There was a variety of shot types, of iron, stone, lead as well as canister. There were also numerous examples of gun accessories such as tampions, rammers, powder scoops, a reamer and a powder dispenser. Two leather buckets, found at the forward end of sector U9, may have carried water to sponge out the guns.

Some barrels were on the deck, but mostly were so damaged in the wrecking process that it was impossible to determine how they were stowed.

Tools comprised a significant category of finds, and although the metal ends had mostly corroded away, the shapes of the handles suggest their original use. Wooden mallets were also found with several wooden shovels.

U7
A loaded bronze culverin, and above it a wooden gun carriage upside down, were found at the U7 gunport. Nearby were shot, bills, a pike, a chest of arrows and a chest of longbows, nearly empty. Otherwise there was a

Figure 12.13 Margaret Rule and Alexzandra Hildred examining a chest containing longbows (Mary Rose Trust)

bucket, a sounding weight and a decorative panel. Two fairly complete human skeletons were also found.

U8

A bronze demi-cannon, made by Francesco Arcanus in 1535, lay alongside the hull but originated from the port side of the ship. Other weapons equipment includes shot and a chest of longbows. A complete log-reel was found sitting upright under a barrel on the Upper deck in this sector. A chest, a tankard, a bucket and a decorative panel are amongst other items that may have collapsed there during the sinking. There were five fairly complete human skeletons.

U9

Weapons in this sector included a handgun, pikes, bills, and shot. The pikes were found wedged against the starboard side among numerous pieces of ship's structure. They stretched across the forward half of sector U9 in the soft grey silt, and were piled one above the other in four or five layers. It seemed that they had originally been standing upright, butt down, against the Upper deck and had toppled as a group against the starboard side of the ship.

Nearby were pieces of decorative panelling, suggesting that they were part of the castle structure.

Figure 12.14 Adrian Barak with the first longbow (Mary Rose Trust)

One segment had two cracked arched panels repaired by a wooden batten nailed to the back.

Four chests were found in sector U9, all were broken. One was small and in a poor condition, and lay along the forward edge of sector U9. Its dovetailed corners had split open and the contents had begun to spill out, revealing personal possessions. These included a small wooden box containing a balance scale, an octagonal wooden plate painted white and some peppercorns, presumably for use as a food flavouring (Fig. 12.16). A compass was found in this sector, with barrels, a basket, a brush, bucket and shovel. There were eighteen fairly complete human skeletons, two more at the junction of U8 and U9, and another at the junction of U9 and U10.

U10

This was a difficult sector to excavate because the artefacts were concreted to the ship. In order to remove them it was necessary to use an air tool and several

122

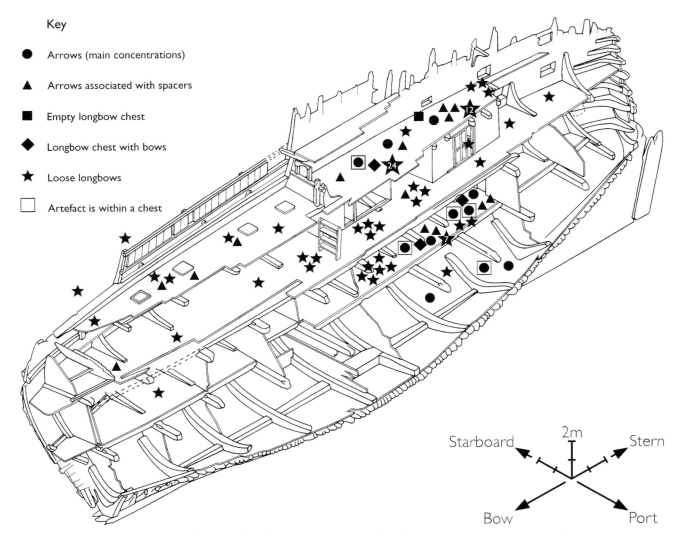

Key

● Arrows (main concentrations)

▲ Arrows associated with spacers

■ Empty longbow chest

◆ Longbow chest with bows

★ Loose longbows

☐ Artefact is within a chest

Starboard ← 2m → Stern

Bow ← → Port

Figure 12.15 Isometric showing the main distribution of arrows and longbows, and chests containing them

small explosive charges. The use of explosives was considered most carefully, and was restricted to small charges simply to loosen the concretion around a badly degraded iron gun in front of a gunport. The first explosive charge revealed a number of bones, a mallet, several parts of an iron gun, and a truck wheel. The iron of the gun initially appeared as new but quickly oxidised upon exposure. A second explosive charge disclosed more skeletal material, fragments of an iron gun and axle, and a leather pouch.

A wooden wheel was firmly embedded against the upper deck and was surrounded by skeletal fragments and shot canister. An important find was a rare chamber pot, the only one found in the ship. Otherwise there were three ship's decorative panels. In a chest were found two dividers, a sounding weight and a compass. There was one fairly complete human skeleton.

U11

Miscellaneous finds include two ship's decorative panels, a cooking pot and handguns.

Sterncastle Deck (C7–9)

A narrow portion of the Sterncastle deck had survived and on it, in sector C7, was a bronze gun on its carriage facing forward. It was a bastard culverin made by R. and J. Owen in 1537 (Fig. 12.17). Shot was also found.

Figure 12.16 Perfectly preserved peppercorns (Photo ref.: 85.0011)

79A1232/1241

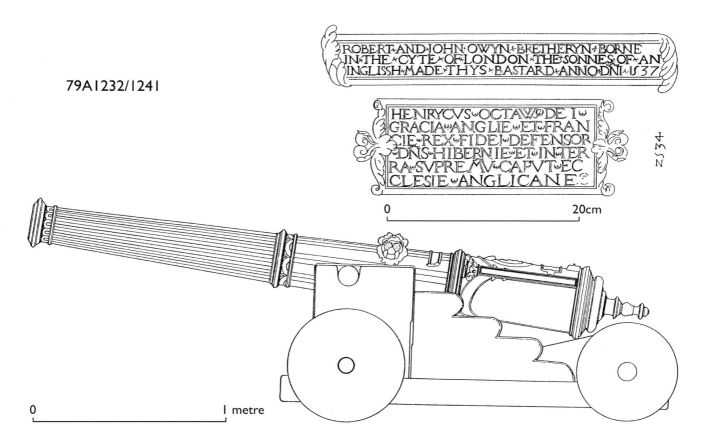

ROBERT·AND·JOHN·OWYN·BRETHERYN·BORNE
IN·THE·CYTE·OF·LONDON·THE·SONNES·OF·AN
INGLISSH·MADE·THYS·BASTARD·ANNO·DNI·1537

HENRYCVS·OCTAVVS·DE·I
GRACIA·ANGLIE·ET·FRAN
CIE·REX·FIDEI·DEFENSOR
DNS·HIBERNIE·ET·IN·TER
RA·SVPREMV·CAPVT·EC
CLESIE·ANGLICANE

0   20cm

0   1 metre

Figure 12.17 Bronze bastard culverin and carriage from the Sterncastle, made in 1537

Summary of the human remains

The location of human bones found throughout the wreck was very carefully recorded by the archaeological team, and this has enabled extensive research to be undertaken by Ann Stirland into the crew. The results of her study are briefly summarised here, but details are given in *AMR* Vol. 4 (forthcoming), and are to be found in her book, *Raising the dead: the skeleton crew of Henry VIII's great ship, the 'Mary Rose'* (Stirland 2000).

The bones represent a minimum of 179 individuals, about 40% of the original crew. Of these it has been possible to analyse 92 fairly complete skeletons. Whereas some bones had stayed fairly close together, others from the same skeleton were widely scattered. A skull from one deck, for example, matched its jawbone from three decks below.

The 92 more complete skeletons were fairly evenly distributed around the ship (Fig. 12.18), though the largest number were on the Upper deck. This suggests that the sinking occurred suddenly, giving the men below no time to escape. The fairly complete skeletons *may* reflect something of the approximate disposition of the men on each deck at the moment of sinking though, of course, their bodies would drift around for some time afterwards.

The bones represent a crew mostly of young men in their late teens and early 20s, with an average height of 1.71m (about 5ft 7in), and facial appearances similar to those of today. They had fairly good teeth, and were strong and robust.

Eighty-eight of the fairly complete skeletons could be aged with confidence: 1 juvenile (age *c.* 12–13); 17 adolescents (age *c.* 14–17); 54 young adults (aged *c.* 18–30); 15 middle-aged adults (aged *c.* 30–40); and 1 older adult (age 40+). Their heights ranged from 1.59m to 1.80m (*c.* 5ft 1in-5ft 11in), showing that the men were no shorter than most men today.

An analysis by Dr Lynne Bell of oxygen isotopes in a small random sample of teeth showed that about 25% of the sample originated away from Britain. This is based upon the fact that oxygen isotopes vary according to latitude, and suggests that the crew of the ship included a substantial proportion of foreigners from southern Europe. It is significant that the only identified person amongst the small number of survivors was a Fleming.

Other studies of 143 individuals show that the crew had a better matching of teeth between the two jaws than have men today, though there was more wear implying a coarser diet. Of these individuals 119 (83%) had caries (tooth decay), 18 (13%) had abscesses, and 52 (36%) had a loss of teeth.

Diseases of malnutrition were indicated, including healed childhood rickets causing bowed lower leg bones, and adult osteomalacia, a condition also causing bone deformities. Some men had suffered dietary deficiencies as children and others as adults. There

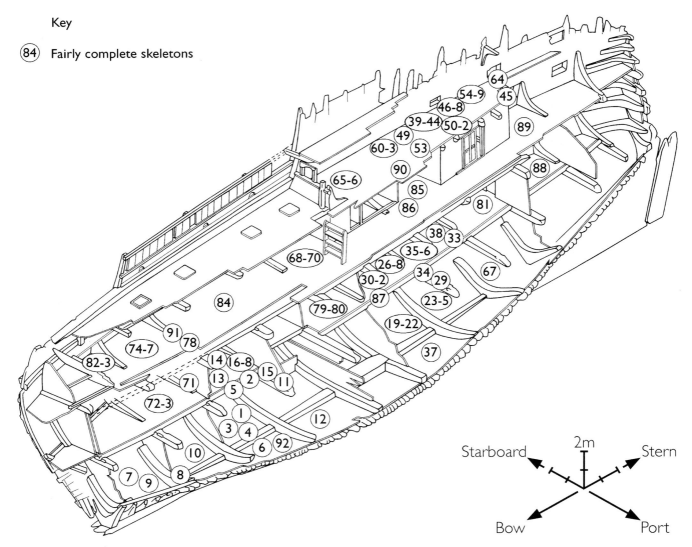

Key

(84) Fairly complete skeletons

Figure 12.18 Isometric showing the distribution of 92 fairly complete human skeletons

were traces of possible adolescent scurvy which resulted in changes to the bones of the eye sockets and left evidence of blood clots along some long-bones. Maybe these reflect the famines which were a problem in Europe during the early sixteenth century, such as occurred in the severe winter of 1527–8. Some adult teeth had horizontal bands or patterns of pits in the tooth enamel (enamel hypoplasia) caused by interrupted growth in childhood between 18 months and 6 years. These were due either to dietary deficiency or to common viral diseases such as measles and mumps.

There was little evidence of infectious disease since they do not usually last long enough to affect bone. Some longer lasting infections, such as syphilis, leprosy and tuberculosis, may affect the skeleton, but of these only traces of respiratory disease were apparent, perhaps tuberculosis, on the surface of some ribs.

Fractures were found in three ankles and there was one severely strained ankle. Three fractured nasal bones were also noted, one of which had not healed and may have occurred at the time of death. Otherwise there

were two healed fractures of the breastbone, and seven healed rib fractures, four belonging to one man. Two skeletons had severely affected right elbow joints, one so bad that the arm could not have been straightened at the elbow.

Fourteen cases of head injuries were noted, some being shallow depressions on the surface of the skulls, whilst others were penetrating wounds, perhaps from missiles. One penetrating wound was partly healed and must have been recent.

Other examples of damage were found, particularly in the form of 'avulsion fractures' in which a piece of bone had been traumatically torn away leaving an unhealed lesion. Six were found at the knee, twelve at the elbow, and eleven on the edge of the foot. It is possible that these resulted from climbing, hauling and running in the unstable shipboard environment.

Occupational deformities exist in some skeletons. In particular, whereas in 3–6% of the modern population the 'acromion' (a spine of bone on the back ('inside') to which major arm muscles are attached) of the shoulder blade (scapula) does not fuse until the age of 18 or 19,

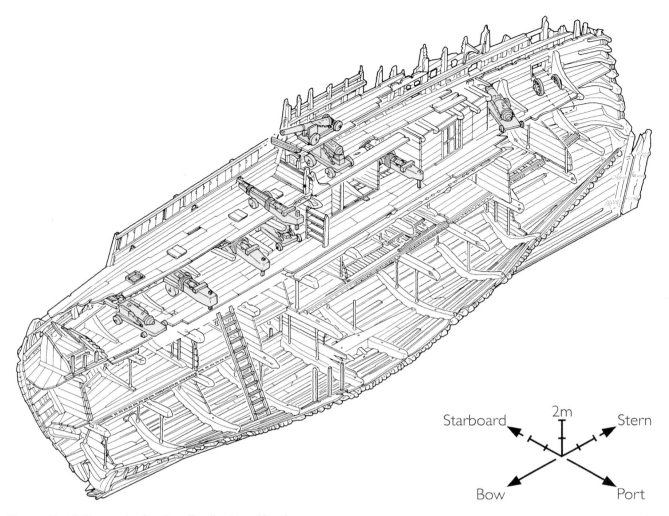

Figure 12.19 Isometric showing distribution of in situ *guns*

19% of those in the *Mary Rose* had not fused. Since this frequency is well above the modern average it may have been due to the long-term use of the war bow, a view also suggested by evidence for more developed thigh and buttock muscles. Ten of 52 complete pairs of shoulder blades had 'Os acromiale', represented by six on both sides, three on the left side and only one on the right side.

Although osteoarthritis had affected very few of the crew's spines, as would be expected in this group of adolescents and young adults, there were a few where some ossification of vertebrae had occurred, possibly due to occupations onboard ship which involved a great deal of heavy manual labour. Particularly interesting was a group of six skeletons found close to a large bronze gun in sector M3 of the Main deck. All six were young (early to mid 20s) ranging from 1.6m to 1.75m in height. Apart from one skeleton, all had been strong, well muscled robust men, though their skeletons had been stressed, especially the spines of three men. The spine of one man had fused vertebrae and had been subjected to such push-pull forces that it resembled the spine of a much older man. Another skeleton had bowed tibia leg bones indicating that he had probably

suffered from rickets in childhood, and yet another skeleton had an arthritic elbow. The odd skeleton in this group was of a man in his mid-20s, who was shorter and had more delicate bones with a lack of build-up of muscle attachments. Apart from him, this group of five men, and their location near a large gun, suggests that they may have comprised a gun crew.

Overview of the guns

The success of the *Mary Rose* as a warship depended primarily on the strength of her guns to immobilise or sink an enemy vessel, and the efficiency of her armed crew to engage the enemy in close combat. The former is reflected by the guns and shot, and the latter by the hand weapons. The armament of the *Mary Rose* will be described in the forthcoming *AMR* Vol. 3 by Alexzandra Hildred.

The guns found in the *Mary Rose* in the nineteenth and twentieth centuries are of 'brass' and 'iron', but their number is incomplete as some were salvaged in 1545 (Figs 12.19, 12.20). Although some of the iron guns found both by Deane and by the Mary Rose Trust

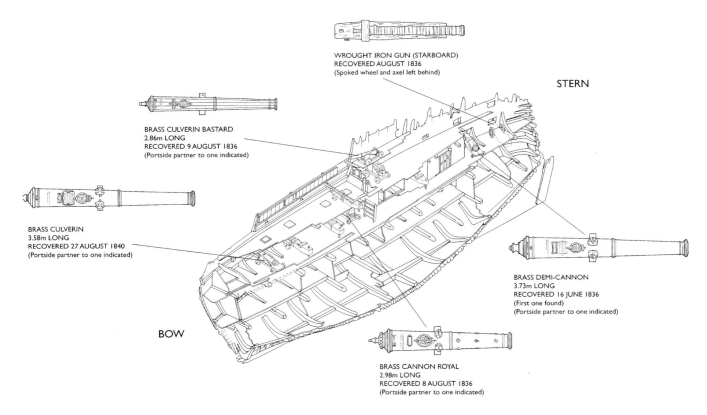

WROUGHT IRON GUN (STARBOARD)
RECOVERED AUGUST 1836
(Spoked wheel and axel left behind)

STERN

BRASS CULVERIN BASTARD
2.86m LONG
RECOVERED 9 AUGUST 1836
(Portside partner to one indicated)

BRASS CULVERIN
3.58m LONG
RECOVERED 27 AUGUST 1840
(Portside partner to one indicated)

BRASS DEMI-CANNON
3.73m LONG
RECOVERED 16 JUNE 1836
(First one found)
(Portside partner to one indicated)

BOW

BRASS CANNON ROYAL
2.98m LONG
RECOVERED 8 AUGUST 1836
(Portside partner to one indicated)

Figure 12.20 Guns recovered by Deane

are broken, a sufficient number was found to reconstruct much of the armament of the ship.

The *Anthony Roll* of 1546 lists all the guns, shot and hand weapons supposedly in the *Mary Rose*. However, this is a little different from what was found in the ship. The *Anthony Roll* states that the *Mary Rose* had the following ship's guns:

Brass guns

Cannons	2
Demi Cannons	2
Culverins	2
Demi Culverins	6
Sakers	2
Falcon	1
TOTAL BRASS:	15

Iron guns

Portpieces	12
Slings	2
Demi Slings	3
Quarter Slings	1
Fowlers	6
Bases	30
Top pieces	2
Hailshot	20
TOTAL IRON:	76

The guns were originally situated on the Main and Upper decks, and in the Forecastle and Sterncastle.

The ten bronze guns found in the ship do not precisely match up with the fifteen guns listed on the *Anthony Roll*. Two more large guns (a demi-cannon and a culverin) were found than are listed, and the three smaller guns, the sakers and falcon, are unaccounted for and may have been salvaged in 1545.

The bronze guns, all cast muzzle-loading weapons with bores ranging from about 112mm to 210mm, were mounted on timber carriages with four wheels. Inscriptions on some of the guns include the date, the name of the gunfounder, and even the type of gun. The gunfounders were the brothers John and Robert Owen, the Frenchman, Petrus Bowdus, and the Italian Arcana family. The dates range from 1535 to 1543 and the types of gun recovered include demi-culverins, culverins, demi-cannons and cannons.

The salvaged iron guns are not inscribed, so their types are not specified. They have two types of construction – wrought iron and cast iron, the large guns and the swivel guns being of wrought iron, and the small hailshot guns being of cast iron.

The larger wrought iron guns were fashioned from iron bars held together by wrought iron rings shrunk around the barrel. Each gun barrel was mounted on a bed of hollowed out timber, with a pair of timber wheels. At the inboard end was a socket in the timber bed into which a breech chamber, primed with gunpowder, was lowered and held in position against the barrel. The gun was fired at the touch hole in the breech chamber, and once fired the chamber was quickly replaced by another for the next shot.

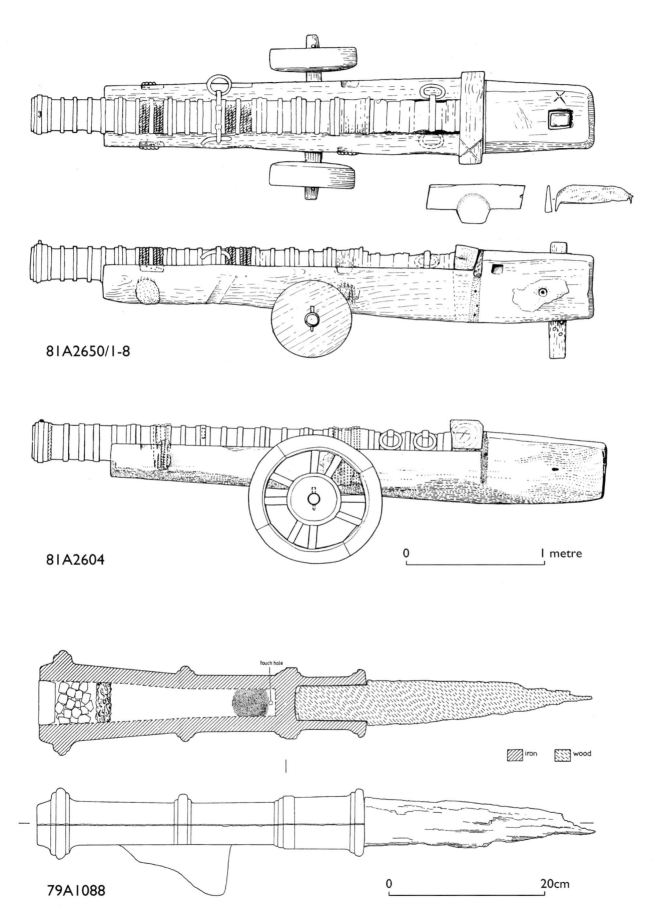

81A2650/1-8

81A2604

0   1 metre

touch hole

iron   wood

79A1088

0   20cm

Figure 12.21 A selection of large and small iron guns

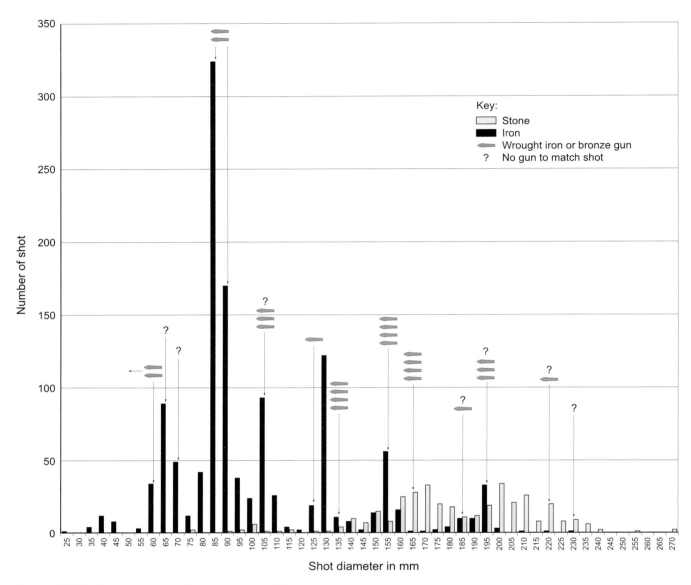

Figure 12.22 Shot sizes in relation to gun bore diameters

Consequently, each gun had a number of associated breech chambers.

The larger wrought iron guns were termed 'port pieces', and have bores of approximately 152mm, 170mm and 203mm. Four were found by the Mary Rose Trust and four by Deane.

'Slings', 'Demi slings' and 'Quarter slings' all used iron shot, according to the *Anthony Roll*, and were smaller in size than the portpieces. They are represented by a number of guns with bores of approximately 40mm, 60mm, 80mm and 110mm.

The thirty 'Bases' were the swivel guns that were used on yokes pivoted on a wale on the ship's side. One of these guns was found at the stern, and at least eleven fragments were found in the scour pit below the bow. They had bores of approximately 35mm, 40mm, 45mm, 50mm and 60mm. The *Anthony Roll* lists the 'Bases' as firing lead shot, and this matches the discovery of one found loaded.

Four of the 20 'hailshot pieces' were found (Fig. 12.21, lower) and are identified by their rectangular shaped muzzle. They are listed on the *Anthony Roll* as having been loaded with 'dyce of iron', and this corresponds with the finding of a loaded hailshot gun.

A value of having recovered and recorded all the shot surviving in the wreck is that they give an overview of the ship's entire armament, and can even suggest what guns are missing. Although the bore diameters of the guns and the diameters of the shot may be only approximate, the overview is shown by plotting the numbers of shot and their diameters on a graph (Fig. 12.22). Peaks in numbers of shot at certain diameters match the bore sizes of the guns, though the gun bores are mostly slightly larger than the shot to allow for 'windage' in the gun barrel. It also shows that the type of shot mostly intended to be used had a diameter of 80–90mm.

Of particular interest is the peak in the iron shot with diameters of 63–67mm, since this does not correspond with any gun found. However, it does correspond with the missing bronze 'Falcon' listed in the *Anthony Roll*, which would have had a bore of about 69mm (Rule and Hildred 1984, 18–19).

From the point of view of the layout of guns in the ship it is important to note that the *Mary Rose* guns often occur in pairs according to their bore diameters, indicating that opposite sides of the ship were similarly armed. Where a single gun or an odd number of guns exists, as for example at around 60mm, 95mm and 152mm, it is reasonable to conjecture that the pair is missing.

13. The Loss of the *Mary Rose*

Archaeology is able to add significant new information to the documentary record about the loss of the *Mary Rose* on 19 July, 1545 (Fig. 13.1). This information, particularly about the loaded state of the guns, may not have been available to those who saw her sink, and suggests that the cause of the loss was not as simple as contemporary accounts state.

There were two contemporary views: the French, on the one hand, who believed that they had caused the sinking by gunfire; and the English, on the other, who believed that the *Mary Rose* sank because she was overloaded by heavy guns and, as she turned to fire her guns, was suddenly caught by a strong gust of wind that heeled her over. The recovery of the ship has disclosed no trace of damage by French gunfire, so the French eyewitness, Martin du Bellay [150], was probably incorrect.

The English view is no doubt derived mainly from survivors, one of whom was interviewed immediately after the sinking by the German Ambassador, Van der Delft:

'the disaster was caused by their not having closed the lowest row of gun ports on one side of the ship. Having fired the guns on that side, the ship was turning, in order to fire from the other, when the wind caught her sails so strongly as to heel her over, and plunge her open gunports beneath the water, which flooded and sank her.' [149]

For a ship that was over 30 years old and in 1512 had fought in the Atlantic ocean off Brest in rough weather [167] her loss is very strange, for the *Mary Rose*

was inherently a stable vessel. The explanation given in Hall's *Chronicle* [151] only three years after her loss, stated that the *Mary Rose* was sunk:

'by to much foly … for she was laden with much ordinaunce, and the portes left open, which were low, … so that when the ship should turne, the water entered, and sodainly she sanke.'

Hollingshed's account [169] many years later, in 1577, tells the same story and shows that this explanation was firmly established:

'One of the King's shippes, called the Marye Rose, was drowned in the myddest of the haven, by reason that she was overladen with ordinaunce, and had the portes lefte open, whiche were very lowe, and the great artillerie unbreeched, so that when the ship shoolde tourne, the water entred, and soddainely she sunke. In hir was Sir George Carewe, knight, and foure hundreth souldioures under his guidyng. There escaped not paste fortie persons of all the number.'

Richard Hooker's biography of Sir Peter Carew [168], written after 1575, appears to embellish the story and therefore must be treated with caution. Some details that can be checked differ significantly from other accounts and cast doubt on its accuracy. In particular he says that 700 men were in the ship whereas contemporary accounts only give about 400. He also states that she sank soon after getting underway, whereas Van der Delft clearly states that she had already engaged the French in gunfire, as is confirmed by the French records. This means that where Hooker described things that cannot be checked, such as the verbal exchange between Sir George and Sir Gawen Carew, he must also remain suspect. He wrote that:

'Sir George Carewe being entered into his shippe, commaunded everye man to take his place, and the sayles to be hoysed, but the same was noe sonner donne, but that the Marye Roose beganne o heele, that is, to leane one the one syde. Sir Gawen Carewe beinge then in his own shipp, and seeinge the same, called for the master of his shippe, and tolde hyme there of, and asked hyme what it mente? who awensweared, that yf shee did heele, she was lycke to be caste awaye. Then the sayd Sir Gawen, passing by Marye Roose, call-

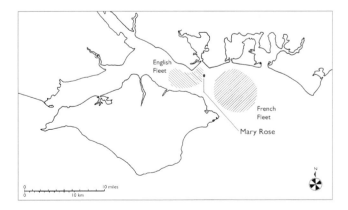

Figure 13.1 Position of the Mary Rose *wreck site in relation to the estimated positions of the English and French fleets, 19 July, 1545*

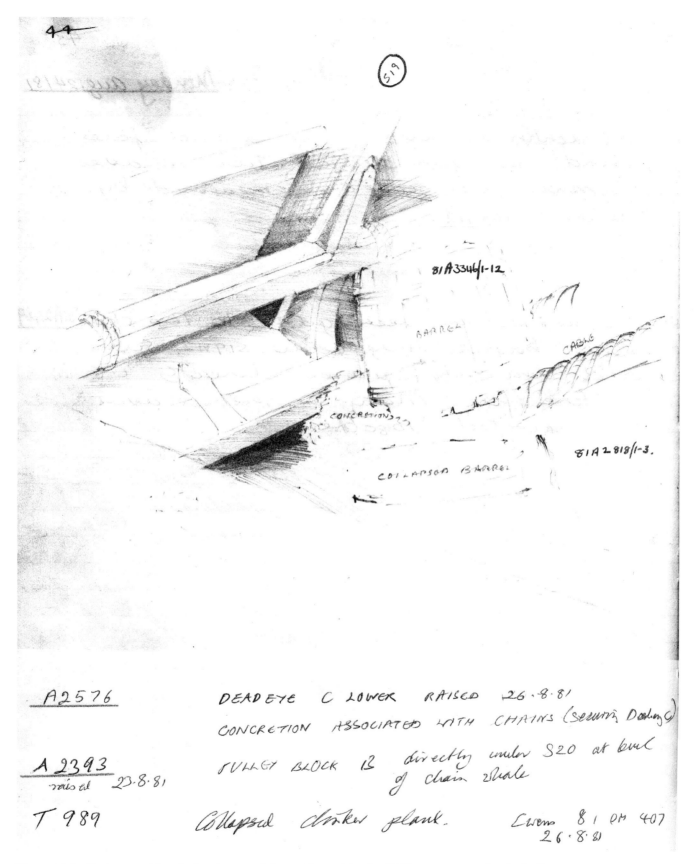

Figure 13.2 Underwater sketch showing surviving cable used in the 1545 attempt to raise the hull

Figure 13.3 Detail of the Cowdray engraving showing the sinking Mary Rose *(© Society of Antiquaries of London)*

ed oute to Sir George Carewe, askeinge hyme howe he did? who answered, that he had a sorte of knaves whom he could not rule. And it was not lounge after but that the sayde Mary Roose, *thus heelinge more and more, was drowned, with 700 men wiche were in here, whereof very fewe escaped.'* [167]

The ship was found on the seabed heeled to starboard, indicating that it was the starboard side lowest gunports, on the Main deck, that were open and had allowed the sea to flood the vessel. The excavators recorded that the Main deck gunports were found in an open position with the guns protruding out of the ports, but whether or not they were fastened open has yet to be established.

It is of course just possible that the ship's angle of heel as found was caused after the ship had sunk, and was the result of the abortive attempts to raise her. The two sixteenth century lifting cables found under the hull amidships (Fig. 13.2) show that salvage had reached an advanced stage, but as the ship's contents had slumped to the starboard side it is most likely that the heel to starboard was the result of the capsize. This is also indicated by the angle of the *Mary Rose*'s mast shown protruding from the sea in the eighteenth century engraved copy of the destroyed sixteenth century Cowdray painting [173] (Fig. 13.3). The French fleet is shown to the east of the wreck, and as the *Mary Rose* was lying north–south on the seabed, the enemy was clearly on her starboard side (Fig. 1.15).

The sixteenth century records state that a contributory factor in the loss of the *Mary Rose* was that she carried guns that were heavier than usual. This possible extra weight has not yet been quantified, but may be calculated from the several gun lists that exist for the ship.

Judging from the Van der Delft account, then, the loss of the *Mary Rose* could be reconstructed as follows: She had fired her starboard guns at the French and, before the gun crews could close the gunports, she had begun to turn so as to bring her port side guns to bear on the enemy. As she turned she heeled over to starboard, and was caught by an unexpectedly strong gust of wind that heeled her over still further so that the sea poured through the open lower gunports and flooded the vessel. The discovery of many of the *Mary Rose* main guns (ie. those mostly with a bore of over 150mm), particularly from the starboard side, means that it is possible to check some details of the cause of her sinking.

The guns show that at the moment of sinking most of her main guns on the starboard side of the main deck were loaded and ready for use:

Main gun	Deck & Sector	Loaded/unloaded
Bronze gun (81A1423)	Main deck M3	Loaded
Iron gun (81A2650)	Main deck M4	Loaded
Iron gun (81A2604)	Main deck M5	Loaded
Bronze gun (81A3003)	Main deck M6	Unknown
Iron gun (81A3001)	Main deck M8	Loaded
Bronze gun (80A3000)	Main deck M10	Loaded

Probably at least three of the four Main guns from the Upper and Castle decks on the starboard side were also loaded:

Main gun	Deck & Sector	Loaded/unloaded
Iron gun (81A0645)	Upper deck U6	?loaded
Bronze gun (80A0976)	Upper deck U7	Loaded
Bronze gun (81A3002) (a port side gun)	Upper deck U7–9	Unknown
Bronze gun (79A1232)	Castle C1	Loaded

Some of the main guns were found both in damaged areas of the wreck or where they had fallen out of the ship. Some of these too were loaded, the status of the remainder being unknown:

Main gun	Deck & Sector	Loaded/unloaded
Iron gun (70A0001)	Bow	Loaded
Iron gun (71A0169)	Stern	Loaded
Iron gun (77A0143)	?01–02	Unknown
Iron gun (82A1603)	Scourpit SS8	Loaded
Iron gun (82A2700)	?03	Unknown, gun broken
Iron gun (90A0126)	Scourpit S02–3	Unknown, gun broken

Some main iron guns were found by Deane in the 1830s in the upper part of the wreck where most are likely to have been derived from the collapsed port side. These too were found loaded:

Iron gun	Loaded/unloaded
(80A2003)	Loaded
(80A2004)	Loaded
(Woolwich)	Loaded
(Greenwich)	Loaded

The fact that so many of the main guns on the starboard side were loaded, and also that the port side guns found by Deane in the nineteenth century were all found loaded, casts doubt on the need for the *Mary*

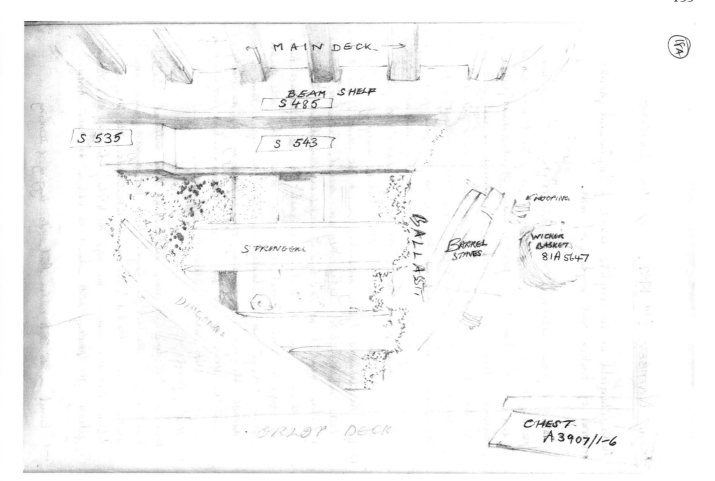

Figure 13.4 Underwater sketch of the area between the Main and Orlop decks in Sector 6, showing the distribution of ballast

Rose to have turned to present the guns on the other side.

An alternative explanation which better fits this new evidence is that, after just a few of the starboard side guns had been fired, as was reported by the survivor, both the survivor and the people watching the disaster erroneously thought that the *Mary Rose* was intending to turn. This was not the case, however, since with many of her starboard side main guns still ready for firing there was no need to turn. This would explain why the starboard side gunports were left open.

Neither the Tudors who watched the tragedy nor the ship's survivors who would be in the upper part of the ship could know of the exact loaded state of the starboard side guns. It would seem, then, that the main cause of the sinking was because she was unexpectedly heeled over by the sudden strong gust of wind, and that perhaps when combined with over-heavy guns, once the Main deck gunports were plunged underwater the ship quickly flooded.

It is difficult to imagine otherwise why a professional crew did not close the starboard gunports had an order to turn been given, and the best explanation is that no such order was given – because the ship was not intending to turn. It was easy for the biographer of Sir Peter Carew, many years later, to pass the blame of the sinking onto the 'knaves whom he [Sir

George Carew] could not rule' since they had died. It is more likely that it was simply a terrible unforeseeable accident.

The archaeological study of the contents of the ship tell us something about what happened next. Large quantities of the contents slid over to the starboard side, including barrels, shot and guns, as the ship heeled over. This extra weight helped maintain the angle of heel, and allowed water to continue flooding the vessel.

The contents of the ship show a degree of violent movement that may have been due either to heeling or to landing on the seabed. The gravel ballast was thrown to the starboard side of the Hold with such force that it displaced planks and penetrated into the Orlop deck (Fig. 13.4). The galley, of mortared bricks, collapsed as the bricks were also thrown to the starboard side, leaving very little mortared structure standing. Even a galley cauldron was thrown right up onto the Orlop deck landing upside down on top of a collapsed partition. The archaeological records reflect other evidence of violent damage, such as on the Main deck, amidst a concentration of personal chests, a chest had been smashed and broken against the wheel of a gun carriage. On the Upper deck another chest was thrown against the starboard side of the ship in sector U11 with such force that its sides were broken. When the ship

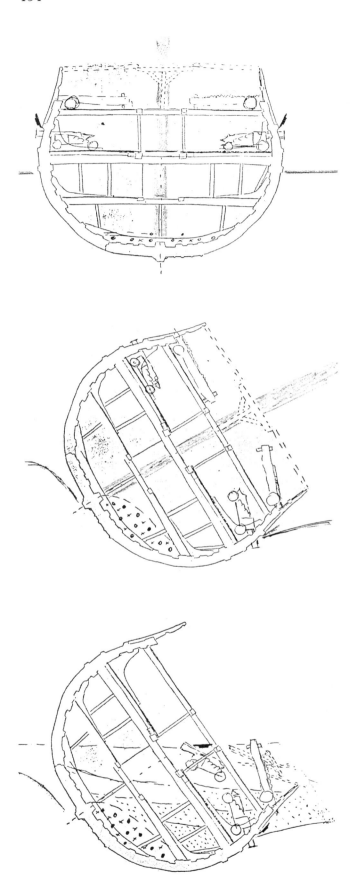

struck the seabed, it pushed up a wave of seabed clay on the port side (Fig. 13.5).

The entire tragedy occurred very quickly, and the locations of the fairly complete skeletons show that many men were down in the Hold collecting supplies, and others were on the Orlop deck. Relatively few men were on the Main deck perhaps because this was where guns were being fired. The greatest number of men, however, was on the Upper deck under the Sterncastle, possibly preparing for a forthcoming hand fight with the French.

The locations of the skeletons seem to reflect the chaos and the panic to escape that must have occurred amongst the crew as the ship heeled over and the equipment and supplies were thrown over to starboard. For example the supervisor of the excavation of the Upper deck in sector U9, under the Sterncastle, commented on the fact that the remains of four or five men lay amidst a jumble of chests, and perhaps were crushed by them. Even in the Hold the concentration of skeletons apparently around a hatchway suggests that the men were caught whilst scrambling to safety.

But with more of the skeletons found on the Upper deck than on any other, it seems curious that only about 30–40 men survived out of a crew of about 400. The answer was found in the waist, particularly in sectors U3–U6 of the Upper deck, where fragments of rope anti-boarding netting were found. This was originally draped over the upper decks of the ship, and many of the men must have been drowned under the netting, but within sight of the surface. The survivors were those who were above or outside the netting, and they will have been unable to help their colleagues struggling just below.

The impact of the tragedy on the numerous families cannot now be quantified as the names of almost all of the men are unknown, but there is no doubt that it was considerable and lasting. It is fitting that a memorial to the dead of the *Mary Rose* exists in Portsmouth Cathedral, and that every year a wreath is placed there by the Mary Rose Trust on the anniversary of the disaster.

Figure 13.5 A series of archive sketches to show the process of sinking

14. The Historical Significance of the *Mary Rose*

The *Mary Rose* was built at a watershed in human history. Until the end of the fifteenth century, Europe was 'the world' to most Europeans but in those last few years major sea routes to the rest of the globe were discovered. Life and politics changed for ever. In 1497–8, just thirteen years before the *Mary Rose* was completed, the Portuguese explorer Vasco da Gama rounded southern Africa and sailed into the Indian Ocean to open up the sea route to the riches of the Far East. In the same year, 1497, the Genoese seafarer John Cabot, sailing from Bristol, reached Newfoundland and by chance found the great cod fishing grounds of Grand Banks. Only months later Christopher Columbus, also born in Genoa, landed in what is now Venezuela. And just two years afterwards, in 1500, the Spanish seafarer Vicente Pinzon and the Portuguese navigator Pedro Cabral independently discovered Brazil.

Suddenly the political map of Europe had a global dimension, and trade and empire-building in the new-found lands beyond the oceans increasingly dominated European ambitions and created intense international rivalries. Rivalries that would need effective ships and efficient navies.

The existence of the new American lands was made personally known to Henry VII when in 1502 three 'savage men' who had been 'taken in the new found island' were presented to him at the Palace of Westminster. 'They were clothed in beasts' skins, and ate raw flesh, and spake such speech that no man could understand them; and in their demeanour like to brute beasts' (Porter 1983, 1).

The importance of these momentous events was underlined just ten years after the *Mary Rose* was fitted out for service. One of the most epic voyages in history was completed in July 1522, while the *Mary Rose* lay at her moorings in an English Channel port after having completed two naval campaigns. Nearly 1000 miles (1600km) southwards, the battered ship *Vittoria* struggled into the Spanish port of Seville having completed the first voyage around the world. She had set out four years earlier, with the support of the king of Spain, with a crew of 270 men under the command of the Portuguese navigator Ferdinand Magellan. Magellan was killed in the Philippines, and his pilot Juan del Cano brought the ship home, with only 31 survivors.

All of this exploration was made possible by men of vision, particularly in Portugal, and by enormous developments both in European shipbuilding technology and in new methods of ship propulsion and

Figure 14.1 The Seal of Paris (© National Maritime Museum, London)

Figure 14.2 The fourteenth century Seal of Winchelsea (© National Maritime Museum, London)

Figure 14.3 Fourteenth century cogs in a sea battle (by permission of the British Library MS Roy. 10.E.IV, f.19)

steering. The survival of the *Mary Rose* gives a remarkable insight into the development in one of the most important ship types of the time, the 'carrack'. The builders of the *Mary Rose* had abandoned the overlapping clinker planking construction technique that had been in use for a thousand years in northern Europe and instead had adopted the edge-to-edge carvel planking long used in the Mediterranean. This change required fundamentally different methods of shipbuilding and enabled larger and more heavily armed warships to be constructed with guns that were able to fire from gunports. Equally important, they had abandoned the medieval technique of sailing with a single mast and square sail, normal until around 1400, and had developed several masts and sails, including the more versatile lateen sail, that made it possible for large ships to be more manoeuvrable (Figs 14.1–3).

The significant developments in ship design had started three centuries before the *Mary Rose* was built, at a time when English ships were mostly relatively small open vessels propelled by a square sail on a single mast. The thirteenth century saw many of the larger ships of northern Europe being provided with castles at bow and stern, and this coincided with the development of the Cinque Ports of south-east England. These ports loaned ships to the king for his navy, in return for which they received considerable rights. In effect the merchant ships with castles temporarily became warships, and so expertise was gained from which would develop the mighty castles of the *Mary Rose*.

The creation of large purpose-built English warships was first established by Henry V (1410–1422) who needed to dominate the English Channel and oppose the French who were not only reclaiming English possessions in northern France, but were also attacking and burning English ports. On land, Henry invaded Normandy in 1415 and crushed the French army at Agincourt, and at sea he reinforced his control

by building four great ships, the *Trinite Royale* (500–540 tuns burden), *Holigost* (740–760 tuns burden), *Jesus* (1000 tuns) and *Grace Dieu* (c. 1400 tuns burden) (Friel 1993, 16).

Amongst the new types of vessel that emerged in the latter half of the fourteenth century was the 'carrack' (Fig. 14.4) which had been developed in the Mediterranean particularly by the Genoese (Hutchinson 1994, 42–4). The main characteristics of this ancestor of the *Mary Rose* were a large sterncastle

Figure 14.4 A carrack (© Ashmolean Museum, Oxford PA1310)

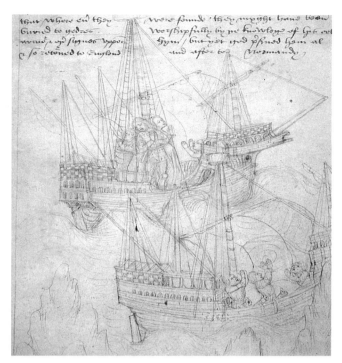

Figure 14.5 A battle at sea in the fifteenth century (by permission of the British Library Julius EIVart 6f 18v)

inboard, a huge bowcastle overhanging the stem and, in the Mediterranean, edge-to-edge carvel planking.

Documentary and pictorial evidence show that carracks were clinker built in northern Europe during much of the fifteenth century, even though shipbuilders of the north certainly knew of the carvel planking tradition from the many voyages to and from the Mediterranean, such as those by the Crusaders. Carvel planked galleys had even been built in northern France during the thirteenth century and Genoese carracks were captured by the English in 1416–17. But in spite of all this, the preferred shipbuilding tradition of northern Europe then remained clinker (*ibid.*, 44–6).

As the largest ships increased in size, the northern shipbuilders of the fifteenth century enthusiastically experimented with new methods of propulsion. The number of masts and sails increased, at first with two masts, the second mast being either a mizzen near the stern or a foremast near the bow. Then there were three-masts with ships carrying fore, main and mizzen masts each with sails. Experimenting with propulsion methods even continued into the sixteenth century with some ships, including the *Mary Rose* completed in 1512, having four masts each with sails.

The armament of warships also changed greatly during the fifteenth century. Before that ships relied mainly on hand weapons, swords and bows and arrows, but by the early fifteenth century, inventories show that some ships had a few iron guns (Fig. 14.5). For example, the *Marie of Weymouth* in 1409–11 had two, the *Bernard de la Toure* of 1410–11 had two, the *Holigost* in 1415 had two guns but by 1420 these had increased to seven, and in 1420 the *Grace Dieu* had three guns (Hutchinson 1994, 156). Although it is not clear if these inventories are complete, the general pattern then was that ships had few guns. Contemporary illustrations show that they were mounted on the upper deck in the waist and were fired over the gunwale, and were also located in the castles. The difficulty was that overlapping clinker planking did not easily allow for gunports to be cut in the sides of ships, as they would have weakened the hull structure, so guns could not be positioned below the uppermost deck.

The fortunate survival of part of a medieval warship, believed to be Henry V's *Grace Dieu*, in the River Hamble near Southampton (Fig. 14.6), makes it possible to study the size, shape and construction of the bottom of an early fifteenth century vessel.

The *Grace Dieu* was the largest medieval ship built in England, though her type is not recorded in contemporary documents (Friel 1993). When she was ready to put to sea in 1420 the king had control of the

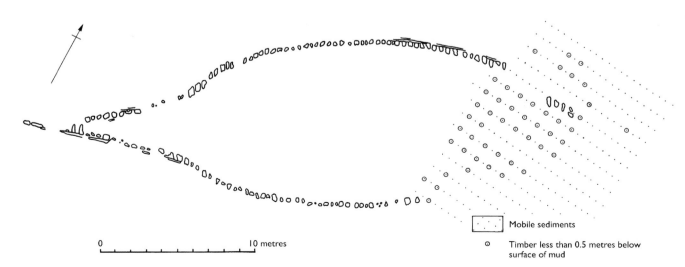

0   10 metres

☐ Mobile sediments

○ Timber less than 0.5 metres below surface of mud

Figure 14.6 Plan of the wreck site in the R. Hamble, believed to be the Grace Dieu (after an archive plan in the National Maritime Museum, London)

Figure 14.7 Bench end from the Chapel of St Nicholas, King's Lynn, c. 1415–20 (© National Maritime Museum, London)

Channel so she was soon retired to a mooring in the Hamble River with a maintenance crew. It was there that she was struck by lightning on the night of 6–7 January 1439 and destroyed by fire. Nowadays the wreck is only visible at extreme low tide when her burnt timbers can be seen.

Although built only 90 years before the *Mary Rose*, the *Grace Dieu* had a construction that could hardly have been more different. Contemporary records show that she was clinker built and apparently had a main mast about 2m in diameter (*ibid.*, 17). She was so large that, even at a time when two masts with sails were

relatively new, it was necessary for her to have three masts, one a 'great mast', and two others one of which had a 'mesan' sail, the term probably derived from the Arabic 'mizan', a balance or adjustment. She also had a bowsprit. Although no picture exists of this great ship, contemporary representations of other vessels show that her main and mizzen masts and sails probably resembled those depicted on a carved bench end of about 1415–20 in the Chapel of St Nicholas, Kings Lynn, Norfolk (Fig. 14.7).

The surviving bottom of the ship, 11.4m wide and just over 38m long, has oak clinker planking nearly 0.30m wide constructed in three layers with a combined thickness of 0.13m, held together by iron rivets with a caulking of moss. The oak frames, about 0.20m wide and 0.13m thick, are closely spaced and notched to accommodate the overlapping planks held to the frames by 36mm diameter treenails (Fig. 14.8).

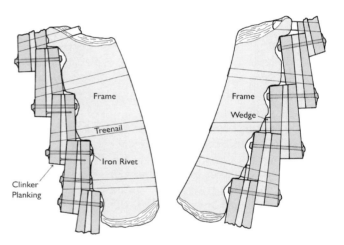

Figure 14.8 Cross-section through outer planking and frame fragment of the Grace Dieu *(after a watercolour by Michael Prynne)*

The keel is about 38m long, compared with about 32m for the *Mary Rose*. The main mast-step, situated forward of amidships, is a rectangular socket 0.83m long, 0.29m wide and 0.20m deep cut in a rectangular timber 1.67m long and 0.89m wide, laid on top of the frames. If the reported mast diameter of 2m is correct, the frames must also have supported the mast in some way (Fig. 14.9). The ballast was of water-worn flints as was the ballast of the *Mary Rose*. The only identifiable part of the ship's upper structure found is the end of a broken deck beam with rebates for the clinker planking, and this originally projected 0.20m beyond the ship's side (Fig. 14.10).

Understanding the structure of this important ship is still at an embryonic stage for the wreck has hardly been excavated. It is not known if she ever had riders like the *Mary Rose*, and this can only be established after very careful cleaning of the timbers, for even though they may have been removed in later salvage their fittings can still be identified.

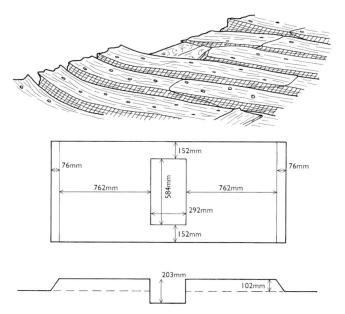

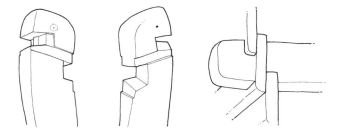

Figure 14.10 The Grace Dieu - projecting end of beam showing rebate probably indicative of clinker planking, shown with suggested reconstruction (right) (after Anderson 1934, 168, fig. 9)

Figure 14.9 The Grace Dieu (top) frames on the port side showing scarfs; (bottom) the mast step

The change from clinker to carvel construction, partly to accommodate guns, occurred at the end of the fifteenth century, and may be reflected by the remains of another great warship dating from around 1500 found at Woolwich Power Station in 1912 beside the River Thames, in south-east London (Salisbury 1961, 89).

The bottom of this great carvel built vessel is believed to be Henry VII's three-masted warship *Sovereign*, built only 25 years before the *Mary Rose*. A sailing contemporary of the *Mary Rose*, she took part in the race around North Foreland off north-east Kent in 1513, at which time Admiral Edward Howard described her to Henry VIII as 'the noblest ship of sail of any great ship at this hour that I trow be in Christendom' [55]. The identity of the Woolwich wreck as the *Sovereign* is made more certain by the discovery of the *Mary Rose*, not only because her general construction is so similar, but also because the documented *Sovereign* is the only vessel that fits the wreck's size and location in the riverbank at Woolwich.

The *Sovereign* is described in a document of 1525 as being of 800 tons, whereas in the same document the *Mary Rose* was given as 600 tons (*CSP* 17 Henry VIII, 22 Oct. 1525, 1714). The same document also states that the *Sovereign* then lay in a dock at Woolwich, and that she must be rebuilt from the keel upward:

> *'the form of which ship is so marvelous goodly that a great pity it were she should die, and the rather because that many things there be in her that will serve right well'.*

There are no later documentary references to the ship, so it is assumed that she was abandoned and allowed to 'die' after all.

The Woolwich ship is often quoted as representing the change-over from clinker to carvel building (Salisbury 1961; Hutchinson 1994, 46; Rule 1982, 22; Marsden 1997, 80) on the basis that at least one frame in the wreck had once been stepped to accommodate clinker planking. It was assumed, therefore, that the ship was originally clinker built but was rebuilt with carvel planks, probably during a major refit in 1509–10. This is about the time the *Mary Rose* was constructed with carvel planking.

This interpretation is now unlikely, for a document has been identified which orders the *Sovereign*'s construction in 1487 and states that she was to be built from the broken-up timbers of the earlier king's ship *Grace Dieu* (a later vessel than the one burnt at Bursledon) (Oppenheim 1896/1988, 36). This *Grace Dieu* had been built by Edward IV in 1473 (*ibid.*, 33) at which time when she would have been clinker built.

What is interesting is that that this *Grace Dieu* was only fourteen years old when she was broken up by Henry VII, perhaps because he considered her clinker hull unsuited to accommodate the increased number of guns required by his embryonic navy (*ibid.*, 35).

There are no contemporary illustrations of the *Sovereign*, but she is well documented and shows that Henry VII favoured more guns in warships than at the start of the fifteenth century. Hand weapons were still very important, as is dramatically illustrated by an early sixteenth century German silver table decoration, known as a 'nef', in the form of a carrack (Oman 1963, pl. xv–xvii; Laughton 1960, 242–85). This may well have resembled the scene only a decade later when the *Mary Rose* was first engaged in battle.

In 1495 the *Sovereign* had 141 guns, including 20 'stone guns' in the waist (ie, guns to fire stone shot), 11 stone and 21 serpentine guns in the summer castle at the stern, and 24 serpentines under the forecastle. She also had 25 serpentines on the 'deck over the summer castle', 20 serpentines on the poop, and 16 serpentines on the forecastle (Hutchinson 1994, 160; Laughton 1960, 246–7). None was on a lower main gun deck, unlike the *Mary Rose*, so she evidently had no lower gunports.

140

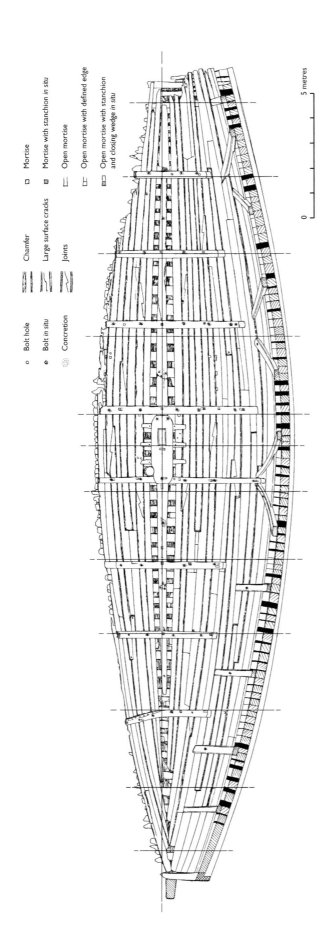

Bolt hole

Bolt *in situ*

Concretion

Chamfer

Large surface cracks

Joints

Mortise

Mortise with stanchion *in situ*

Open mortise

Open mortise with defined edge

Open mortise with stanchion and closing wedge *in situ*

0   5 metres

Figure 14.11 Plan of the Hold of the Mary Rose

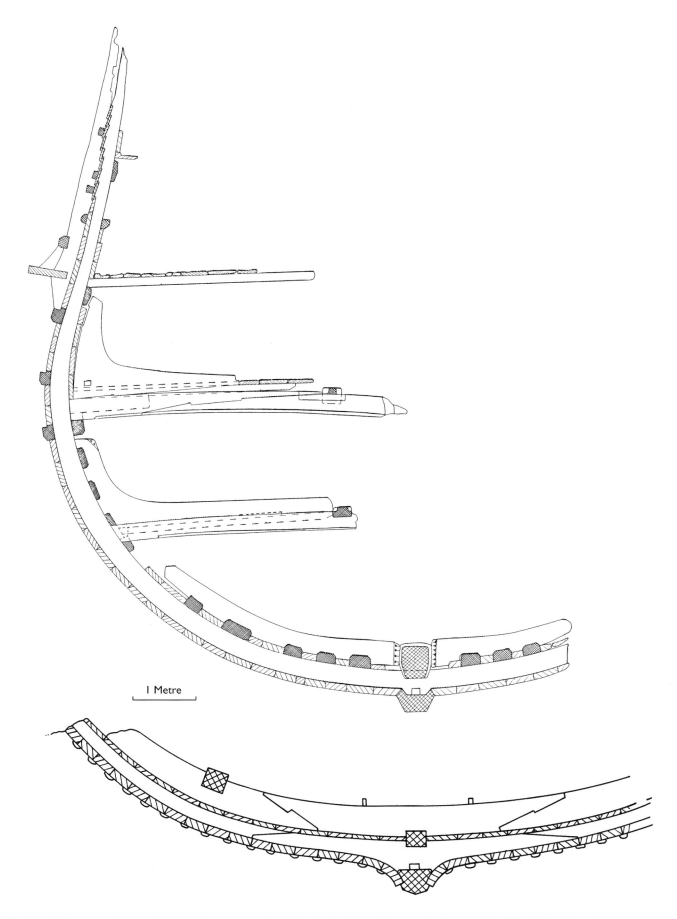

1 Metre

Fig 14.12 Comparative sections, to the same scale, of (top) the Mary Rose *and (bottom) the* Woolwich ship *(*Sovereign*)*

Another major change that occurred around 1500 was the introduction of the flat transom stern or 'square tuck' to replace the rounded stern since this would allow stern gunports to be constructed. Although it is not known if the *Sovereign* had a rounded stern like other ships of the fifteenth century, what is clear is that the *Mary Rose* had the flat stern by 1545 and reflects the then more 'modern' design (Laughton 1961, 100–105).

A comparison between the holds of the Woolwich ship and the *Mary Rose* shows structural similarities in the frames, the carvel planks, the laths covering outboard seams, the mast-step in a long keelson, and transverse riders strengthening the hull bottom (Figs 14.11, 14.12). There are important differences too which show that the *Mary Rose* had improvements in her construction. The most obvious feature of the Woolwich ship was the lower 3m of the main mast, a massive composite structure 1.32m in diameter, constructed from several timbers bound together and set in a rather complex mast-step. Perhaps its thickness was partly to support fighting tops that were larger than those in the *Mary Rose*. By comparison the foot of the main mast in the *Mary Rose*, probably about 0.80m in diameter, was set in a simple mast-step. The bottom of the *Mary Rose* was stronger than the Woolwich ship in that alternate ceiling timbers were thick and thin giving considerable longitudinal strength, whereas in the Woolwich ship the ceiling planks were all thin, though two stringers at the side of the hold gave longitudinal strength.

It is important to remember that the structure of the *Mary Rose* is as she was in 1545 after much alteration, and not necessarily as she was when built in 1511–12 when she was a companion of the *Sovereign*. Consequently, we may not be comparing like with like. The future study of the *Mary Rose* may identify clues to her earlier construction and form. Maybe she originally had a rounded stern, and her main deck was not fitted with gunports. Whatever the case it is clear that the *Mary Rose* can now provide answers to some of the great uncertainties about Tudor warship design, construction and armament at a crucial time in history, as was discussed at length by Laughton 40 years ago (Laughton 1960).

Since warship design is constantly evolving, it is worth considering what happened to naval architecture after the *Mary Rose*. Records of English warships are few until the 1580s by which time carracks had been wholly replaced by a much more sleek type of warship, the galleon. In particular the huge forecastle projecting over the stem in carracks had been replaced by a small forecastle wholly inboard, though having four masts in the largest ships continued into the seventeenth century until warships settled on having three masts (Clowes 1959, 38–55).

No English warship structure of the latter half of the sixteenth century has yet been found to compare with the *Mary Rose*, and it is not until the second half of the seventeenth century that substantial warship remains are found in England, such as with the 70-gun *Anne* of 1690 sunk in a beach near Hastings. The best major ship find illustrating the galleon is the Swedish warship *Vasa* sunk in Stockholm harbour in 1628, and now preserved in a museum in that city.

Social issues relating to the maritime community that served in the *Mary Rose* are reflected by the 19,000 objects found in the wreck. These are discussed in *AMR* Vol. 4, and reflect rank and status of command, living arrangements, sanitation and entertainment in the *Mary Rose*. Some general matters of the Tudor navy, such as sailors clothing, victualling, pay and handling the sick have already been studied from documentary records alone (Oppenheim 1896/1988, 72–82), but now the archaeological evidence from the *Mary Rose* enables these to be illustrated and analysed.

Research into the *Mary Rose* and her contents is still at an early stage, and there is much for future generations to study. For example, the articulated parts of human skeletons and associated objects, particularly clothing, have still to be described in full, but already they seem to show that in the weeks following the sinking, the decaying articulated bodies gradually disassembled in the cold dark silty water within the hull, until some still articulated parts, perhaps held together by clothing, were buried in the silt. In order to interpret even this macabre evidence it will be necessary to understand the processes of the decay of human remains underwater so as to reconstruct the once living people.

The documentary records referring to the *Mary Rose* (Appendix) also need comprehensive study; and to put them into a broad context it is necessary to compare them with the records of other contemporary warships in Henry VIII's navy, particularly the sister ships *Sovereign*, *Regent* and *Peter Pomegranate*.

It is also important to seek the wrecks of other warships that were contemporaries of the *Mary Rose* so as to draw comparisons. One site, still undiscovered, is potentially of outstanding importance: the wreck of the *Regent* sunk off Brittany in 1512. As she was engaged in battle against a French warship which was also sunk, the careful examination of the site should reveal information highly relevant to the *Mary Rose*. The armament, in particular, will help clarify what types of guns were then in use, and these may be compared with those listed as being in the *Mary Rose* in 1514.

Much of the historical significance of the *Mary Rose* is preserved in the huge volume of data in her historical and archaeological archive. This enables a unique window to be opened on English maritime life over 450 years ago. Twenty years after the ship was raised, the process of exploring that history is being undertaken by the Mary Rose Trust but, because it is a charity with limited funds, the work can only proceed at a pace that is slower than many would wish. Nevertheless, the Trust's archives are open to scholars and specialists in many fields who themselves can make important contributions to knowledge.

15. The *Mary Rose* and Nautical Archaeology

The 'Mary Rose Project' represents a significant stage in the development of nautical archaeology not only in Britain but also worldwide. This is because the Mary Rose Trust and its team sought to achieve ideals in the investigation, preservation and public presentation of the maritime heritage that were thought to be almost unattainable in the private charitable sector. At a time when other historic shipwrecks found in Britain, such as the British warship *Association* (1707) and the Dutch East Indiaman *Hollandia* (1743), were having parts of their collections sold by auction as was required by British and Dutch law at the time, the team sought to preserve the Mary Rose collection and archive in its entirety, and to create a museum in which to house and exhibit it.

The objectives of nautical archaeology are no different from those of archaeology on land, except that they are focused on maritime themes. They are to investigate, record, reconstruct and preserve the physical evidence of the maritime past and to publish the results both to an academic audience and to the public at large. 'Publication' is here used in its widest meaning and includes museum exhibition, television and radio programmes and posting information on the Internet, as well as preparing articles for magazines and journals and writing books.

In about 1970, when the *Mary Rose* was discovered, the wreck made its first important contribution to nautical archaeology by helping, with other sites, to convince the government of the day that historic shipwrecks in British territorial waters should be protected as historic monuments. No such legislation then existed, so the passing of the *Protection of Wrecks Act* in 1973 was a landmark. Two other more visible wrecks also made an impact then, the Dutch East Indiaman *Amsterdam* sunk in the beach at Hastings in 1749, and the bottom of the fifteenth century English warship *Grace Dieu* lying in the Hamble River, near Southampton. These three sites together were amongst the first historic wrecks to be protected under the *Act* in the UK (Fenwick and Gale 1999).

The general public's perception of the *Mary Rose* has always been centred on the drama of excavating and raising the ship which, during 1979–1982, cost £2.8 million. The academic perception is different for it is interested in the publication of the archaeological information, and seeks access to the archive of objects and records for research purposes.

Although the two perceptions are inexorably linked, all too often, with other historic shipwrecks, the public view has been satisfied but not the academic need. This particularly applies to those wrecks where the recovered antiquities have been sold to pay for the salvage. As a result, the public has sometimes been unable to separate archaeological investigation from treasure or wreck hunting operating under the guise of 'archaeology'. By ensuring that archaeology of the *Mary Rose* was the primary objective of the project, the Trust made a very clear public statement that clarified the difference.

Those objectives are set out in the aims of the Mary Rose Trust: 'to find, record, excavate, raise, bring ashore, preserve, publish, report on and display in Portsmouth'... 'all for the education and benefit of the nation'. This meant that, following the excavation and recovery of the ship, the next major step was to develop the educational value of the vessel and its contents in a museum. Since the museum opened on 9 July 1984 it has received over five and a half million visitors.

The successful outcome of this seemingly 'impossible' project is the result of the vision and inspired leadership by the discoverers of the ship, the Trustees and its officers, by its Patron, HRH Prince Charles, as well as by those many individuals and companies who donated equipment and specialist time and expertise. Had the *Mary Rose* been left to await government funding, she would still be lying in the sea-bed, as are all the other protected historic shipwrecks in British waters. She might also have been partly excavated and some of the more valuable contents sold. The enormity of the task that the Mary Rose Project set itself is shown by comparison with the parallel efforts at Hastings to raise and preserve the eighteenth century Dutch ship *Amsterdam*, the best preserved East Indiaman known in the world. These failed in spite of the efforts of British archaeologists, the Dutch 'Amsterdam Foundation' and the support of the City of Amsterdam.

Each key person on the Mary Rose project, whether Alexander McKee, Margaret Rule or any one of a number of others, has a story to tell about why they became involved. HRH Prince Charles has kindly written that he became involved:

'because I have a well-developed sense of history; I was interested in archaeology having studied it

at Cambridge in my first year; I felt people would be fascinated to see Henry VIII's great ship on display; I felt Portsmouth could benefit from the Mary Rose *being on display; I* mind *about our heritage and feel that artefacts, such as the* Mary Rose, *help to provide an important link in understanding the past and thus helping to interpret the future.'*

By setting high standards of British nautical heritage management in respect of a great post-medieval shipwreck, the Mary Rose Trust had to consider carefully what it sought to achieve. It recognises that there is still a long way to go, for the conservation and restoration of the ship will not be completed for many years. Moreover, the description, analysis and publication of the ship and its contents, as found, is only at an interim stage. The publication of five interim volumes now will one day be superseded by more definitive publications, once the conservation and restoration of the ship has been completed.

The Mary Rose Project has broken much new ground in developing safe management techniques of submarine archaeological excavation using hundreds of volunteers. Twenty-eight thousand dives were monitored in what is one of the biggest underwater archaeology projects ever undertaken anywhere. The result was that training procedures were developed that gave a huge number of people an understanding of archaeological processes. Some of these went on to become involved in other projects, such as the partial excavation of the wreck of the eighteenth century Dutch East Indiaman *Amsterdam* at Hastings. Others established an internationally approved amateur diver training programme and accreditation scheme in underwater archaeology through the Nautical Archaeology Society (NAS) (Figs 15.1, 15.2).

The quality of supervisory diving on the *Mary Rose* had to be professional, and this was aided by the loan of costly professional equipment that would not normally have been freely available. This equipment was tested in circumstances that could not have been foreseen by companies such as Comex Houlder Ltd (now Stolt Comex Seaway).

As the *Mary Rose* site was mostly obscured by muddy water, it was necessary to create an effective system of recording archaeological features in the sea-bed environment. With help from companies and from specialists, it was possible to develop a number of high-technology systems. Sub-bottom sonar profilers and side-scan sonar located the site; colour and monochrome video systems were loaned by Marconi for recording, teaching and public relations; and ultra sonic cameras were tried that could 'see' through deposits.

Measuring the wreck underwater was a huge problem in low visibility. Measuring tapes were unreliable over long distances as they were distorted by

Figure 15.1 NAS trained diver recording a cannon in Scallastle bay, Scotland (courtesy of the Nautical Archaeology Society)

currents and drifting weeds. The acoustic rangemeter and acoustic transponders lent by Sonardyne International Ltd were amongst the solutions, and they were also used in the docking system during the lifting of the ship. The Direct Survey Method, developed by Nick Rule to record key measurements, became a cornerstone of the underwater survey of the ship.

New techniques were constantly being tried to achieve the same objectives in underwater excavation as occurred on land excavations. Around 1980 it was often claimed by others that it was not possible to record a major underwater site in the detail that was normal on sites on land. In particular it was thought impossible to cut sections through strata underwater, and to record them. On the *Mary Rose* site this was found to be untrue, and key sections were recorded showing the stratigraphy in and around the wreck. Moreover, the excavation was also undertaken layer by layer.

Substantial airlifts were mostly used on other historic shipwreck sites as digging tools, but on the *Mary Rose* a different technique was employed that gave better results. Instead, the hand or trowel was the digging tool and the airlift was used simply to remove the spoil. This ensured that the diver strictly controlled the process of excavation.

The method of lifting the *Mary Rose* was both innovative and completely different from that used on the seventeenth century Swedish warship *Vasa* sunk in Stockholm harbour. The archaeological team, faced with an open hull that would be damaged if lifting straps had been placed underneath, examined alternative solutions and devised a system of lifting from above. Other well-preserved historic wrecks around the world now have two alternative tried methods should they consider lifting another historic ship.

Until the *Mary Rose* was excavated the normal practice in Britain was for salvors of other historic

Figure 15.2 Diver briefing during an NAS course at Horsea Island Dive Centre (courtesy of the Nautical Archaeology Society)

wrecks to recover only a selection of objects. Iron cannons and shot were normally left on the seabed as they were difficult to conserve and had little salvage value. Only the more valuable bronze guns were recovered, often for sale. By seeking to recover everything in the excavation area, the Mary Rose Trust has enabled scholars to evaluate the story of the ship in a much more comprehensive way. For example, by recovering all shot it was found that they peaked in quantities at certain diameters that matched the guns of similar bore diameters. This showed what guns and shot were intended to be the main types of firepower in the ship. Of interest, also, were peaks of shot that did not relate to any guns found, indicating the former presence of guns that had been salvaged in the past. Such work had never been carried out before or since on a British historic wreck site.

Handling over 19,000 artefacts and 3533 samples from the wreck was new to underwater archaeology in Britain. The sheer scale made it necessary to establish careful recovery and storage systems, and to create a post-excavation archive management system which not only dealt with the objects themselves but also with the extensive documentation of drawings, written reports, dive records and photographs.

The storage and conservation of the ship, one of the largest waterlogged wooden structures of archaeological importance ever recovered from a tidal submarine site in the world, required processes that had not been developed on this scale in Britain. The Mary Rose Trust led the development of long-term methods somewhat following techniques already used on other large ships recovered from the inland waters of Sweden and the Netherlands. This subsequently resulted in the Trust creating a national 'centre of excellence' in conservation, with one of largest freeze-driers in Britain for handling waterlogged objects. It has recently marketed a service in conserving waterlogged objects, a particularly important project being to preserve the 3500 years old Bronze Age boat from Dover. For a

while there could be seen in the Mary Rose Museum's laboratory the oak planks of this, one of the oldest discovered plank-built boats in the world. Only minutes away was the huge oak planked seagoing ship *Mary Rose*, young by comparison, showing how shipbuilding had developed in the intervening three millennia.

The involvement of the public in the project was and still is central to the Trust's success, with a result that there was an enormous public response to fundraising. The lead taken by HRH Prince Charles was crucial, as he modestly writes:

> *'Obviously, my patronage might help draw more attention to the project; help unlock funds; create a bit more publicity and public knowledge; perhaps my connection with Henry VIII might help make the project more interesting'.*

The Trust developed an excellent relationship with the media, and over 60 million television viewers saw the ship being raised in 1982. The dramatic partial collapse of the lifting frame leg as the wreck was lifted above the surface underlined the fact that the Trust was working at the cutting edge of technology, and that there was no precedent for the recovery method.

At the time the *Mary Rose* was raised there were no major historic shipwreck museums in Britain. Some maritime museums existed with miscellaneous collections, and there was a growing number of 'commercial' museums, established by divers, which combined the exhibition of shipwreck artefacts with selling antiquities from underwater sites. In time the British government instituted nationally a museum accreditation scheme of 'registration' to identify the properly established museums, such as the new Mary Rose Museum, that could receive public funds. When this occurred, the Mary Rose Museum was one of the first to be accredited. Since then public support and success in sponsorship and fundraising has remained central to the project, and the Trust has worked hard to involve the public, particularly through their Friends organisation and events programmes.

In the twenty years since the *Mary Rose* was raised, various academic issues have been considered. First, it has become general practice for much smaller ancient vessels, such as the Saxon boat from Graveney in north Kent, to be dismantled and raised so that they could be completely recorded and interpreted in detail in a museum environment. Although it would have been possible for the *Mary Rose* to be recorded in 'general' terms whilst underwater, much construction detail would have been missed simply because of the difficulties of access. Also the involvement of specialists who did not dive would have been lost, so the quality of the analysis of the ship would have been limited. Moreover, the long-term exposure to the underwater environment would have resulted in the ship timbers becoming degraded by currents and marine life.

Raising the *Mary Rose*, therefore, was essential to achieve a high quality of record of the ship.

And secondly, the publication of the knowledge gained about the ship and its contents has remained a central aim of the Trust, but has been left until it could be achieved. After the ship was raised, the Trust had to create the museum and to start conserving the ship. This brought an income to pay staff and assured the project's future. Simultaneously, much basic cataloguing of the ship's contents, parts of the ship and the archive records took place over many years. From the excavation phase alone there are about 25,000 'dive log' sheets each of which recorded the work undertaken on each dive; about 6500 pages of 'site books' compiled by the archaeological supervisors; about 1000 sheets of 'finds books' recording objects recovered from the sea-bed, and 200 sheets of 'shore logs' which recorded the shore based excavation of material.

Publication has now been addressed by the Trust, but as no other major post-medieval warship like the *Mary Rose* has ever been published, there is no experience upon which to base the publication. Consequently the Trust's Editorial Committee, under the Chairmanship of David Price, sought advice. After much discussion it decided that five volumes would give a sound interim statement. These are: volumes 1, the history and site archaeology; 2, the ship; 3, the arms and armament; 4, the remaining finds; and 5, conserving the ship and its contents. The experience gained in working to such a format could form a basis for the investigation and publication of other historic wrecks (Fenwick and Gale 1999).

Much detailed analysis of the excavation records still remains to be done in the years ahead, particularly to compile a set of drawings of the ship and its contents as found underwater. At present the drawings of the ship are as it is in the museum, and the location of objects is only by its broad sector within the vessel. Preparing drawings of each sector 'as found' is an enormous undertaking that requires the integration of many records, including computer processing and plotting out the DSM measurements.

The human remains comprise a special category of object from the ship, and they require comment as they represent nearly 200 people who were lost in known circumstances. Even though their locations within the ship and associations have yet to be plotted out in detail, the Trust has always been sensitive to the need for these bones to be treated with reverence, but still be available for scientific study. There is no legal basis for the care of human remains from historic shipwrecks, except from recent warships protected under the *Protection of Military Remains Act* 1986. Neither the Ministry of Defence nor the Police and the Coroner, nor even the Receiver of Wreck has authority in this area. Human remains cannot in law be 'owned', but as their care is such a sensitive issue the Trust has formulated a policy which seeks to treat the remains with reverence and to make them available for specialist study in a restricted storage area. Recognising their importance, the Trust undertook the internment of an unknown member of the ship's company in Portsmouth Cathedral on 19 July 1984, just ten days after the Mary Rose Museum opened. Each year on that anniversary date the Trust lays a wreath on the tomb.

The *Mary Rose* has given the public a view of maritime life over four centuries ago, and students of the history of warships a unique insight into naval development at a time when no scale drawings of vessels exist. She was one of the earliest carvel built ships that became commonplace later. She was also one of the first English warships with lidded gunports, thereby enabling heavy guns to be placed on a lower deck – though managed with disastrous results. In other ways she reflects the creation of the modern navy and its administration by Henry VIII. It is most appropriate that her resting place is in the Royal Navy dockyard at Portsmouth near where she was built, within sight of both HMS *Victory* and modern warships together with their naval personnel – the successors of those who perished so tragically in 1545.

Bibliography

Adams, J. 1986. Excavation strategy and techniques. In Gawronski, J (ed.), *Stichting VOC Schip Amsterdam 1985*. Amsterdam: Stichting VOC Schip

Adams, J. & Rule, N. 1991. DSM – an evaluation of a three dimensional method of survey on underwater sites. In Reinders, R. (ed.), *Sheepsarchaeologie: prioriteiten en lopend onderzoek. Proceedings of the Glavimans Symposia 1986 and 1988*. Rijksdienst Ijsselmeerpolders, Flevobericht 322

Anderson, R. 1934. The Bursledon ship. *Mariners' Mirror* 20, 158–70

Anderson, J. 1969. A new technique for archaeological field measuring. *Norwegian Archaeological Review* 2, 68–77

Bear, B. 1989. *Days, Months and Years: a perpetual calendar for the past present and future*. Diss: Tarquin Publications

Bevan, J. 1996. *The Infernal Diver*. London: Submex

Bradford, E. 1982. *The Story of the Mary Rose*. London: Hamish Hamilton

Barnes, R.S.K., Coughlan, J. & Holmes, N.J. 1973. A preliminary survey of the macroscopic bottom fauna of the Solent with particular reference to *Crepidula fornicata* and *Ostrea edulis*. *Proceedings of the Malacological Society of London* 40, 253–75

Chatwin, C.P. 1960. *British Regional Geology: The Hampshire Basin and Adjoining Areas*. 3rd edn. London: HMSO

Clowes, G.S. Laird 1959. *Sailing Ships, their History and Development*. London: Science Museum, HMSO

Collins, M. & Ansell, K. 2000. *Solent Science – a Review*. Amsterdam: Elsevier, Proceedings in Marine Science 1

Collins, K.J. & Mallinson, J.J. 1984. Colonisation of the *Mary Rose* excavation. *Progress in Underwater Science* 9, 67–74

Collins, K.J. & Mallinson, J.J. 1983. *Sublittoral Survey from Selsey Bill to the East Solent*. Report to the Nature Conservancy Council. Contract No: HF3-11-04

Collins, K.J., Herbert R.J.H. & Mallinson, J.J. 1989. Marine flora and fauna of Bembridge and St Helens, Isle of Wight. *Proceedings of the Isle of Wight Natural History & Archaeological Society* 9, 41–85

Collins, K.J. & Mallinson, J.J. 2000. Marine habitats and communities. In Collins & Ansell (eds) 2000, 247-59

CSP: *Calendar of Letters and Papers, Foreign and Domestic of the reign of Henry VIII, preserved in the Public Record Office, the British Museum and elsewhere*. HMSO.

CSP Venetian: *Calendar of State Papers and Manuscripts relating to English affairs existing in the archives and collections of Venice. Volume II, 1509-1519*. Edited by R. Brown. London 1867.

Dean, M., Ferrari, B., Oxley, I., Redknap, M., and Watson, K. (eds), 1992. *Archaeology Underwater, the NAS Guide to Principles and Practice*. London: Archetype/Nautical Archaeology Society

Dixon, I.M.T & Moore, J. 1987. *Surveys of Harbours, Rias and Estuaries in Southern Britain: the Solent System*. Report to the Nature Conservancy Council by the Field Studies Council, Oil Pollution Research Unit, Pembroke, CSD Report 723

Dobbs, C. & Bridge, M.C. . Preliminary results from dendrochronological studies on the *Mary Rose*. In *Down the River to the Sea: Proceedings of the Eighth International Symposium on Boat and Ship Archaeology*, 257–62. Gdansk

Dyer, K.R. 1975. The buried channels of the 'Solent River', Southern England. *Proceedings of the Geological Association of London* 86, 239–45

Eltringham, S.K. & Hockley, A.R. 1958. Coexistence of three species of the wood-boring isopod *Limnoria* in Southampton water. *Nature* 243, 231–2

Eno. N.C., Clark, R.A. & Sanderson, W.G. 1997. *Non-native Marine Species in British Waters: a review and directory*. Peterborough: Joint Nature Conservation Committee

Farnham, W.F., Fletcher, R.L. & Irvine, I.M. 1973. Attached *Sargassum* found in Britain. *Nature* 243, 231–2

Falconer, W. 1815. *A New Universal Dictionary of the Marine*. London

Fenwick, V. & Gale, A. 1999. *Historic Shipwrecks, Discovered, Protected and Investigated*. Stroud: Tempus

Fletcher, R.L. & Manfredi, C. 1995. The occurrence of *Undaria pinnatifidia* (Phaeophyceae, Laminariales) on the south coast of England. *Botanica Marina* 38, 355–8

Friel, I. 1993. Henry V's *Grace Dieu* and the wreck in the R. Hamble near Bursledon, Hampshire, *International Journal of Nautical Archaeology* 22, 3–19

Glasgow, T. jnr. 1970. List of ships in the Royal Navy from 1539 to 1588 – the Navy from its infancy to the defeat of the Spanish Armada. *Mariners' Mirror* 56, 299–307

Hall's *Chronicle* 1548.

Hancock, K. 1969. *Oyster Pests and their Control.* Burnham on Crouch: MAFF, Fisheries Laboratory Leaflet 19

Hollingsworth's *Guide to Portsmouth*, 1840.

Hutchinson, G. 1994, *Medieval Ships and Shipping,* Leicester, University Press

Horsey, S. snr. 1844: *The Loss of the Mary Rose. Republished* 1975. Brightstone: R.J. Hutchings

Kemp, P. 1979. (ed). *The Oxford Companion to Ships & the Sea.* Oxford: University Press

Knighton, C.& Loades, D. 2000. *The Anthony Roll of Henry VIII's Navy.* London: Ashgate.

Knighton, C. & Loades, D. 2002. *Letters from the Mary Rose.* Stroud: Sutton

Laughton, L.G.C.1960. Early Tudor ship-guns, *Mariners' Mirror* 46, 242–85

Laughton, L.G.C. 1961. The square-tuck stern and the gun-deck, *Mariners' Mirror* 47, 100–105

Lundin, E. 1973. Determining the positions of objects located beneath a water surface. *International Journal of Nautical Archaeology* 2, 371–8

Marsden, P. 1972. Archaeology at Sea. *Antiquity* 46, 198–202.

Marsden, P. 1985. *The Wreck of the Amsterdam.* London: Hutchinson

Marsden, P. 1986. The origin of the Council for Nautical Archaeology. *International Journal of Nautical Archaeology* 15, 179–83

Marsden, P. 1994. *Ships of the Port of London, First to Eleventh centuries AD.* London: English Heritage, Archaeological Report 3

Marsden, P. 1997. *English Heritage Book of Ships and Shipwrecks.* London: Batsford/English Heritage

McKee, A. 1968. *History Under the Sea.* London: Hutchinson

McKee, A. 1973. *King Henry VIII's Mary Rose.* London: Souvenir.

McKee, A. 1982. *How we found the Mary Rose.* London: Souvenir

Oman, M. 1963. *Medieval Silver Nefs.* London: Victoria and Albert Museum, HMSO

Oppenheim, M 1896/1988. *A History of the Administration of the Royal Navy and of Merchant Shipping in Relation to the Navy from 1509 to 1660.* Reprinted, Aldershot: Temple Smith

Phillips, T. Sir. 1839. The life of Sir Peter Carew, of Mohun Ottery, co. Devon, *Archaeologia* 28, 96–151

Porter, H. 1983. *The Tudors and the North American Indian.* Hakluyt Society

Quinn, R., Bull, J., Dix, J. & Adams, J. 1997. The *Mary Rose* site – geophysical evidence for palaeo-scour marks, *International Journal of Nautical Archaeology* 26, 3–16

Rule, M. 1982. *The* Mary Rose. *The Excavation and Raising of Henry VIII's Flagship.* London: Windward/Conway.

Rule, M. 1983. *The* Mary Rose. *The Excavation and raising of Henry VIII's Flagship*, 2nd edn. London: Windward/Conway.

Rule, M. 1986. Mary Rose, *a Guide.* Portsmouth: Mary Rose Trust

Rule, N. 1989. The Direct Survey Method (DSM) of underwater survey, and its application underwater. *International Journal of Nautical Archaeology* 18, 157–62

Rule, N. 1995. Some techniques for cost-effective three-dimensional mapping of underwater sites. In Wilcock, J. & Lockyear, K. (eds), *Computer Applications and Quantitative Methods in Archaeology 1993*, 51–6. Oxford: British Archaeological Report S598

Rule, M. & Hildred, A. 1984. Armaments from the 'Mary Rose'. *Antique Arms & Militaria*, 17–23

Salisbury, W. 1961. The Woolwich Ship. *Mariners' Mirror* 47.2, 81–90

Sharples, J. 2000 Water circulation in Southampton Water and the Solent. In Collins & Ansell (eds) 2000, 45–53

Spont, A. 1897. *Letters and Papers Relating to the War with France 1512–1513.* Navy Records Society 10

Stirland, A. 2000. *Rasing the Dead.* Chichester: Wiley

Thorp, C.H. 1980. The benthos of the Solent. In *The Solent Estuarine System, an Assessment of Present Knowledge*, 76–85. NERC publication series C, 22

Thurley, S. 1993. *The Royal Palaces of Tudor England.* Yale: Univerity Press

Velegrakis, A. 2000. Geology, geomorphology and sediments of the Solent System. In Collins & Ansell (eds) 2000, 21–43

Velegrakis, A., Dix, J.K. & Collins, M.B. 1999. Late Quaternary evolution of the upper reaches of the Solent River, Southern England, based on marine geophysical evidence. *Journal of the Geological Society of London* 156, 73–87

Vine. S. 1998. www.maryrose.org/history/history_of_the_mary_rose.pdf

Webber, N.B. 1980. Hydrography and water circulation in the Solent. In *The Solent Estuarine System, an Assessment of Present Knowledge*, 25–35. NERC, Publications Series C, 22

West, I. 1980. Geology of the Solent estuarine system. In *The Solent Estuarine System, an Assessment of Present Knowledge*, 6–18. NERC, Publications Series C22

Appendix: The Historical Sources

The purpose of this Appendix is to collect together as many known contemporary references to the Mary Rose as possible, so as to enable the history of the ship to be reconstructed and the archaeology to be better understood. The list of historical sources is not complete and should be read in association with *Letters from the Mary Rose* by C. Knighton and D. Loades (2002) where some texts are given in full and which includes a few texts not listed here. This important book was published after this Appendix was completed. It is likely that other documents exist that refer to the *Mary Rose*, in which case the Mary Rose Trust would be pleased to add transcripts to the archives. Moreover, as there is some confusion concerning the dates and transcriptions of documents by different scholars, it is particularly important that the contemporary documents are studied in their entirety.

The references give a valuable view of part of the fitting-out process, the working environment of the ship, the voyages, warfare at sea, the activities that determined life on board, and they show that the ship was inherently stable. The loss of the ship in 1545, therefore, was unexpected.

This Appendix relies entirely upon the published and unpublished work of others, and in particular thanks are due to Stuart Vine, Ian Friel and Alex Hildred of the Mary Rose Trust, and to David Loades and Anne Rose of the British Library. Although S. Horsey in 1844 and Alexander McKee in 1982 published useful first attempts at reconstructing the history of the *Mary Rose*, it is Stuart Vine who took this forward and developed a more comprehensive study in his paper *A history of the Mary Rose*, published on the Internet in 1998. Subsequently, these are partly superseded by Knighton and Loades (2002) which lists 84 texts, and includes brief biographies of the people associated with the *Mary Rose* in the sixteenth century.

The main published and unpublished archival sources are:

(1). *Calendar of Letters and Papers, Foreign and Domestic of the Reign of Henry VIII, Preserved in the Public Record Office, the British Museum and Elsewhere.* HMSO. This is abbreviated to 'CSP', and reference is made to the volumes and their parts (eg. Vol. 1 Part 2 is shown as CSP I–II).

(2). *Calendar of State Papers and Manuscripts relating to English Affairs Existing in the Archives and Collections of Venice. Volume II, 1509–1519.* Edited by R. Brown. London 1867. This is abbreviated to 'CSP Venetian'.

(3). CSP *Spanish State Papers.*

(4). Alfred Spont, *Letters and papers relating to the war with France 1512–1513.* Navy Records Society vol. 10, 1897.

(5). S. Horsey, senior, *The Loss of the Mary Rose*, 1844. This book was bound in wood from the wreck that had been sold by Mr Deane on 12 November, 1840. Republished 1975 by R.J. Hutchings, Brightstone, Isle of Wight.

(6). Alexander McKee, *How we Found the Mary Rose, Souvenir Press*, London, 1982, 9–42.

(7). Ian Friel, exhibition notes in the Mary Rose Trust archive.

(8). British Library, notes for a Mary Rose exhibition held in the Department of Manuscripts in 1982–1983.

(9). C. Knighton and D. Loades, *Letters from the Mary Rose*, Sutton, Stroud, 2002.

Dating in the *Calendar of State Papers* is sometimes by calendar date, and sometimes by the year of Henry VIII's reign which commenced on 22 April, 1509. There has been confusion by some authors in rendering the coronation dates into calendar dates. These have been checked where possible, and it is hoped that this confusion has been removed.

The entries in the CSP are given in full, but where Friel, Horsey or McKee give an expanded version of the original text this too is given. The CSP references are often only indicative of the archival sources which contain much more documentary information, and it is clear that there is enormous scope in the future for a full historical study of the *Mary Rose* and her relationship to the development of the Tudor Navy.

In the archival sources there are references to 'Dead Shares' which should be explained. These were an additional allowances of pay to naval officers and men made in the sixteenth and seventeenth centuries, and payment ranged from 50 shares for an admiral to half a share for the cook's mate. It was introduced during the reign of Henry VIII (1509–47) and remained in force until 1733 [Kempe 1979, 234].

CONSTRUCTION & FITTING OUT, 1510–1512

1510

1. *30 Dec., 1509*
A private Venetian letter from England dated 30 Dec. 1509 refers to an increase in the price of tin because the King has bought a great quantity to make 100 pieces of artillery. He wishes to launch and arm four ships which he has been making in Hampton (ie. Southampton). Unfortunately neither the ships nor their tonnage is given. [CSP I–I, 287, p. 133]

2. 29 Jan., 1510

The materials for the construction of the *Mary Rose*, 600 tons, might just be represented by the following document, though the tonnage figures more closely match those of the *John Baptiste* (400 tons) completed in 1513, and the *Peter Pomegranate* (340 tons) completed in 1512:

Warrant for building two new ships, 29 Jan 1510, initialled by Henry VIII: '... *also the said John Dawtrey by our like commandment hath delivered and paid unto the said Robert Brigandyn, clerk of our said ships for timber, ironwork and workmanship of two new ships to be made for us, £700, and the one ship to be of the burden of 400 tons and the other ship to be of the burden of 300 tons ...* (also, payment of £316/13s/4d for): *... all manner of impliments and necessaries to the same two ships belonging ... for sails, twine, marling (-line), ropes, cables, cabletts, shrouds, hawsers, buoyropes, stays shells, buoylines, tacks, lifts, top armours, streamers, standard(s), compasses, running glasses, tankards, bowls, dishes, lanterns, brass sheaves and pulleys, victuals and wages of men for setting up their masts, shrouds and other tackeling for the said two new ships ...*' [PRO-E404/87/1. 5944 (Friel); Knighton and Loades 2002, text 1]

1511

The *Mary Rose* is believed to have been named after the King's favourite sister, Mary, and the Tudor emblem, the rose. Several much smaller vessels with the same name are also referred to in the CSP in various years. The major source for building and fitting out the *Mary Rose* is Daunce's Accounts described as '*Here ensueth the receipts of all such sums of money, obligations and specialities as John Daunce, our servant .... hath received, from the 1st July, the 3rd year of our reign forward ...*'.

3. 9 June 1511

Holograph letter, dated Wolwich, 9 June, from Brigandyn, Clerk to the King's ships, to Mr Palshid, one of the customers of Southampton, about money received for repair of the *Sovereign* and new making of the *Mary Rose* and *Peter Pomegranate*. [CSP I–I, 1393, p. 640; Knighton and Loades 2002, text 2]

4. 29 July, 1511. Portsmouth–Thames

Daunce's accounts, 29 July, 1511: To Robt. Brygandyne, clerk of the King's ships, for the conveyance of two new ships, *The Mary Rose* and *The Peter Granade*, from Portsmouth to the Thames, 120l. [CSP I–II, 3608, p. 1496 (under date 6 Hen. VIII, 1514); Knighton and Loades 2002, text 4]

29 July, 1511, Paid by our commandement to Robert Brigandyne, clerk of our shipps, toward the chardges of the conveyance of our 2 new shipps from Portesmouth to the Ryver of Thames, the one of them called the Marye Rose, the other called the Peter Garnerde . . . cxxl. [Horsey]

5. 29 July 1511–20 Sept. 1512

20 Sept. 1512: Receipts and disbursements by John Dawtrey, John Hopton, Rob. Brigandyne, clerk of the King's ships, for

repairing the *Sovereign* and making the *Regent*. The same for the *Mary Rose* the *Petur Garnarde*, the *Sovereign*, two new barques, and two new row barges from 29 July, 3 Hen. VIII. (1511) to 20 Sept. 4 Hen. VIII. (1512) [CSP I–I, 1393, p. 639]

6. 9 Sept. 1511. Thames

Daunce's accounts, 9 Sept., 1511: To Robt. Brygandyne for the expenses of the two new ships, *The Mary Rose* and *The Peter Granade*, now in Thames, £30. [CSP I–II, 3608, p. 1496]

7. 20 Sept., 1511. Thames

Daunce's accounts, 20 Sept., 1511: To Robt. Brygandyne for the charges of *The Mary Rose* and *The Peter Garnade*, lying in Thames, £50. [CSP I–II, 3608, p. 1497]

8. 24 Sept. 1511. Portsmouth–Thames of London

Daunce's accounts, 24 Sept., 1511: To Richard Palshidde, one of the King's customers at Southampton, for 24 cotes (coates) of white and green for 24 soldiers, employed for the safe conduct of *The Mary Rose* from Portsmouth to '*the Temmys of London*,' and six similar coats of white and green for the master, 4 for the quartermasters and boatswain, at 6s. 10d. a coat; the wages of the said 24 soldiers for a month and a half, at 5s. a man per month; the reward of the said Rich. Palshidde for his attendance on the ship, 40s., and John Clerke, master of the said ship, 20s. [CSP I–II, 3608, p. 1497; Knighton and Loades 2002, text 4]

9. 26 Sept. 1511. Portsmouth–Thames

Daunce's accounts, 24 Sept, 1511: To Robt. Brygandyne for the wages and victualling of the masters, mariners and soldiers, unto the 26 Sept. 3 Hen. VIII., in *The Mary Rose* and *The Peter Granade*, during their conveyance from Portsmouth to the Thames, £8. 2s. 2d. Also to the said Robt. Brygandyne for 35 coats of white and green for the above-mentioned master and 34 of his company, at 6s. 8d. a coat. [CSP I–II, 3608, p. 1497]

Paid by our commandement to the same, in full payment of the wages of the masters, mariners, and soldiours, and the victling of them, unto 26 September, the third yere of our reigne, in our 2 new shipps, the one called the Marye Rose, the other the Peter Garnerde, for the sure conveyance of them from Portesmouth unto the Thames .... viiil iis. iid. [Horsey]

10. 1 Oct. 1511. Thames

Daunce's accounts, 1 Oct., 1511: To Cornelius Johnson, gunmaker, towards new stocking and repairing divers pieces of ordnance in the King's ships in the Thames, viz., *The Mary and John*, *The Anne of London*, *The Mary Rose* and *The Peter Granade*, £20. To the same, for 8 loads of elm for stocking the said ordnance, at 4s. the load. [CSP I–II, 3608, p. 1497; Knighton and Loades 2002, text 4]

11. 18 Oct. 1511

Daunce's accounts, 18 Oct., 1511: To Thomas Sperte, master, and David Boner, purser of *The Mary Rose*, for decking and rigging the same, £66. 13s. 4d. [CSP I–II, 3608, p. 1498; Knighton and Loades 2002, text 4]

12. *16 Nov. 1511*
Daunce's accounts, 16 Nov., 1511: To Thomas Spert, master, and David Boner, purser of *The Mary Rose*, for decking and rigging *The Peter Pounde Granade*, also for victualling her, and mariners' wages retained for her voyage to be made into Zeland, £66. 13s. 4d. [CSP I–II, 3608, p. 1498]

13. *23 Nov. 1511–28 Jan. 1512*
Daunce's accounts, 28 Jan., 1512: To Thomas Sperte, master of *The Mary Rose*, by John Lawden, purser of the same ship, towards her charges from the 23 Nov. 3 Hen. VIII. [1511], £13. 6s. 8d. [CSP I–II, 3608, p. 1499]

14. *23 Nov. 1511*
Daunce's accounts, 8 January 1512: To Thomas Sperte, from 23 Nov., £20. [CSP I–II, 3608, p. 1499]

15. *23 Nov. 1511–13 Mar. 1512*
Daunce's accounts, 13 March 1512: To Th. Spert, master of *The Mary Rose* by John Lawden, purser of the same, towards her charges from 23 Nov., £40. [CSP I–II, 3608, p. 1500]

16. *24 Nov. 1511*
Daunce's accounts, 18 Dec., 1511: To Thomas Sperte, master of *The Mary Rose*, upon his account made before Sir Edw. Howard, 24 Nov. 3 Hen. VIII. [1511], for charges connected with the said ship, 29s. 1.75d. [CSP I–II, 3608, p. 1498]

17. *24 Nov.–20 Dec. 1511*
Daunce's accounts, 20 Dec., 1511: To T. Sperte, master of *The Mary Rose*, for the said ship, from 24 Nov. £20. [CSP I–II, 3608, p. 1499]

18. *26 Nov. 1511*
Daunce's accounts, 26 Nov., 1511: To Cornelius Johnson, gunmaker, upon a book of parcels, signed by Sir Edw. Howard, for mending guns, making iron work and carpenters', sawyers' and labourers' wages for stocking guns for the King's ships, *The Mary and John, The Anne of London, The Mary Rose* and *The Peter Pounde Garnade*, £37. 2s. 6d. [CSP I–II, 3608, p. 1498]

19. *10 Dec. 1511*
Daunce's accounts, 18 Dec., 1511: To Thomas Sperte, master of *The Mary Rose*, in full contentation and payment of all charges for *The Peter Pounde Garnade*, due upon his account made before Sir Edw. Howard, 10 Dec. 3 Hen. VIII. [1511], £71. 9s. 11.5d. [CSP I–II, 3608, p. 1498]

20. *17 Dec. 1511*
Daunce's accounts, 17 Dec., 1511: To Willm. Botrye, of London, mercer, upon a bill signed by Sir Edward Howard for tukes, bokerams, Brussels cloth and chamletes, to make streamers and banners for *The Mary Rose* and *The Peter Pounde Garnade*, £50. 19s. 2d. To John Browne, of London,

painter, upon a book of parcels signed by Sir Edward Howard, for painting and staining banners and streamers for the same, £142. 4s. 6d. [CSP I–II, 3608, p. 1498; Knighton and Loades 2002, text 4]

(Note: D. Hobbs, 'Royal ships and their flags in the late fifteenth and early sixteenth centuries', *The Mariner's Mirror*, 80.4, Nov. 1994, 391, dates this entry to 17 December, 1512).

1512

21. *7 Feb. 1512*
Daunce's accounts, 7 Feb., 1512: To John Lawden, purser of *The Mary Rose*, upon a bill signed by Sir Edward Howard, for ordnance, £48. 3s. 4d. [CSP I–II, 3608, p. 1499]

22. *1 April 1512*
Daunce's accounts, 1 April 1512: To Th. Spert, for *The Mary Rose*, £40. [CSP I–II, 3608, p. 1500]

23. *5 April 1512*
Daunce's accounts, 5 April, 1512: To Th. Spert, for *The Mary Rose*, £24. 18s. 11d. To Cornelius Johnson, gunmaker, upon a book signed by Sir Edw. Howard, for making guns, gunstocks, bands, chambers and other iron work for the ships, £77. 0s. 3d. To John Browne, of London, painter, upon a bill signed by Sir Edw. Howard, for stuff delivered to the ships and for painting the ships, £47. 9s. [CSP I–II, 3608, p. 1500]

THE FIRST FRENCH WAR, 1512–1514

24. *8 April, 1512*
Sir Edward Howard, Admiral, 8 April 1512: Indenture between Henry VIII and Sir Edward Howard, witnessing that the said Admiral shall command the fleet now ready for sea with 3000 men of war, over and above the 700 soldiers, mariners and gunners in the *Regent*. His wages to be 10s., and every captain's, 1s. 6d. per diem; every soldier's, mariner's, and gunner's, 5s. per month wages, and 5s. per month victuals. Coats of every captain and soldier 4s., of every mariner and gunner 20d. Is to return at the end of three months to Southampton to revictual. His fleet to consist of 18 ships (portage and deadshares of each given): the *Regent* of 1,000 tons, the *Mary Rose* of 500 tons, the *Peter Pomegranet* of 400, *John Hopton's* ship 400, the *Nicholas Reede* 400, *The Mary John* 240, *The Anne of Greenwich* 160, *The Mary George* 300, *The Dragon* 100, *The Lyon* 120, *The Barbara* 140, *The George of Falmouth* 140, *The Peter of Fowey* 120, *The Nicholas of Hampton* ten score tons, *The Martenet* 9 score tons, *The Genet* 70 tons, *The Christopher Davy* 160 tons, *The Sabyen* 120. To have 2 crayers for revictualling. Conduct money for soldiers etc. to be 6d. per day from their homes to the place of shipment, accounting 12 miles for a day's journey. Half the prizes etc. to be reserved for the King. Dated 8 April, 3 Hen. VIII. Sir Edward appeared to this indenture before the Chancellor, April 20. [CSP, I–I, 1132, p. 540]

25. *9 April 1512*

Daunce's accounts, 9 April, 1512: To Th. Spert, for *The Mary Rose*, £82. 2s. 6d.; Th. Spert, for *The Mary Rose*, 73s. 4d. [CSP I–II, 3608, p. 540]

26. *17 April 1512*

Daunce's accounts, 17 April, 1512: To John Lawden, purser of *The Mary Rose*, for necessaries 'in this her voyage of war.' £20. [CSP I–II, 3608, p. 1501]

27. *17 April–8 July 1512*

Accounts of Sir Edward Howard, Admiral, with the charges for the 'first three months ', Saturday, 17 April, 3 Hen. VIII to 8 July, 4 Hen. VIII, of warships, and include the following entry for the *Mary Rose*: '*The Marie Roose: – Fyrst to Syr Edward Haward, knyght, chief captein and admyral of the Flete for his wages and vitayle at 10s. a day by the seid iij mounthes amountyng to 42l. Also to Sir Thomas Wyndeham knyght for his vitayle and wages at 18d. by the day by the said iij mounthes, 6l. 6s. Also for the wages and vitayle of 2 lodesmen alias pylottes ych of thiem at 20s. a mounth by the seid iij mounthes 6l. Also for vitayle of 411 souldiours, 206 maryners, 120, gonners 20, and servitours 20, in the same ship, every man at 5s. a mounth by the seid tyme 308l. 5s. Also for wages of the same 411 persons every man at 5s. a mounth by the seid tyme 308l. 5s. Also for 34 deddeshares demi at 5s. a share by the seid tyme 25l. 17s. 6d. Also for toundage aftyr 3d. a ton a weke by the seid tyme 500 ton, nil quia navis Regis*' (Captains who are spears, or paid as spears, are not paid under this account). The ships with their tonnage and captains' names include the *Marie Roose*, 500, Sir Edw. Haward, Sir Thos. Wyndeham. [CSP I–I, 1453, p.663; Knighton and Loades 2002, text 5]

28. *19 April, 1512*

Letter Bishop of Durham to Lord Darcy:

Is busy setting forth of the King's army by the sea that he cannot write often. 10,000 men are being sent into Guienne under my Lord Marquis. Preparations are being made for their landing at Fontarabia. John Stile writes that they will be met by 10,000 men provided by the King of Aragon, of whom half are to be horse. Sir Edward Howard is gone to sea with 5,000 men very well appointed. My Lord Marquis is to be at Hampton to embark with all the army on 4 May; and the French King makes great preparation against them. [CSP I–I, 1147, pp. 543–4]

29. *28 April, 1512*

Daunce's accounts, 28 April 1512: To Humphrey Walker, of London, gunfounder, upon bill signed by Sir Edw. Howard, for gunshot and other things for the ships, £10 13s. 9d. To Cornelius Johnson, gunmaker, upon bill signed by Sir Edw. Howard, for gun-chambers and ironwork delivered to the ships, £38 6s. 2d. [CSP I–II, 3608, p. 1501]

30. *6 May 1512*

Letter Henry VIII to Cardinal Bainbridge:

Has a fleet of 6,000 men at sea, who have already taken 12 Breton and French ships. Is sending 12,000 men to invade Guienne and Gascony under the King of Spain, and has now,

at Hampton, gone on board the ships. Describes the men as marvellously encouraged by the indulgence which the Pope sent and likely to do great things. The Pope must be urged to attack the French strenuously. With a good wind the army should reach Guienne in 15 days. [CSP I–I, 1182, p. 555]

31. *14 June 1512*

William Knight to Wolsey: After leaving the Isle of Wight, on the 3 June, followed by Sir Edw. Howard to sea, to the coast of the Trade. Some of the company were separated from the Marquis 30 or 40 miles, in consequence of the ungoodly manners of the seamen, robbing the King's victuals when the soldiers were sea-sick. [CSP I–I, 1239, pp. 571–2]

32. *1 July 1512. Brittany, Southampton*

Venice, 1 July, 1512: Extract from a letter from a Councillor of the King of England, 1 July, 1512: The King's fleet under Lord Howard has recently distinguished itself by taking many of the enemy's ships and invading his lands. For four days the English remained in Brittany won several battles, slew many enemies, captured many knights and other gentlemen, burnt the towns and villages for 30 miles round and with their small force of 5,000 challenged 15,000 French and Bretons. The latter declined, saying that it was only by compulsion that they were defending the French King against the Pope. Since then Lord Howard was with the King at Hampton, where he is said to remain in consultation, retaining the fleet. He took many ships with wealth of various kinds and artillery sent by the French King to the Duke of Gueldres, for an invasion of Flanders. The King's ambassadors have returned out of Scotland saying that the King himself wants peace but his people are otherwise inclined. [CSP I–I, 1268, 4 Hen. VIII, p. 583; Spont 1897, 26–7]

33. *9 July 1512*

Daunce's accounts, 9 July 1512: To John Clerke, master of *The Sovereign*, upon bill signed by Sir Edw. Howard, for stuff brought of Roger Halle to the use of *The Mary Rose*, £12. 14s. 2d. [CSP I–II, 3608, p. 1502]

34. *9 July – 30 Sept. 1512*

Estimation of charges of the English navy for the second three months.

'Also for the overcharge and excesse of wages and vytayle of 31 men charged and being on Sir Howard's ship, the Mary Rose, over his first muster, with 16 of Thomas Wyndam's servaunts not recovered in his muster, with 5 trumpetts and sertayne mariners and gonners, forasmuch as he ys allowed for 400 men and hath 431, so in excesse for 3 monthes past: £46 10s = £93. Somme: £587 6s.' [Spont 1897, 36; Knighton and Loades 2002, text 8]

35. *26 August 1512*

Wolsey to [Foxe, bishop of Winchester]: Gives an account of a severe sea fight near Brest on Tuesday fortnight, where the *Regent* captured the great carrick of Brest; but both, fouling, were burnt, and most part of the crew in them. Sir Thos. Knyvet and Sir John Carewe slain. Begs he will keep the news secret. Farnham, 26 August. P.S.: The French fleet has fled to

Brest. Sir Edward [Howard] has vowed *'that he will never see the King in the face till he hath revenged the death of the noble and valiant knight Sir Thomas Knyvet.'* [CSP I–I, 1356, p. 628]

36. *5 September 1512*

Antonio Bavarin to Francesco da Pesaro of London. 5 September, 1512: (NB: Antonio Bavarin was the agent or factor of the *'Pesari of London.'* In Mr. Brewer's Calendar, p. 432, date 1 November 1512, there is a note of a payment made to him for bow-staves, probably those already mentioned by Sanuto, date 4 September 1510):

Dated London, 5 September: How 50 sail of the King's ships, which had previously put to sea from Hampton, made for the coast of Brittany. In Brest there were 28 large ships armed to come out; so on the 9th August the English fleet went thither and found the French three miles off the harbour, into which, on perceiving the English, and having cut their cables, they returned, though two ships, the biggest, remained out, one of them being the great carack of Brest of 1,500 [sic] tons, in trim. The wind was high, with a heavy sea, but Master Thomas Knevet, captain of the *Regent*, (although less by 100 tons than the Frenchman,) together with another little English vessel, engaged the big Frenchman; *'the Regent'* poured in shot and prepared to board throwing out her grappling iron. The ships being thus chained together, there was a very long fight, the action lasting 24 hours [sic]; many killed on both sides. At length the French, perceiving the English to be victorious, set fire to the ships to avoid capture, and the two were destroyed. Praises greatly the captain, Knevet. Of the 800 English on board the *Regent*, 170 were saved; and of the 1,500 Frenchmen, 20 were saved and made prisoners.

Another French vessel of 1,000 tons was unable to get into harbour, and after being much battered, stood out to sea, and was chased by an English ship well appointed.

The English fleet put into Dartmouth, some vessels returning to Hampton; when repaired, they were again to go out.

Sends a note of those on board the carack. The English fleet had burnt many places in Britanny and some 24 French ships, and on that day (the 5th) had captured a French ship, on board of which was the captain Drepa [sic], and had also sunk two other men-of-war.

List of men, ordnance, etc., on board the great carack of Brest, belonging to the King of France, of from 1,400 to 1,500 [sic] tons burden, though but a *'bark:'* -
  Mons. de Clermont, high admiral of France.
  Mons. Primauget (Primoia), captain of the ship.
  Mons. Enores de Clarica.
  Mons. Simon de Loy.
  Mons. Vangel.
  300 knights and gentlemen.
50 gunners; 400 arbalast men; 400 pipes (sic) of biscuit; 100 pipes (sic) of salt meat; 16 very large bronze bombards on carriages, besides other bombards, muskets, and harquebuses innumerable; 160 barrels of bombard powder; 2 boats (bati) of 40 butts each, full of 6 bronze ....

Intelligence derived from the pilot and others taken alive.

Moreover, gold chains belonging to the knights and ready money to a very great amount. [CSP Venetian, II, 1509–1519, 199, pp. 80–1]

37. *1512*

A document exhibited at the British Library in 1982–83 was described as follows: Articles against Jacques Berenghier, a gunner in the ship *Mary John*, found guilty of sabotage and sentenced on the flagship *Mary Rose* to have his ears cropped, 1512. The chief accusation against Berenghier, given here in Latin, was that he had overloaded a number of guns. By using two stones wrapped in thick rope (presumably a method of reducing windage), where only one was needed, he had been responsible for the guns bursting and breaking when they were used against the enemy. In addition he was accused of having in his possession flints for making sparks and of carrying gunpowder loose, not just confined in the horn which gunners carried for that purpose hung around their necks. Berenghier was sent back from the flagship to his own ship the *Mary John* to be examined and tortured to discover if others had been involved. Finally he was returned to the *Mary Rose* for judgment by the Admiral, Sir Edward Howard, found guilty of the charges, and sentenced to have his ears cropped. [Brit. Lib: Additional MS. 48012 (Yelverton MS. 12), f. 17v.; Knighton and Loades 2002, text 7]

38. *15 September 1512*

A document exhibited at the British Library in 1982–83 was described as follows: Letter of Margaret of Savoy, Regent of the Netherlands, to Henry VIII complaining of an act of piracy against one of her subjects, Jacques Berenghier, a merchant of Lille; 15 September 1512. This letter gives a different version of the intriguing story of Berenghier's supposed sabotage. While returning home from an expedition to England to sell his wares, Berenghier was seized, his goods plundered and he himself pressed into service as a gunner in Henry VIII's navy. Subsequently, it is claimed, although he had served loyally, the fact that he was French-speaking led the captain of the *Mary John* to persecute him without cause. He was accused of damaging guns and attempting to start a fire, and as a result he was tortured on the rack to such an extent that he lost a foot. After being delivered to the Admiral, he was imprisoned for a long time at Southampton, threatened with hanging and had his ears cropped. All this, it is said, without cause and simply because he was mistakenly thought to be French.

This and the previous document give two very different sides of the story and leave a considerable question mark over the affair. Was Berenghier guilty of sabotage or was he simply a convenient scapegoat after an accident involving damage to the *Mary John*'s guns? [Brit. Lib: Cotton MS. Galba B III, f.22; Knighton and Loades 2002, text 6]

39. *12 October 1512*

News of England, transmitted by Piero Lando, Venetian Envoy, accredited to the Cardinal of Gurk. 12 October, 1512: Departure from Portsmouth on the 9th of August of the Admiral of England with 50 ships and 10,000 men, exclusive of mariners; course steered by him along the English coast as far as the entry of the sea of Spain in quest of the enemy. The coast being clear, left 10 ships in certain harbours, and with the remainder, in the name of '*God and of St. George*,' made for Britanny to give battle. Late on St. Lawrence's eve [9 August] came in sight of the Britanny coast, with a few sail; continued his course during the whole night, and on the following day, towards 11am, off Brest, the look-out man of the Admiral's galley discovered some two leagues off in the mouth of the gulf of Brest a number of ships, which proved to be the French fleet. Chase given with extreme joy by the Admiral in his ship of 500 tons (ie: presumably the *Mary Rose*) and another of 400, commanded by a valiant knight, called Sir Anthony Ughtred (Antonio Utrect), they leaving the other ships a quarter of a league astern, lest the French, who were in force at anchor and so near shore, should sheer off, as they, however, did. The English Admiral cannoned the French, Admiral, compelled him to cut his cables, and put to sea, and with a single shot from a heavy bombard disabled his mast, and killed 300 men, the ship saving itself amongst the rocks. Attack in the meanwhile by the ship of 400 tons on the carack of Brest, called the *Queen*, of 400 tons burden, and carrying 400 men. The former did not grapple, but in a moment riddled the latter so between wind and water by shots from six large '*cortos*', that the French could not keep her afloat. The rest of the English fleet coming up, the *Regent* boarded the carack with 400 men, and she surrendered, but the powder magazine (containing 300 barrels for the use of the French fleet) blew up instantly, the explosion being so furious, that the *Regent*, of 800 tons, caught fire, and both ships were burnt together, though 180 of the *Regent*'s men, throwing themselves into the sea, were saved by the ships' boats of the English fleet; of the French only six escaped, and they were made prisoners. The ship of Sir Anthony Ughtred (Antonio Utrect) with 30 men sheered off (*se tiro*), and during two days the whole of the English fleet remained in this bay of Brest to raise the anchors of the 53 French ships [which had cut their cables]. On the third day the English landed, burned 27 of the said French ships, captured 5, made prisoners to the amount of 800 persons, and set on fire to many places on land.

Return of the fleet to England, on account of the stormy weather.

Englishmen who perished in the *Regent*-
Sir Thomas Knevet, knight, master of the horse of England, and captain.
Sir John Carew, knight.
Soldiers and sailors, 600.

Frenchmen who perished:-
Mons. de Primauget (Promagier), captain.
Mons. Gabriel de Chacho.
Mons. Simon de la Haie.
Mons. Camaugel.
The Seneschal of Morlaix.
300 knights and gentlemen, who on St. Lawrence's Day went on board the carack to make merry with their kinsfolk, some taking their wives with them.

Soldiers and sailors, 800.
Gunners, 50.
Arbalast men, 400.
.... The King had given an order for the construction of four ships of 800 [sic] tons each, the builders being bound to have them completed by Easter next, 1513. [CSP Venetian, II, 1509 – 1519, 200, pp. 81 – 82; Spont 1897, pp. 60–3]

40. *14 Oct. 1512. Southampton–Thames*
14 Oct., 1512: The names of such ships as be appointed to come into the Thames straight from Hampton, viz.:- *The Sovereign*, the *Mary Rose*, the *Petre Pomegranate*, *Hopton's* ship, the *Nicholas Red*, the *Barbara*. These to be victualled to the 14th day of October, wherewith they shall hold them contented. [CSP I–I, 1413, p. 644]

41. *28 Oct. 1512*
28 Oct. 1512. Accounts of Sir Edward Howard, Admiral, as '*governor and conductor*' of the '*King's navy and army by the sea*'. Coats to soldiers at 4s. and jackets to mariners at 20d., giving under each ship the numbers of soldiers under captains named, the number of mariners and the amount paid. These include – The Marie Roose: Sir Edward Howard 220, trumpets 5, Sir John [sic] Wyndeham 26 – £50. 4s.; mariners 120, gunners 20, servitors 20, – £13. 6s. 8d. [CSP I–I, 1453, p. 662]

42. *28 Oct. 1512–11 Feb. 1513*
Accounts of John Hopton for expenses of the Navy, 1514: Expenditure on the Mary Rose from 28 Oct. to 11 Feb, 4 Hen. VIII, possibly including wages of labourers and others making a new dock. [CSP I–II, 3318, p. 1396]

£132 4s. 3 1/2d. spent by John Hopton, at Blackwell, 28 Oct. 1512–11 Feb. 1513: '*unto John Browne, painter, of London, for flags wit St. Georg's crosse at 3s. the pece, for 14 of them*'. [Spont 1897, pp. 80–1]

43. *28 Oct.–25 Nov. 1512. Southampton*
Accounts of Sir Edward Howard, Admiral, with necessary and foreign charges. These include pay for Thomas Spert, master of the *Mary Rose* and John Cloge, master of the *Peter Pomegarnet*, for seven days, coming and returning from Southampton to Eltham in October to advise the King as to stowing the ships for the winter and other causes. [CSP I I, 1453, p. 664; Spont 1897, p. 68; Knighton and Loades 2002, text 9]

1513

44. *1513*
Exchequer Accounts give *The names of the ships, captains, and masters, with the number as well of soldiers as mariners and tons, which be appointed to be in the King's army royal by the sea this next year.* These include *The Mare Rose*, Sir Edward Haward captain; Thomas Spert master. Victuallers for the said army include *The Christopher Davy* victualler to the *Mary Roose* (though this victualler's entry has been crossed out). [CSP I–I, 1661, p. 749]

45. *1513*

A duplicate document has corrections and additions by the King, and includes the following – *The Mary Rose*, portage (tonnage) 600; Sir Edward Haward captain, 200; Thomas Spert master; 200 mariners. Victuallers for the said army include: *The Baptist of Harwich* to the *Mary Rose*. [CSP I–I, 1661, pp. 750–1]

'*The Mary Rose, portage 600.*
Sir Edward Howard, capitayn of his awne retynew .. 200 [men])
Thomas Spert, maister   }*Sum 401*
Maryners .... 200 [men])
                                    Wherof 40 gunners'
                                    [Spont 1897, 80]

46. *1513*

A further arrangement of the ships exists with the following entry: *The Mary Rose*, 600 t.; Sir Edward Haward captain; William Fitzwilliam; Thomas Spert master, 402. The bark to the *Mary Rose*; Sir Edward H. captain; Davison master, 68. [CSP I–I, 1661, pp. 751–3]

47. *1513*

Navy, 1513: '*Divers prests prested unto the Lord Admiral and unto divers men by his warrants*,' viz. to Thomas Spert, master of the *Mary Rose* upon wages of soldiers and mariners £27. 14d., by the hands of the said Thomas upon the making of '*gables*', £10. etc. Other ships are mentioned. Total: £551. 15s. 11.5d. [CSP I–I, 1661, p. 754]

48. *14 Feb. 1513*

Daunce's accounts, 14 Feb., 1513: To John Lawden, late purcer of *The Mary Rose*, in full payment of necessaries in her last voyage of war, as shown by a book signed by Sir Edw. Howard, £13. 7s. 5d. [CSP I–II, 3608, p. 1502]

49. *1513*

Wolsey Memoranda, Intended Expedition to Britanny. 1513:

ii. Memorandum: '*20 gunners at 8d. the day the piece; 6 surgeons whereof one master at 2s. by the day and the remnant at 12d.*'; one herald at 4s., and one trumpet at 16d.

iii. Captains and men to be taken out of the navy and army now under the Lord Admiral '*to land with the Lord Lysle*,' viz.: Lord Ferrys 400, Sir Wm. Trevenyan 300, Courtney and Cornewall 300, Sir Weston Browne 150, Sir Th. Wyndam 150, Ant. Poyntz 100, Wyseman 100, Fras. Pygot 100, James Dallabere 100, Matth. Cradoke 100, John Baker 60, Nic. Draper 100, Ric. Mercer 80, ... 60, [Lov]eday 60, James Clyfford 100, Barnard 60, Ric. Bardysley 60, Wowell 60, George Wet[wom]be 60, George Trogmerton 150, Ychyngham 100, West 60, Alexandyr 100, Pyrton 150, Wallop 150, Eldercare 100, Barkeley 100, '*Flemynges petycapteyn*' 200, James Knevet 50, '*Sir Edward Howard's, late Lord Admiral*,' 100. [CSP I–II, 1869, p. 852]

50. *1 Mar.–1 April 1513*

Navy, 1 Mar.–1 April, 1513: There is a detailed statement of the ships with their captains entitled '*The charges of the army by sea of our sovereign Lord King Henry the VIII.th*' for one month from 1 March, 4 Hen. VIII [1513], to 1 April following [1513]. These include the *Mary Rose* and give in columns the names and '*portage*' of the ships, and for each ship the names and wages of the captains and masters, the number and wages of the soldiers and names of those by whom they were furnished, the number and wages of the mariners, the number of dead shares and allotment of them among the crew from master down to the cook's mate, the number and wages of the gunners and the monthly reward to gunners. [CSP I–I, 1661, p. 753]

Horsey gives this entry as follows: '*The chargis of the Armye by see of our soverayne lorde Kynge Henry the VIIIth for one hoole moneth, begynnyng the firste day of Marche, the fourthe yere of his most noble reigne, unto the first, day of Aprile then nexte folowyng, accomptyng xxiii daies for the moneth. The Mary Rose of the portage ... Dc Sir Edward Howard, Capytayne, at xviiid. the daye ... xliis. His Retynewe every man vs. a monthe ... xx ... cs. Thomas Spert, Master ... v s. Maryners every man v s. a monethe, ciiii, xx ... xlv l. Deade sharis proporcioned in like maner as in Gabrielle, xxvii. di.– vil. xvii s. vi d. Gonners every man v s. a mollethe, xx ... c s. Rewardis for the seide Golmers proporcioned in like maner as in the Cabrielle ... xl s. x d. Summa of the memle ... ccccii. dede sharis ... xxvii. di. money ... cxi l. v s. iiii d.*' [Horsey]

51. *14 Mar. 1513. Thames*

Daunce's accounts, 15 March 1513: To Th. Spert, upon a bill signed by Sir Edw. Howard, for '*lodemanshippe of The Mary Rose into the Temmys*,' 60s. [CSP I–II, 3608, p. 1033]

52. *1512–1513. Portsmouth*

'*John Read twinne with his brother Thomas was drowned in ye Mary Rose at Portsmouth anno [4 of] H. 8 [1512–1513]*'.

[See '*Read of Ludgershall, Visitation 1566*' in *Additional Pedigrees of a Visitation of Buckinghamshire in 1634*, pub. Harleian Society, vol. 58, 1909. Quoted in Stirland 2000, 61. Also, see Sir Henry Twynam's *History of the Twyynam Family*, 32–3; M. Rule, *Mary Rose, A Guide*, Mary Rose Trust, 1986, 20]

53. *14 Mar.–16 July, 1513. Woolwich, Sandwich, Dartmouth, Southampton, Portsmouth, Sandwich*

Warrant by Thomas, Lord Howard, [6] (162–5): '*The charges of the good ship called the Mare Rosse*' from 14 March to 16 July, 1513, viz. at Wolweche (18 March) Sandwehe (25 March), Dartemuth, Plumht (10 May to 23 May), Hampton (4 June), Porttsmuht (8 June) and Sandwehe (22 June to 15 July). [CSP I–II, 2305, 1032–4]

54. *19 Mar. 1513*

Letter from Sir Edward Howard to Wolsey, 19 March, 1513: By your letter, I perceive that you have sent my fellow Keby with a clerk to view the victual here. '*Sir, without I should lose a tide it cannot be*'; and, as those who delivered the victuals at

London can say what they delivered and most of our pursers are left behind to hasten the victuals, I send Keby back to you. *'And I have sent a guest up to the King, that was taken in the Marya de Loretta. I pray you let him be well twitched, for I ween he can speak news'.* Has received the satin of Bruges. Will write when he comes to the Downs. *'Written in the Mary Roos this Saturday'* . Add.: To Master Amner be this delyvered in hast. Endd.: My lord Admiral. [CSP I–I, 1688, p. 772; Knighton and Loades 2002, text 12]

55. *22 Mar. 1513. Gyrdelar Hed, Deeps, Goodwin*

Letter from Sir Edward Howard to Henry VIII, 22 March, 1513: Informs him that on Saturday, in the morning, after the King had left the fleet, they were to have gone into the Deeps, but on coming to Gyrdelar Hed the wind veered from W.N.W. to E.N.E., and obliged them to anchor for that day. He had commanded [such] of the small ships as would go next day to the Downs to get them over the Land's End, and there went that way both the new barks *The Lesard* and *The Swalow*, and eight more of the small ships; the residue kept with the writer through the Deeps. All Palm Sunday they stirred not, for the wind was E. by S. , *'which was the right course that we should draw to ... On Monday the wind came W.S.W., which was very good for us; and* [that night?] *we slept it not; for at the beginning of the flood we were all under sail.'* (Here a whole line is lost) ... *'slakyng, where the Kateryn Fortaleza saylyd very weel.'* ... *'Your good ship, the flower, I trow, of all ships that ever sailed, reckoning ... every ship, and came within three spear length of the Kateryn, and spake to John Flem*[ming and to] *Peter Seman, and to Freman, master, to bear record that the Mary Rose did fetch her at the tay*[l on her] *best way and the Mary's worst way; and so, Sir, within a mile sailing left her an fly ... at the sterne; and she al the other, savyng a v. or syx smal shipps which cut o*[ver the] *Forland the next wey. And, Sir, then our curs chanched, and went hard uppon a bowlyn ... the Forland, wher the Mary Rose, your noble shyp, fet the Mary George, the Katerryn Prove, a bark ....* Lord Ferys hyryd, the Leonard off Deartmowth; and som of them weer iiij. long myle afore m[e] or ever I cam to the Forland. The next shipp that was to me, but the Sovereyn, was iij. myl behynd ... but the Sovereyn past not half a myle behynd me. Sir, sche is the noblest shipp of sayle* [of any] *gret ship, at this howr, that I trow be in Cristendom.'* When the admiral came to anchor he wrote down the order in which the other vessels came up. The first after the *Mary Rose* was the *So[vereyn]*, [then the] *Nycholas*, then the *Leonard of Dertmouth*, the *Mary George*, the *Herry of Hampon*, the *Anne* [of Greenwich], the *Nycholas Montrygo* called the *Sancheo de Garra*, the *Kateryn*, the *Mary* [Fortune]. *'Sir, one after another, there was a fowle tayle between the Mary Roos and the aftermest* [which] *was the Marya de Loretta. And the Crist was one of the wurst this day. She may beer* [no more] *sayl, no mor may the Katerryn.'* The wind rising, they left the Foreland and tried to get into the Downs through the Gowlls. Between the Brakks and the Goodwin the wind veered and put them in danger. Some of the vessels were fain to put about. Hopes the victual will come safe. The ships of Bristol are with him; *'one that Antony Poynges is in upon a ix. score.'* Such a fleet was never seen in Christendom. Excuses the length of his letter, but the King commanded him to send word how every ship did sail. Has written to Master Almoner for victuals. Desires a warrant to Ble[wbery] to deliver Hopton 200 harness. Written in the *Mary Rose*. Signed. Addressed: To the King's noble grace from the Admiral. [CSP I–I, 1698, 22 March, 1513, pp. 777–8; Spont 1897, 94–8; Knighton and Loades 2002, text 13]

Friel gives a modern version of the document as follows:

'... the Mary Rose, your noble ship, fet(?) the Mary George, the Katherine Prowe, a bark (that?) Lord Ferrers hired, the Leonard of Dartmouth, and some of them were four miles afore me, before ever I came to the Foreland. The next ship that was (near) to me, (apart from) the Sovereign, was three miles behind, but the Sovereign passed not half a mile behind me ... ... When I came to an anchor, I called for pen and ink to mark what ships (came) to me, for they all came by me to an anchor. The first next the Mary Rose was the So(vereign, then the) Nicholas, then the Leonard of Dartmouth, then the Mary George, then the Henry of (South)hampton, then the Anne, then the Nicholas Montrygo (also) called the Sancheo de Garra, then the Katherine, then the Mary J(ames), Sir, one after another. ... ... I beseech your Grace not (to be) miscontent that I make so long a matter in writing to you and of no matter of substance, but that you commanded me to send your Grace word how every ship did sail, and this same was the best trial that could be, for we went both slacking and by a bowline, and a cool ...(?) a course and a bonnet, in such wise that few ships lacked no water in over the lee wales ...' [Sir Edward Howard, Lord High Admiral, to Henry VIII, 22 March 1513. Brit. Lib: Cotton MS. Caligula D. VI, f. 103]

56. *24 Mar. 1513*

Naval ordnance, 24 Mar. 1513: Account of Cornelius Johnson, the King's gunmaker, of the repair of guns and ironwork, from 22 Jan. to 24 March, 4 Hen. VIII (1513), provided for warships, including the *Mary Roose*. [CSP I–I, 1704, p. 779]

This document was exhibited at the British Library in 1982–83, and the accompanying description described it as: Work for the *Mary Rose* includes *'bynding of a greate bras with Iron'* and supplying 6 *'mychcis'* (wedges for the sighting of guns), 6 bolts, 18 gun hammers, and 18 *'pykaxes for gonne stonnis'*. [Stowe MS. 146, f.27]

57. *1513*

Sir Edward Howard to Wolsey. 1513: The money that the treasurer had will not stretch to next month's wages, by £1,000, and there is victualling and other necessaries besides. *'Wherefore, send a proportion, against the payment of the next month, of £1,000 at least and ye shall see that there was never penny laid out but of force it must needs be.'* For tidings refers to his letter to the King, and begs credence for Sabien, who, although a poor man, *'shal show grounds of wealth and honour to my master if ye will hear him.'* To Master Amner, in haste. [CSP I –I, 1772, p. 808]

58. *5 April, 1513. Plymouth*

Letter of 5 April, 1513 from Sir Edward Howard to Wolsey: Is now in Plymouth Road. Has sent a ship of Compton's to bring in such of the King's ships as are now at Hampton. Has no news of the Spaniards in the Thames. Expects an engagement within five or six days, as he hears that 100 sail are coming towards him. Trusts in God and St. George to have a fair day on them. The victuals are bad and scanty, and will not serve beyond 15 days. Has been much troubled in victualling the *Katharine Fortileza*, no provisions having been sent for her. Would he had never a groat that he might keep the West till he and the enemy meet. Begs him, for God's sake, to make provision of biscuit and beer, that they not be compelled to go into the Downs, and so the French escape. Bodell (?), the carpenter, bored so many holes in the *Katharine Fortileza* that she leaks like a sieve. The hoyes sent to take the pipes are not to be trusted; all the pursers were left in London. Atclif had ordered the stewards should be paid 4d. for drawing every tun – a perilous example! Wishes the victual should come to Dartmouth; there is plenty at Sandwich, and three or four Spaniards will carry much. Begs Wolsey will commend him to the King, and desires his Grace to trust no tidings till he hears from the Admiral, who, if he lives, will be the first to write. *'Sir, I pray you, recommend me to the Queen's noble grace; and I know well I need not pray her to pray for our good speed; and to all good ladies and gentlewomen; and to my fellows, Sir Charles and Sir Henry Gilforde; and, Sir, specially recommend me to my Lord my father, beseeching him of his blessing.'* In the *Mary Rose*, 5 April. PS – Never saw worse storms, but only one galley is lost. Sends in this packet a letter for his wife. [CSP I–I, 1748, pp. 798–9]

'Maister Amner, in my hartiest wise I can I recommende me unto you, certifying to you that I am now, at the writing of this my letter, in Plimowthe rode, with all the Kyng's fleet, saving the shippes that be at Hampton [NB: 10 ships, including probably the Peter Pomegranate. Also the Sabyn, as W. Sabyn, her captain, delivers to Th. Wyndham, captain of the John Baptist £1000 from customs of Southampton, 2 April], wich I loke for this nyght, for when I cam open on the Wighth I wolde not goo in, but sent a shippe of Compton's to cause them to comme in all hast, and the wynd has been ever syns as good as was possible.

And as for our Spaniards, that should come oute of Thamys, I here no worde of them. Godde sende us good tydyngs of them.

Sir, I thynke our besynes wil be tried withyn 5 or 6 days at the furdest, for an hulke that cam straight from Brest shewith for a certente that ther be redy commyng forward a 100 shippes of warre, besides the galeis, and be prest upon the first wynde, and sais that they be very well trimmed and will not faill to comme owte and fight with us.

Sir, thies be the gladdest tydyngs to me and all my capytayns and all the residew of the army that ever cam to us, and I trust on God and St. George that we shall have a fair day on them, and I pray Godde that we lynger no longer, for I assure you was never army so falselie vitailled. They that received ther proportion for 2 monthes flesche can not bring about 5 wekes, for the barells are full of salt, and when the pecis kepith the nowmgre, when they shuld be peny peces, they be scant halfepeny peces, and wher 2 peces shulde make a messe, 3 will do but serve. Also many cam owte of Themys with a monthe's bere, trusting that the vittelers shulde bringe the rest, and here commyth none. I send you word for a sewrty here is not in this army, one with another, past 15 dais.

Sir, the Kateryn Fortileza hath troubled me beyonde reson, she browght owte of Themys but for 14 dais vitaill, and no vitelar is vomme to helpe her, and so have I vitailled her with beere ever sens,

and so brings my vitallyng bak, for it is no small thing that 500 men spend daily, and no provision here for her.

I have sende to Plimouth on myne owne hedde to gete somme vitaill if it be possible, I trust ye will allow for hit. I wolde I had never a grote in England that I might kepe thies west parties till they and I meate.

Sir, ye Mylords of the Kyng's moost honorable Counsell wrote to me od a proportion that shulde be all redy delivered. Sir, if some be well vitailled, the moste parte be not, and ye know well, if half shulde lakke, hit wer as good in a maner that all lakked. In consideration to kepe th' army together, Sir, for Godd's sake, sende by post all along the coste that they brew bere and make biskets that wee may have some refresshyng to kepe us togedor upon this cost, or els we shal be driven to come again into the Downes and let the Frenchemen take ther pleasure, and Godde knowith when we shall gete us up so high Westward again. I had ever, then that we shulde be driven to that yssew, to be put all the dais of my life in the peynfullest prison that is in Cristendome.

Sir, the Kateryn Fortileza hath so many leakis by reson of Bedell, the carpynter that worked in her at Wolwiche, that we have had moche to do to kepe her above water; he hath bored an 100 agore hoolis in her and left unstopte, that the water cam in as it wer in a seve. Sir, this day I have all the calkers of th' army on heer. I trust by to morrow she shall be more stanche.

Sir, wher ye write to me that ye send hois to take our pipes, Sir, thei ar such men that they wolde throw them that ye sent with the vitaill over boarde, and when the pipes had been brought and they goon from us, they throw them over borde and gotte into Flawnderes. Sir, I know no mannys proporcion but myn awne, nor one capitayn knowith what his purser hath receved, for we lafte all our pursers at London to hast furth our vitall, and nother here of our pursaris nor our vitaillis. And well I note that I have geven such ordre in despendyng of our vitaill that ther was never army so striated, not by one drynkyng in a day, which I knew well hath byn a grete sparyng, but for all this we be att yssew that I shewed you befor.

And wheras ye write that it were no reason that the Kyng shulde pay for his awne good, Sir, I am of the same opinion. But, Sir, or ever I had knowlage of any man, the delyverars of vitell had received dyvers foists of diverse shippes, and geven the stewards 4d. for every ton drawing. Wich I thought a parelouse example, howbeit one that Atclif sent for the sealyng of certayn commissions for the takyng and preservyng of the foists showed me that maister Atclif had commaunded them to pay every man 4d. for the drawyng of a ton. And, Sir, if that had not byn, I shulde have seen all delivered withoute any peny takyng; but, Sir, never man complayned to me of any such thyng.

Sir, all the vitaill that shall com to us, let it come to Dartmouth, for ther it may lie redy for us, and sewre inough. Sir, ther ys moche vitall at Sandwich, and they have no vessels to bring it to us. Fill some of your Spanyards shippes ther bellies full, 3 or 4 of them will cary much, and spare not to spende vitaill upon us this yere. For, with Godd's grace, the fleete of Fraunce shall never do us hurte after this yere, and if they be so redy as the hulke hath showed us for a certente, I truste to Godde and St George that ye shall shortlie here good tydyngs. And, howsoever the matter gooth, I will make a fray with them, if wynde and wedar will serve, or 10 days to an ende.

Therfor I pray you recommende me to the kyng's noble Grace and show him that he trust no tydyngs till here worde from me, for I shalbe the first that shall know it if I leve, and I shalbe the first that shall sende hym word. Sir, I pray you recommende me also to the qwene's noble Grace, and I know well I nede not to pray her to pray for our good spede, and to all good ladies and gentlewomen, and to my felowes sir Charles and sir Henry Gilforde, and, Sir, speciallie recommende me to mylorde my father, besechyng him of his blessyng. And, Sir, I pray you to knyt up all, with have me moost humbly recommended to the kyng's noble Grace as his most bounden servaunte as knowith Our Lord, who ever more sende hym victory of his enemyes, and you, my speciall frende, your most hart's desire.

Written in the Mary Rose, the 5th day of Aprile, by your to my litill power

Edward Howard.

Sir, I neede not to write unto you what stormys we hadde, for you know it well inough. Sir, I saw never worse, but, thanked be God, all is well, saving the loss of one of our galeis. All ill go with her. Sir, I send you in this paquet a letter to my wife; I pray you delyver it to her. [Spont 1897, 103–7; Knighton and Loades 2002, text 14]

59. 1513

By 12 April Howard was blockading Brest. He landed 1500 men to burn and pillage. The French sent galleys, led by Pregent de Bidoux, who sank master Compton's ship and crippled a new bark. [CSP I–I, 1786, p. 813]

60. 12 April, 1513

[Sir Edward Howard, Admiral] to Henry VIII. 12 April, 1513: On Sunday last, the 10th, [they] moved out of Plymouth. On Monday last the wind rose so sore at N.N.E. they were fain obliged to set in with the Traad, and went in at the Broad Sound. Before St. Matthew's, there lay at road 15 sail of '[m]en a war,' who *'fled like cowards'* to Brest Water as soon as they spied the English. Before the writer could get as far as St. Matthew's the wind shifted E.N.E., and prevented them getting further than the mouth of Brest Water, where they descried the fleet of France to the number of 50 sail. Here they dropped anchor, determining next morning, if they could have wind *'to lay it on aboard'; 'for, Sir, these ships cannot get in by* [the cas]*tell but at an high water and a drawing wind. Sir, the wy*[nds hav]*e blown so at E.N.E. that we cannot as yet come no … Sir, we have them at the greatest advantage that ever men had.* [Sir, God] *worketh in your cause and right, for upon a 5 or 6 days* [ere we came to] *the Traad Pery John, with his galleys and foists, for skan*[tiness of victual went] *to St. Maloo's, and a 5 or six small barks* [keep the] *sea between the fleets; and all their trust* [is in their galleys but they] *shall never come together; with God's* [help] *… them to leave them …* [th]*ys yssew. Sir, the first wind that ever cometh …* [they shall] *have broken heads that all the world shall speak of it. Sir,* [I beseech you] *let ships resort with our victuals into the Traad, setting their course as f*[or] *… along the coast of England or they hal over. And if they hear no* [other] *news there, then let them come over, on God's name, commyn at the Broad* [Sound] *for they be enough to beat Percy John and all his fleet, I warrant your Grace, having them a sea board.'*

This Tuesday, at night, hearing that a ship of fourscore lying in Croydon Bay and four small craft had run aground, he sent out the *Lizard*, the *Genet*, the *Baptist of Harwich*, and his own boat. They burnt the big ship, and brought in the rest; one that was laden with salt he had despatched to England with this letter. *'And, Sir, I have sent a letter a … ships of Spain and victuallers, if so be they be come on the coast* [or be] *come to your Grace, that they shall resort hither with all diligence. Sir, if* [God thinks] *good to send us any wind not having no part of the e*[ast in it, the na]*vye of France shall do your Grace little hurt all the …e shall not tarry long here for it. For, Sir, that we w… in two days, with God's grace. And it pleased God, I w… we had done our business with the army t… and also with all Brittanny, for here is … that is full little and'* ★ ★ ★ Praises the captains, soldiers, and mariners, whose only study is how they may best grieve the enemies; and if victual serve, they are determined this year to '[make] *a bar coost al the remale off Frans that bowndeth on the see co*[st, that they] *shal never recover it in our days. Therfor, for no cost sparyng, let pro*[vision] *be maad; for it is a weel-spent peny that saveth the pownd.'* Whilst he was writing the latter end of the letter the *Lyzard*, the [*Genet*, the] row galleys and row barges, went in to them with the flood, rowing [agains]t them, and caused them to come to their sails, *'and so cam larg* [as though they would ha]*ve com and fowgth with us, and so I weyd and cam to sailes,'* but the wind failed. *'Sir, Seynt George to borowgh … he yit for x. days heer; and* ★ ★ ★*'. 'To the Kyngis noble Gras.'* [CSP I–I, 1171, pp. 807–8 Knighton and Loades 2002, text 15]

61. 17 April, 1513

[Sir] Edw[ard Howard], Lord Admiral, to Henry VIII. 17 April, 1513: The day after he [wrote] to the King, made a pretence of landing beside Brest. About 10,000 of the enemy appeared on the coast. His men, though not more than 1,500, would have attacked them. To divert their minds, as they are hardly handled in the distribution of victuals, he skirmished there past two hours. Passed over to the other side of Brest, *'that New Droydon stood on,'* crossing the neck of land; and, to anger the enemy and show he was not afraid, burned all the houses that stood in their sight. To prevent their attacks the enemy have moored hulks against the mouth of the haven. If he can get horses sufficient to carry two pieces of good ordnance with the cart, will sink the ships where they lie. *'Sir, as for the galeys, we mak gret wa*[tch for] *them, as Master Arthur can shew your graas,'* and if any come the boats and small vessels shall lay them sharply aboard. 'And rather then th[ey shall] skape us I have assyngyd Herper, the Thomas of Hul, my bark, [Treve]nyans bark and two or thre smal shipps not to spar to geve c[ause to] stand, thow they should ron them a grownd for to make them [stand].' Marvels at not hearing of 'our thre Spaniards' that were to come from the Thames. If their victual come not to-morrow they will despair. The wind has been the fairest possible. Makes sure that Sabien has informed the King. *'Sir,* [I have] *taken all Master Arthur's folks, and bestowe them in the arme, wher I* [may by] *reson of deth, by casualte and othervoys. And, Sir,* [I have given him liber]*te to go hoome; for, Sir, when he was in the extreme danger* [and hope gone] *from hym he called upon Our Lady of Walsingham for help and comf*[ort, and made] *a vow that, and it pleased God and her to deliver him owt off that pe*[ril, he w]*old never eet fleshe nor fyche tyl he had seen heer. Sir, I a*[ssure you] *he was in mervelous danger, for it was merveil that the shipp bey*[ng under] *al her sayls strikyng full but a rok with her stam that she br*[ake] *not on peces at the first strok.'* His absence will be a great loss to them. Recommends him highly to the King. Hopes he will give him comfortable words for his bravery. Wishes to know news from Scotland. St. Matthew's, 17 A[pril]. *'To the King's grace, in all possible haste, from my Lord Admiral.'* [CSP I–I, 1786, p. 813; ; Knighton and Loades 2002, text 16]

62. *28 April, 1513*

Pregent de Bidoux to [Robertet ?], 28 April, 1513: Tells how, after leaving Brest on 13 March, he was compelled by sickness among his men to apply to M. de Chillou, vice-admiral of Britanny, for new men. On Friday, the Eve of St. George, after leaving Bar le Duc, was met at the Croix Primoguet by some 50 English ships. Describes the fight ending in the flight of the English, who lost a ship of 300 sunk in his sight, another sunk behind the point and two others which sank in the night. On Monday following, St. Mark's day, some 60 ships and boats, with Admiral Lord Howard in the first galleasse, assailed him and many men were slain on both sides; but the English finally drew off. As the two prisoners he took, viz., a Fleming, since dead, and an Englishman, both said the Admiral was among those who boarded the galley, and described him; Pregent made search and today recovered his body. Sent word of this to the Grand Master and Laval, at St. Mathieu; and the former immediately sent to learn from the King and Queen how the Admiral should be buried. Meanwhile embalms the body. Want of money and men. As the Queen gave him a whistle he sends her the Admiral's, and to Madame Claude the Admiral's clothes. Since the English arrived there have been continual alarms. Writes to the King. Conquet, 28 April. [CSP I–II, 1825, p. 835]

63. *5 May, 1513*

Edward Echyngham to [Wolsey]. 5 May, 1513: *'The news of these parts be so dolorous that unneth I can write them for sorrow. How be it I have found you so good master unto me that* [it] *hath pleased you to cause the King's most noble grace to write unto me.'* On Friday, 22 April, 6 galleys and 4 foysts came through part of the King's navy, sank the ship that was master Compton's, and strake through one (? the *Lesse Barke*) of the King's new barks, of which Sir Stephen Bull is captain, in seven places, so that she was with difficulty kept above water. Then the ship boats took one of the foystes and the residue of the galleys, went into Whitsand Bay beside Conkett, and there lay all Saturday. On Sunday my Lord Admiral appointed 6,000 men to land between Whitsand Bay and Conkett, and so come upon the rear of the galleys; but in landing espied Sabyn coming under sail, on which he abandoned the project, and sent Mr. Fythwilliam to tell all the captains of great ships to return into the Treade before the haven of Brest, to prevent the French fleet getting out, while the small ships ... upon the galleys. And the small ships and the great lay 4 miles [asunder].

On St. Mark's day, 25 April, the Admiral appointed four captains and himself to board the [galleys]. The Admiral himself, with 160 men, went in [the one galley] and in the other [my lord F]erris; and in one of two small crayers [went Thomas Cheyne and Wa]llop and in the other went Sir Henry [Shirborne] and [Sir] William Sidnaye. These enterprised to win the French galleys with the help of boats, the water being too shallow for ships. The galleys were protected on both sides by bulwarks planted so thick with guns and crossbows that the quarrels and the gonstons came together as thick as hailstones. For all this the Admiral boarded the galley that Preyer John w[as] in, and Charran the Spaniard with him, and 16 others. By advice of the Admiral and Charran they had cast anchor into ... of the French galley, and fastened the cable to the capstan, that if any of the galleys had been on fire they might have veered the cable and fallen off; but the French hewed asunder the cable, or some of our mariners let it slip. And so they left this [noble Admiral in the] hands of his enemies. There was a mariner, wounded in eighteen places, who by adventure recovered unto the buoy of the galley, so that the galley's boat took him up. He said he saw my lord Admiral thrast against the rails of the galley with morris pikes. Charran's boy tells a like tale, for when his master and the Admiral had entered, Charran sent him for his hand gun, which before he could deliver, the one galley was gone off from the other, and he saw my lord Admiral waving his hands, and crying to the galleys, *'Come aboard again! Come aboard again!'* which when my lord saw they could not, he took his whistle from about his neck, wrapped it together and threw it into the sea. To ascertain whether he was alive or dead, they sent a boat to the shore, with a standard of peace, in which went Thomas Cheyne, Richard Cornewaile, and Wallop. On their landing they were challenged; and, after hostages of France had been taken into the boat, Cheyne and his company landed, there met Preter John on horseback, and inquired about his prisoners, who answered: *'Sirs, I ensure you I have no prisoners English within* [my] *galley but one, and he is a mariner, but there was one that lept into my galley with a gilt target on his arm, the which I* [saw] *cast overboard with morris pikes; and the mariner that I have prisoner told me that the same man was your Admiral.'* Lord Ferrers shot away all his ordnance. The lesser row-barge followed and had her master slain. Then came Thomas Cheyne and Wallop in their crayer, and then Sir Henry Shirborne and Sir William Sidnaye, who rushed into Pryer John's galley and broke part of his oars, but being left alone, and thinking the Admiral safe, returned. All were full of sorrow at the Admiral's death, *'for there was never noble man so ill lost as he was, that was of so great courage, and had so many virtues, and that ruled so great an army so well as he did, and kept so great order and true justice.'* Need for a new admiral. Frere Barnardyn at Burdews. The writer and Harper commanded to go to Hampton. Many sick and wounded; many dead of the measles. Saturday, the last day of April, the whole navy came to Plymouth, and on Sunday he himself saw a boat of sick men sent out of a ship of the army; and two of these men so soon as they felt ... of the earth fell down dead. The letter describes a later sea engagement from Echyngham's ship, and ends: *'Written at Hampton, the 5 day of*

M[ay].' [CSP I–II, 1844, pp. 842–3; see also Spont 1897, 154–8]

64. *7 May, 1513. Plymouth*
Letter, 7 May 1513. From Thomas Lord Howard to Henry VIII:

'Please it your most noble Grace to understand yesternight I cam unto Dertmouth at 9 of the clok, and this daye at oon of the clok I cam hydder as wery a man of rydyng as ever was any. At which tyme I assembled in the Mary Rose my lorde Ferrers and all oder noblemen and capeteynes and most expert masters of your army, and ther rehersed unto them your commandement yeven unto me, and after that I enquired of them the cause of their comyng from the parties of Breten without your commandement. Unto which they answered with oon hole voyce and all in oon tale they did it upon dyverse and resonable groundys. Oon was they~ had grete defawte of vyttell and had not in their borde for 3 days, notwithstandyng that Sabyan brought with him 9 crarys ladyn with vittells. And such vittellers as were appoynted for them, came from London hydder and to Dertmouth, and here remayned till the cummyng hidder of your armye, without cummyng to them.' Oon other 'cause was, all your capiteynes and masters generally sey, that, and they had contynued there and oon day of calme had cum, if the galyes being within 3 myle of them wold have doon their werst unto them, as it is to suppose they wold have doon, they shuld not a fayled to have sonke such of your ships as they list to have shot ther ordinance unto: which ordinance, if it be such as they report, is a thynge mervelous. Without that your said armye could in anywise have anoyed them. Whereupon [I] resoned with your masters, seying if the galyes had cum forth and that your 2 gallies and 2 rowbarges with the help of the boats had sett on them, what they thought they had been able to have doon to the said galies. And with oon accorde they answered me that oon of the galies in a calme wolde distresse your 2 galies and rowbarges and to drown with their oorys as many bootys as cam within the reche of them. And also all the masters saye that, if the wynde had blownen streynably at S.W., or W.S.W., or W. and by S., ther had been no remedy, [and by] force they must have renne into Croydon Baye, wher they shuld have ly ... nere, the shorys of both sidys beying allredy soor bullewerked, that, without [they] had been able to have betyn the Frenchmen from the londe, the said French[men with] their ordenaunce myght have destroyed all your fflete lying ther. And as [accordyng] to the actuell ffeitys of all such noblemen and gentylmen as were pr[esent], my broder, the Admyrall, was drowned (whom Jesu perdon!) I assure your [Grace] herforth as I can be anywise understande, they handelid them self as [well as ever] men did to opteyne their Masters pleasure and favor.

Syr, ther w[er with my brother] 175 men, of whome wer left on life but 56, and of those [beyng wyth] my lord Ferrers, men 25 slayne and 20 hurte, and may galye had not fallen on grounde beyng nere the shoore, then the od[er in like]wise borded as the oder dyd and of lyklyhode ferre had escaped ... Sherborne and sir William Sydney borded a galie, they beying in a small [crayer], and yet by fortune had but 3 men slayne and 7 hurte ... Thomas Cheny and Wallop beying in a littell crare borded in lykewise and yet they had no man slayne nor hurte. William Tolly and his broder Sir Robert B ... of all men and had 12 men slayne and above 20 hurte. Wiseman m... borded not, but he had all his men slayne or hurte. Sir Wystan Bro[wne had] 3 men slayne, and dyverse oder

bootys had many men slayne and hurte. [Please] your Grace that, as ferre as I can understand by any mannys report, [it was] the most daungerfull enterprise that ever I harde of, and the most manly handeled of the setters on, insomuche that I see no lyklyhode [nor] possybillyte to brynge the maryners to rowe the galies or bootys to s[hore without] other bargen. Sir I had forgetyn 2 men that did aswell as was possibi: [it] was Gurney beying in the Jenet Purwyn, and good Lewes with the oon ... in the Elizabeth of Newecastell, as well apperyd by the slaughter of ... and bowgyng of their ships. And all oder gentilmen which had [part] of the enterprise ar the most angrye men in the woride that they ha[ve] ... therof.

Also, Sir, plees it your Grace to understande I have declared ... unto all the capitaynes and masters howe your Grace wold I shuld [with the] armye retourne unto the Trade, demaundyng of them what servyce ... shall be possible for us to do your Grace ther. And as well the capitaynes [as the] masters have answerd me that, consyderyng the gret fortifycation out ... the gret daunger of the galies if a calm cum, the great daunger o[f the] wyndys afore rehersed, if they fortune to blow streynably, they all [beyng of one] mynde say precysely they see no lyklyhoode nor possybyllite but that o[ur retourne] there shall rather tourne to our great reproche, losse of ships and [men than] oderwyse. And also they all thynke it not possyble, the premysses consi[derd] anythynge that may redounde to the honour of your Grace, your re[alin and] oure poore honesties, oonless that your Grace wold so furnysshe us with [all, that] we myght be able both to kepe our shippes and also to defend [them against] your enemyes for 5 or 6 dayes: which doon, all the expert cap[teyns and] masters thynk veraly your Grace shall not oonly cause us to d[estroy the ships] of Fraunce with the galies, but also put your enemyes to the ... that ever they had in Bretyn.

Sir, I haue not wretyn unto [your Grace] the premysses, but that the noblemen and capiteynes of [the navy] signed with their handys the copy of the same. And nowe, Sir, in my most humble [waye], I beseche your Grace that with all possyble diligens I may knowe howe your pleasure shal be, that I shall order myself, and that I may have answer from your Grace by Wednysdaye at nyght, before which tyme it shall not be possyble for me to departe hens, consyderyng that your army wold not have their vittell in before that tyme, and also a great part of your armye is sparkylled abrode on the londe, and slayne, and departed from the armye I am sure not so fewe as 500. At which tyme, if I have no worde from your Grace, the wynde serving with Goddys grace, I shall see the Trade. And if I can perceyve any thynge that may be doon, I shall accomplyssh the same to the best of my power, and if it may stande with your pleasure that I shall seke along the cost of Breten beyond the Trade howe I maye most anoye your enemyes, I beseeche your Grace I maye be advertised thereof, for, Sir, if your pleasure shal be to send us no gretter nowmbre of men, as ferre as I can perceyue by all your masters, the gretter displeasures that we may do your enemyes shal be beyonde the trade to Rochell ward, wher if your Grace woll that we shall medill with the yles patessed, as they have doon with yours, I dowte not to do them great hurte. And as towchyng the flete that lyeth at Brest, they dare not come forth toward the west parties of your realm, for, and they did, that wynde that shuld serue them shuld serue me to clap betwene them and home, which I pray God to geve me grace onys to see. And as for vittelers, your seruantys from Hampton beyng come to me I dowte not to be well furnesshed [for] 2 moneths. And if they wold go to

Normandye warde, then I wold trust your Grace shuld shortly haue your pleasure of them. Syr, I can saye no more unto your Grace. Myn poore advise shalbe heryng so moche as I have herd, that eyther your Grace shall send us a sufficient company to londe or ells to let us seke oure best ad[vantage], for in the Trade, if your masters may be trustyd, is nothyng to be doon, and in the letter wich I send Master Awlmesner, your Grace shall understande [more] and thus our Lord preserue your most noble Grace.

Wryten in the Mary Rose, in Plymouth havyn, the 7 day of May, at 11 a clok at nyght.

[Endorsed:] *To the kyng's Grace.*

Delyvered the post at mydnyght.

My Lorde Admyrall. [Spont 1897, 154–8; see also CSP I–II, 1851, pp. 845–6; Knighton and Loades 2002, text 17]

65. *7 May, 1513. Plymouth*

Letter from Thomas, Lord Howard, to Wolsey, dated 7 May, 1513: Will not write again what he has written to the King. Found the army very badly ordered; more than half on land, and a great number, he fears, stolen away. Heard of their leaving at his coming to Exeter, and has sent to bring them in again. All are in great fear of the galleys, and had as lief go to Purgatory as to the Trade. Trusts to be here by Friday. The captains are greatly discouraged by the King's letters. The galleys might have been burnt, but his brother would *'suffer no man to cast in wild fire.'* The shores were well bulwarked, but the galleys did little hurt. Begs that some favourable letter may be sent the captains. Intends to punish two men who behaved badly at the late engagement, Coke the Queen's servant, and Freman his brother's servant. Cannot understand the reason of the men's unwillingness to go again to the Trade. Cannot leave before Thursday. The *Anne Galaunt* is not seaworthy. In the *Mary Rose*, at Plymouth, 7 May. Addressed: To Mr. Almoner, with the King's grace. [CSP I–II, 1852, p. 846; Knighton and Loades 2002, text 18]

66. *9 May, 1513*

Naval payments, warrant by Thomas, Lord Howard: [2] 9 July, 1513, (267) Edward Braye whom *'I have appointed'* captain of the *Mary Rose*, two months' wages at 18d. a day from 9 May. [CSP I–II, 2305, pp. 1032–4; Knighton and Loades 2002, text 19]

67. *9 May, 1513*

Naval payments, warrant by Thomas, Lord Howard: [4] (272) One month's wages from 9 May, 1513, to 111 soldiers whom Howard was commanded to bring but could not bestow in the *Mary Roose* until the retinue of his *'brother Sir Edward Howard, late Admiral,'* was despatched, dated 18 June. [CSP I–II, 2305, pp. 1032–4; Knighton and Loades 2002, text 20]

68. *13 May, 1513*

Henry VIII to Lord Howard, Admiral of England, and to Lord Lyle. Intended expedition to Britanny. 13 May, 1513: Instructions given by the King to the Lord Howard, Admiral of England, and to the Lord Lyle (altered from *'Sir Charles Brandon, knight'*) for *'making an enterprise as well by land as water for the distrussing of the navy of France now being in Bretayn.'* Draft, with corrections in Wolsey's hand: Lord Lisle, who is to be chief captain of the enterprise by land, shall, with his retinue, join the Admiral at Southampton by the – (blank) day of this month [altered from an order to take shipping at Southampton and *'resort to Plymouth or Dertmouthe, where the King's navy now is,'* with authority to act as admiral when not in the company of the Admiral of England]. The Admiral and Lord Lisle to call a council of the captains and expert mariners and devise with them about the safeguard of the navy and the place and manner of landing. The Admiral must arrange to make an attack on the navy of France, while Lord Lisle and his retinue are landing and provide for the safety of the rest of the navy in his absence. Lisle has a bill of the captains and soldiers he shall take to assist him out of the navy, but it is remitted to the discretion of the Admiral and him to modify such arrangements on the spot. [CSP I–II, 1869, p. 851]

69. *13 May, 1513. Plymouth*

Letter from Thomas, Lord Howard to Henry VIII, dated 13 May, 1513: Thanks for letter received to-day at 11 a.m., dated 12 May, whereby it appears that my cousin Sir Charles, and many other noblemen shall be sent to us. *'Sir, I doubt not, God and the wind serving,'* you shall obtain the destruction of the French navy and a great part of the coast of Brytainge; but this is the most dangerous haven in England for so many ships (and they *'nightly fall together'*), and when the wind is southwards it is impossible to leave. A council of the most expert masters advises the assembling at Hampton, where wind that would bar us in here would carry us to Brytainge. For Sir Charles to come from Hampton hither would be clean out of his course; and a south wind might keep him here in harbour until all his victual was spent, and thus break *'your noble pretended enterprise.'* Therefore, if wind serve, I will draw to the Isle of Wight and ride before Portismouth. Understanding that my Lord Broke and Sir Piers Edgcombe shall come with my said cousin, to save charges and the wearying of their men, I will ship them here. We can also make shift to take in some of my cousin's men if he lack shipping, and I undertake that at Hampton none of our company shall come on land. If the coming forth of the French is unlikely, as I wrote yesterday, our remaining here is useless. Your letters directed to Lord Ferres and other captains have marvellously rejoiced them. As commanded, I have sent Fitzwillyam, *'which is right sore against his mind to have departed till he had done you some other service,'* and I am sure he will always do hardy service. While writing this, I had news that 20 Spaniards with 6,000 men are come to Fawmouth. Scribbled in the *Mary Rose* at Plymouth, 13 May, at noon. [CSP I–II, 1870, p. 852–3; Knighton and Loades 2002, text 21]

70. *14 May, 1513. Plymouth*

Letter from Thomas, Lord Howard to Wolsey, dated 14 May, 1513: Intends, as he wrote the King yesterday, as soon as the wind serves, to come with the whole navy, men of war and victuallers, to Hampton; but this is the worst haven in England to get out of, for the army lying in three parts, and all within Plymouth Sound, no wind but North can bring all forth without warping. Prays God bring the wind out of the

South. *'Here we lie, victuallers and men of war I am sure above 100 sail; and Gonstone is yet at Dartmouth, and yet he went hence before my coming and in no wise can get to Hampton.'* None of the ships you named in Dalaber's bill, nor of the victuallers, are yet departed, although both they and we are ready when God sends wind; and therefore it were well to cause *'all soldiers that shall come with Sir Charles'* to tarry about Salisbury, Winchester and other places, and not to come to Hampton until the ships come, or they will waste provisions which should serve the army. Scribbled in the *Mary Rose*, at Plymouth, 14 May, 1513. Addressed: To Master Almoner with the King's Grace; delivered at Plymmouth at 5 at afternoon. [CSP I–II, 1875, p. 854; Knighton and Loades 2002, text 22]

71. *15 May, 1513. Plymouth*

Letter from Thomas, Lord Howard to Wolsey, dated 15 May, 1513: Windbound, together with the *Peter* and other great ships, in Katt Water, which prevents him from following the King's pleasure. The *Sovereign* and others are at St. Nicholas' Island. Intends to go to Asshe Water, and send the victuallers to Hampton with Anthony Poynes, Wisman, and Draper. Desires a letter on his arrival at Southampton enjoining no captain or seaman to go [ashore]. Has made a pair of gallows at the waterside, where some will *'towter'* to-morrow. Sends a writing in Spanish given him by a merchant of Bristol, who heard it proclaimed in Cadiz 10 days ago, and brought it for his safeguard against Frenchmen. The King shall speed better if he trust his own ... Is informed by Sabyan that Brest Castle was won by Mons. de Rohan in consequence of his threatening the Bretons in the castle with destruction of their lands. Hopes, when he and Sir Charles come to Hampton, to find there my Lord of Winchester to debate with him. Trusts to *'rype'* him well in every cause; *'for when I am not occupied'* he says, *'it is my most business to be instructed of them that can skill.' 'I had rather the posts toke payne in sporring their horsis than I shud be fownd to slow in wryting or workyng when tyme shall require.'* On Tuesday night the victuallers will be at Hampton and the men of war about the [K]ow and the Wight. In the *Mary Rose*, at 1 in the afternoon. [CSP I–II, 1883, p. 856; Spont 1897, 163–6; Knighton and Loades 2002, text 23]

72. *16 May, 1513. Plymouth*

Letter from Thomas, Lord Howard to Wolsey, dated 16 May, 1513: Whereas I wrote yesterday of our departure to Hampton; this day at 10 o'clock, when most of the ships in the Sound were ready to weigh anchor, the wind, *'being at west shot southerly and blew so rudely'* that all the ships were forced to come in again. Doubtless you will see the matter of the waste of victuals which Sir Charles's company would make at Hampton. I send the Spanish letter of which I wrote, which my servant forgot to enclose. This day came two ships of Flanders from Rochell reporting peace proclaimed between France and Spain and 5 ships of Spain at Rochell and 9 at Bordeaulx lading wine for Flanders. If we meet them or any Flemings with wine, shall I send them into England or let them go free, and shall I make them a price, and what price, as well Gascon as Rochell? I fear *'ye be weary of my often writing, but I had rather be judged too quick than too slow.'* In

haste at 2 o'clock in the *Mary Rose*, 16 May. Addressed: To Master Almoner with the King's grace. [CSP I–II, 1886, pp. 859–60; Knighton and Loades 2002, text 24]

73. *18 May, 1513. Plymouth*

Letter from Thomas, Lord Howard to Henry VIII, dated 18 May, 1513: At 10 a.m. on the 17th I received your letters of the 15th ordering certain ships to the Narrow Seas; and have accordingly victualled them and appointed the *Peter of Foway* to go with them in the *Mary of Brixam*'s stead, with two gentlemen of mine for captains. Both they and the rest have been ready to depart these six days, but for two or three days the wind, at W.S.W., the best wind to bring us to Hampton, has blown so strainably that we have been forced to lay out shot anchors and have broken many anchors and cables. Your new cables are of the worst stuff that ever man saw. At my coming to Hampton I will send you an *'ensample.'* You may reckon on our being there within a day and a night after this tempest is done, coming along the coast of Normandy, so that seeing us draw towards England they may think we *'intend no more to come in Bretaynge,'* and be the more unprovided. I trust your pretended enterprise be not known to your enemies, lest they withdraw their ships from Brest to Rochell or Bordeaulx; for those who know Brest think it will be impossible for them to save ship or galley if we find them there. Scribbled in the Mary Rose, 18 May, at Plymmouth, *'where I pray God defend me for ever coming again with such a royal army.'* [CSP I–II, 1894, p. 862; Knighton and Loades 2002, text 25]

74. *19 May 1513*

Richard [Fox] Bp. of Winchester to Henry VIII. 19 May, 1513: Has received a letter from the Almoner, stating that the King lately wrote to the Admiral to come to Portsmouth and wait there for Sir Charles Brandon; and that, if he reaches there before this Thursday, Fox is to advise the King by post to Windsor, that the King may visit Portsmouth secretly. The Admiral is not yet come, as he is wind-bound in Plymouth haven. Advises the King to come to Hampton, not to Portsmouth. There is no shipping fit for Sir Charles Brandon, except two Spaniards. Sir Charles is expected here today. The despatching of the army will require time. John Dawtrey has made provision for the Admiral and his company. Lacks only empty pipes. Understands that victual for Sir Charles's men comes from London. Hampton, Thursday, 19 May, 9am. To the King's grace at Windsor. [CSP I–II, 1898, p. 864]

75. *19 May 1513*

Richard [Fox] Bp. of Winchester to Wolsey. 19 May, 1513: Received this morning his letter dated London, 17 May (by which Wolsey will perceive the speed of the posts), and thereupon wrote to the King that neither my Lord Admiral nor any of that army have arrived at Portsmouth or here. Hears they are windbound in the haven of Plymouth. No ships or victuallers have come out of the Thames or from Sandwich. Will learn from John Dawtrey's letters all about ships, victualling and wages. Hopes that ships will be sent at once to scour the Narrow Seas, and waft the hoys to Calais. It is too great a shame to lose those that be lost, and he trusts Wolsey will venture no more until he has wafters. Thinks he might man some of the Spaniards at Sandwich for this purpose. When my Lord Admiral comes the writer will ask him to send to the Narrow Seas such ships as are named in Wolsey's letter. Sir Charles [Brandon] has not come, nor any captain save Bruges. Has provided lodgings for the companies two days' journey in the country. [CSP I–II, 1899, pp. 864–5]

76. *19 May 1513*
John Dawtrey to Wolsey. 19 May 1513: Has received his letter desiring to know whether he can pay the army under the Lord Admiral for three months and the men under Sir Charles Brandon for two. Has no such warrant. Had only expected to provide victuals for the great army, payments for the beerhouses at Portsmouth, the Sowchyvers, etc.; and has little over £6,000 in hand. Hampton, 19 May. PS – Here be no ships come as yet save the *Mawdelyn of Pole*, 100 tons. Sent to: To, etc., Master Wulcy, the King's amner. [CSP I–II, 1900, p. 865]

77. *May–Aug. 1513*
The Navy: File of receipts by pursers, captains and others of various ships, including the *Mary Rose*, for victuals received from John Dawtrey between May and August, 5 Hen. VIII (1513). [CSP I–II, 2217, p. 992]

78. *20 May 1513*
Thomas Lord Howard to Wolsey. 20 May, 1513: Encloses a letter sent him yesterday. The bringer, who was in Guernsey this day sen'night, says that, on 11 May, there passed from Britanny towards Normandy above 60 sail, and on the 13th 18 sail, and that divers ships of Britanny, with wine and linen, come into Gurensey. These Bretons say they have taken the ordnance out of their ships into the castle [of Brest] and for this year will defend the land, *'but against next year they will make ships enough to defend the sea'*; also that Friar Barnardyne is looked for in Britanny with ten galleys. This I cannot believe, as I never heard he had more than one galley and a foist. The Normans are bringing their goods to Guernsey for fear of the King's landing there; and say that if the English come, and do not burn the country, Base Normandy will yield to them.

A Breton here who came with English prisoners, 7 May, from Seint Poul de Lion, says he heard from mariners who stole away from Brest *'that the ships of war were come forth fro the castle and would return to their countries, and that the hulks that were at Brest said that they would go homeward and convey the Admiral to Hownflew, where he intended to lay up his ship for this year.'*

He says the French could not be victualled to come forth in two months and that *'ships of Brytainge that be at home be hauled up into creeks and digged in pits not thinking to come to the sea this year.'* The Council should debate these things, for if the French navy have dispersed from Brest the *'enterprise pretended there'* should be of small profit. I have sent three good barks along the coast of Britanny either to bring me a fisherman who can tell the truth of the premises or else to learn from Weston, at Guernsey if any men of war have gone towards Normandy.

Commendations to the King and Queen, his father and other friends. Regrets his long abode here, but cannot make ships sail against wind. Plymouth, 20 May, *'warping with much pain fro Cat Water to the Sownde.'*

To Master Almoner with the King's grace; delivered at 3 at afternoon. [CSP I–II, 1907, pp. 867–8; Knighton and Loades 2002, text 26]

79. *20 May 1513*
Venice. Sanuto. 20 May, 1513: The Papal ambassador, on 20 May, showed a letter from Florence, of the 15th, announcing that, by letters from Blois, of the 3rd, the French and English fleets had fought, and the latter were worsted and lost a man of high rank [ie. Sir Edward Howard]. Similar news came from Rome on the 23rd. [CSP I–II, 1911, p. 868]

80. *28 May 1513*
Thomas Lord Howard to Henry VIII. 28 May, 1513: This morning at 5 o'clock came to me Sabyn, whom I sent with two other ships to the Brytaynge coast (where they have taken 13 sail laden with salt and brought them within the Needles), saying that one whom Weston sent out of Alderney to Normandy reports that on Thursday last *'he left the Lowys, the ship of Loboyle(?) and the ship of Depe and divers other ships without Homflew in the road. And, Sir, I think it shall not be possible for them to get in these neap tides; wherefore, with God's grace, I will forth this day, so that I may be with them in the morning by day.'* The prisoners say that all the men of war *'were coming to Normandy to revictual and at Briake took their council, and so the ship of Bordeaulxs, the ship of Rochell, the ship of Rone, with 12 sails returned to Brest, and the rest went towards Normandy.'* Also that the Queen is come to Nauntes and has sent three months' wages and a ship of 80, with powder and ordnance, to Brest; and that the French King has sent Mons. de la Mote to Scotland to pay wages of 5 Scottish ships and 18 of Denmark, and with him went two ships laden with flour, by the west parts of Ireland. Scribbled in great haste, 28 May, at 6am, *'bt your humble subject and admiral, Thomas Howard.'*

'To the King's most noble Grace, and in his absence to my lords of his most honorable Council. Haste, post, on thy life.' [CSP I–II, 1936, pp. 876–7; Knighton and Loades 2002, text 27]

81. *5 June 1513*
Thomas Lord Howard to Wolsey. 5 June, 1513: Has found him so kind, he can do no less than write to him from time to time, as never poor gentleman was in greater fear to take rebuke than he. His late brother was exposed to calumny, *'many men putting fear what he durst do, which opinions the day of his death he well proved untrue.'* Before the King, it was debated whether he should burn the ships at Brest Castle or destroy the haven there by sinking ships; and the King bade him spare not to enter the great water of Brest. Since his departure the Lords Winchester and Lisle have, in the King's name, countermanded the order. Thinks the French will not come abroad unless they are joined by the Scots and Danes. If they will not, the army had better be discharged. The Spaniards here would fain be home, since they heard of the

truce. Begs his friendly advice from time to time. Hampton, 5 June. *'To Mr. Almoner, with the King's grace.'* [CSP I–II, 1965, pp. 891–2; Spont 1897, 167–70; Knighton and Loades 2002, text 28]

82. *6 June 1513*

[Wolsey] to Thomas Lord Howard. 6 June, 1513: My lord Admiral. As the Council are now writing, and his hands are full, forbears writing for the present. Is to take such habiliments for war as were appointed for Lord Lisle, leaving the rest with Ric. Palshyde, to whom Wolsey has written to deliver Howard all the bows he has. It is not possible to convey anchors or cables by land. Has shipped them by four hoys four days ago. Begs he will be sparing of the victuals. Written at my poor house at Bridewell, the 6th day of June. [CSP I–II, 1969, p. 892]

83. *6 June 1513*

Thomas Lord Howard to Wolsey. 6 June, 1513: This morning at 8 o'clock, Calthorp and Harper, whom I sent to the Normandy coast for tidings, brought me the master of a fisherman (of seven men) whom they had taken, who says that, 15 or 16 days past, 18 ships came out of Brytaynge to Homflew and are laid up under the town, and the mariners and soldiers gone home *'saying they will no more go to the sea this year without the Scots and Danes come, whom they look daily for.'* He says they make no preparation for revictualling, save that Hob a Barton has men mustered for his new ship and a bark that shall go with her to the north parts; also that Normandy was in great fear of an English landing and that all *'would gladly yield themself English so that their country were not robbed nor 'brenned.' The French King had so pilled them, with more larger 'tayles' by the third part than ever he had done, that they would gladly be English and to be out of his thraldom; saying that, and the war continue one year, Normandie shall be utterly destroyed.'* Wisman, who was with Calthrop and Harper, has brought a hulk which long ago, coming with wines from Bordeaulx, was carried to Dieppe, because the master was an Englishman long resident in Flanders, but is now suffered to depart unladen. The master confirms what the Frenchman says, save that he says Hab a Barton is already departed northward with 12 small ships to seek his profit. *'I pray God he meet not with the Iceland fleet.'* The Englishman says also that one of the ships from Britanny, of more than 200, *'fell on a leak and was brought to Herflew, and bring (sic) her on ground 'waltred' on the one side and is perished.'*

The premises heard, I took horse and rode hither to tell my lord of Winchester and Lord Lizle, and will forthwith return to the ships. I look hourly for news from Brytayne, where I have three ships. Cannot yet certify the time of my departure, for *'there is slow lading of beer at Portismouth'*, but tomorrow I take musters and will make all haste *'to Brytaynge ward.'* Winchester, 6 June, 1pm. *'Sir, as yet I hear no word of anchors nor cables fro you.'* To Master Almoner with the King's Grace. [CSP I–II, 1971, p. 893; Knighton and Loades 2002, text 29]

84. *8 June 1513*

Thomas Lord Howard to the Council. 8 June, 1513: On 7 June *'I received your letters at midnight of the 6th day.'* As to your first article, answering what I wrote touching my return to Brest; no man can be more joyful than I to go thither, for I see not how otherwise I may do service unless the Scots and Danes come. I will do my best to save the King's navy, *'but without some adventure none exploit of war will be achieved.'* Has enquired how so great a number of bows and arrows have been wasted and finds that *'the greatest number were 'wechyn' bows of whom few would abide the bending.'* Cannot undo the past, but will henceforth prevent waste. Foists were assuredly wasted, but not since his coming. As to discharging unnecessary victuallers, Winchester and Lord Lizle can show that of 140 he has taken under 30 and would not have taken more than 14 save only to bring back the empty foists. Began yesterday to take musters and hopes to finish by noon tomorrow. Fears that many are gone without licence. Lord Ferres, whose men mustered 311, is sure that 100 are wanting and has arrested two who were going away. If it be proved that they *'were departed'* they shall be hanged tomorrow. He says that Hereford gaol is full of his men who have run away. The King should command some of them to be executed, and others to be brought hither against my return, to be executed here. Lading of beer alone delays his departure; for there are but two cranes and the crayers can only come in and out to them at full sea. In consultation with Wm. Pawne and Palshide, suggests the use of lighters as in the Thames. Two or three of the greatest in Thames should be towed hither by crayers, 'and with making them higher with a strake of board we doubt not they shall come safe hither.' The brewhouses here are the goodliest he has ever saw, and already brew 100 tuns a day. As there is no place to store it but the streets, where hot weather would destroy it, he has commanded Wm. Pawne to have great trenches digged and covered with boards, turf and sedges. The beer which came for Lord Lisle has been mostly sent back to London; for Heron's servants, who deliver it, say that the brewers are bound to take back *'unable stuff.'* I know not what the King pays, but *'much of it is as small as penny ale and as sour as a crab. I doubt not your Lordships will see the brewers punished.'* ... Portismouth, 8 June. Delivered at 11 am., *'haste, post, haste, haste.'* [CSP I–II, 1978, pp. 896–7; Knighton and Loades 2002, text 30]

85. *13 June, 1513. Qwar Abbey, near Fishbourne, NE Isle of Wight*

Letter from Thomas, Lord Howard to Fox, Surrey and Wolsey, dated 14 June, 1513:

To-day, at 3p.m., I received yours of 12 June, touching the wages of the ships in the Narrow Seas; but the *Caryke of Savona*, the *Kateryn Forteleza* and the *Mary George* were already gone out of sight toward the Narrow Seas, with many small men carrying *'the King's mowntes of the New Forest'* and other necessaries sent from Hampton or going to *'convey the King's army over,'* and they will be in the Downs ere you receive this letter. Upon what you write of the ship of Denmark in Flanders and the galleys in Dieppe, I have sent three small ships after the said carricks to carry them a letter of warning and help them against the galleys, from which they would be in danger if a calm came. We are here strong enough to encounter the whole fleet of France, and, had the wind served, had been gone towards Brest ere now. Scribbled in the *Mary Rose* before Qwar Abbey, *'abiding to know the King's pleasure.'* Addressed: To my lord of Wynchester, my lord Treasurer and Master Almoner; delivered at Portismouth at 4 at afternoon the 13 day of Juny. [CSP I–II, 1992, p. 900; Knighton and Loades 2002, text 31]

86. *18 June, 1513*
Naval payments, warrant by Thomas, Lord Howard: [3] 18 June (268) *Mary Roose*, for oars. [CSP I–II, 2305, pp. 1032–4; Knighton and Loades 2002, text 32]

87. *4 July – 28 Aug. 1513*
Naval payments. *'Costs and charges of vittelers of the Kinges armye by see'* paid by Sir Thomas Wyndam, treasurer of the said army. For fighting ships, these give names and tonnage of the ships, names of the captains and masters, number of soldiers, mariners, dead shares and gunners, the rate of pay of each man and the payments made under each heading, the entries being signed in the margin by the captains or their servants. For the month 4 to 31 July, 5 Hen. VIII (1513), these include the *Mary Rose*, 600t., Thomas lord Howard, admiral of England, Edward Bray, captain of the ship, 402. Also, the *'bark to the Mary Rose'*, 80t., Wm. Davison master, 66. For the month 1 to 28 August, 1513, there are similar accounts which include the *Mary Rose*. [CSP I–II, 2304, 3; pp. 1029–30]

88. *12 July, 1513*
Naval payments 1513, warrants: [7] (264–5) Various costs relating to Howard's order dated *'in the Mary Rose'*, 12 July. [CSP I–II, 2305, pp. 1032–4; Knighton and Loades 2002, text 34]

89. *13 July, 1513. Plymouth*
War expenses, 1513: For the month beginning 13 July, 5 Hen. VIII. (1513), payment to Rob. Symson, surgeon of the *Mary Roose*, dated Plymouth, 20 June, 5 Hen. VIII., for his pay from 14 March 5 Hen. VIII [CSP I–II, 3614, no. 179, p. 1520; Knighton and Loades 2002, text 35]

90. *7 Nov. 1513*
Accounts of John Hopton for expenses of the Navy, 1514: Expenses, by the King's command made *'upon all his ships within his havens and rivers of Temmys, Portsmowthe, Hambl Rysse and elsewhere within this realm of England'* and paid by John Hopton, clerk controller of the King's ships, beginning 7 Nov. 5 Hen. VIII. (1513), on the King's ships, including the Mary Rosse. [CSP I–II, 3318, p. 1396]

91. *1513*
Naval payments 1513, warrants, addressed by the Lord Admiral to Sir Thomas Wyndham, as treasurer of the army by sea, for payment by pursers and others for incidental expenses. The undated 1513 *Mary Rose* entries include the following:

Warrants by Sir Edward Howard –
[1] (322). Master of the *Mary Roose*, for dead shares *'which John Dancy left unpaid for the first month'*.
Warrants by Thomas, Lord Howard –
[5] (316) *Mary Rose*.
Warrants by the Earl of Surrey –
[8] (172) John Brerely, purser of the *Mary Rose*, 29s. 10d.
[9] (238) Andrew Fysche, one of the gunners of the *Mare Roose* *'to heal him of his hurts'*, 13s. 4d.
[CSP I–II, 2305, pp. 1032–4; Knighton and Loades 2002, text 36]

92. *1513*
Naval expenses 1513: Payments as well as wages for divers ships of war of the King's army royal, include *The Mary Rose*, Thomas Pert master; 101 mariners; 6 gunners; 27.5 deadshares allowed to the master and mariners, at 5s. a deadshare; – total, £34. 2s. 2d. [CSP I–II, 2478, p. 1092]

93. *1513*
Repairs to the kitchen probably of the *Sovereign* (but the *Mary Rose* has been suggested by Friel), between 1512 and 1513. The cumbersome and repetitive language of the account, typical of the period, gives an idea of laborious work of Tudor administrators. They also had the problem of addition and subtraction using Roman numerals. Arabic numerals were known in England at this time, but their use was not widespread. The lead and solder were probably used to repair the lead lip around the cooking cauldrons. The oven found in the wreck of the *Mary Rose* had two cauldrons and was built with bricks:
'Stuff [materials] and mending of the kitchen [margin]
Also the said John Hopton hath paid in likewise to Robard Adams, plumber, for 354 lb [161 kg of] lead at 6s the hundredweight – 21s 3d; in solder at 5d the pound, for 92 lb [42 kg] – 38s 4d. So by the said John Hopton provided and bought, occupied (used), employed and annexed and repairing of the furnace (oven) in the said ship in time of this account all amounting to – 59s 7d.
Also paid in likewise unto (two) plumbers in repairing of the said furnace by the space of 8 days at 6d the day – in time of this account in all amounting to – 8s.
Purchase of stuff [margin]
Brick [margin]
Also the said John Hopton hath paid for brick for the said furnace at 6d the hundred for 1000 of them. 5s. So paid and occupied, employed and annexed to the use and behove of the said ship in time of this account. In all amounting to – 5s.

Lime & sand [margin]
Also paid in lime for the said furnace for one hundred (weight?), 6s 8d; for 2 loads of sand, price the load 6d., for the 2 loads, 12d. So paid and occupied about the furnace for the use and behove of the said ship within the time of this account, in all amounting – 7s. 8d.

Masons' wages [margin]

Also paid in likewise to Steven Wastell, Bricklayer, for 8x9 days at 8d the day – 6s. His servant (assistant) at 6d the day by 9 working days, 10s. 6d., and for 2 labourers that laboured with the said bricklayers at 4d the day by 8 working days, either of them 5s. 4d. – 15s. 10d.' [PRO-XC2495 CL. E36/12. p. 103–4]

1514

94. *1514. Newcastle*
The Earl of Surrey, Thomas Lord Howard, Admiral of England [see CSP 2651, p. 1157], (? Jan/Feb) 1514: *'Money that I, Thomas earl of Surrey, Admiral of England, doth ask allowance of for such charges as I and my company were at from the time we landed at New Castell into the time we took the sea again, by space of 16 days.'* Included amongst the 15 ships, giving under the ships, the names and wages of their captains and the numbers and wages of the soldiers and mariners, is the *Mary Rose*, Edw. Bray, captain (here were also twelve gunners of Dansk, taken out of a hulk to serve for the journey by land, whose wages, with reward to seven of them who were hurt, amounted to £13. 6s. 8d.). The wages of the foresaid captains, being at Hull for four days *'afore they landed at Newcastell toward the Scottish field'*, each taking 4s. a day, 12l. [CSP I–II, 2652, p. 1158; Knighton and Loades 2002, text 37]

95. *1514*
The Navy: *'The names of the shi[ps], captains, mariners, soldiers and gunners, which be appointed to be in the King's army by the sea this next year.'* Showing the name of each ship, its *'portage'*, the name of the captain and the number of soldiers, mariners and gunners, and finally the total number of the crew: Included is the *Mary Rose*, 600t., Sir Henry Shernburne, 350. [CSP I–II, 2686, p. 1179]

96. *1514*
Ordnance for the Navy, 1514: *'Ordnances particularly set out needful for furnishing the army royal pretended to be set to the sea in'* 5 Hen. VIII (ie. 22 April 1513–21 April 1514): viz – the bows, arrows, etc. required for each ship, including the *Marie Roose*. [CSP I–II, 2687, p. 1180]

97. *2 March 1514*
The Navy, 1514: Three warrants on the same paper by Sir T. Wyndham to Mr. Dauncey to pay John Brown, master of the *Mary Rose*, John Ysham, captain of the *Christopher Davy*, and John Parryn, master of the *Barbara*, for wages of certain men from 2 March. Signed by T. Wyndham. [CSP I–II, 2764, p. 1203]

98. *4 March 1514*
The Navy, 1514: Musters were taken on 4 March 5 Hen. VIII (1514) of various warships, including the *Mary Roose*. [CSP I–II, 2702, p. 1184]

99. *25 April, 1514*
Expenses of the war, 25 April, 1514: *'Paymentis of mony for the Kingis Riall Armye by see for oon moneth bygynnyng the xxv daye of Apryll anno vjto R. Henr. viij vi, which shall eende the xxij daye of Maye then next after, the first and the last dayes includyd, accomptyng xxviij dayes for the moneth.'* Included are many ships, with *The Mary Rose*, Sir Henry Sherburn, captain ('nil' wages); 185 soldiers, 200 mariners, 20 gunners. Total, £110. 3s. 4d. [CSP I–II, 2842, p. 1235]

100. *23 April, 1514*
The Navy, exchequer accounts: Accounts of victuals (ie. beer) delivered (apparently by Rich. Palshid) to the Navy showing in the case of each ship the name of the purser, the number of men and the number of tuns of beer: *'Beer delivered to the King's army by sea for six weeks'* beginning 23 April, 6 Hen. VIII (1514), including to John Brereley, Mary Roose, 350m. [CSP I–II, 3148, p. 1343]

101. *2 May 1514. Harwich, Thames (Blackwall), Portsmouth, Dover*
John Wodlas, 2 May, 1514: Petition to the Council by John Wodlas, of Harwich, for his reasonable expenses in the following service. He conveyed the *Maryrose* over *'a danger in the sea called the Nase,'* and, upon countermand, brought her back to Harwich. Then, within five days, he was commanded to convey her through *'a place in the sea called the Slade,'* to meet the King coming from Calais, and so did, and then conveyed her out of the Downed, through the Blake Depes, into Tamys. He *'now last'* brought the *Mary Rose* from Blake Wale to Portesmouth. Other work followed for the ship *Libbeke*. This petition is subscribed with an order, in Wolsey's hand, to Mr. Dawnce to pay Woodeles, 20 mks. Signed: T. Lincoln. It ends with Wodlass's receipt for 20 mks. from Sir John Daunce on 2 May, 6 Hen. VIII (1514). [CSP I–II, 2865, p. 1248; Knighton and Loades 2002, text 38]

102. *23 May–19 June, 1514*
The Navy, 23 May, 1514: *'Costs and charges of the King's ships in his army royal by sea'* for the month, beginning 23 May, which *'shall end'* 19 June next. Giving, under ships, the names and wages of the captains (who sign the entries) followed by the numbers and wages of soldiers, mariners, and gunners, the number and cost of deadshares and amount of *'rewards for gunners'*; and totals. Included is the *Mary Roose*, Sir Harry Sharborne. [CSP I–II, 2938, p. 1268–9]

103. *27 May 1514. Dover*
Thomas Earl of Surrey to the [Privy Council], 27 May, 1514: Came yesterday to Sandwich, hoping to have found the ships in the Downs, but they were not there, and by 7 o'clock he came to Dover. The vice-admiral had sent over Sir Henry Sherbourne and Sir Stephen Bole, with ten sail of small men, and the row barge, galleys, and others, well manned, in as good order, to his mind, as possible. The wind was N.N.E.; the haze great. With the flood they *'drew over with Scalis Clyves,'* and then with the ebb came with a good *'blower'* to St.

John's Road, and sent forward Sir Stephen Boole, Thomas Vaughan, and three others. '*Prior John*' rode at the point of St. John's Road, towards Calais, five miles from Boleyne. At sight of these five ships the French fled with sails and oars, and got beyond reach. '*The wind at midnight forced them to return; and my cousin Wyndam in like* [manner with] *20 sails with him; and at this hour I see him with them … coming again unto us.*' Has appointed Sir Henry Sherborne with 10 sail, and Wiseman and Wallop with other 10 sail, if wind come before midnight, Sir Henry to get between Boulogne and the galleys and Wiseman to come along the shore from Calais. If he had 2,000 or 3,000 soldiers, such as are now at Calais, shipped in the haven there to be landed with other 3,000 within two miles of Boulogne the galleys might be taken. Has ordered Sir Thomas West to stay at Sandwich till the King's further pleasure. Has sent two good ships to Seland to waft the fleet, and appoint nine to go northwards when the wind serves. Written in the *M[ary Rose]* in Dover Road, 27 May, at 7 at night. [CSP I–II, 2946, pp. 1274–5; Spont 1897, 202–5; Knighton and Loades 2002, text 39]

104. *1514, probably about 27 May. Dover*
Surrey to Norfolk, Fox and Wolsey, 1514: Wrote yesterday how he had appointed an enterprise against the galleys. This morning the wind came N.W., so that ships dare not venture within St. John's Road; but with next fair wind the writer will go over in the King's Less Bark with a company of small ships and if the galleys remain outside the bulwark he trusts '*to displease them without great loss. And if they go within the bulwark as far as I can understand it is as dangerous as it were to enter within Risbanke Tower; which is not to be adventured with none but with them that will cast themself away wilfully.*' As it does not seem honourable for all the army to remain here for fear of the galleys, and they must shortly go to the Wight for victualling, he suggests that the ships named in the enclosed bill should, under Sir Wistan Browne, defend the passage and encounter the galleys while the rest of the army draws '*westward to do the most annoyance to the Frenchmen they can.*' (Here the first leaf ends with the note that the captains have seen '*this side of the leaf*' and desired him so to write, '*but none is privy to the other side.*')

If '*this Frenchman* [footnote: 'apparently the General of Normandy, Thomas Boyer'] *that now is come*' should conclude a peace when the great ships have gone westward the wind might come so that it should cost £2,000 more to bring them into Tamys. Doubtless as you see cause you will '*either shortly stop or else haste forward as well the King's great ship, with her victuals, as also such victuals as John Dawtre shall prepare more for this army.*' If the matter of peace will be concluded within a fortnight it were better to keep the great ships here and send small ships westward; for the ships here are victualled for a fortnight and more, '*and those that go northward for a month.*' Desires answer in the premises '*by post,*' so that if he is to tarry here he may send for more servants, having but 18, '*which is too few.*' Scribbled in the *Mary Rose* in Dover Road. PS: '*Yesterday, in the calm, Preer John with his galleys and foists chased a small balinger of ours but he would never come two mile*

fro the shore.' Addressed: To my lords of Norfolk, Wynchester and Lincoln. End: My lord Admiral's letters. [CSP I–II, 2959, p. 1277–8; Knighton and Loades 2002, text 40]

105. *14 June, 1514. Portland, Cherbourg*
Surrey to the Council, 14 June, 1514: Landed yesterday in Normandy three miles west of Cherbourg, and burned [four] miles west, three miles east, and more than [two] inland as far as any house might be seen for great woods, leaving nothing unburnt but abbeys and churches. Burnt many gentlemen's country houses, '*well builded and stuffed with hangings and be … of silk, of which neither they nor our men have little pr*[ofit]*, for all or the more part was burnt.*' Re-embarked without the loss of a man. The night before I landed, to requite the burning of Preer John, I sent Walope, Gonstone, Sabyan, and 700 men to land thirty miles west of me. They have not yet returned, and were so far on our lee that they cannot be here till night, but they burnt the country so sore that we lost sight of the high hills of the Hag. Thinks the King should write a letter of thanks to the Vice-admiral and captains. Never saw men of better will to serve. Sends his servant Edw. Bray for their further information. Thinks Dover and Hastings should be warned for fortify themselves; for if Preer John intend any new business, he will meddle with one of those places, and could [burn] either without danger. When the wind is favourable, I shall send six more ships to those parts to encounter him. In the *Mary Rose*, before Portland. 14 June. [CSP I–II, 3001, p. 1295; Knighton and Loades 2002, text 41]

106. *27 July, 1514. River Thames*
Survey of the Navy: (6). Inventory of '*stuff, tackle, apparel, ordnance, artillery and habiliments of war*' in the King's ships 27 July, 6 Hen. VIII (1514), viewed by Sir Henry Wyat, Sir Andrew Wyndsore, George Dalyson and Thomas Tamworth, commissioners, and delivered by indentures, the tackle in every case to John Hopton and the ordnance and artillery as follows: every mast, pulley, yard, stay, etc., and among the ordnance all guns, pikes, shot, etc., are entered under each ship's name – including the *Mary Roose* (John Browne, master, and John Bryarley, purser). Knighton and Loades (2002, 74) date this document to 9 August 1514 (see [107] below) [CSP I–II, 3137, pp. 1338–40; Knighton and Loades 2002, text 43]

Friel has transcribed (6) as follows:
Inventory of the Mary Rose, taken in the River Thames, 27 July 1514:
p. 55:
'*The King's Ship called the Mary Rose*
Stuff (materials), *tackle and apparel delivered to John Hopton by indenture as aforesaid, that is to say –* [margin]

Main masts – 1
Main yards – 1
Main sails, a course (main part of sail) *and 2 bonnets – 1*
Tacks –2

Sheets – 2
Bowlines – 2
Parrals – 1
Trusses – 1
Dryngs – 2
Braces – 2
Tyes – 1 pair
Halyards to the same – 1
Lifts –2
Jeers – 1
Stays – 1
Shyrwyns – 1
Shrouds – 26
Chains of iron to the same – 26
Swifting tackles – 8
Polankers – 8
Garlands – 3
The main top – 1
The top mast – 1
Yards to the same – 1
Top sails – 1
Bowlines – 2
Sheets – 2
Lifts – 2
Braces – 2
Tyes – 1
Halyards to the same – 1
Stays – 1
Shrouds – 10

p. 56
Yet the Mary Rose
Yet stuff and tackle delivered to John Hopton by indenture as
aforesaid, that is to say – [margin]
Trusses – 1
The Top Galant
Masts to the same – 1
Sails – 1
Yards to the same – 1
Parrals – 1
Bowlines – 2
Sheets – 2
Braces – 2
Lifts – 2
Stays – 1
Shrouds – 6
Foremasts – 1
Yards to the same – 1
Parrals – 1
Sails, a course and 2 bonnets – 1
Tacks – 2
Sheets – 2
Bowlines – 2
Lifts – 2
Braces – 2
Lifts – 2
Trusses – 2
Shrouds – 16
Chains of iron with bolts, to the same – 16

Pulleys – 4
Stays – 1
Tyes – 2
Halyards – 1
Fore tops – 1
Topmasts – 1
Sail yards – 1
Sails – 1

p.57
Yet the Mary Rose
Yet Stuff and Tackle, etc. [margin]
Bowlines – 2
Sheets – 2
Lifts – 2
Braces – 2
Tyes – 1
Halyards to the same – 1
Stays – 1
Parrals – 1
Bowsprit – 1
Yards – 1
Spritsails – 1
Bonnets to the same – 1
Truss – 1
Lifts – 1
The main mizzenmast – 1
Yards to the same – 1
Parrals – 1
Sails – 1
Tyes – 1
Halyards to the same – 1
Truss – 1
Sheets – 1
Braces – 2
Lifts 1
Stays – 1
Shrouds – 12
Iron chains with bolts, to the same – 12
The main mizzen top – 1
Top mast – 1
Sailyards – 1
Parrals – 1
Sails – 1

p. 58
Yet the Mary Rose
Stuff and Tackle, etc. [margin]
Truss – 1
Lift – 1
Shrouds – 8
Bonaventure mast – 1
Yards to the same – 1
Parral – 1
Sails – 2 (sic)
Tyes – 1
Halyards – 1
Truss – 1
Sheets – 1

Stays – 1
Shrouds – 8
Brass sheaves to the halyards of the bonaventure mast – 4
Brass sheaves to the main mizzenmast – 4
Brass sheaves to the tackles over starboard (side) – 4
Brass sheaves for the garnets of the same – 1
Brass sheaves in the tackles of the ladboard (port) side – 13
Brass sheaves in the garnets of the same – 4
Brass sheaves for the lift pulleys – 3
Brass sheaves for the topsail sheets – 1
Brass sheaves in the sheets knights – 2
Brass sheaves in the ramhead – 1
Brass sheaves in the lifts – 1
Brass sheaves for the topsail sheets – 1
Brass sheaves in the jeers – 3
Brass sheaves in the halyards of the foremast – 4
Brass sheaves in the tackles over both sides – 4
Brass sheaves in the sheets – 2
Brass sheaves in the tye of the (bow)sprit – 1

p. 59
Yet the Mary Rose
Yet stuff and tackles, etc. [margin]
Brass sheaves for the main bowlines – 2
Brass sheaves in the davits of the forecastle – 2
Brass sheaves in the davits of the destrells – 1
Brass sheaves in the cats – 1
Iron sheaves in the cats – 1
Iron sheaves in the davits – 1
Spare brass sheaves, great and small – 3
Compasses – 3
Running glasses (hourglasses) – 2
Sounding leads – 2
Sounding lines – 1

Anchors called {*Shet anchors – 1* }
{*Bowers – 2* }
{*Destrells – 2* } *7*
{*Caggers – 1* }
{*a new sheet anchor – 1* }

Cables { { {*for the sheet anchors – 2* } }
{ *New* {*for the starboard bowers – 2* } }
{ {*for the ladboard (port bowers) – 2* } } *15*
{ }
{ {*and worn – 3* }
{ *Old* {*junks – 4* }
{ {*lagging (cagging?) cables – 2* } }

Cat–hooks – 2
Fish–hooks – 2
Luff–hooks – 2
Leech–hooks – 2
Warping hawsers – 6
The Boat – 1
Masts to the same – 1
Sails to the same – 1
Oars to the same – 20
The cock (–boat) with mast, sail and 6 oars – 1

p. 60
Yet the Mary Rose

Ordnance, artillery & habillaments (implements) *of war left in the said ship in the charge and custody of John Browne master, & John Bryarley purser, of the same, by indenture as is foresaid, that is to say –* [margin]
Great curtows of brass – 5
Murderers of brass – 2
Chambers to the same – 3
Falcons of brass – 2
Falconets of brass – 3
Great murderers of iron – 1
Chambers to the same – 1
Murderers of iron of another sort – 2
Chambers to the same 4
Cast pieces of iron – 2
Chambers to the same – 4
Murderers of iron of another sort – 1
Chambers to the same – 2
Slings of iron called demi–slings – 2
Chambers to the same – 4
Stone guns – 26
Top guns – 3
Chambers to the same – 75
Serpentines of iron – 28
Chambers to the same – 107
Forelocks for stone–guns, top–guns and serpentines – 94
Myches (swivels) to the same – 80
Stone shot, great and small – 500
A little gun of brass without (a) chamber – 1
Hammers for guns – 13
Picks for stone – 22
Heads for arrows of wildfire – 8
Hocks for arrows of wildfire – 29
Strings – 600
Bags of leather – 9
Parchment skins – 20
Lead – 2.25 sows and certain cast (lead)
Charging ladles of copper – 2

p. 61
Yet the Mary Rose
Yet stuff and tackle, etc. – [margin]
Ladles of iron for casting pellets – 2
Bolts of iron – 17
Streamers (flags) for the top(s) – 3
Gilded flags – 18
Small flags – 28
Top–armours – 3
Standard staffs for flags (flagstaffs) – 15
Trivets of iron – 3
Spits of iron – 1
Cob–irons – 1
Grid–irons – 1
Frying–pans – 1
Tar kettles – 1
Pitch–kettles – 1
Kettles for the cook–room (kitchen) – 1
Cauldrons in (the) furnace, with their gear – 2
Hooks for hanging kettles – 1
Iron cressets – 1

Shovels – 5
Scoops – 5
Leather buckets – 3
Baskets – 4
Lime–pots – 1
Bells – 1
Bows – 20
Arrows – 20
Bills (hand–weapons) – 20

p. 62
Yet the Mary Rose
Artillery and habillaments for the war delivered to John Millet
& Thomas Elderton by bill signed by with the hands of the
foresaid commissioners, that is to say – [margin]
Hacbusshes (muskets) – 91
Iron shot of diverse sorts – 457
Iron shot with cross–bars – 120
Lead pellets, great and small – 1000
Pellets for hacbusshes – 900
Iron dice (for shot) – 1500
Arrows of wildfire (incendiaries) – 74
Balls of wildfire – 2
Salets (helmets) – 180
Breast (-plates) – 206
Back (-plates) – 206
Gorgets (armoured neck-pieces) – 146
Splints (leg-armour) – 172 pairs
Gun-powder – 21.5 barrels
Gunpowder cartridges – 1 chest–full
Charging-ladles for falcons and curtows – 7
Sponges to the same – 6
Stamps – 3
Iron crow(-bars) – 14
Bows of yew – 123
Chests to the same – 2
Arrows – 504 sheaves
Chests to the same – 11
Bills – 218
Stakes for the field (pointed wooden stakes) – 149
Morris pikes – 159'

107. *9 August, 1514*
Survey of the Navy: (11). Indenture, 9 August, 1514, witnessing delivery to John Hopton by Sir Henry Wiatt, Sir Andrew Wyndesore, Sir Thomas Wyndam, George Dalison and Th. Tamworth, commissioners to view the stuff remaining in the King's ship the Mary Rose. [CSP I–II, 3137, pp. 1338–40]

There is uncertainty about the year for an extract of what is probably this document is published under the date 9 August, 1515 (D. Hobbs, 'Royal ships and their flags in the late fifteenth and early sixteenth centuries', *The Mariner's Mirror* 80.4, Nov. 1994, 388–94), and shows that the *Mary Rose* carried the following flags: *'a banner of St. Katherine in metall; 5 banners of the arms of Boulonge in metall; 4 banners of the arms of England and Castile in metall; 4 banners of the Rose and Pomegranite in metall; One of St. Peter in metall; 2 of the Castell in metall; 1 streamer of St. George in colour; 1 streamer of*

the red lyon in colour; 1 streamer of the Castell in colour'. The *Mary Rose* carried 18 banner staves [PRO SPD Henry VIII 230/229]

108. 1514. Blackwall
Survey of the Navy, 1514:
(5). Inventories of ordnance and tackle in warships, including the *Mary Rose* (ordnance).
(15). A brief abstract and calendar concerning the viewing of the King's ships taken by Sir Henry Wyat, Sir Andrew Windsor and others, at Erith 7 ships, Woolwich 3 ships, at the Blackwall where there are the warships *The Mary Rose, The Peter Pome Granade* and *The Great Elizabeth*, and at Deptford 1 ship. [CSP I–II, 3137, pp. 1338–1340]

IN ORDINARY, 1515–1520.

REPAIRS 1517–1518

1515
(No references)

1516
(No references)

1517

109. *9 June 1517*
Document exhibited at the British Library 1982–83 where it was described as follows: In this agreement, dated 9 June 1517, John Hopton, Comptroller of the King's Ships, undertook for the sum of 600 marks to *'make and cast a pond'* in a meadow at Deptford, co. Kent), large enough to float the *Great Galley*, the *Mary Rose*, the *Peter Pomegranate*, the *Great Barke* and the *Lesser Barke*. Building was also to include: *'a good hable and suffycient hed for the same ponde and also certeyn hable Slewsis thurgh the whiche the watir may have renre and course into the foresaid ponde as well at Spryng tydes as at nepetydes.'* [Brit. Lib: Additional Charter 6289; Knighton and Loades 2002, text 44]

110. *8 October 1517–28 December, 1521. Thames*
Wages paid by John Hopton to the keepers of ships now in the Thames, from 8 Oct. 9 Hen VIII. (1517) to 23 March 12 Hen VIII (1521). These include The *Mary Rosse*, Wm. Mewe and 4 men. Note that Thos Sperte is now master of the *Herry Grace Diew*, but the ship is in ordinary [CSP III–II, 1911, dated 28 Dec. 1521, p. 817]

1518

111. *August 1518*
The *Kings Book of Payments*, under August 1518: John Hopton, for repairing and caulking the great galley, the *Mary Rose* etc., £100 [CSP II–II, p. 1479]

112. *26 Nov. 1518*

Navy Accounts, 26 Nov., 1518: Payments by John Hopton, clk., comptroller of the King's ships, including for caulking (Oct. 9 Hen. VIII) several warships including *The Mary Rosse*, £15. 3s. 7.5d. The caulking of 6 ships, including the *Mary Rose*, two row barges and two galleys occurred between 5 Aug and 26 Nov. 1518 [CSP II–II, 4606, p. 1407]

1519

(No references)

MEETING THE KING OF FRANCE 1520

1520

113. *June 1520*

Field of the Cloth of Gold, 1520: A memorial of things necessary for the transporting of the King for the interview between him, the French king, their queens, queen Mary dowager of France, and the mother of the French king. These extensive preparations include the *Mary Rose*, the King's *Greate Barke*, the *Litle Barke*, and two other small ships are to scour the seas from time to time during the passage of the King; their rigging and victualling are committed to Sir Wm. Fitzwilliam, Sir Wistan Browne and John Hopton, clerk to the King's ships. Sir John Daunce to issue money for the purpose. [CSP III–I, 704, p. 239]

114. *2 Oct. 1520*

Shipping, 2 Oct., 1520: Amongst very many expenses, which include a great variety of fittings in the King's ships very relevant to the *Mary Rose*, is : to 7 men who helped to '*plumpe*' the *Mary Rose* for a day and night, 2s. 8d. [CSP III–I, 1009, p. 372; Knighton and Loades 2002, text 45]

IN ORDINARY 1520–1522

1521

(No references)

SECOND FRENCH WAR, 1522

1522

115. *4 June, 1522: Downs*

Fitzwilliam to Henry VIII, 4 June, 1522: On Friday last, the day the King left Dover, the wind changed to W.S.W., and blew so hard that they were obliged to go into the Downs and stay there all Saturday and Sunday. On Monday the wind changed to W. by N. Started for Hampton, intending to have stopped at every flood, and gone on with the tide. Was obliged to put back to the Downs, as the wind went back to S.W., in which quarter it keeps still. Will go to Hampton by the next wind. The *Henry Grace Dieu* sailed as well and rather better than any ship in the fleet. She weathered them all, save the *Mary Rose*; and on a wind, there would be a '*hard chose*' between them. The galley was next them, but if she '*may vyere the shit, she will go from us all.*' All yesterday the wind blew '*sore and strainably;*' but the *Henry* rode as still and gently at anchor as the best ship in the fleet. Consulted Brygandenne, Gonson and the wisest masters in the fleet, about laying her up for the winter. All agreed the Cambre was not suitable, but, to make certain, sent John Browne, master of the *Mary Roose*, and John Clogge, of the *Peter Pondegarnet*, who sounded it with John Fletcher and John Swanne, two of the wisest masters in Rye, but could find no place fit for her. All say that Portsmouth or Dartmouth are the fittest places, and that it would be dangerous to bring her into the Thames again. In the Downs, Wednesday, 4 June. [CSP III–II, 2302, p. 975; Knighton and Loades 2002, text 47]

116. *21 June, 1522. Isle of Wight*

Earl of Surrey to Henry VIII, 21 June, 1522: Embarked here with the army on Thursday, at noon, and waits only for lack of wind. It still blows S.W. and W., the direction in which we ought to go. The King has been deceived about the victual. The whole complement for 5,000 men, the beer from Portsmouth, and the rest from Hampton, was promised by the last of May; and now, the 20th of June, we have with much difficulty been provided with flesh, fish and biscuit for two months, from Hampton, and we can get no more than one month's beer from Portsmouth. The Vice-admiral was promised his whole complement before today, but few of his ships are victualled for more than three weeks, some for only eight days, and most of them for a fortnight. Thirteen or fourteen crays have come to the Vice-admiral, with victual from London, and the victuallers have caused the masters to indent with them for the proportions they have received, not advertising either myself or the Vice-admiral of what is sent, nor when the rest shall come. They say they have been hindered about the beer for want of casks, but are as far behindhand with flesh, fish and biscuit as with beer; which I think comes from negligence. We cannot do what we intend unless we are better furnished, both from London and Portsmouth, and it would be a pity to spend so much without doing some great displeasure to the enemy which we see good likelihood of doing if wind and victual serve '*doubting much more of the victual than wind.*' Begs the King to send some substantial man to London to hasten it, and have it shipped in the *Christopher Davy* and other ships, and sent within the Wight in charge of Thos. Vaughan. A wise man should be sent to see about the beer at Portsmouth. Has left Wm. Symonds, with 100 men, to come in the ships from London with the victuals from Hampton, London and Portsmouth. He and Wingfield went to Portsmouth to see the ordnance and bulwarks, and consult about the fortification. None of the ordnance can be fired, the stocks being rotten, '*the welling clearly consumed,*' and much of the iron work '*failed.*' As Palshid had no money to pay the brewers, without which they refused to work, and there was no money for making bulwarks and repairing ordnance. Surrey gave him 200 mks. of his own. Thinks Pawne, or some other expert man, should be sent down to see to all matters here. James Worsley should return to the Wight, to see that watch is made for any hostile ships that beacons are made there and at Portisdowne, and the country warned to repair to Portsmouth when they are fired. Jenyns will tell the King tomorrow of the whole state of the army. In the *Mary Rose*, within the Isle of Wight, 21 June. [CSP III–II, 2337, pp. 991–2; Knighton and Loades 2002, text 48]

117. *23 June, 1522. St. Helens*

Thomas Earl of Surrey to Wolsey, 23 June 1522: While writing I am under sail off St. Elyn's, with a good wind, but not much of it. I beseech you to command the victuallers at Hampton, Portsmouth and London to send the rest of the victual after me with all speed; and to write to Christopher Coo to follow Harper's advice, and *'in no wise come within havens.'* The London victuallers will tell you for how long he is victualled. Thos. Clere has beer for one month, and other victuals for two months, at Hampton. I ask you also to write to Thos. Vaughan to convey the London victuallers into the Wight, and then to return. When in the narrow seas, he must keep more the coast of Calais than the Downs. At nights he must lie near Calais, for the French steal away that way in the night, both northward and from the north. *'Scribbled in the Mary Rose,'* 23 June. Addressed: To my lord Legate's good grace. [CSP III–II, 2341, p. 993; Knighton and Loades 2002, text 49]

118. *c. 24 June, 1522. St Helens*

Earl of Surrey to Henry VIII, (no date) 1522: Friel has transcribed part of this as follows: *'Pleaseth it your most noble grace to be advertised that at the writing hereof I was under sail going forwards, the wind being at north, which is good but it is very little wind. Most humbly beseeching your grace to cause our victuals to be sent after us as well from London, as from Southampton and Portsmouth. It were pity that we should be let (prevented from) to accomplish that we intend to attempt only for lack of victuals ...Your most humble subject, T. Surrey'.* [Thomas, Earl of Surrey, aboard the *Mary Rose* off St. Helen's, Isle of Wight, to Henry VIII, about 23 June, 1522. PRO- SP1/25; see also CSP III–II, 2342, p. 993; Knighton and Loades 2002, text 50]

119. *27 June, 1522. St Helens. Portland*

Earl of Surrey to Henry VIII, 27 June, 1522: Friel has transcribed this as follows: *'Pleaseth it your grace to be advertised that on Tuesday last we departed from St. Helen's, the wind being contrarious and with force of the ebbs stopping the floods* (tide), *be this present hour come before Portland. And so from tide to tide intend to do unto the time we may get as far as Dartmouth, where we must of force abide unto the time God will send wind to serve us to run over to the coasts of your enemies. Sir considering how little victual we have on board, contrary* (against) *the minds of the* (ship-) *masters of the Army* (fleet) *we have thus plied the tides to the intent something might be done against the enemies before our victual be spent. Most humbly beseeching your grace that the rest of our victual might be with haste sent after us ...'* [To Henry VIII, off Portland, Friday 27 June, 1522. PRO– SP1/25; see also CSP III–II, 2351, p. 995; Knighton and Loades 2002, text 51]

120. *30 June, 1522. Dartmouth*

Surrey to Henry VIII, 30 June, 1522: Last night I came to the Road. As divers of my company were in sight, and could not come on till this tide, and as we were all in want of water, I thought best to remain here today: so I, with Wingfield, Fitzwilliam and Jerningham, Hopton, Gonson, Sabyan, John Brown and others, took a boat and went to Dartmouth, to see what places we could find to lay in your great ships this winter. Never saw a goodlier haven after all our opinions. At the entry there is a blockhouse of stone, with an old castle on the same side, and another old castle on the other side, besides another blockhouse, and a chain ready to be laid. The town is not two arrows' shot thence, and the ships may lie two miles further within the haven, under John Gilbert's house, and have at least five fathom at low water. The chain that is at Portsmouth may be laid within the other chain, so that it will not be possible for any ships to enter. The only danger is, if the enemy were to land at Torbay, only two miles from the place where the ships will ride, they might cast fire into them, or some fellow in the night might steal near them, and throw wildfire into them. To avert this, you had better write to the bishop of Exeter, and the best gentlemen in Devonshire, saying you are informed they are making a blockhouse besides Briksame, within Torbay, and if they would make another at Churston, within the same bay, you would help them with ordnance and powder. I see by the gentlemen who have been aboard today, they would do it at their own cost, and, once done, no army could land there. If three or four acres of low wood, growing by the shore, were cut down, and a stone wall made, over 800 paces long, and, within the wall, great bandogs allowed to go loose at night, there would be no fear of wildfire cast by stealth. Thinks it would be well to get two or three experienced men to view the harbour and its fortifications more closely than he has been able to do ... hundred pounds would make them perfectly secure. Within four miles of where the ships are to lie, you have a park called Dertington, containing 2,000 goodly oaks, which would furnish timber for repairs. They will spend less in tackling here than at Portsmouth, by as much as all the charges of making here will amount to. If the ships are to be kept here it would [not be right] to spend much for repairs at Portsmouth, *'but whi*[le the Emperor] *should pass into Spain, to cause the Henry Grace a Dieu to* [keep him] *company thus far, and then to be brought in hither, f*[or] *I am informed there will be gathered together here, of your* [army], *within 24 hours, 9,000 or 10,000 men, for their defence ag*[ainst the French].' (What follows is in Surrey's hand) – At the closing of this letter all of the ships were under sail. If the wind hold, we shall land tomorrow on the enemy's ground. Sends with this letter Nicholas Semer, mayor of Dartmouth, a very wise man who can tell you about this haven. I have asked divers of those who were at the viewing of this haven to put their hands to this. In the *Mary Rose*, in Dartmouth Road, 30 June. Signed by Surrey, Sir. Ric. Wingfield, Hopton and Gonson. [CSP III–II, 2355, pp. 997–8; Knighton and Loades 2002, text 52]

Friel has transcribed part of this as follows: *'Pleaseth it your grace to be advertised that yesternight I came to the Road and because of diverse of my company were within sight and might not come so far forth unto this tide and also for lack of fresh water whereof we were all destituted, (I) thought (it) best to abide here this day. And so with Richard Wyngfeld, William Fitzwilliam, Sir Richard Jermyngham, Hopton, Gonson, Sabian, John Browne and diverse others took a boat and went into Dartmouth Haven to view and see what places we might find to lay in your grace's great ships this winter, and advertise to your grace as (to what) we have seen. In my life I saw never a goodlier haven ...'* [To Henry VIII, Dartmouth Road, Devon, Monday 30 June 1522]

121. *3 July, 1522. Morlaix*

The Earl of Surrey to Wolsey, 3 July, 1522: I have informed the king of the taking of Morles, and other occurrences here. I trust you have sent more victuals after us, for we need them. Many of Fitzwilliam's ships are without flesh and fish, and I have to lend him some of mine. I have only beer for twelve days. It would be a pity to leave undone what we intend to assay for want of victuals, and it is dangerous to go further without. As soon as we have a wind, we shall depart hence, and *'draw beyond the Trade,'* and we will not return as long as we have any beer, *'though in return we should drink water.'* I wish letters of thanks to be sent to the lords and gentlemen here, who have deserved it highly. *'Scribbled in the Mary Rose, within the haven of Morles.'* Thursday, 3 July. [CSP III–II, 2362, p. 1002; Knighton and Loades 2002, text 53]

(Friel): *'Pleaseth it your grace to be advertised that at this time I have advertised the king's grace of the taking of Morlaix with the circumstances of much part of that hath been done since my coming hither. Whereof I do forbear to write to your grace because I know the same shall come to your hands. I trust [before] this time your grace hath caused more victuals to be sent after us which shall be very welcome for we have need thereof. Sir William Fitzwilliam his company is now without flesh (meat) and fish in a great number of his ships, and so am fain [I have] to lend him part of mine. And all my company have beer but for 12 days ...'* [To Cardinal Wolsey, Morlaix Haven, Brittany, Tuesday 3 July, 1522. PRO-SP1/25]

122. *4 Aug., 1522*

Fitzwilliam to Wolsey, 4 August, 1522: Received today, about one o'clock, your letter dated Westminster, 3 Aug., enclosing a bill of the names of the captains and ships appointed to keep the sea. Yesterday the lord Admiral left for Calais, with a fair wind, and will probably be there tomorrow. Sends a book with names of the ships and captains whom he has appointed to keep the sea. It cannot be altered, as there are no other ships here; and those appointed have two months' victual on board, which was left from that provided for the army, and their wages are paid for a month. The ships for the North have been dispatched. Those for the west will go tomorrow, except the *Gabrell of Topsham* and the *Trinitie George*, which were to be equipped with the crews and victuals of the *Mary Roose* when she is laid up. Will send out those for the narrow seas immediately, except the *Mary Roose* and the *Grete Barke*, which cannot be ready for three days. I wish to know what I am to do, as Pointz has gone with the Admiral. If you wish to have the *Mary Rose* and the *Peter Pondegarnet* laid up to keep the sea, the *Gabrell of Topsham* and the *Trinitie George* must be discharged, or fresh victuals and money for wages provided for them. If the former ships are appointed, this will not be

needed, and no more great ships will be wanted, except the *Grete Barke*, the *Mary James*, and the *New Spanyard*, unless you hear for certain that the French king is preparing an army, when any of the ships at Portsmouth might soon be got ready.

The *Gabrell of Topsham* and the *Trinitie George* would do better service in the West Sea, as well for the return of the fishermen from the New Found Land, as for the going of the French into Scotland, than the others in the narrow sea. As to my going to Calais, will not refuse to go wherever the King commands. If he does order it, I wish to know it as soon as possible, that I may send my folks thither, and provide what I need, and that you would write to the Admiral to keep the tent appointed for me. If I go, is Gonson to be Admiral according to the book the lord Admiral brought from the King? Mr. Hert is not here, and there are only 50 gunners, but I will tell Westowe to take up as many as he can, up to 100. My lord Admiral has taken the *Maglory* with him to convey Lord Fitzwalter's folks to Calais, but she is at liberty when they are disembarked. In the *Mary Rose*, 4 Aug. Addressed: To my lord Cardinal's grace. [CSP III–II, 2419, p.1021; Knighton and Loades 2002, text 54]

123. *?1522*

Horsey relates that the fleet is needed to protect convoys for the Calais bridgehead. There are lists of stores embarked and paid for, and lists of crews. The *Great Harry* is the flagship of Sir Thomas Howard, Lord Admiral. The *Mary Rose* is the second ship of the fleet and was the flagship of the Vice-Admiral, Sir William Fitzwilliam (at 6s. 8d. per day). Also on board is the fleet treasurer, Sir William Sydney (paid 2s. per day). The Master is John Browne (paid 5s. a month). There are 126 soldiers, 244 mariners, 30 gunners, 2 'surgeons' at 23s. 4d the pair of them.

'A declaracione made by John Jenyns of all the chages of the Kynges armye roialle, nowe beyng one the see, as welle in his navye and llete roiall, beyng there in the retynue of my Lorde Admyralle [Thomas Howard, Earl of Surrey] *as in the retynue of Syr William Fitz-William, Knyghte, Vice-Admyralle, that is to wete for oone hole monethe.'* This was probably drawn up in the year 1522, and the rating &c., of the *Mary Rose* is given as follows: *The Mary Rose. vic. tonne. Sir William Fitz-William, Vice-Admyral at vi s. viii d. by the day ... ix l. vi s. viii d. Sir William Sydney, Treasurer, at ii s. by the day ... 1vi s. John Browne, Maister, for a monethe ... v s. Soldiours, cxxvi .... xxxi l. x s. Maryners, ccxliiii. ... 1xi l. Dedesharys, xxv, & di ... vi l. vii s. vi d. Gonners, xxx .... vii l. x s. Rewardes to Gonners ... 1vii s. vi d. Surgyons, ii.... xxiii s. iiii d. Somllle of menne ccccv. Of money xxii l. xvi s.* [Horsey].

This document was exhibited at the British Library in 1982–83 and was described as follows: Extract from a list of wages due to the crews of twenty-one ships on active service, fourteen of which had been appointed to *'kepe the narrow sees with the viceadmyrall'.* The list is undated but must relate to the period 1522–4.

The list is headed by the *Mary Rose*, flagship of Vice-Admiral Sir William Fitzwilliam. He receives £9. 6s. 8d. (6s. 8d. per day over a period of twenty-eight days). Sir William Sidney, his treasurer, grandfather of Sir Philip Sidney, is paid 56s. A flat rate of 5s. per month goes to the master of the ship and to each of her 126 soldiers, 244 mariners and 30 gunners. A further 5s. is allotted to each of the 25.5 deadshares (wages paid in respect of non-existent members of the ship's notional complement and divided out amongst the existing crew) and 57s. 6d. is accounted for as rewards to gunners. The ship's two surgeons receive 23s. 4d. between them. As the single surgeon aboard the next ship is paid 10s., this probably indicates that the *Mary Rose* carried one more senior surgeon who merited the higher rate of 13s. 4d. [Brit. Lib: Royal MS. Appendix 89, f.5]

IN ORDINARY 1523–1526

1523

124. *?1522–1523*
A document exhibited at the British Library in 1982–83 where it was described as follows: '*A BOKE OF THE KYNGES NAVIE ON THE SEA.*' A list of the twelve ships in Henry's navy with their '*portage*' (ie. tonnage), captains and complement. The list is undated but the contents suggest it relates to the period 1522–3. The *Mary Rose* appears second in order after the Italian-built 700 ton *Gabriel Royal*. Her captain is given as John Hopton and her master as John Browne. The ship's complement is given as 126 soldiers, 244 mariners, and 30 gunners. [Brit. Lib: Royal MS. 14 B XXXI]

1524

125. *17 March–13 April, 1524. Portsmouth*
Ships, 13 April, 1524: List of the crews of the ships in Portsmouth Harbour, mustered by Richard Palshed, for one month from 17 March to 13 April 15 Hen. VIII (1524) includes – The *Mary Rosse*, Fadere Conner, 17 men. The other ships include: *Henry Grace a Dewe, The Grette Galley, The Grette Galley* [?the *Less Galley*], *The Mary Grace, The Grette Barbara, The Peter Pomgarnot, The Grette Barke, The Mary James, The Mary John, The Mary George,* and *The John of Grenwich.* All had skeleton crews. [CSP IV–I, 244, p. 96]

126. *17 July, 1524*
Navy, 17 July, 1524: A reference to the *Mary Rose* in the list of the keepers of ships. [CSP IV–I, 512, p. 217]

127. *1524*
List of ships at various ports, with tonnage: ... [place lost] The *Henry Grace Diew*, the *Gret Galey*, the *Mary Rosse*, the *Petir Pomgarnet*, the *Gret Nycolas*, the *Gret Barke*, the *Lesse Barke*, the *Kateryn Fortun*, the *Mary George*, the *Mary James*, the *Sweepstake*, the *Swallow*. [CSP IV–I, 974, p. 426]

128. *26 Nov. 1524–1 Sept. 1525. Portsmouth*
The King's Ships, 5 Jan. 1530: (1). Payments made for wages and victuals for shipkeepers on various ships, including the *Mary Rose*, all kept in the haven of Portsmouth for part of the period from 26 Nov. 15 Hen. VIII. (1524) to 1 Sept., 16 Hen. VIII. (1525). [CSP IV–III, 6138, p. 2739]

1525

129. *3 July, 1525*
Dover, 1526: '*The shift of the ferry box for one quarter ended at Midsummer, chested among these ships following, 3 July 17 Hen. VIII*' – The *Barbara*, 3l., The *Marye Roose*, 3l., The *Gabryell*, 2l. 16s. 8d. Also extra payments for same ships for masters for several voyages. [CSP IV–III, Appendix 90, p. 3112]

130. *22 Oct., 1525. Deptford*
Ships, 22 Oct., 1525: Names of the King's ships within the port and haven of Portsmouth and the river of Thames, 22 Oct. 17 Hen. VIII (1525), include:

The *Gabryell Royall*, 700 tons 16 years of age.
The *Marye Rosse*, 600 tons, 14 yrs. of age.
The *Petur Pomgarnet*, 340 tons, 14 yrs.
The *John Baptiste*, 400 tons, 13 yrs.
The *Grette Bark*, 200 tons, 12 yrs.
The *Lesse Barke*, 160 tons, 12 yrs.
The *Mary James*, 260 tons, 16 yrs.
The *Mary George*, 240 tons, 15 yrs.
The *Minion*, 180 tons, new.
The *Maudelen of Depforde*, 120 tons, 3 yrs.
The *Katerine Barke*, 100 tons, 3 yrs.
The *Mary Impercall*, 120 tons, 2 yrs.
The *Barke of Bullen*, 80 tons, 14 yrs.
The *Trinitie Henrye*, 80 tons, 6 yrs.
The *Barke of Murlesse (Morlaix)*, 60 tons, new.
The *Sweepstake*, 65 tons, 3 yrs.
The *Swalowe*, 60 tons, new.
The *Gryffyn*, 80 tons, 14 yrs.
The *Grett Sabra*, 50 tons, 3 yrs.
The *Lessere Sabra*, 40 tons, 3 yrs.
The *John of Grenewyche*, 50 tons, 12 yrs.
The prize taken by Thos. Sperte, 60 tons, 15 yrs.
The *Hulke*, 160 tons, 3 yrs.
The *Mary Gylforde*, 160 tons, 1 yr.

This is followed by another document that is '[An account of how ma]*ny ships the King* [hath, this] ... *year of his reign, what portage* [they be of, and w]*hat state they be in the same day;* [also where th]*ey ride and be bestowed:*' -

There follows the *Great Henry Grace Dieu*, 1500 tons (though another document on this page lists the *Henry Grace de Dieu* as 1000 tons and 12 yrs old), riding at Northfleet, being in good reparation, except caulking. Next is *The Sovereign*, 800 tons, in a dock at Woolwich. She must be new made from the keel upward; '*the form of which ship is so marvellously goodly that great pity it were she should die, and the rather because that many things there be in her that will serve right well.*' Then there is the *Gabriel Royal*, 650 tons which lies off Erith. She needed extensive rebuilding. Next there follows '*Item, the Mary Rose, being of portage 600 ton, lieth in* [dock] *at Deptford beside the storehouse there, which must* [be]... *and calked from the keel upward, both within and without.*' Other warships are listed, including the *John Baptist*, the *Barbara* and the *Great Nicholas*, each of 400 tons; the *Mary George*, 250 tons, and other ships. [CSP IV–I, 1714, p. 762]

Horsey transcribes part of this document as follows: '*The names of alle the Kinges schipps, as welle that rydethe within the portte and havene of Porttesmothe, as thoo that rydethe within the ryvere of Themmys, the xxiith of Octobur, xvii. Henry Vlll, [1526]*'; in which we read: '*The Marye Rosse, of the tonnege of vi c. tonne, ande of the age of xiiii yeres.*'

131. *November 1525*
Horsey gives the following reference: '*An abstracte of the daily charges for the Kynges shippes yet of Novembre, in the xviii remaynyng, the xvi. yere of his reigne [1525] ...The Mary Rose. For wages and vitailles of viii. maryners, her kepars every moneth, iiii l. xii s. viii d. that is, in a lyke yere, ix l. iiii s. viii d.*'

(NB: This might be part of 126)

1526

132. *1 March 1526–12 Dec. 1527*
Navy Warrants, 12 December, 1527: Warrants from the King, Arthur lord Lisle, and Wm. Gonson, to Sir John Daunce, general surveyor, for payment of money to Th. Jermyn, clerk of the King's ships, to be expended on various ships, including the *Mary Rose*, and other purposes. Dated from 1 March 17 Hen. VIII (1526) to 12 Dec. 19 Hen. VIII. (1527). [CSP IV–II, 3656, p. 1641]

133. *16 Nov. 1526*
The Navy, 16 Nov, 1526: Estimate for a year's wages for mariners to keep the following ships, and for the number of cables that each will consume:- included is the *Mary Rose*: for 8 mariners to keep her, £4. 12s. 8d. a month; for 6 cables, £42 [CSP IV–II, 2634, p. 1166]

This document was exhibited at the British Library in 1982–3 and was described as follows: An abstract of expenses for keeping several of the ships of Henry VIII's navy laid up, 16 November 1526. The *Mary Rose* is second on a list of eleven ships which also includes the *Henry Grace à Dieu*, the *Gabriel Royal*, the *Peter Pomegranate* and the *Great Barke*. Wages and victuals are to be provided for eight mariners, keepers of the ship, at a cost of £4. 12s. 8d. per month. It is estimated that she may need as many as six mooring cables in a year, at a total cost of £42. The *Gabriel Royal*, a larger ship than the *Mary Rose*, has a caretaker crew of ten and may need eight cables at a cost of £80. The *Great Barke*, considerably smaller, has a crew of four and her extimated six cables cost only £30. [Brit. Lib: Royal MS. 14 B. xxii. c.]

134. *1526*
The Navy, 1526: Account of the state of the King's ships, and their yearly cost. The *Greate Galey*, the *Mary Rose*, the *Peter Pomegarnet*, the *Greate* and *Lesse Barkes*, and the two *Robarges*, cost yearly £39. They are good for the wars, or else for the King's pleasure, but their overlops, summer castles, and decks must be caulked shortly after March. Before these ships were brought into dock they cost about 700 mks a year. The *Sovereyn*, the *Greate Nicholas*, the *Mary Jamys*, and the *Harry of Hampton* must have 'a new makyng' before they do any service. [CSP IV–II, 2635, p. 1167]

REPAIR 1527–1528

1527

135. *28 Feb.–3 June, 1527*
(iii). Payments to labourers making a dock for the *Mary Rose*, etc., beginning 28 Feb. 18 Hen. VIII. (1527), 2d. a man each tide. And again, from 3 June 19 Hen. VIII (1527). [The King's Ships, 5th Jan. 1530. CSP IV–III, 6138, p. 2739]
iii. Payments of laborers at the dock where the Henry Grace de Dieu lies, at divers times when the water broke into the dock, beginning 28 March 18 Hen. VIII [1527]. Others, 4 June 19 Hen. VIII [1527]. Laborers making dock for the Mary Rose, and c., beginning 28 Feb. 18 Hen. VIII [1527], 2d. a man each tide. And again, from 3 June 19 Hen. VIII [1527]. [The King's Ships, 5 Jan. 1530. CSP IV–III, 6138, p. 2739]

136. *5 June–July 1527*
(vi). Payment for the repair of the *Mary Rose* and other ships in June and July, 19 Hen. VIII [1527]. [CSP IV–III, 6138, pp. 2738–40]
Friel transcribes this as follows:

'*Hereafter followeth all such stuff with other necessaries provided by me Thomas Jermyn, Clerk of our sovereign lord the King's ships for the reparation of the Mary Roose and for caulking of her overlop & decks fore and aft within board and likewise for searching and caulking from the keel upward without board and repairing and trimming of her boat the 5th day of June in the 19th year of the reign of our sovereign lord King Henry the viiith.*

First paid for 37 feet of plankboard 5 inches (thick) at 8s the hundred the sum monteth – 3s
Item more for 120 feet of overlop board 2 inches thick at 3s.4d the hundred, sum – 4s
Item more for 46 feet of square timber at 3s.4d the ton – 4s
Item more for 6 cloven boards at 4d a board – 2s
Item for 55lb of carvel spikes at 1.5d the lb – 6s.10.5d
Item for 150 of overlop nails at 3s per hundred – 4s.6d
Item more for 150 of overlop nails at 2s per hundred – 3s.
Item for 150 of overlop nails at 16d per hundred – 2s.
Item more for 600 of 6d nails – 3s.
Item more for 100 of 5d nails – 5d.
Item for 400 of 4d nails – 16d
Item for 100 of 3d nails – 3d
Item for 600 of scupper nails – 2s.
Item for two loads of burning – 2s. [Reeds burnt under the hull to soften the old caulking material before re-caulking].
Item for 6.75 hundredweight of oakum [old rope used in caulking] *at 7s.8d the hundredweight – 51s.9d.*
Item for 6 dozen? of thrums – 12d. [sheepskins used in caulking].
Item for 2 hoses – 15d.
Item more spent in pitch – 8 barrels
Item in tar – 2 barrels
Sum of the page £4 13s. 31/2d.43
[Friel modern ref – PRO E315/317; Knighton and Loades 2002, 99–100, text 55]

137. *25 June, 1527. Portsmouth*

(2). Payment of wages for making a new dock *'for the grounding of the Mary Rose, the Peter Pomegarnet, and the John Baptist.'* labourers at the dock and the Storehouse at Portsmouth, called the Long House, making 'vices' for winding aground the King's ships ... from the 25 June 18 Hen. VIII (ie. 1527). Also payment for wages and victuals of carpenters and caulkers, hedging and ditching and making gates for enclosing nine acres bought for the King, on which the dock and storehouses are made. [The King's Ships, 5th Jan. 1530. CSP IV–III, 6138, p. 2739]

IN ORDINARY 1528–1544

1528
(No references)

1529
(No references)

1530
(No references)

1531
(No references)

1532
(No references)

1533
(No references)

1534
(No references)

1535
(No references)

1536

138. *1536*

Cromwell's Administration, 1536: In Cromwell's hand: Things done by the King's highness sythyn I came to his service: include – he purchased Hampton Court, ... He has repaired the tower of London; new made the *Mary Rose*, the *Peter Powngarnerd*, the *Lyon*, the *Katheryn Galye*, the *Barke*, the *Mynyon*, the *Swepestake*. ... He has most costly wars in Scotland, and has had great wars in Ireland. He has borne most costly charge at the coronation of queen Anne. He has

maintained the great and sumptuous house of the lady Catharine Dowager. Etc. [CSP X, 1231, p. 513]

1537.
(No references)

1538
(No references)

1539

139. *26 Jan., 1539. Thames*

The King's Ships, 26 Jan., 1539: The number and state of the King's ships in the Thames, 26 Jan. 30 Hen. VIII (1539). These include – The *Mary Rose*, the *Peter*, and the *Minion*, *'new made, standing in their docks there, masts ready but not set up, who cannot be made ready to sail under three months time after commandment given.'* ... Other ships mentioned are the *Primrose*, the *Great Galley*, the *Less Bark*, the *Genet*, the *Lyon* and the *Trinity*. It will be hard to have shipwrights, calkers, and mariners, to furnish all these ships at once, for they must occupy 500 persons. ... The King has no place convenient to lay the cordage which he has ordered from Dansik; but room might be made in the storehouse at Deptford. [CSP XIV–I, 143 pp. 51–2]

1540

140. *1 Oct., 1540: Thames*

Marillac to Francis I, King of France, 1 October, 1540: London, 1st Oct., 1540: Letter includes an answer to the questions of how many ships of war Henry VIII has, how they are manned, and whether any are being newly prepared for sea; and how many, with those of his subjects, he could make at need. Answer is that he commonly has 30 or 40 of his own at the most, and last year, when there was a suspicion of war, they were put in such order that they are still well equipped. Three of them, which are much larger than the rest, in this river, viz: the *Great Harry*, of 1500 tons, and the *Marie Roze* and *Pomme Grenade*, of 900 tons or 1000 tons each. [CSP XVI, 110, p. 56]

1541

141. *13 Feb., 1541*

Ordnance, 13 Feb., 1541: '*A book*' of the King's ordnance etc. in the Tower of London and other places, and in the King's ships, within the realm of England and at Calais, 13 Feb., 31 Hen. VIII (1541). These include the armament in each ship given, including the *Mary Rose*. [CSP XV, 196, p. 71]

'Yet the Kyngs shypes
The Mary Rose

Peces of Brasse
Demy canons 4
Culveryns 2
Demy culveryns 2
Sakers 5
Ffawcons 2
                    peces 15

Peces of Iron
Port peces 9
Slyngs 6
ffowlers 6
Bases great and small 60
                    eces ... 91' (NB: this is a mistake
in 1541, it should total '81'). [PRO–E101/60/3]

1542
(No references)

1543

142. *31 July, 1543*
Chapuys to the Queen of Hungary, 31 July, 1543: A modern transcript of a foreign document refers to extreme diligence being made by Henry VIII in equipping the rest of the ships and putting in them an incredible quantity of artillery. Amongst other pieces the *Great Henry* will carry 12 double cannons and the *Marie Roze* 6; and within these two ships will go 1,200 men at least. Written from London, 31 July, 1543. [CSP XVIII–I, 973, p. 522]

1544
(No references)

THIRD FRENCH WAR, 1545

(1). 1545, BEFORE THE SINKING

143. *1545, but dated 1546*
The *Anthony Roll* list of the ships in the king's navy includes the only contemporary picture of the *Mary Rose*, but it is dated 1546, the year after the ship had sunk. Anthony Anthony was an officer in the Board of Ordnance in which each ship is listed with 'ordnance, municions and habillments of war'.

The *Mary Rose* shown on the *Anthony Roll*
'The Mary Rose, Tunage vij (700). Men: souldiours, clxxxv (185); marrynars, cc (200); gonnars, xxx (30) – iiijcxv (415). For the Mary Rose: Ordenaunce, artillary, munitions, habillimentes for the warre, for the armyng and in the deffence of the sayd shyppe to the see.
Gonnes of brasse: Cannons, ij (2); Demy cannons, ij (2); Culveryns, ij (2); Demy culveryns, vj (6); Sakers, ij (2); Fawcons, j (1). Somma, xv (15).

Gonnes of yron: Porte pecys, xij (12); Slynges, ij (2); Dewi slynges, iiij (3); Quarter slyng, j (1); Fowlers, vj (6); Baessys, xxx (30); Toppe pecys, ij (2); Hayle shotte pecys, xx (20); Handgonnes complete, l (50).
Gonnepowder: Serpentyn powder in barrelles, ij (2) last; Corne powder in barrelles, 3 last.
Shotte of yron: For cannon, (l) 50; For demy cannon, lx (60); For culveryn, lx (60); For demy culveryn, clx (140); For sakers, lxxx (80); For fawcon, lx (60); For slyng, xl (40); For demy slyng, xl (40); For qwarter slyng, l (50); Dyce of yron for hayl shotte, [blank].
Shotte of stoen and leade: For porte pecys, cc (200); For fowlers, clxx (170); For toppe pecys, xx (20); For baessys, shotte of leade, iiijc (400); For handgonnes, shotte of leade, jm (1000).
Bowes, bowestrynges, arrowes, morrys pyckes, byllys, daertes for toppis:
Bowes of yough, ccl (250); Bowestrynges, vj (6) groce; Livere arrowes in shevis, cccc (400); Morrys pykes, cl (150); Byllys, cl (150); Daertes for toppys, in doussens, xl (40).
Munitions: Pyckehamers, xij (12); Sledgys of yron, viij (8); Crowes of yron, xij (12); Comaunders, xij (12); ampions, iiijml (); Canvas for cartowches, xx (20) ellys; Paper ryall for cartowches, j (1) qwayer; Fourmes for cartowches, vj (6).
Habillimentes for warre: Ropis of hempe for woling and brechyng, x (10) coylles; Naylis of sundere sortes, jml (1000); Bagges of ledder, viij (8); Fyrkyns with pursys, vj (6); Lyme pottes, x (10) doussen; Spaer whelys, iiij (4) payer; Spaer truckelles, iiij (4) payer; Spaer extrys (axel trees), vj (6); Shepe skynnys for spongys, xij (12); Tymber for forlockes and konnys, c (100) foete.'
[Archive refs: PL 2991, first roll, pp. 6–7, Pepys Library, Magdalene College, Cambridge; second roll, BL Add. Mss. 22041; Knighton and Loades 2000; Knighton and Loades 2002, text 58]

144. *1545, probably about 20 June*
The Navy, 1545: A list of ships with their tonnage and men, including *Mary Roos*. Total ships, 14; men, 3,250. ... A list of captains, for ships:- Sir George Carewe, etc. [CSP Addenda I–II, 1697, p. 569]

145. *1545, probably about 20 June*
Friel describes this as an English fleet list of spring–summer 1545. This order of battle probably dates from about 20 June 1545, and seems to relate to Lord Lisle's plan to attack the French invasion fleet gathered in the mouth of the Seine. The plan failed, chiefly because of bad weather. The letters '*b*' and '*w*' in the margins mean 'battle' or 'wing', the tactical positions of the ships. The battle was the main body, with most of the largest ships; the wing (or wings) was to one side of the battle, and had most of the highly manoeuvrable oared vessels. Most of the ships listed above belonged to the king. It is probably the last surviving battle-plan to list the *Mary Rose* for within a month she had been lost.

The order of battle upon the sea (written on back of document)

b The Henry (Grace a Dieu).......................1000 tons
b The Mary Rose ....800 tons
b The Peter (Pomegranate)..........................600 tons

b The Jesus of Lubeck ....*700 tons*
b The Matthew Gonson ....*500 tons*
w The Great Galley ....*500 tons*
b The Paunsey ....*400 tons*
w The Strewse ....*450 tons*
w The Mary of Hamburg ....*400 tons*
w The Sweepstake ....*300 tons*
w The Minion ....*300 tons*
b The Swallow ....*200 tons*
w The Salamander ....*280 tons*
b The Unicorn ....*200 tons*
w The Less Galley ....*300 tons*
b The Venetian ....*800 tons*
b The Argosy ....*500 tons*
b The Saviour ....*340 tons*
b The Painted Hulk ....*500 tons*
w The Ship of Dover ....*260 tons*
b The Ship of Montrego ....*260 tons*
w The New Galleon of Kent ....*300 tons*
w The Less New Galley ....*250 tons*
b All the ships of Bristol
w All the king's small ships
b The Galley Subtle
Of thus there is of 500 (tons) and upward *9*
Of 300 (tons) and upward *8*
Of 200 (tons) and upward *6*
b Item, all the new hulks

[PRO-SP1/245, pt1. 5635; see also CSP Addenda I–II, 1698, p. 569]

146. *1545*

The War with France and Scotland. 1545: *'This 37 year, 1545, about the 20 of July, the lord Donybalte, Admiral of France, came with 200 sail afore the Isle of Wight, the King's Majesty being there near at Portsmouth* (where Sir George Carew was drowned in the *Mary Rose), and certain of the Frenchmen landed in the Isle of Wight, where their captain* [The Chevalier d'Aux] *was slain and they driven to their ships.'* [CSP XX–II, 494, p. 213]

147. *24 June, 1545: Downs, Portsmouth*

Lisle to the Council, 24 June, 1545: Having been tormented with storms and strainable winds; and on Sunday night last the 21st, while lying *'a quarte seas over towards Bechiff,'* divers of the hulks attempted to steal away in the darkness. They were perceived and followed by the swiftest ships of the fleet, whereof Sir John Barkleye in the *Lesse Galley*, being foremost, thought to stop them by firing a saker, but it burst and he was stricken through the body with a fragment of iron, as will have been already reported by the captain of Portsmouth. It was 9 o'clock next morning, and they were *'a kennying'*

beyond the Wight, before the hulks were collected again. That night rough weather compelled the fleet either *'to hold up again with the Narrow Seas or else put ourselves in with the Wight'*; and so, to join the rest of the army coming out of Thames and the *Henry* and *Mary Roose* in the Downs, they come hither, arriving yesterday afternoon. ... [CSP XX–I, 1023, p. 494; Knighton and Loades 2002, text 59]

(2). 1545–1549 CONTEMPORARY DESCRIPTIONS OF THE SINKING OF THE MARY ROSE, 19 JULY 1545

148. *23 July, 1545*

Horsey describes this as follows: Lord Russell to Sir William Paget, Secretary of State. Bodnam, 23 July, 1545: *'I am verie sory of the unhappy and the unfortunat chawnce of the Mary Rose, whiche, throwghe suche rechenes and great negligence, shulde be in suche wise caste awaie, with tho that werre within her, whiche is a great losse of the men and the shipp also; notwithstanding ye give me good hope by your letters that the shipp shal be recovered againe, which I praye God may be so.'* [see also CSP XX–I, 1255, p. 623; Knighton and Loades 2002, text 61]

149. *24 July, 1545*

Van der Delft, German Emperor's Ambassador, to Charles V, 24 July, 1545: *'... Next day, Sunday [19 July], while the King was at dinner on the flagship, the French fleet appeared. The King hurriedly left the flagship and the English sailed to encounter the French, shooting at the galleys, of which five had entered the harbour while the English could not get out for want of wind. Towards the evening the ship [the Mary Rose] of Viceadmiral George Carew foundered, all the 500 men on board being drowned save about 25 or 30 servants, sailors and the like. Was told by a Fleming amongst the survivors that when she heeled over with the wind the water entered by the lowest row of gun ports which had been left open after firing. They expect to recover the ship and guns ...'* [CSP XX–I, 1263, p. 627]

Alternative version:
23–24 July, 1545

'After dinner the admiral [Viscount Lisle, John Dudley] *told me that he had the King's orders to take me to his Majesty, as he would rather see me that afternoon, in consequence of the whole of his time being occupied the next day visiting his ships and dining on the flagship.*

On the following day, Sunday, whilst the King was at dinner on the flagship, news came that the French were only five short leagues away. This turned out to be true, for within two hours their fleet in great force was seen in front of this port, and the King hurriedly left the flagship. The English fleet at once set sail to encounter the French, and on approaching them kept up a cannonade against the galleys, of which five had entered well into the harbour, whilst the English could not get out for want of wind, and in consequence of the opposition of the enemy.

Towards evening, through misfortune and carelessness, the ship of Vice-Admiral George Carew foundered, and all hands on board, to the number of about 500, were drowned, with the exception of about five and twenty or thirty servants, sailors and the like, who escaped. I made enquiries of one of the survivors, a Fleming, how the ship perished, and he told me that the disaster was caused by their not having closed the lowest row of gun ports on one side of the ship. Having fired the guns on that side, the ship was turning, in order to fire from the other, when the wind caught her sails so strongly as to heel her over, and plunge her open gunports beneath the water, which flooded and sank her. They say, however, that they can recover the ship and guns'. [NB: The loss of the *Mary Rose,* with Vice-Admiral Sir George Carew, is described in exactly similar terms to this in the *Spanish Chronicle of Henry VIII*, the probable author of which (de Guaras), if he did not accompany the ambassador in his journey to Portsmouth, certainly obtained his information from the same source].

'On Monday the firing on both sides went on nearly all day, and could be plainly witnessed from here. Some people say that at nightfall the English did some damage to a French galley.

Apparently the French fleet consisted of over 300 sail, without counting the 27 galleys they had; but still these people here seem determined to give battle, as soon as they get their ships together and the wind is favourable.' [CSP., Spanish State Papers, Henry VIII, pp. 185–94; Knighton and Loades 2002, text 62]

150. *1545*

An account by Martin du Bellay, a French eyewitness, describing the battle and the loss of the *Mary Rose*: 'In the morning with the help of the sea which was calm, without wind or force of current, our galleys could be steered and manoeuvered at will to the detriment of the enemy, who, not being able to move through lack of wind, lay openly exposed to the fire of our artillery, which could do more harm to their ships than they could to the galleys, more so because they are higher and bulkier, and also by their use of oars, our galleys could run away, avoid danger, and gain the advantage. Fortune supported our force in this way for more than one hour. During this time, amongst other damage suffered by the enemy, la Marirose, one of their main ships, was sunk by gunfire, and out of five or six hundred men who were on it, only thirty-five were saved'. [McKee 1982, 25–6; Knighton and Loades 2002, text 63]

151. *1545*

Extract from Hall's Chronicle, entitled '*The Union of the two noble famelies of Lancastre and Yorke*', etc.,: originally printed in 1548, only three years after the loss of the *Mary Rose*.

'In June [1545], the Lord Lisle, Admirall of Englande, with the Englishe fleet, entered the mouthe of the river of Sain, and came before Newehaven [now, Havre-de-Grace], where the greate armie of Fraunce laie, whiche wer CC saile of shippes and xxvi galies of force, whereof the bishop of Rome had sent xx, well furnished with men and money, to aide the Frenche kyng. Th'Engleshemen beying but a clx. saile, and all greate shippes did not determyne to set on the whole navie, but shot certayne peces of ordinaunce at theim, whiche caused the galies to come abrode, and shot at the Englishemen, whiche galies had greate advauntage, by reason of the calme wether. Twise eche part assaulted other with ordinaunce, but sodainly the wynde rose so greate, that the galies could not indure the rage of the seas; and th'Englyshemen wer compelled to entre the main seas, for fear of flattes and so sailed unto Portesmouthe, where the kyng then laie; for he had knowlege by his espialles, that the Frenche army entended to land in the Isle of Wight, wherfore he repaired to that cost, to se his realm defended.

After the departyng of th'Engleshe navie from Newhaven, the Admirall of Fraunce, called the Lords Donibalt, a man of greate experience, halsed up his sailes, and with his whole navie came to the poynt of the Isle of Wight, called S, Helenes poynt, and there in good ordre cast their ankers, and sent xvi of his galies daily to the very haven of Portesmouthe.

Th'Englyshe navie liyng in the haven, made them prest, and set out towardes them, and still the one shot at the other. But one daie above all other, the whole navie of the Englishmen made out, and purposed to set on the Frenchmen; but in their settyng forward, a goodly ship of Englande, called the Mary Rose, was, by to much foly, drouned in the middest of the haven, for she was laden with much ordinaunce, and the portes left open, which were very low, & the great ordinaunce unbreached, so that when the ship should turne, the water entered, and sodainly she sanke. In her was Sir George Carewe, knight, Capitain of the saide shippe, and foure hundred men, and much ordinaunce.

At the same tyme certain of the Frenche menne landed in the Isle of Wight, where the Capitaine was slain and many other, and were, bothe to their greate losse and pain, driven again to their galies.' [Horsey]

(3). *1545–1549, SALVAGE OF THE MARY ROSE*

152. *31 July, 1545*

Suffolk to Paget, 31 July, 1545: Will with speed set men to the weighing of the *Mary Rose*. Portesmouth, last of July 1545. [CSP XX–I, 1325, p. 651; Knighton and Loades 2002, text 65]

153. *1 Aug., 1545*

Horsey describes this as: Charles, Duke of Suffolk, to Paget at Portsmouth, 1st August, l545. '*And as concernyng the Mary Rose, we have consulted and spoken together with them that have taken uppon them to recover her, whoo desyreth to have, for the saving of her, suche necessaryes as is mentyoned yn a Sedule herein enclosed; not doubting, God willing, but they shall have all things redy accordingly, soo, that shortely she shal be saved. A remembraunce of things necessarye for the recoverye, with the help of God, of the Mary Roose. Fyrst – 2 of the greatest hulkes that may be gotten; more the hulkes that rydeth within the havyn. Item, 4 of the gretest hoys within the havyn. Item, 5 of the gretest cables that may be had. Item, 10 greate hawsers. Item, newe capsteynes with 20 pulleys. Item, 50 pulleys bounde with iron. Item, 5 doseyn balast baskettes. Item, 40 lbs. of talowe, Item, 30 Venezians maryners, and one Veneziane carpenter. Item, 60 Inglisshe maryners to attende upon them. Item, a greate quantitie of cordage of all sortes. Item, Symond, patrone and Master in Foyst, doth aggree that all thynges must be had for the purpose aforseyd.'* [see also CSP XX–II, 2, p. 2; Knighton and Loades 2002, text 66]

154. *1 Aug., 1545*

Suffolk to Paget, 1 August, 1545: Trusts that by Monday or Tuesday the *Mary Rose* shall be weighed up and saved. Two hulks, cables, '*pulleces*,' etc., are ready for the weighing of her. Portesmouth, 1 Aug. 1545. [CSP XX–II, 3, p. 2; Knighton and Loades 2002, text 67]

McKee (1982, 34) quotes this as follows: '*I trust by Monday or Twisday, at the furthest, the Mary Rose shall be wayed upp, and saved. There be twoo hulkes, cabulles, pulleces and other things made redy for the waying of her.'* Dated Saturday, 1 August, 1545

155. *2 Aug., 1545*

Suffolk to Paget, 2 Aug., 1545: All is ready for the weighing of the *Mary Rose* tomorrow. ... Portesmouth, 2 Aug., 1545. [CSP XX–II, 14, p. 6; Knighton and Loades 2002, text 68]

156. *2 Aug., 1545*

Horsey gives this as: John, Viscount Lisle, to Sir William Paget, Knight, Portchemouth, 2nd August, 1545: *'We have moche adoe to frame every thinge for the Mary Rose, but all that may be possible do don, ys don tbr the same. The worst ys, we muste torbere thre of the greteste hulkes of the flete, tyll the thinge be don, which muste be emptyed of all her vitayles, ordnance, and baliste, during the busynes, which wil be a great weakening to the navye, yf any thing in the meanetyme shall happen.'* He adds at the end, that the fleet remains stationary, in the place where they were at anchor the day the King left the town, except the *'Gret Venezian'*, which was brought nearer to the haven, to take in ballast, and the *'too hulkes, the Jhesus and the Sampson, which ys brought unto the Mary Rose, becaus they muste wey her upp.'* [see also CSP XX–II, 16, p. 7; Knighton and Loades 2002, text 69]

157. *5 Aug., 1545*

Horsey gives this as follows: The Duke of Suffolk and others to Paget, Portesmouth, 5th August. *'And as touching the Mary Rose, her sailes and saile-yardes be layd on land; and to her mastes there is tyed three cables with other ingens to wey her upp, and on every syde of her a hulk to sett her uppright, which is thought by the doers thereof God willing, to be doon to-morowe one tyme in the day, and that doon, they purpose to discharg her of water, ordenaunce, and all other things, with as moch deligence as is possible, and by littell and littell, to bring her nerer to the shore; and as we shall, from tyme to tyme, woork with her, to save her, his Majeste shal be advertised accordingly.'* [Knighton and Loades 2002, text 70; see also CSP XX–II, 38, p. 17]

158. *5 Aug., 1545*

Horsey gives this as follows: Lisle to Paget, Portesmouth, 5th August. *'The Mary Roos, which I trust with the leave of God, shal be brought upp right again one tomorowe, hath so chardged all the Kynge's Majesties Ship-wryghtes with makyng engyns for the same, that they have had no leasure t' attend any other thyng sithens his Majesties departure hence, which I beseche you to signifie unto his Highnes.'* [Knighton and Loades 2002, text 71; see also CSP XX–II, 39, p.18]

159. *7 Aug., 1545*

Horsey's description is: The Duke of Suffolk to Paget Portesmouth, 7th August. *'My Lorde Admyrall, being this present Friday at dynner with me, told me, that he had a good hope of the waying upright of the Mary Rose, this afternone or tomorow.'* [Knighton and Loades 2002, text 72; see also CSP XX–II, 61, p. 30]

160. *9 Aug., 1545*

Lisle and St. John to Paget, 9 Aug., 1545: This day the Italians who had the weighing of the *Mary Roos* signify that, by the method they have followed they cannot recover her and have broken her foremast. They came to declare this to my lord Great Master, but he had already departed hence. Now they ask six days' proof to try dragging her into *'shallow ground.'* The great hulks which have been occupied about weighing her cannot well be spared out of the army; and, yet, considering the importance of the ship and the goodly ordnance that is in her, the lord Admiral has appointed the two hulks which were stayed to go forth with the fleet to serve towards recovering her, for, to be of use in the army, they *'must have sparre deckes and wast nettyng with pourtes cut'*, to finish which will take longer than was thought. The lord Admiral stays returning the book of the ships with the captains' names until he has word again of the King's pleasure for placing one captain or two to the charge of the rowing pieces. Portsmouth, 9 Aug. [CSP XX–II, 81, p. 39]

This has been partly transcribed as follows: Sunday, 9 August, *'Master Secretary, Theis shalbe tadvertise you, that this daye thitalians which had the doyng of the wayeng of the Mary Roos haue been with my Lord Chamerlayn and me to signify vnto vs that after this sourt which they haue followed hetherto they can by no meanes recouer her, for they haue alredye broken her foremast ... And now they desyr to prove an other waye, which ys to dragg her as she lyeth vntill she come into shallow ground, and so set her upright, and to this they axe vj days prouf.'* [McKee 1982, 36; Knighton and Loades 2002, text 73]

161. *1545*

22 tuns of beer were consumed during the salvage work. [Pipe Office Declared Accounts 2477, quoted in Oppenheim 1988, p. 67]

162. *25 Aug., 1545*

Wriothesley to Henry VIII, 25 Aug., 1545: Of the two boats which are ready to lead them, one shall serve for the *Mary Rose* and the other remain as a lighter at Portesmouth. ... Ely Place, 25 Aug. [CSP XX–II, 211, p. 93; Knighton and Loades 2002, text 74]

163. *3 Sept., 1545*

Harvel to Paget, 3 Sept., 1545: *'Although th'infortunable case of Sir George Carow is by negligence so miserablye successid,'* it is the fortune of war and hitherto the King has had prosperous success. ... Venice, 3 Sept., 1545. [CSP XX–II, 288, p. 133; Knighton and Loades 2002, text 75]

164. *8 Dec., 1545*

The Privy Council, 8 Dec., 1545: Meeting at Westminster ... and another warrant to pay Petre de Andreas and Symone de Maryne, Venetians, 40 mks. in reward for their pains about the weighing of the Mary Rose. [CSP XX–II, 951, p. 473; Knighton and Loades 2002, text 76]

165. *1547*

Rolls entry:1547: Pay Peter Paule, an Italian, £50 11s. 5d for recovering ordnance from her. [McKee 1982, 36]

Oppenheim (1988, 67) refers to this as: Up to 30 June 1547, the whole amount expended in the various attempts to salvage the Mary Rose was £402 6s. 8d, and this may have included £57 11s. 5d (NB. McKee p.36 says £50 11s. 5d) to Peter Paul, an Italian, for the recovery of some of her guns, which was paid within the time for which the total was made up but appears in other papers [Pipe Office Decld. Accts 2588, and Acts of the Privy Council 17 May 1547; Knighton and Loades 2002, text 77]

166. *1549*
Another £50 paid to Peter Paul for recovering ordnance. All hope of salvaging the *Mary Rose* appears to have been lost thereafter [McKee 1982, 36; Oppenheim 1988, 67, quoting Acts of the Privy Council, 3 Aug. 1549; Knighton and Loades 2002, text 79]

(4). LATER ACCOUNTS OF THE SINKING OF THE MARY ROSE

167.
Lediard in his Naval History records D'Annebault's version of the sinking:

It was ordered that at daybreak the galleys should advance upon the British whilst at anchor and, by firing at them with all fury, provoke them into engagement and then retreating endeavour to draw them out of their hold towards the main battle. This order was executed with a great deal of intrepidity and the weather favoured our attempt beyond our wishes for it was proven in the morning a parfect calm. Our galleys had all the advantages of working which we could desire to the great damage of the English who for want of wind not being able to stir laid exposed to our cannon and being so much higher and bulkier than our galleys hardly a shot missed them while they, with the help of their oars, shifted at pleasure, and thereby avoided the danger of the enemy's artillery. Fortune favoured our fleet in this manner for above an hour during which time, among other damages the English received, the Mary Rose, one of their principal ships, was sunk by our cannon and of 5 or 600 men which were on board only 5 and 30 escaped. [Lediard, T., *The Naval History of England* (Wilcox 1735), quoted in Rule (1983, 36–7)]

168. *After 1575*
Richard Hooker, the contemporary biographer of Sir Peter Carew, after 1575 wrote '*The Lyffe of Sir Peter Carew, late of Mohonese Otrey, in the countie of Devon, Knyghte, whoe dyed at Rosse, in Irelande, the 27th of November, 1575, and was buryed at the Cettie of Water Forde, the 15 of December, 1575; collected by John Vowell, al's Hoker, of the Cetie of Excester, Gent. partly upon the credyble reporte of others, and partly wch he sawe and knewe hyme selffe*' (This is published by Phillips (1839, 96–151). The following extract is from pp. 109–11):

'*Not longe after, the seas beinge waxed calme, and the weather verie fayre, the Frenche gallyes, havinge wynde and weather at will, they woulde also needes raunge and scower the seas; and fyndinge theyme cleare, and the Englishe navie to be lede upe in harborow, they came alonge alle the southe coostes of Englande, even unto the Isle of Weight, where some of theyme landed, and did miche harme; and some of theyme came unto the haven of Portesemouth, and theire rowed upe and downe; theire beinge never a shipp at that instante in that redynes, nore anye suche wynde to serve yf they had bynne in redynes, to empeache theyme. The Kynge, who, upon the newes here of, was come to Portesemouthe, he*

fretted, and his teethe stode one ane edge, to see the braverye of his enymyes to come soe neere his noose, and he not able to encountre wth theyme, wherefore immediatly the beakens were sett one fiere throughte the whole coases, and forthwith suche was the resorte of the people as were sufficiente to garde the lande from the entringe of the Frenche men, lykewise comaundementes were sente out for alle the Kyng's shippes, and all other shippes of warre, wch were at Loundon and Queneborow, or eles where, that they shoule with all speede posyble make haste and come to Portesemouthe, which things were accordinglye performed. The French men, perceivinge that they could doe noe good by tarieinge theire, departed agayne to the seas. The Kynge, as sone as his whole fleet was come togethere, willeth them to sett all things in order, and to goe to the seas; which things beinge donne, and every shippe crosse sayled, and every captayne knoweinge his chardge, it was the Kyng's pleasure to apoynte Sir George Carewe to be Vyce Admyrall of that journye, and had apoynted unto hyme a shippe named the Marye Rose, wch was as fyne a shippe, as strounge, and as well apoynted as none better in the Realme. And at theire departure the Kynge dyned aborde with the Lorde Admyrall [This was Sir John Dudley, created Viscount Lisle, 12th March, 1542–3, and appointed Lord High Admiral 27th January 1543–4] *in his shippe, named the Greate Henry, and was theire servid by the Lorde Admyrall, Sir George Carewe, this gentleman, Peter Carewe, and their uncle, Sir Gawen Carewe, and with suche others onlye as weare apoynted to that voage and servyce. The Kynge, beinge at dynner, willed some one to goe upe to the topp, and see whethere he coulde see anye thing at the seas: the woorde was noe soner spoken but that Peter Carewe was as forwarde, and forthwith clymmythe upe to the tope of the shipp, and theere syttinge, the Kynge asked of hyme, what newes? Who tolde hyme that he had syght of three or foure shippes, but as he thoughte they were marchauntes; but yt was nott lounge but he hade ascryed a greate nomber, and then he cryed out to the Kynge, that theire was, as he thought, a fleete of men of warre. The Kynge, supposinge them to be the Frenche men of warre, as they weare in deede, willed the borde to be taken upe, and every man to goe to his shippe, as also a longe boote to come and carrye hime one lande. And firste he hath secreat talkes with the Lorde Admyrall, and then he hath the licke with Sir George Carewe, and at his departure frome hyme, toke his chayne from his necke, with a greate whistle of gold pendante to the same, and did put it aboute the necke of the said Sir George Carewe, gevinge hyme also therewith many good and comfortable wordes. The Kynge then toke his boote, and rowed to the lande, and every othere captayne went to his shippe appointed unto hime. Sir George Carewe being entered into his shippe, commaunded everye man to take his place, and the sayles to be hoysed, but the same was noe sonner donne, but that the Marye Roose beganne to heele, that is, to leane one the one syde. Sir Gawen Carewe beinge then in his own shipp, and seeinge the same, called for the master of his shippe, and tolde hyme there of, and asked hyme what it mente? who awensweared, that yf shee did heele, she was lycke to be caste awaye. Then the sayd Sir Gawen, passinge by Marye Roose, called oute to Sir George Carewe, askeinge hyme howe he did? who awnswered, that he hade a sorte of knaves whom he could not rule. And it was not lounge after but that the sayde Mary Roose, thus heelinge more and more, was drowned, with 700 men wiche were in here, whereof very fewe escaped. It chaunsed unto this gentleman, as the common proverbe is, 'the more cookes, the worse potage'. He had in this shipp a hundrith maryners, the worste of theyme beinge hable to be a master in the beste shippe within the realme, and these soe maligned and dysdayned one the other, that, refusinge to doe that wch they should doe, were carelesse to doe that that they oughte to doe, and soe contendinge in envie, perished in frowardness. The Kynge this meane whyle stode one the lande and sawe this tragedie, as also the Lady the wiffe to Sir George Carewe, who, with that syght, felle into a soundinge. The Kynge, beinge oppressed with sorowe of every syde, comforted her, and thancked God for the other, hopinge that of a harde begynnynge their would folowe a better endinge. And notwithstandinge this looste, the service apoynted wente forewarde, assone as wynde and weather woulde serve; and the resydewe of the fleete, beinge aboute the number of one hundred and fyve seales, toke the seas. The Frenche men perceivinge the same, licke as a sorte of sheepe runnynge into the foolde, they shifted awaye, and gate them into theire harborowes; thinckinge it better to lye theare in a salffe skynne, than to encontre with theyme of whome they shoulde lytle wynne.'*

169. *1577*

Extract from Hollinshed 's Chronicle, first published in *1577*: '*After this, the eighteenth of July* [1545], *the Admirall of France, Monsieur Danebalte, holsed uppe sayles, and wyth his whole navie came foorthe into the seas, and arryved on the coast of Sussex, afore Brythamsteed, and set certaine of his soldiours a land, to burne and spoile the countrey; but the beacons were fired, and the inhabitantes thereaboutes came downe so thicke, that the Frenchemenne were driven to flee, with losse of divers of their number, so that they did little hurte there. Immediatly hereupon they made to the point of the Isle of Wight, called Saint Helen's point, and there in good order upon their arrivall they cast ankers, and sent daily xvi of their galleis to the verye haven of Portsmouth. The Englishe navie, being there in the same haven, made them readye, and set out towards the ennemies, and still the one shotte hottelye at the other; but the winde was so calme that the Kyng's shippes could beare no saile, whiche greatly greeved the minds of the Englishmen, and made the ennemies more bolde to approch wyth their galelis, and to assayle the shippes with their shot, even within the haven.*

Yet the twentieth of July, the whole navie of the Englishemen made out, and purposed to sette on the Frenchmen, but in setting forward, through to much follye, one of the King's shippes, called the Marye Rose, was drowned in the myddest of the haven, by reason that she was overladen with ordinaunce, and had the portes lefte open, whiche were very lowe, and the great artillerie unbreeched, so that when the ship shoold tourne, the water entred, and soddainely she sunke. In hir was Sir George Carewe, knight, and foure hundreth souldioures under his guidyng. There escaped not paste fortie persons of all the number. The morrowe after, aboute two thousand of the Frenchmen landed in the Isle of Wight, where one of their cheife Capitaynes, named Le Chevalier Daux, a Provencos, was slayne, with manye other, and the residew wyth losse and shame driven back agayne to their galleyes.' [Edit. 1577, vol. ii p.1602. Horsey]

170. *1593*

In 1593 Sir Richard Hawkins wrote of the sinking, having suffered from open gunports in his own ship: The *Mary Rose* '*which was overset and suncke at Portsmouth, with her captain,*

Carew, and the most part of his company drowned in a goodly summers day, with a little flawe of wind; for that her ports were all open, and making a small hele, by them entered their destruction; where if they had been shut, no wind could have hurt her, especially in that place'. [McKee 1982, 28; Knighton and Loades 2002, text 83]

171. *1623*

Sir William Monson (born 1569) published a reference in 1623: '*The Mary Rose, next to the Regent in bigness and goodness, after this was cast away betwixt Portsmouth and the Isle of Wight. Part of the ribs of this ship I have seen with my own eyes; there perished in her four hundred persons.*' [McKee 1982, 36; Knighton and Loades 2002, text 84]

172.

There is believed to be a reference to a Roger Grenville drowning in the *Mary Rose*, amongst the records of Talland Church, near Looe, Cornwall, connected with the Killigarth family. This has not been checked [Rule 1986, 20]

173.

An engraving exists in which shows the sinking of the *Mary Rose* which took place on the 19th of July, 1545. This representation is a copy of a sixteenth century painting formerly at Cowdry House, Sussex; an account of which is given by Sir Joseph Ayloffe, in *Archaeologia* 3, 261. The painting was engraved in 1778 at the expense of the Society of Antiquaries, and an original copy of the engraving is now in Portsmouth City Museum (Fig. 1.15).

King Henry is shown joining the army at Portsmouth, and gives a view of the harbour, town, and fortifications of Portsmouth, of Southsea Castle, Spithead, the Isle of Wight, and part of the adjacent county of Hampshire, as also of the French and English fleets, and of part of the English camp. The King, mounted on a horse is represented as riding from the town of Portsmouth, and just entering Southsea Castle, in his way to the camp. Behind the King are two persons on horseback, that on the right hand is the Duke of Suffolk, the King's lieutenant in this expedition, mounted on a black horse. The other is Sir Anthony Brown, the King's master of the horse, mounted on a white courser. On the back of the Isle of Wight, off Bembridge Point, and thence stretching along shore to St. Helens road, is the French fleet, all under their top-sails. Off that part known as No Man's Land, are several French galleys firing at the English fleet, then at Spithead. The four last mentioned galleys are undoubtedly placed here, to represent and point out the position of those, which, as we are informed by Du Bellay and Florenge, the French Admiral had detached from his fleet, under the conduct of Baron de la Garde, to provoke the English fleet, and bring on a general engagement.

Between the Spit and the entrance into Portsmouth Harbour, lies the sunken *Mary Rose* with two of her tallest masts rearing out of the sea, and a man calling from a masthead. The ship lies at an angle, and around are the floating bodies of drowned men and parts of rigging, and one man swimming towards a rescue boat.

Index

Barbara Hird

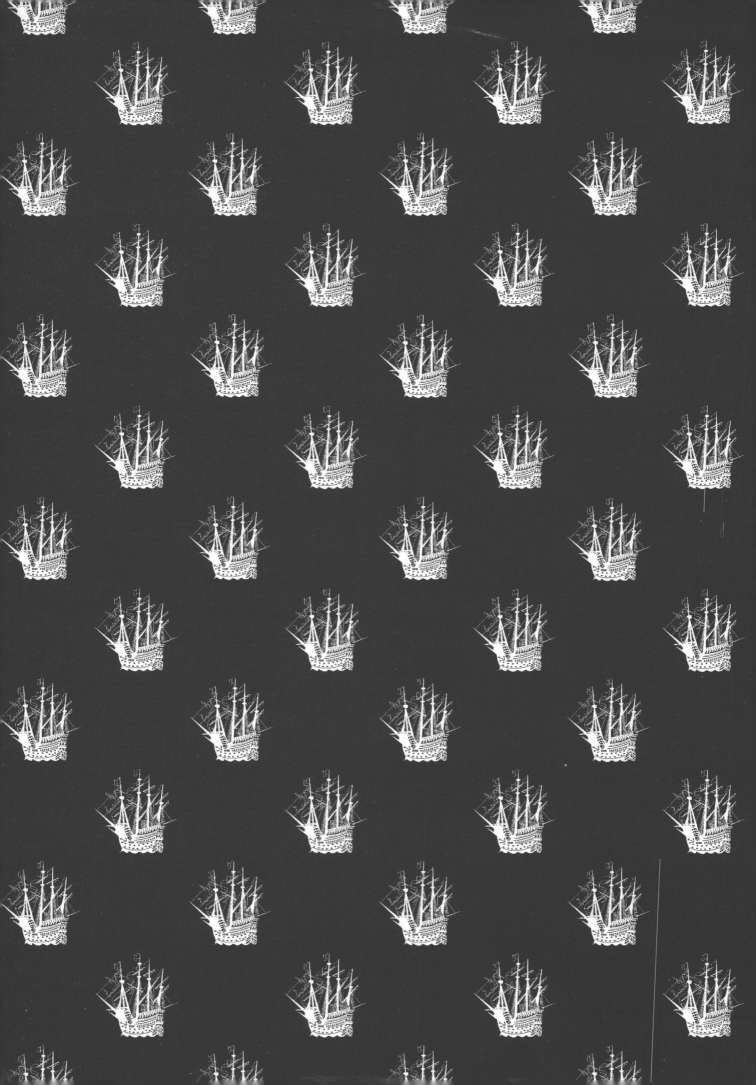